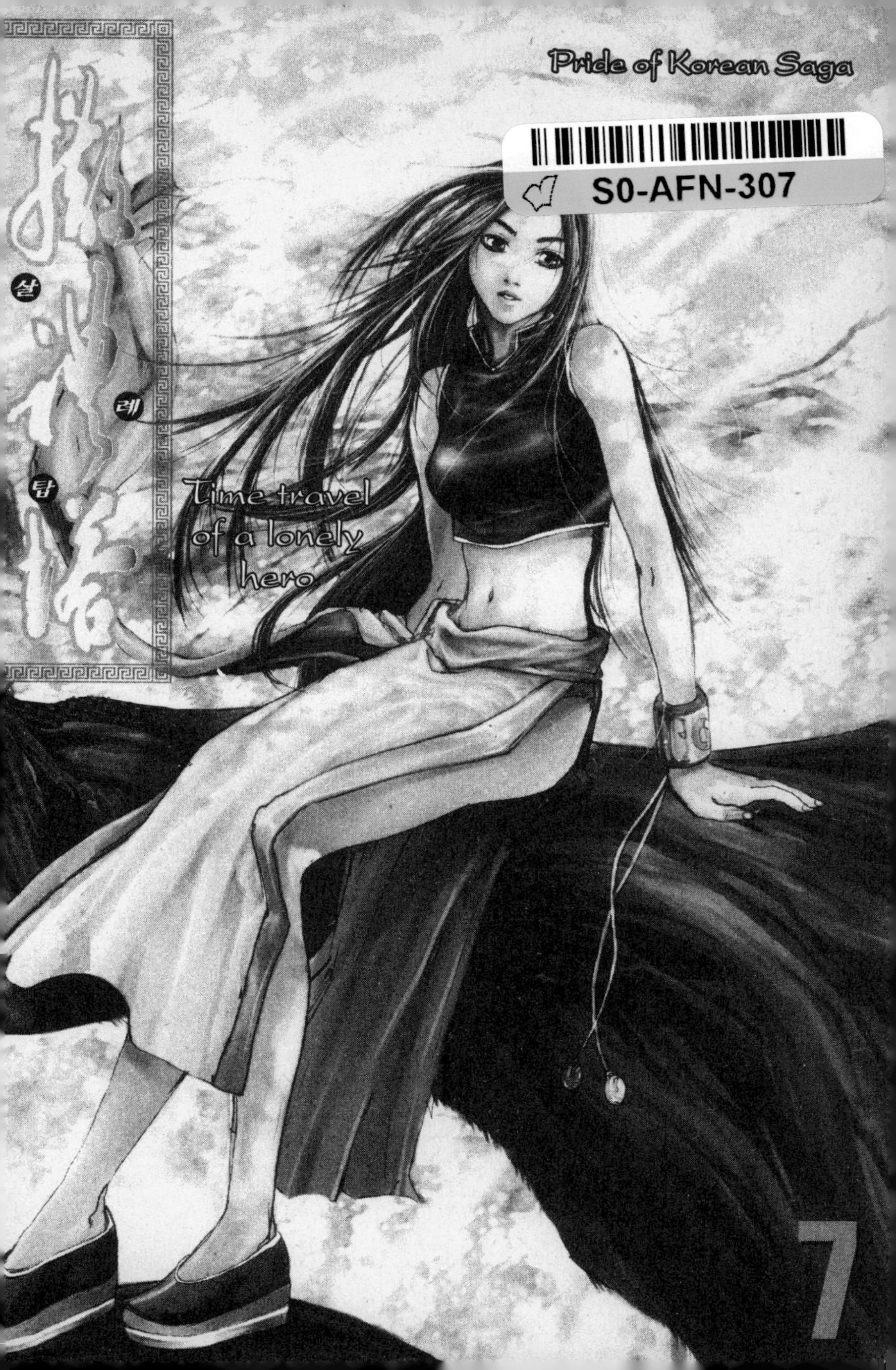
Pride of Korean Saga
살 레 탑
Time travel of a lonely hero
7

Threads of Time Vol. 7
created by Mi Young Noh

Translation - Jihae Hong
English Adaptation - Frank Marraffino
Retouch and Lettering - Camellia Cox
Production Artist - Camellia Cox
Cover Design - John Lo

Editor - Luis Reyes
Digital Imaging Manager - Chris Buford
Production Managers - Jennifer Miller and Mutsumi Miyazaki
Managing Editor - Lindsey Johnston
VP of Production - Ron Klamert
Editor-In-Chief - Rob Tokar
Publisher - Mike Kiley
President and C.O.O. - John Parker
C.E.O. and Chief Creative Officer - Stuart Levy

A  Manga

TOKYOPOP Inc.
5900 Wilshire Blvd. Suite 2000
Los Angeles, CA 90036

E-mail: info@TOKYOPOP.com
Come visit us online at www.TOKYOPOP.com

ISBN: 1-59532-038-4

First TOKYOPOP printing: June 2006
10 9 8 7 6 5 4 3 2 1
Printed in the USA

Threads of Time

撒神塔

Volume 7

By

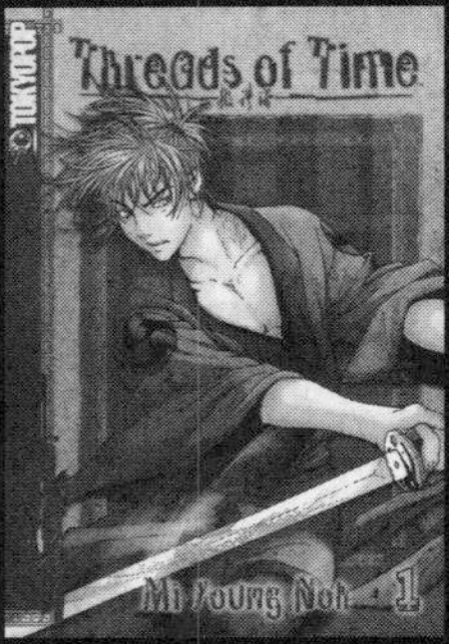
TOKYOPOP
Threads of Time
Mi Young Noh 1

Threads of Time Vol. 1

High school kendo champion Moon Bin Kim suffers from a recurring nightmare in which he lives as Sa Kyung Kim, the son of a prominent warrior family in 13th Century Korea (Koryo). After a freak accident at the school swimming pool, Moon Bin falls into a coma, but his modern-day personality resurfaces in the distant past when Sa Kyung revives miraculously after years of unconsciousness. As if being displaced in medieval Koryo isn't enough, Moon Bin finds himself at the very brink of war. From his deathbed, Genghis Khan decreed that Koryo should be conquered. Sali Tayi, the most brutal and feared general of the Mongol army, is appointed to lead the invasion into the peninsula. Opposing him is Moon Bin's 13th Century father, the legendary warlord Kim Kyung-Sohn.

Threads of Time Vol. 2

Using her clever wiles and substantial might, the stunning granddaughter of Genghis Khan, Atan Hadas, is made second-in-command to the ruthless Sali Tayi. Her first mission is to be sent into the heart of Koryo to gather intelligence on the defensive forces. In the woods near Ghu Zhu Palace, Moon Bin happens upon the princess while she is bathing in a waterfall, and is smitten immediately by her beauty. At the same time, Kim Kyung-Sohn discovers the true identity of Atan Hadas, and orders her arrest. Unaware that she is a princess and a spy of the enemy, the impetuous Moon Bin helps her escape capture. Returning to Sali Tayi, Atan Hadas learns that a full-scale invasion of Koryo has begun.

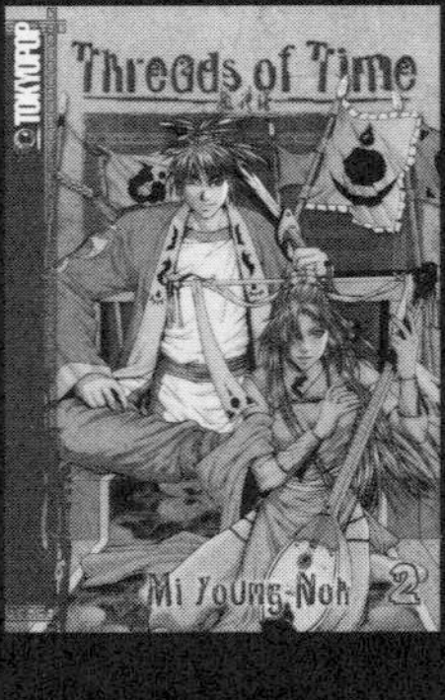
TOKYOPOP
Threads of Time
Mi Young Noh 2

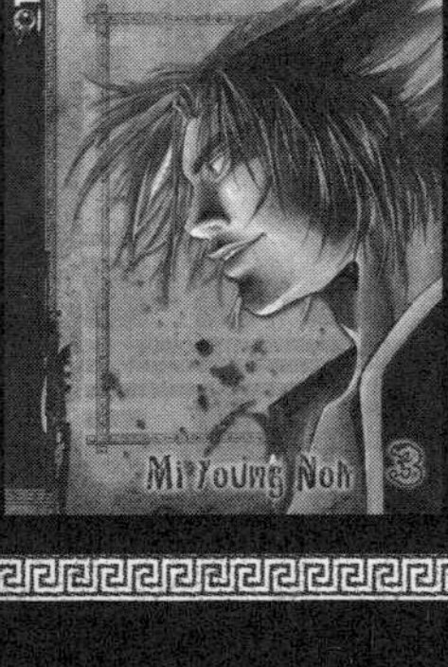
TOKYOPOP
Threads of Time
Mi Young Noh 3

Threads of Time Vol. 3

In an all-out assault, the Mongol army ravages the northern towns and outposts of the land. With their howling war cries, the invaders cut a bloody swath toward Ghu Zhu Palace, the stronghold of Koryo's defense. General Sali Tayi offers Koryo an ultimatum: surrender to the devastating ferocity of the Mongol army or go to war with it. With his valor unmoved by the Mongol's threats, Kim Kyung-Sohn upholds a remarkable resistance. Despite facing overwhelming enemy forces, the Koryo palace weathers the storm of a vicious Mongol siege. On the field of battle, the two commanders engage one another in personal combat and Kim Kyung-Sohn astonishingly perseveres—keeping the hopes of a successful resistance alive for one more day.

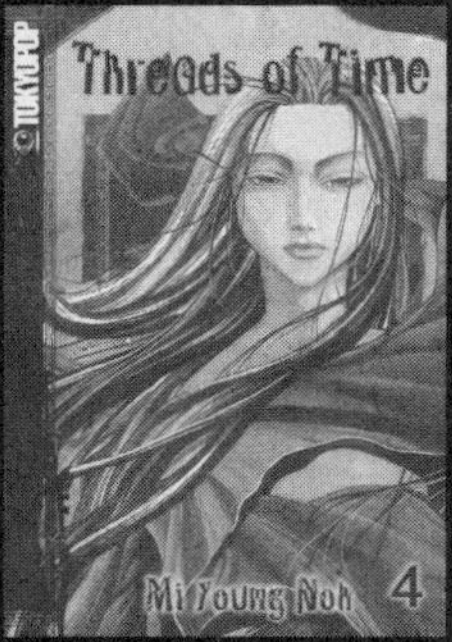
Threads of Time
TOKYOPOP
Mi Young Noh 4

Threads of Time Vol. 4

Having had both his body and his pride injured, Sali Tayi orders the rape and massacre of Kim Kyung-Sohn's Household. Witnessing the brutality of her fellow soldiers, Atan Hadas begins to doubt the glorified honors of the Koryo conquest. Walking again in the woods outside Keh Kung, she is reunited with the equally pensive Moon Bin. Seeking to repay Moon Bin for his earlier assistance, Atan Hadas warns of the slaughter and counsels that he should flee the land and save himself. Unable to abandon his 13th Century family, Moon Bin returns to his home to find that everything he knew in this new reality has been destroyed...

Threads of Time Vol. 5

Reacquainted with Chung-War, Moon-Bin is convinced to dress as a woman to better hide among the Koryo people and avoid the murderous clutches of the Mongols. Meanwhile, the Koryo ruler turns over control of the country to the Mongol hordes, much to the shocking surprise of General Kim Kyung-Sohn, who has fought fiercely for the preservation of his country only to be betrayed by its leaders.

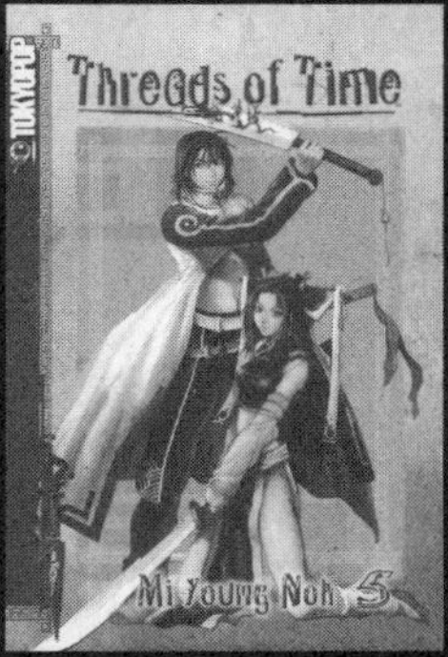
Threads of Time
TOKYOPOP
Mi Young Noh 5

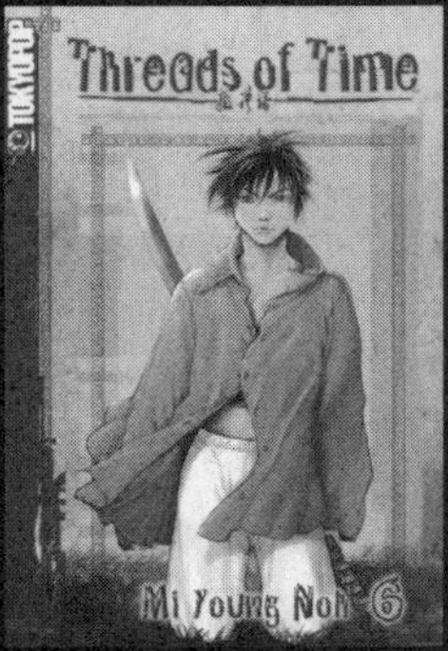
Threads of Time
TOKYOPOP
Mi Young Noh 6

Threads of Time Vol. 6

With the haunting and heroic death of General Kim Kyung-Sohn, the last substantial Koryo resistance to the Mongol army is felled, leaving smattering groups of Koryo soldiers and commanders to lead smaller resistances throughout the countryside. Moon Bin is discovered as a man and tossed into the ranks of the Slave Corps, Koryo citizens who will be trained as Mongol soldiers to fight their own on the battlefield.

contents

Threads of Time 7

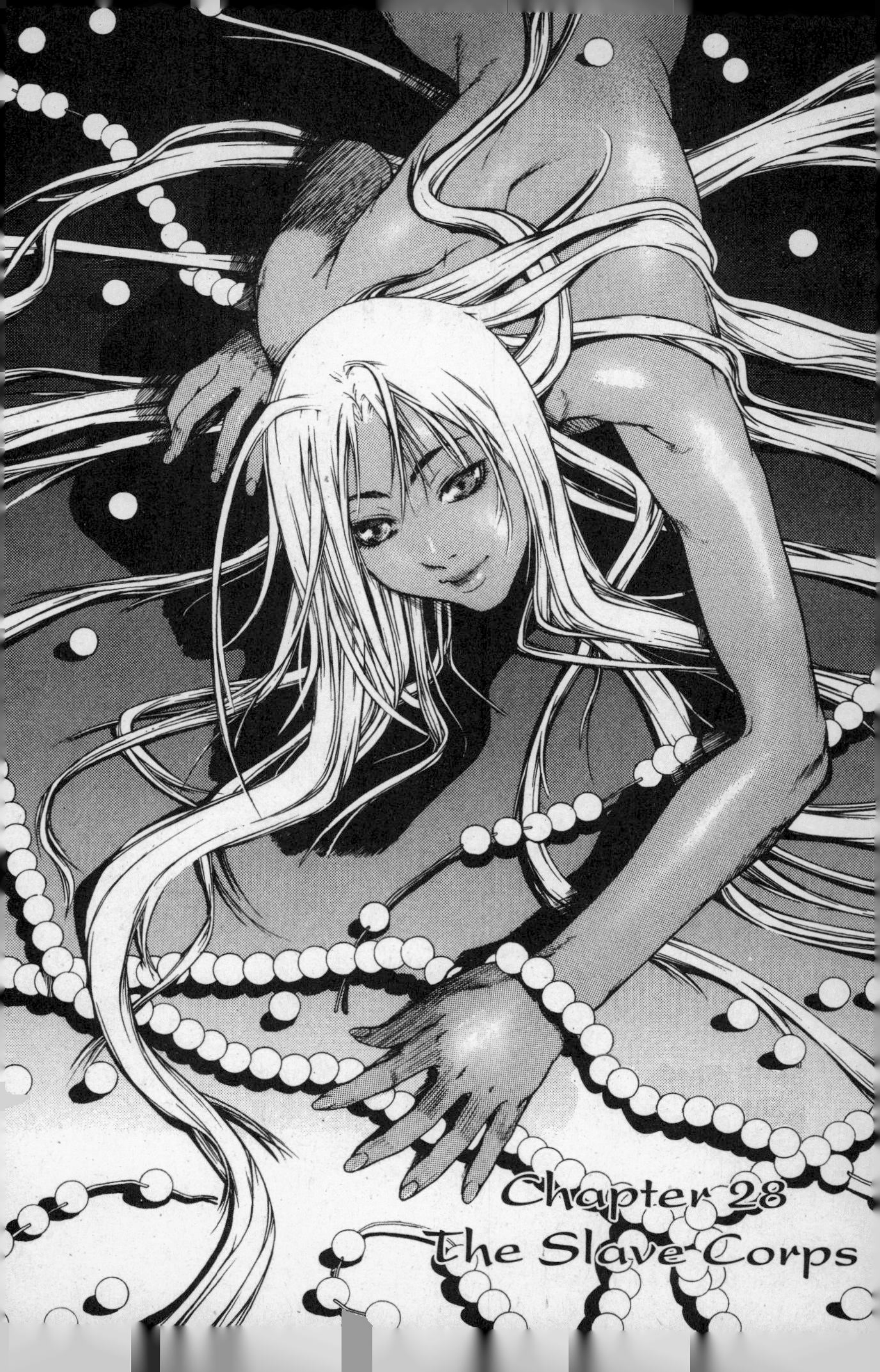
Chapter 28
The Slave Corps

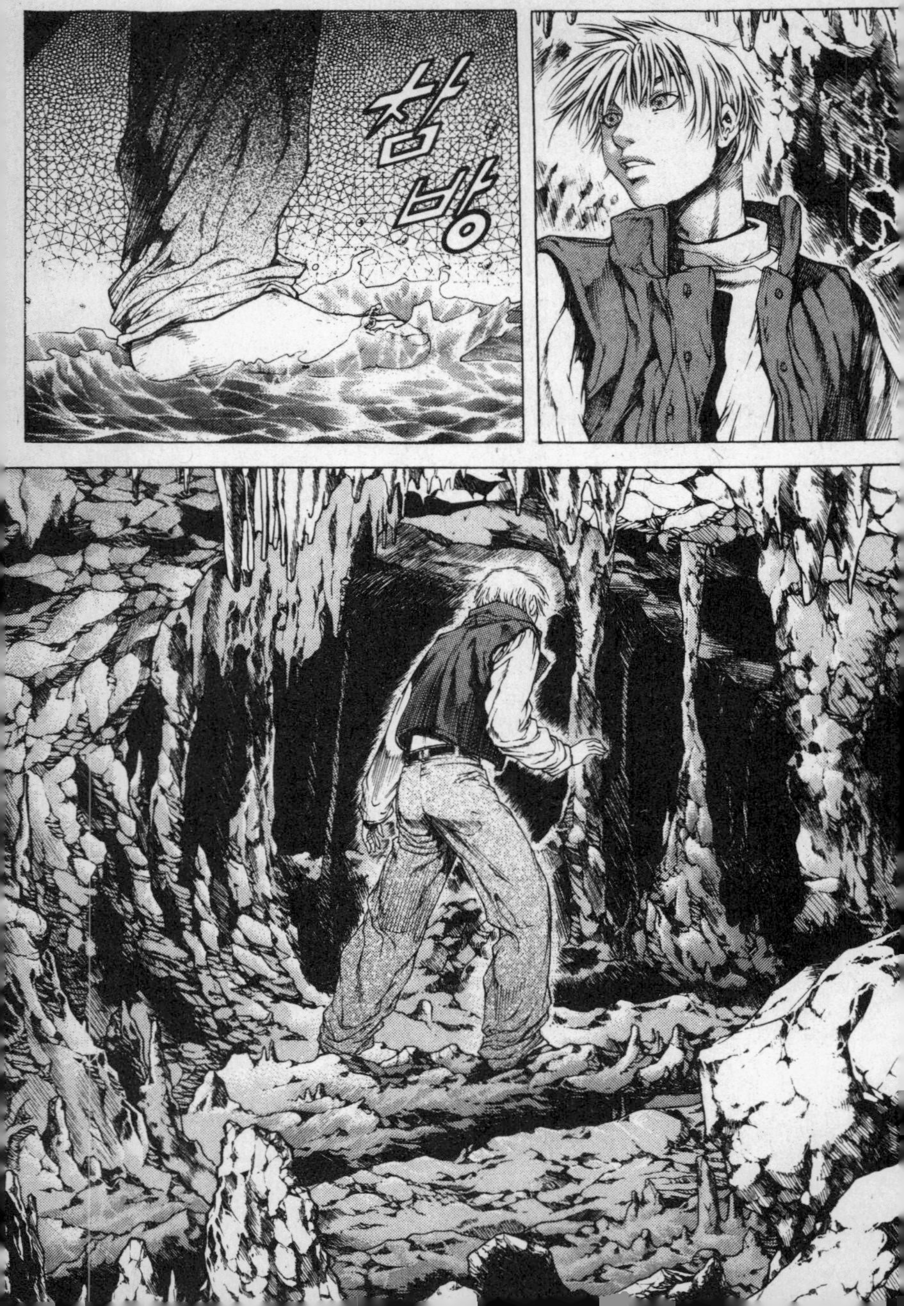
참방

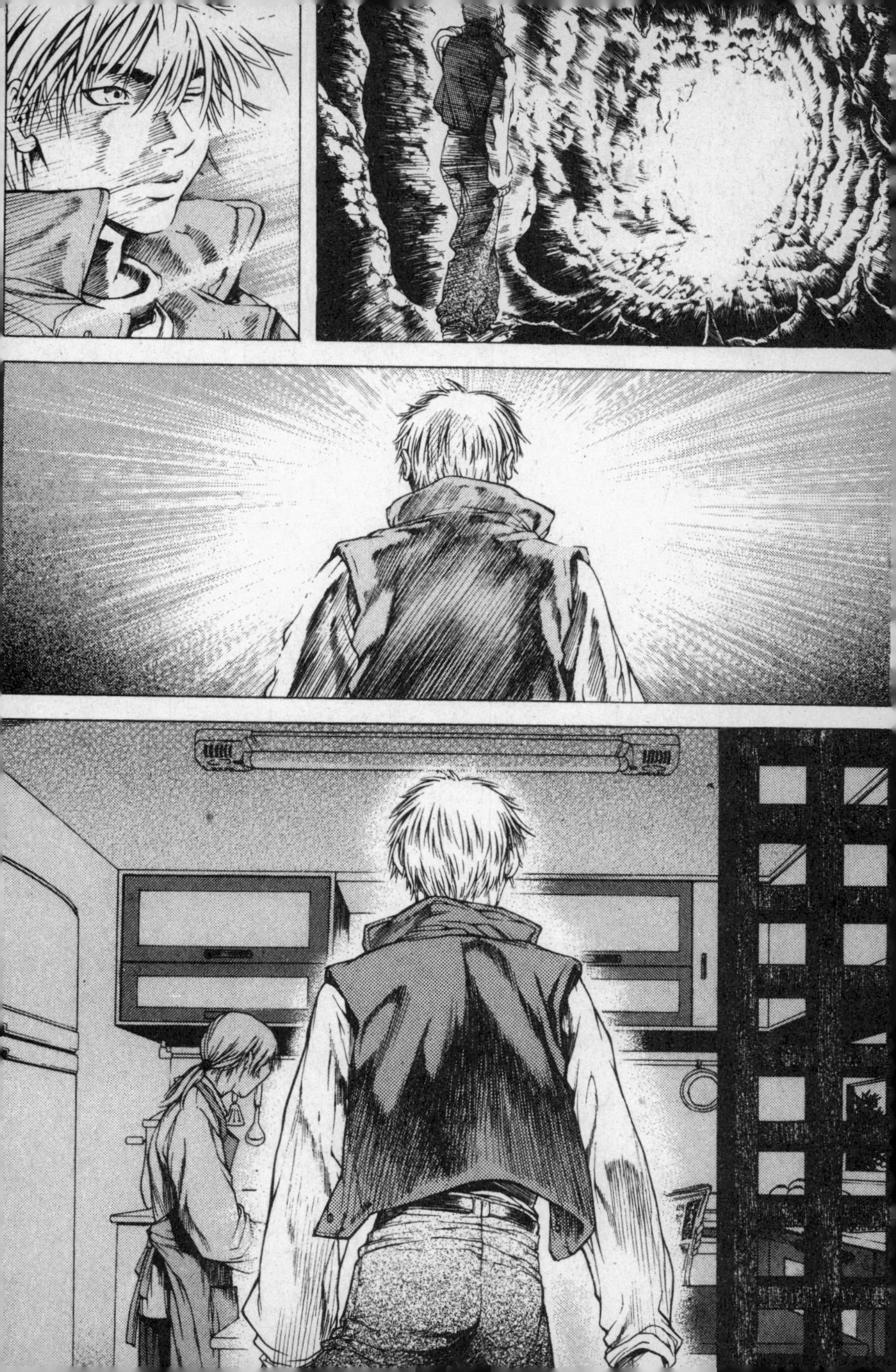

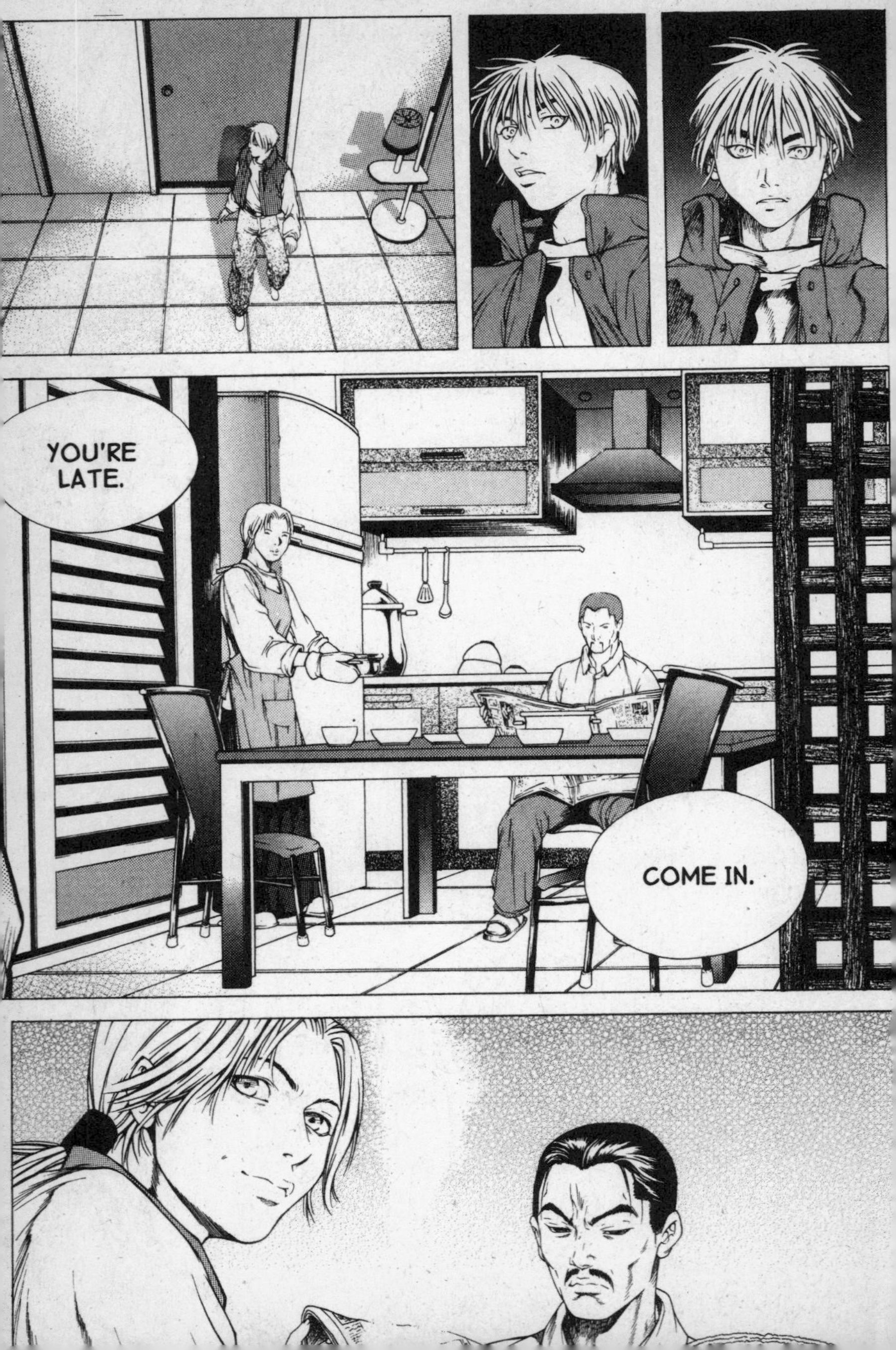
YOU'RE LATE.
COME IN.

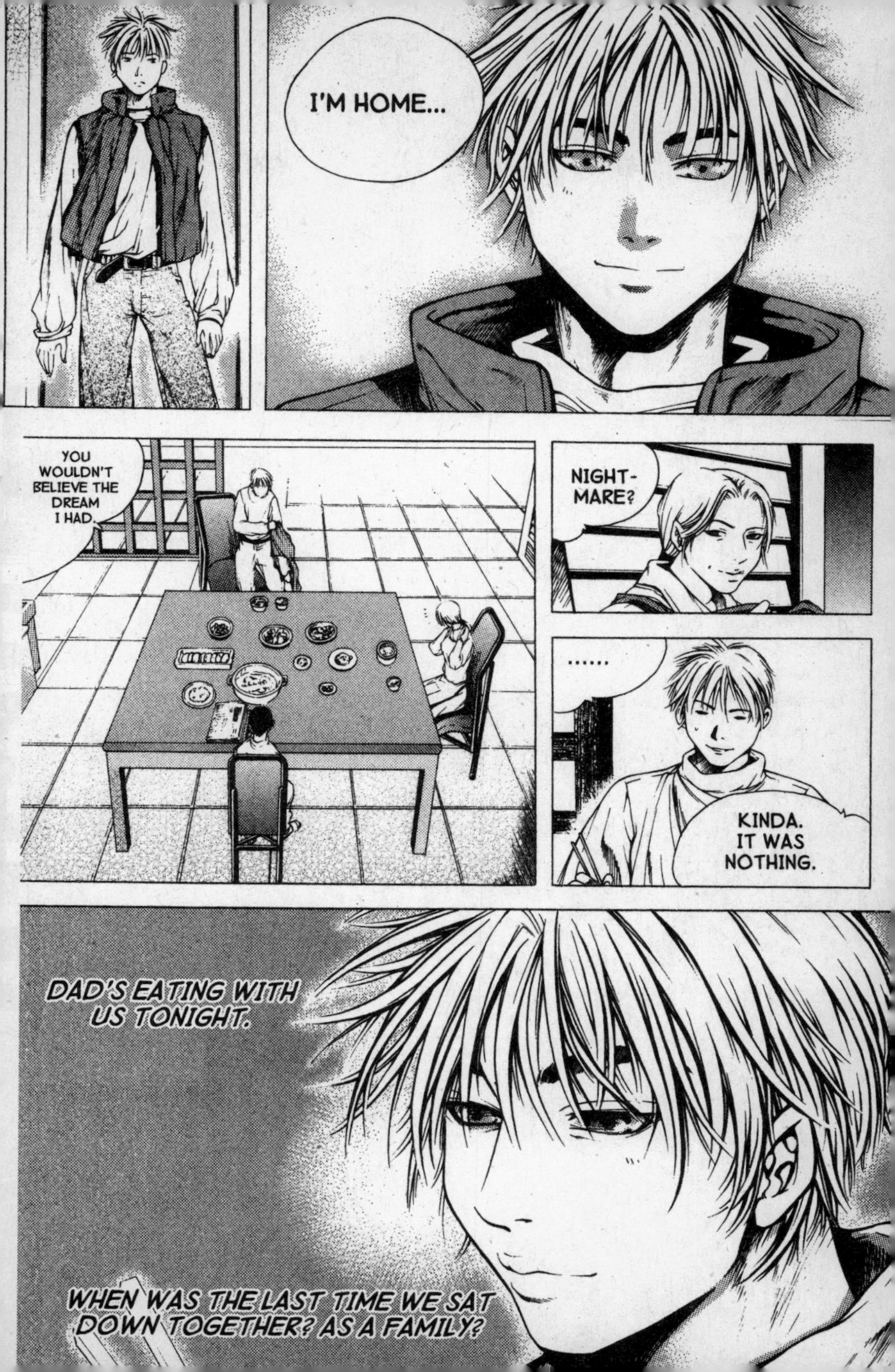
I'M HOME...
YOU WOULDN'T BELIEVE THE DREAM I HAD.
NIGHT-MARE?
......
KINDA. IT WAS NOTHING.
DAD'S EATING WITH US TONIGHT.
WHEN WAS THE LAST TIME WE SAT DOWN TOGETHER? AS A FAMILY?

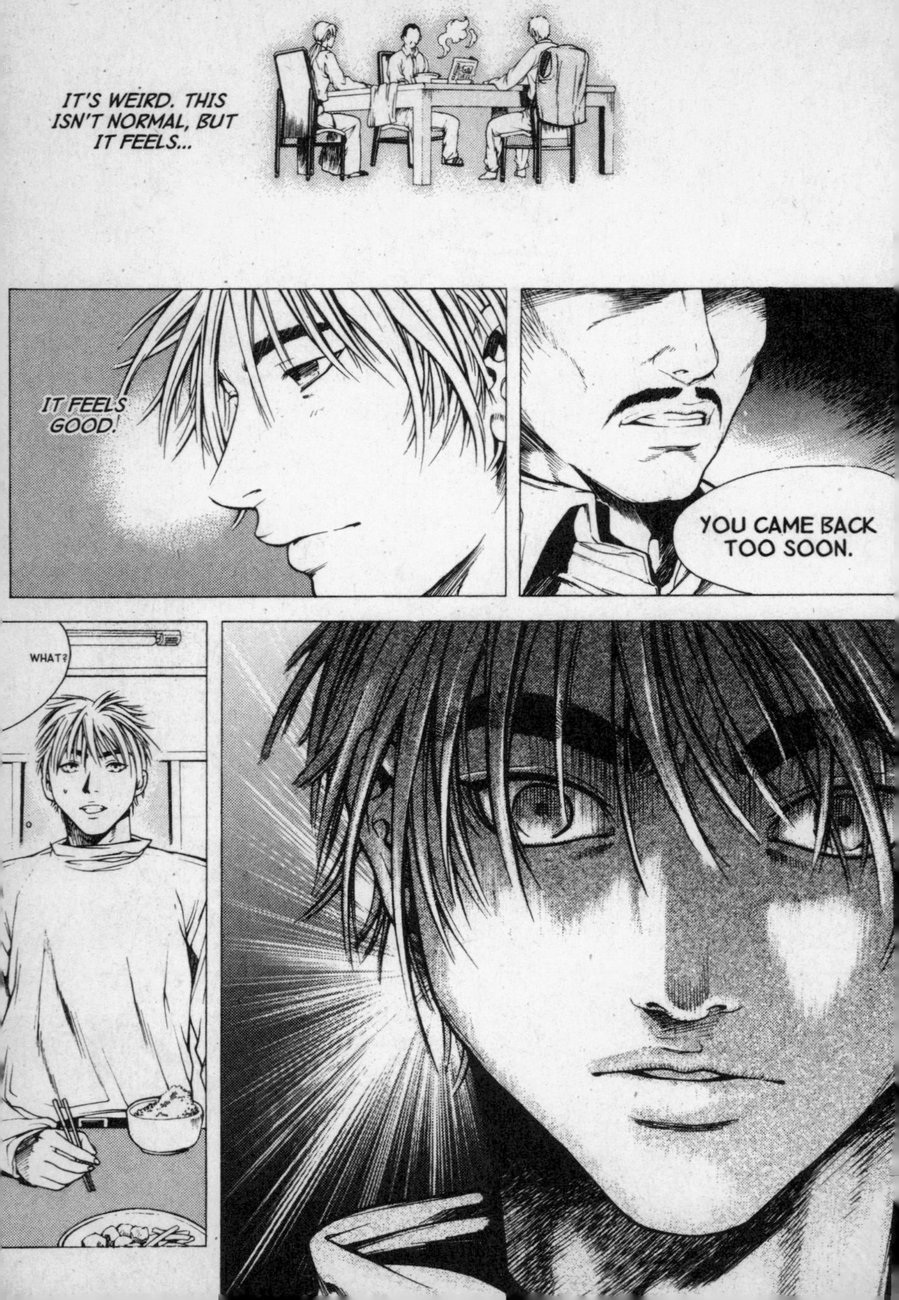
IT'S WEIRD. THIS ISN'T NORMAL, BUT IT FEELS...
IT FEELS GOOD.
YOU CAME BACK TOO SOON.
WHAT?

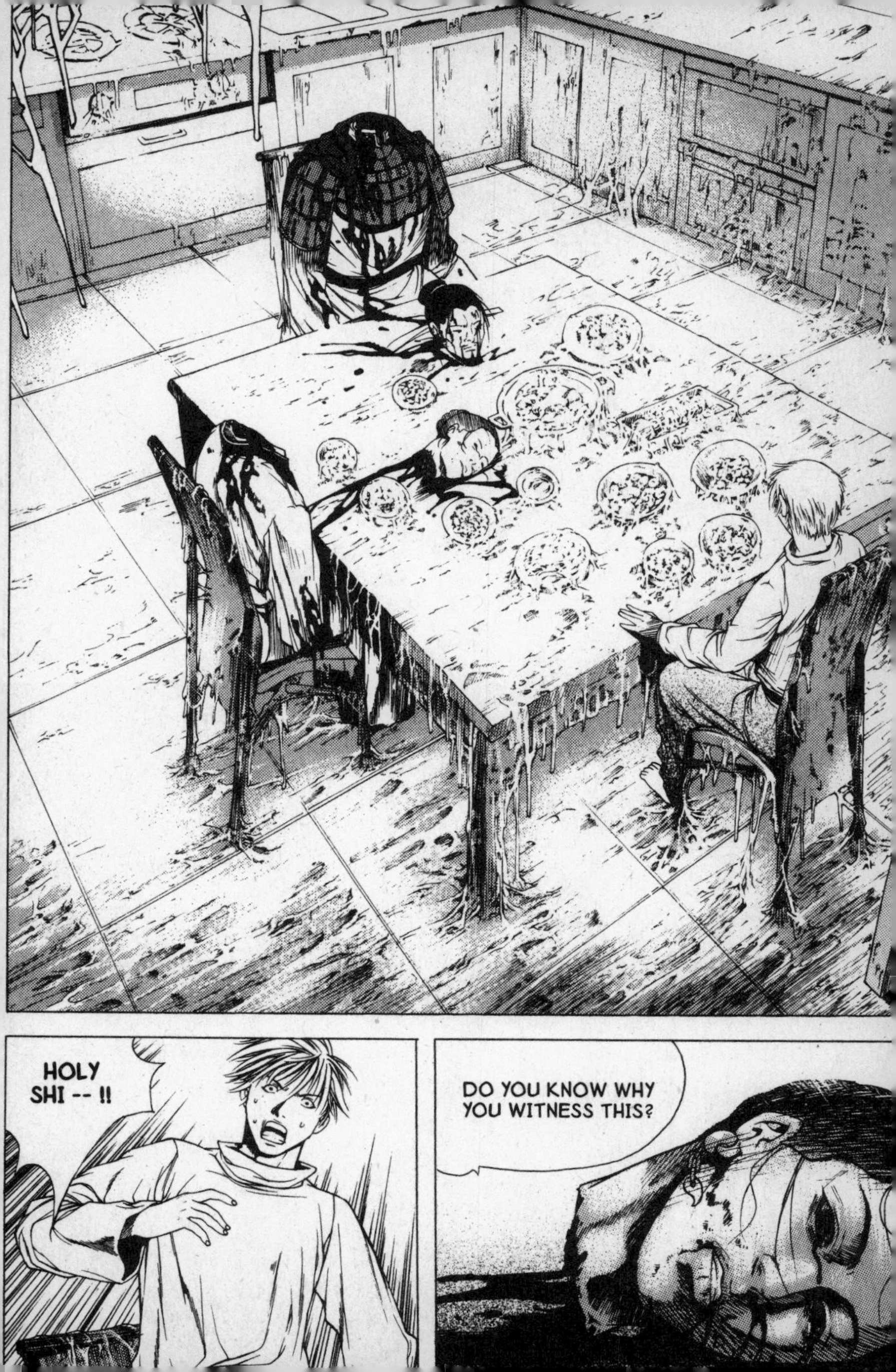
HOLY
SHI -- !!
DO YOU KNOW WHY
YOU WITNESS THIS?

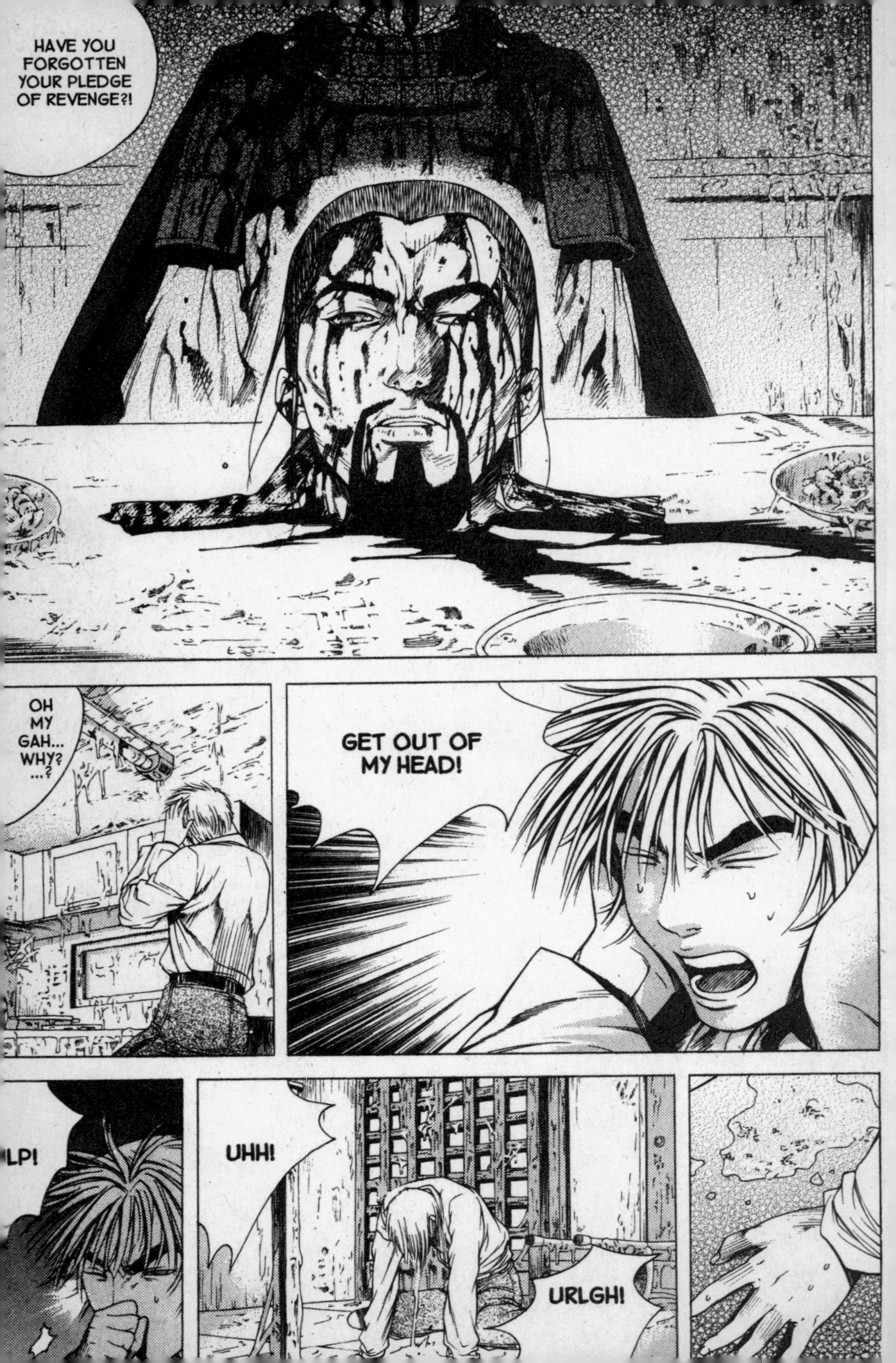
HAVE YOU FORGOTTEN YOUR PLEDGE OF REVENGE?!
OH MY GAH... WHY? ...?
GET OUT OF MY HEAD!
LP!
UHH!
URLGH!

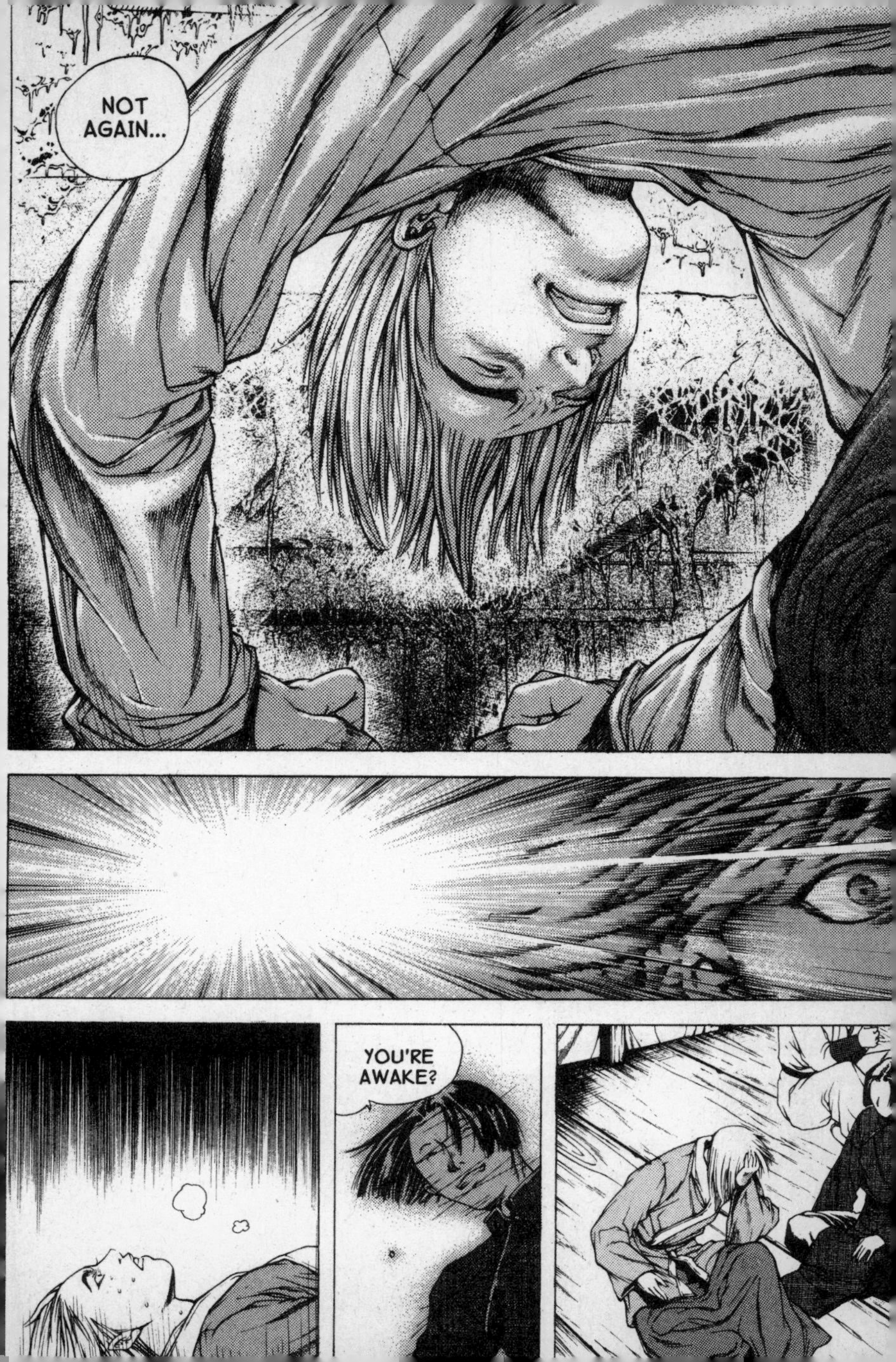
NOT AGAIN...
YOU'RE AWAKE?

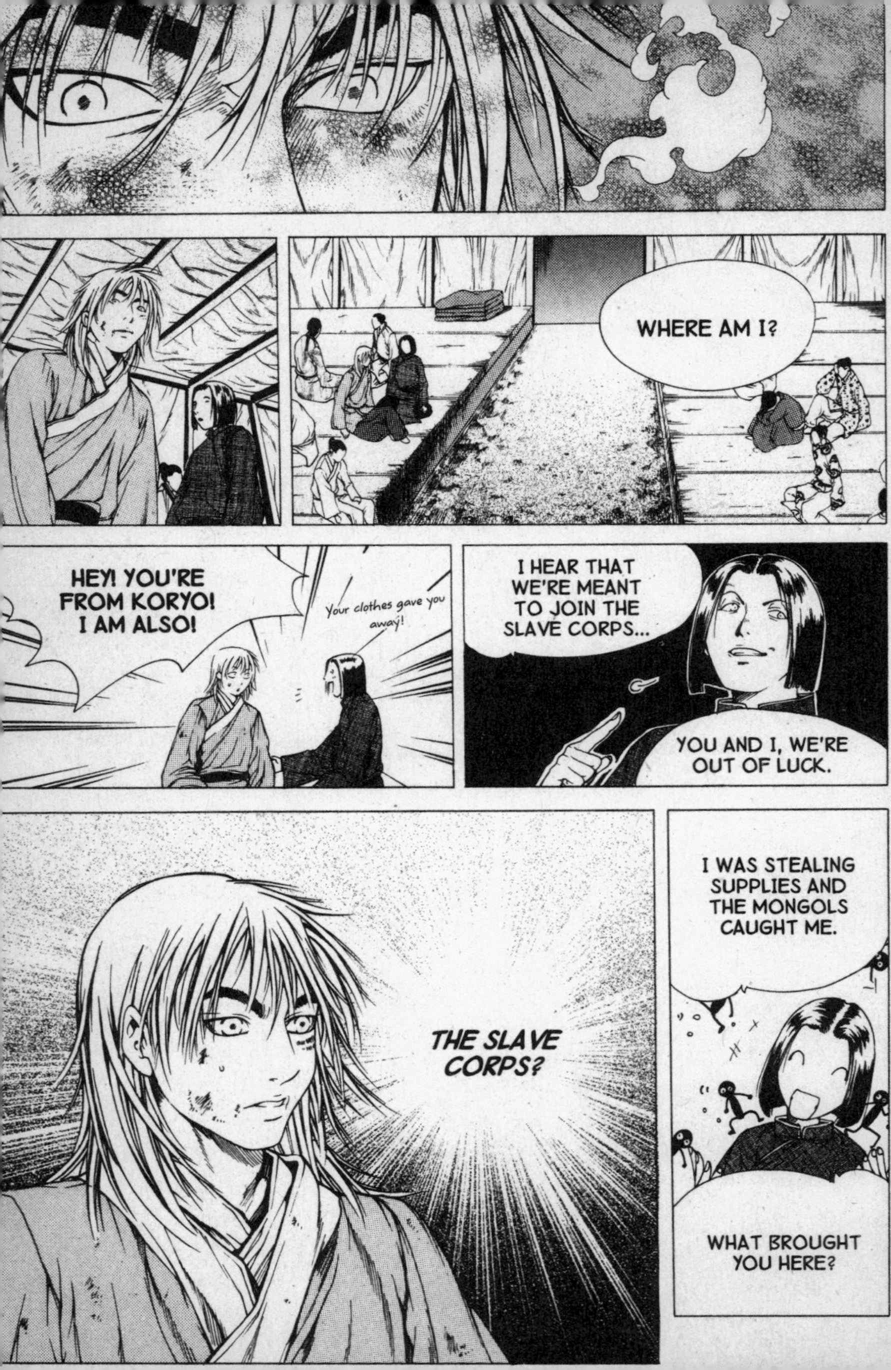
WHERE AM I?
HEY! YOU'RE FROM KORYO! I AM ALSO!
Your clothes gave you away!
I HEAR THAT WE'RE MEANT TO JOIN THE SLAVE CORPS...
YOU AND I, WE'RE OUT OF LUCK.
THE SLAVE CORPS?
I WAS STEALING SUPPLIES AND THE MONGOLS CAUGHT ME.
WHAT BROUGHT YOU HERE?

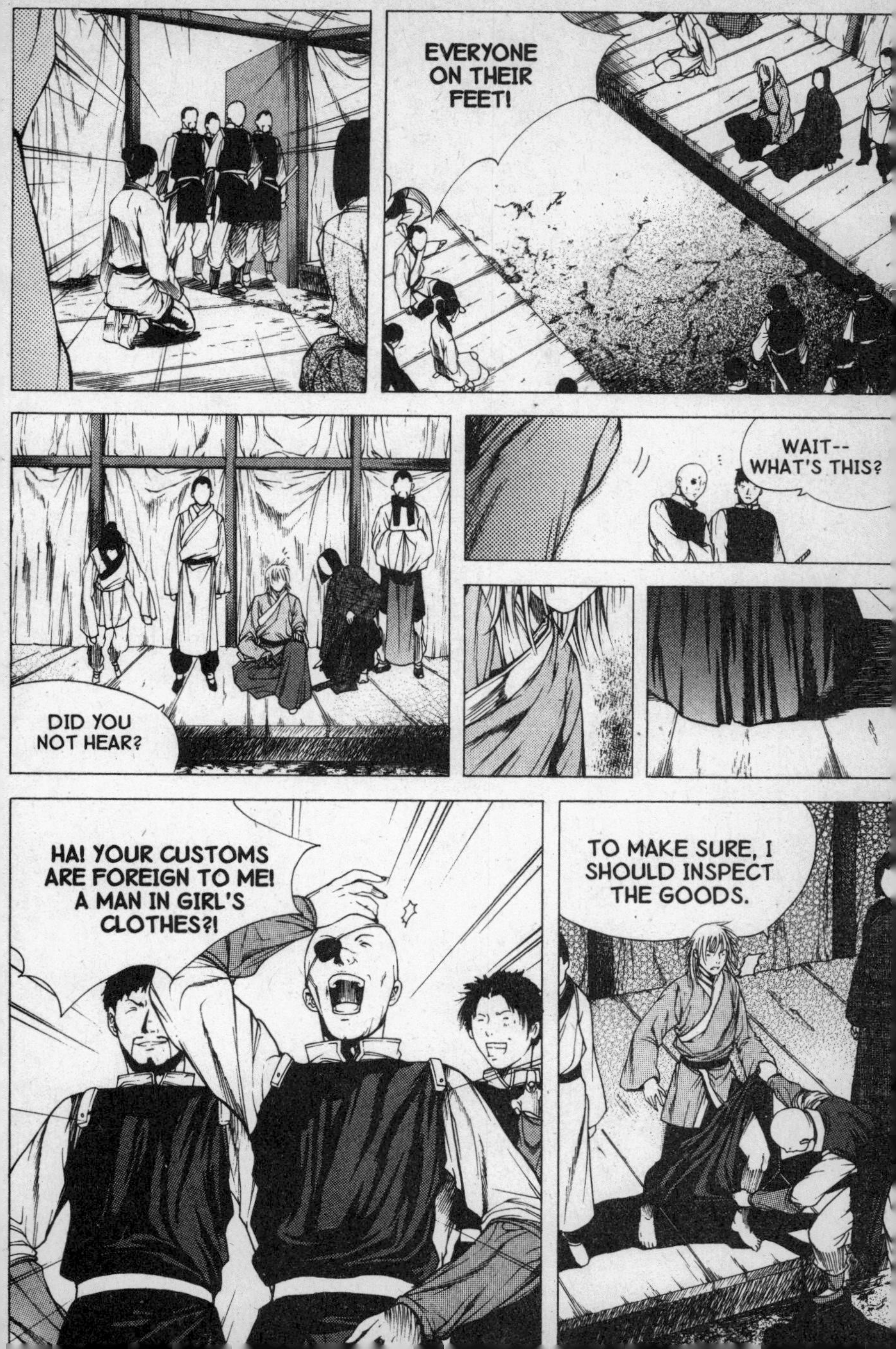
EVERYONE ON THEIR FEET!
DID YOU NOT HEAR?
WAIT-- WHAT'S THIS?
HA! YOUR CUSTOMS ARE FOREIGN TO ME! A MAN IN GIRL'S CLOTHES?!
TO MAKE SURE, I SHOULD INSPECT THE GOODS.

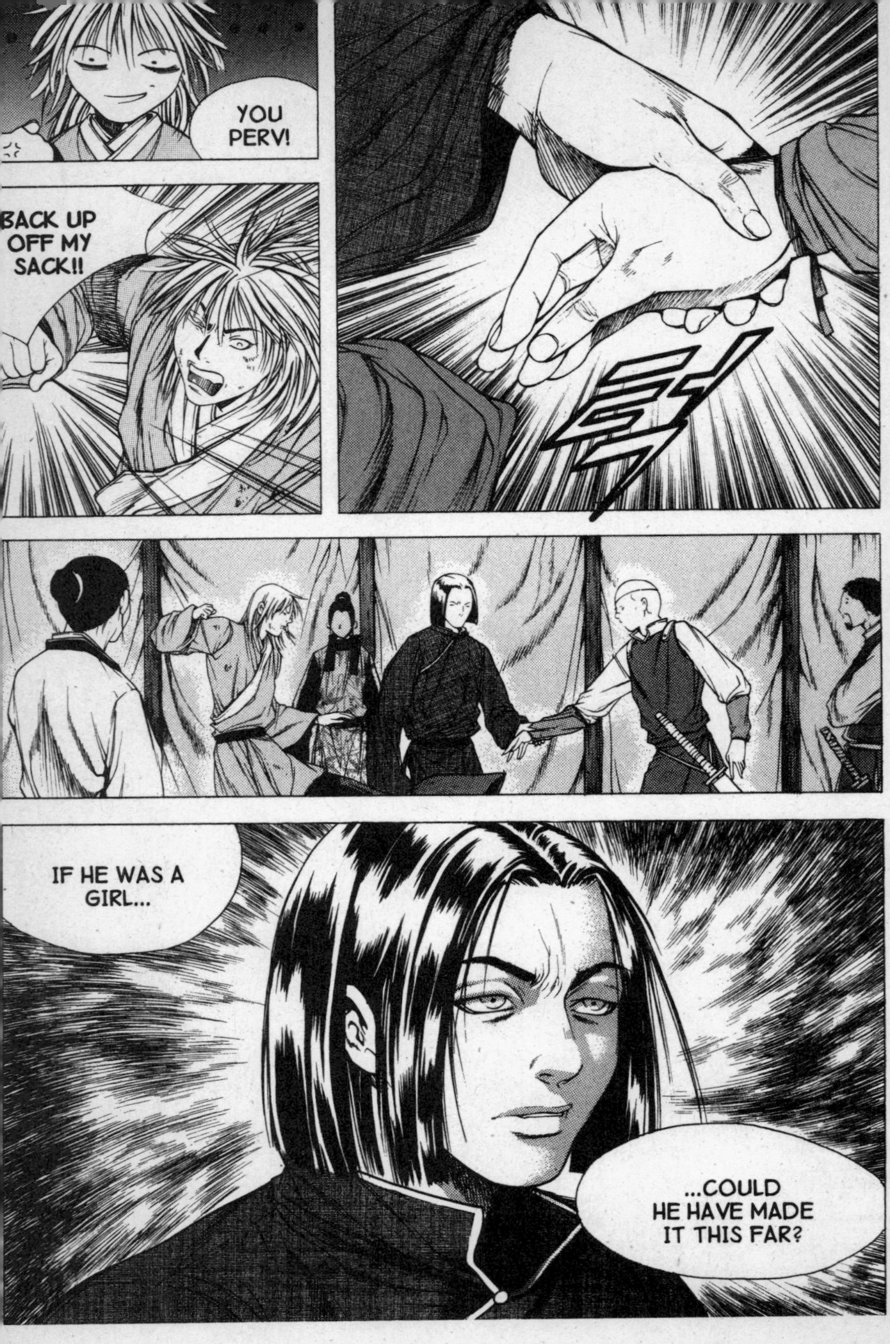
YOU PERV!
BACK UP OFF MY SACK!!
IF HE WAS A GIRL...
...COULD HE HAVE MADE IT THIS FAR?

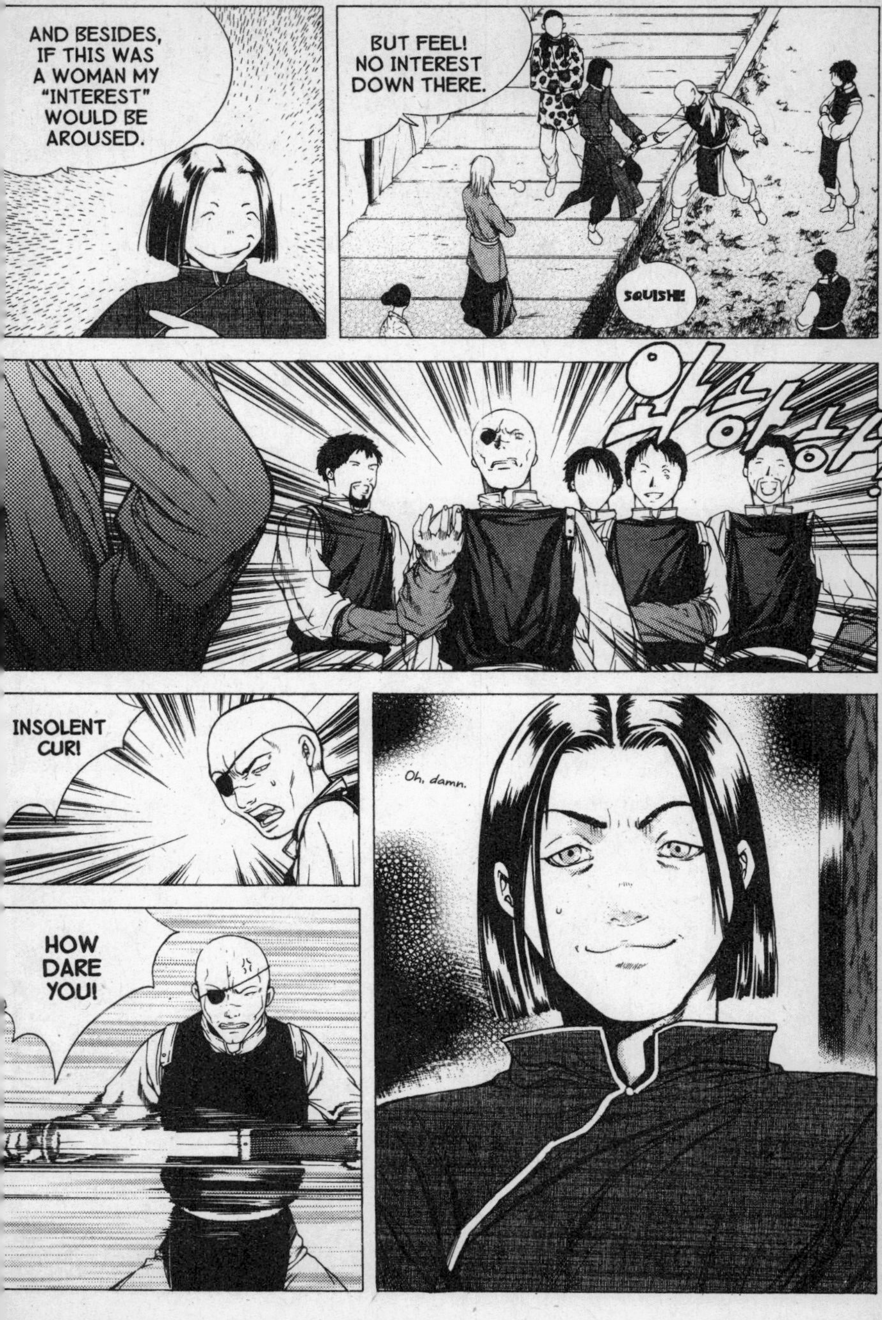
AND BESIDES, IF THIS WAS A WOMAN MY "INTEREST" WOULD BE AROUSED.
BUT FEEL! NO INTEREST DOWN THERE.
SQUISH!
와하하하!
INSOLENT CUR!
HOW DARE YOU!
Oh, damn.

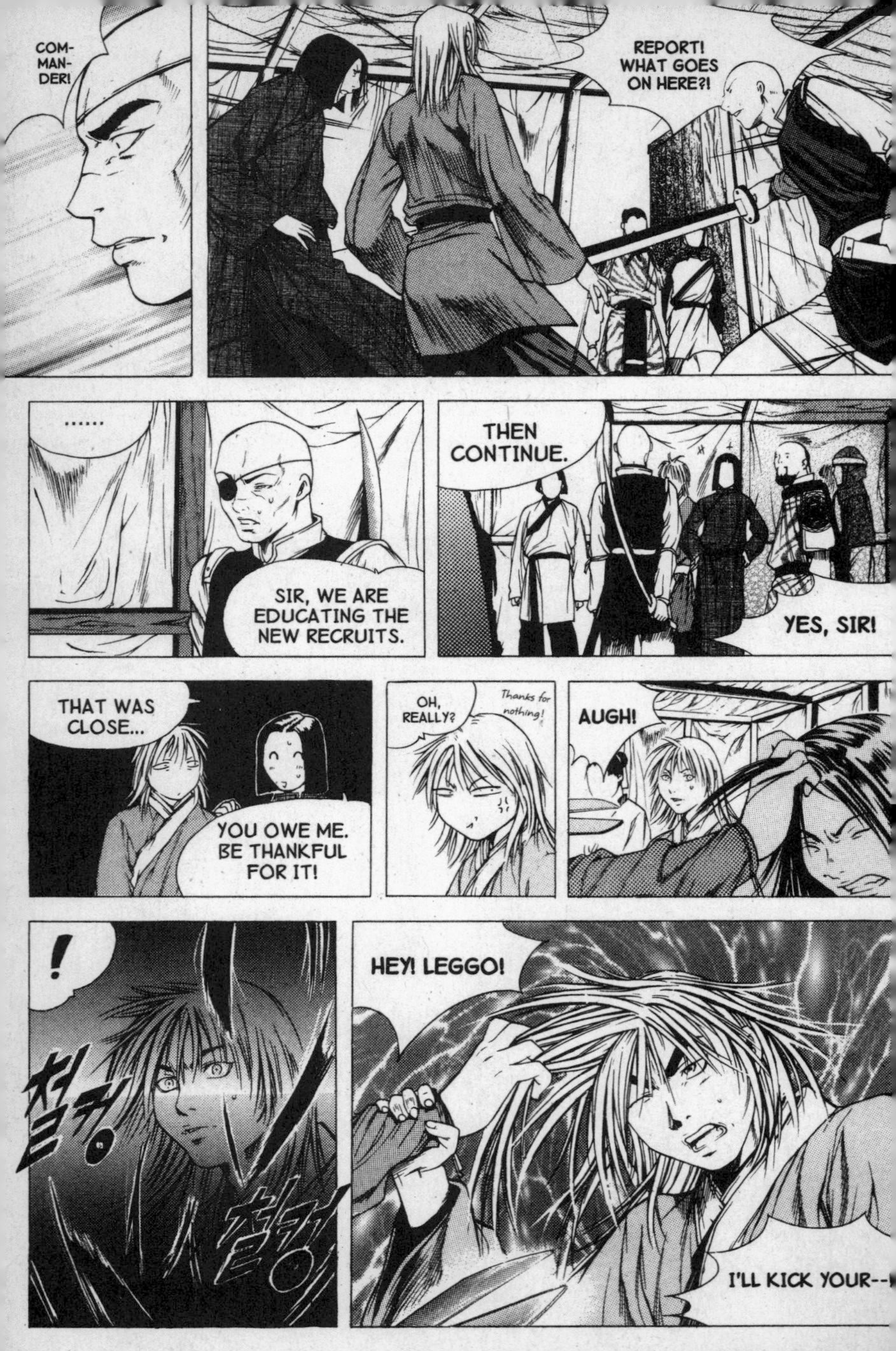
COM-MAN-DER!
REPORT! WHAT GOES ON HERE?!
......
SIR, WE ARE EDUCATING THE NEW RECRUITS.
THEN CONTINUE.
YES, SIR!
THAT WAS CLOSE...
YOU OWE ME. BE THANKFUL FOR IT!
OH, REALLY?
Thanks for nothing!
AUGH!
!
HEY! LEGGO!
I'LL KICK YOUR--

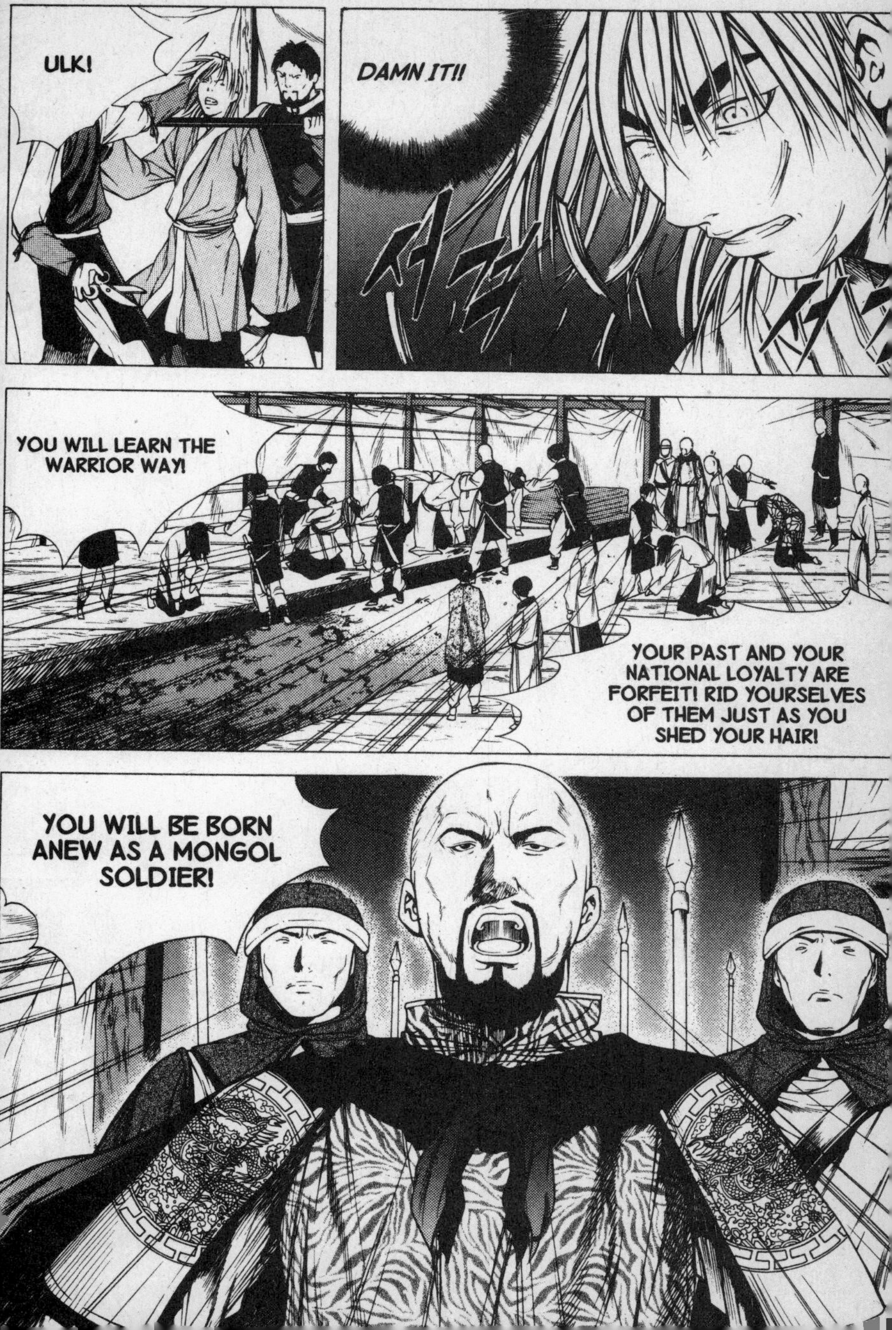
ULK!
DAMN IT!!
YOU WILL LEARN THE WARRIOR WAY!
YOUR PAST AND YOUR NATIONAL LOYALTY ARE FORFEIT! RID YOURSELVES OF THEM JUST AS YOU SHED YOUR HAIR!
YOU WILL BE BORN ANEW AS A MONGOL SOLDIER!

CONSIDER YOUR NEW STATUS WITH PRIDE AND HONOR!

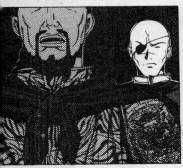

ME? A WARRIOR? FOOLISHNESS...

THINK OF THE GLORY TO BE ACHIEVED! AND RICHES!

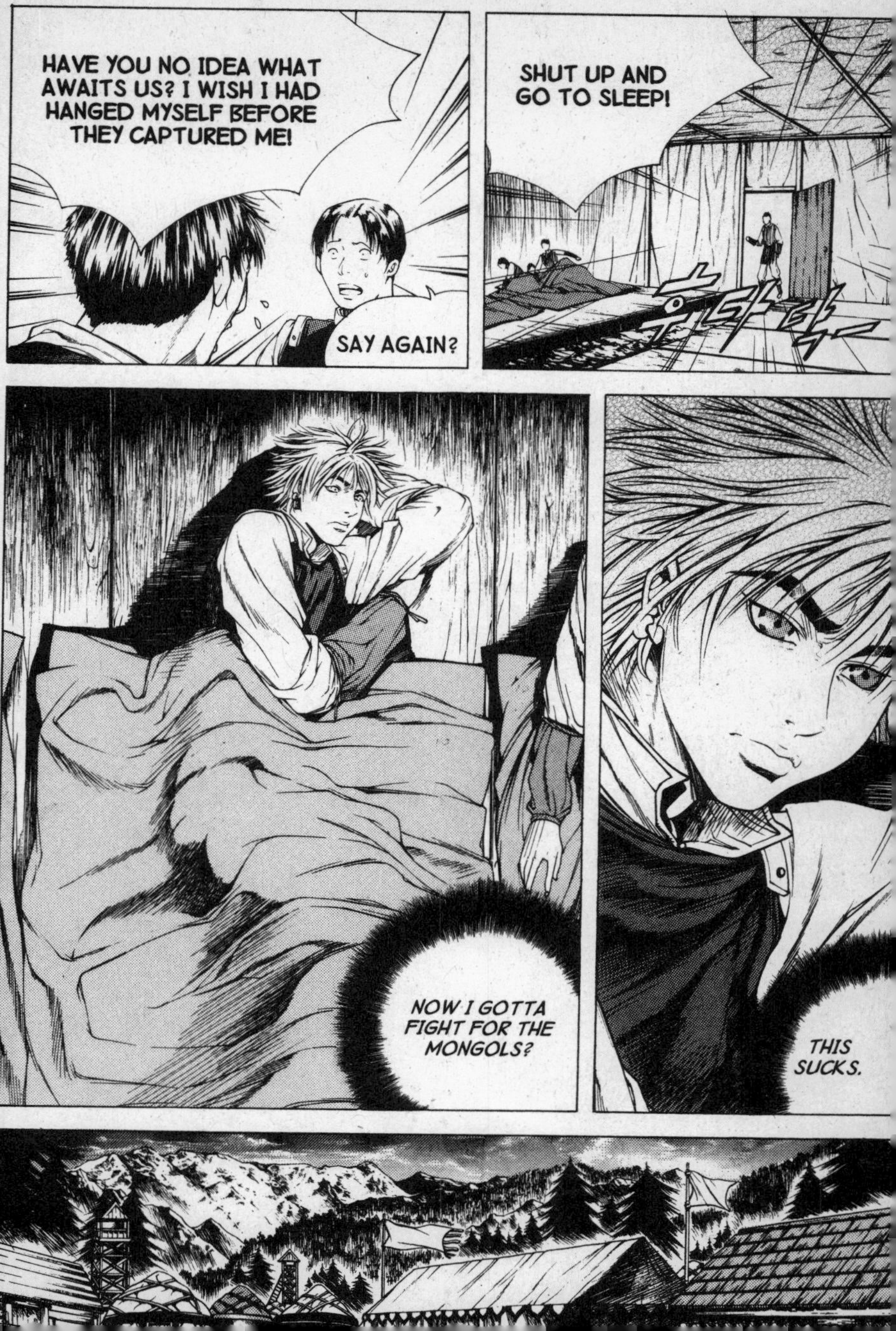
HAVE YOU NO IDEA WHAT AWAITS US? I WISH I HAD HANGED MYSELF BEFORE THEY CAPTURED ME!
SAY AGAIN?
SHUT UP AND GO TO SLEEP!
NOW I GOTTA FIGHT FOR THE MONGOLS?
THIS SUCKS.

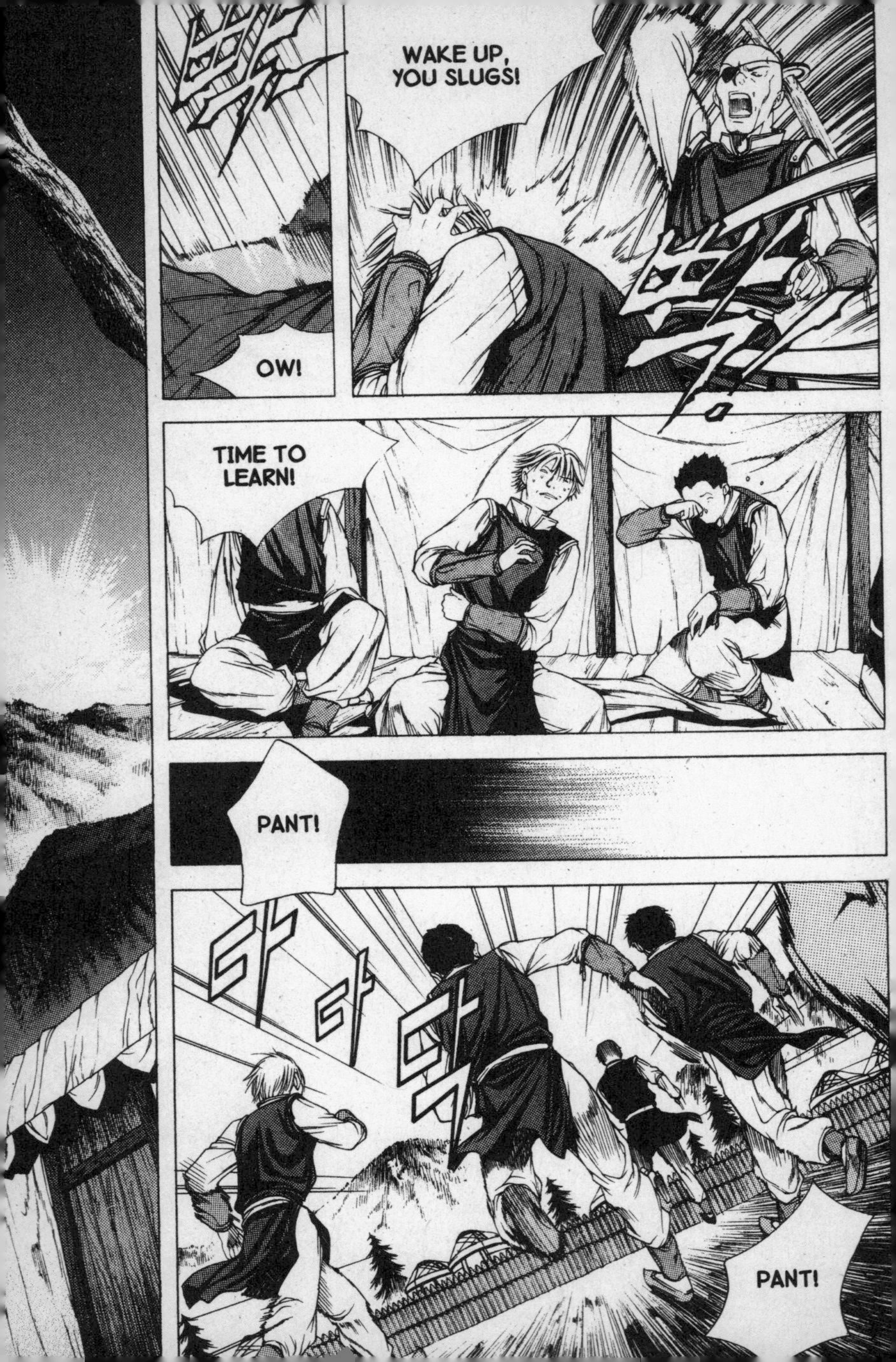
빡
OW!
WAKE UP, YOU SLUGS!
빡
TIME TO LEARN!
PANT!
PANT!

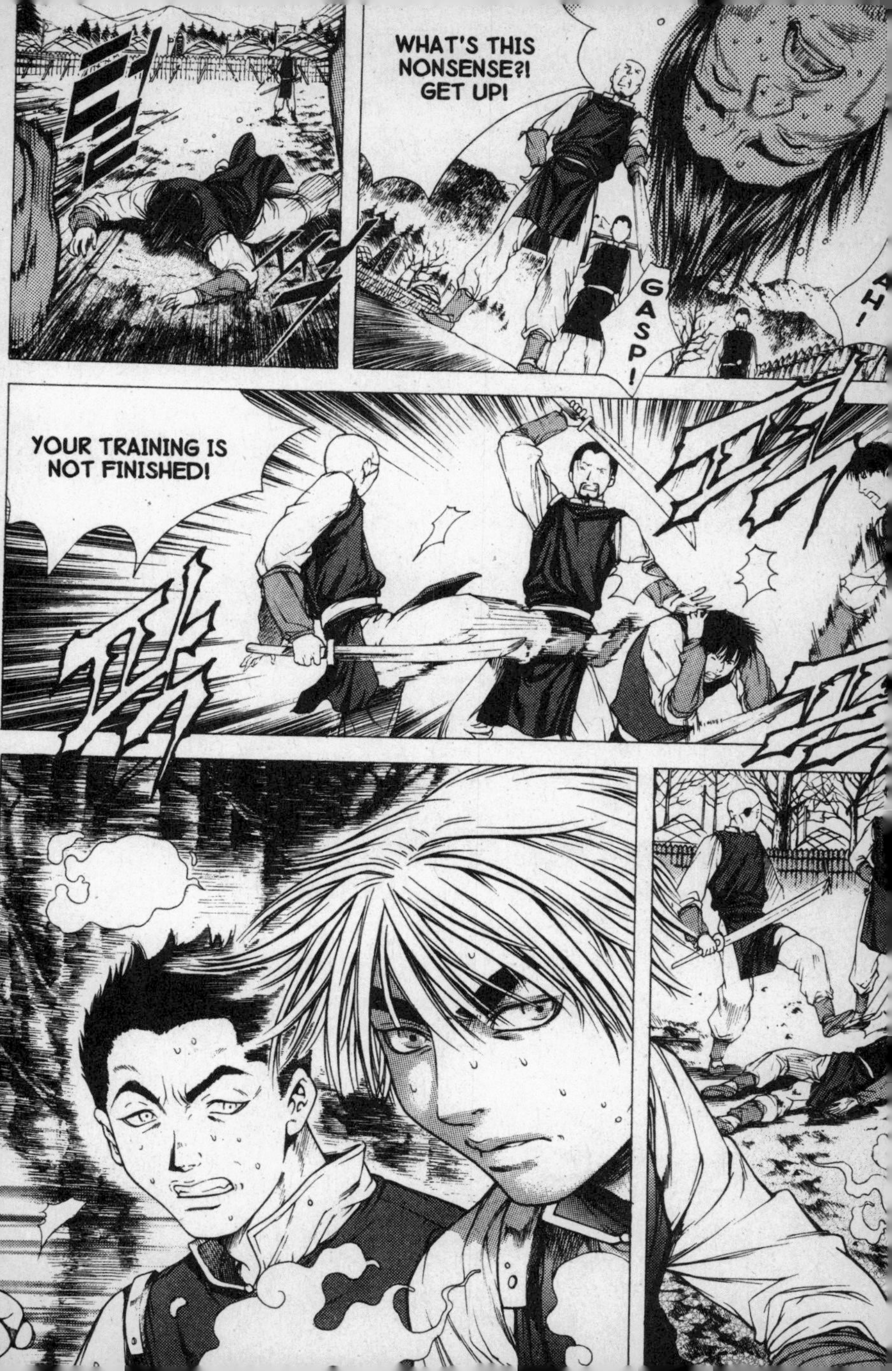
WHAT'S THIS NONSENSE?! GET UP!
GASP!
AH!
YOUR TRAINING IS NOT FINISHED!

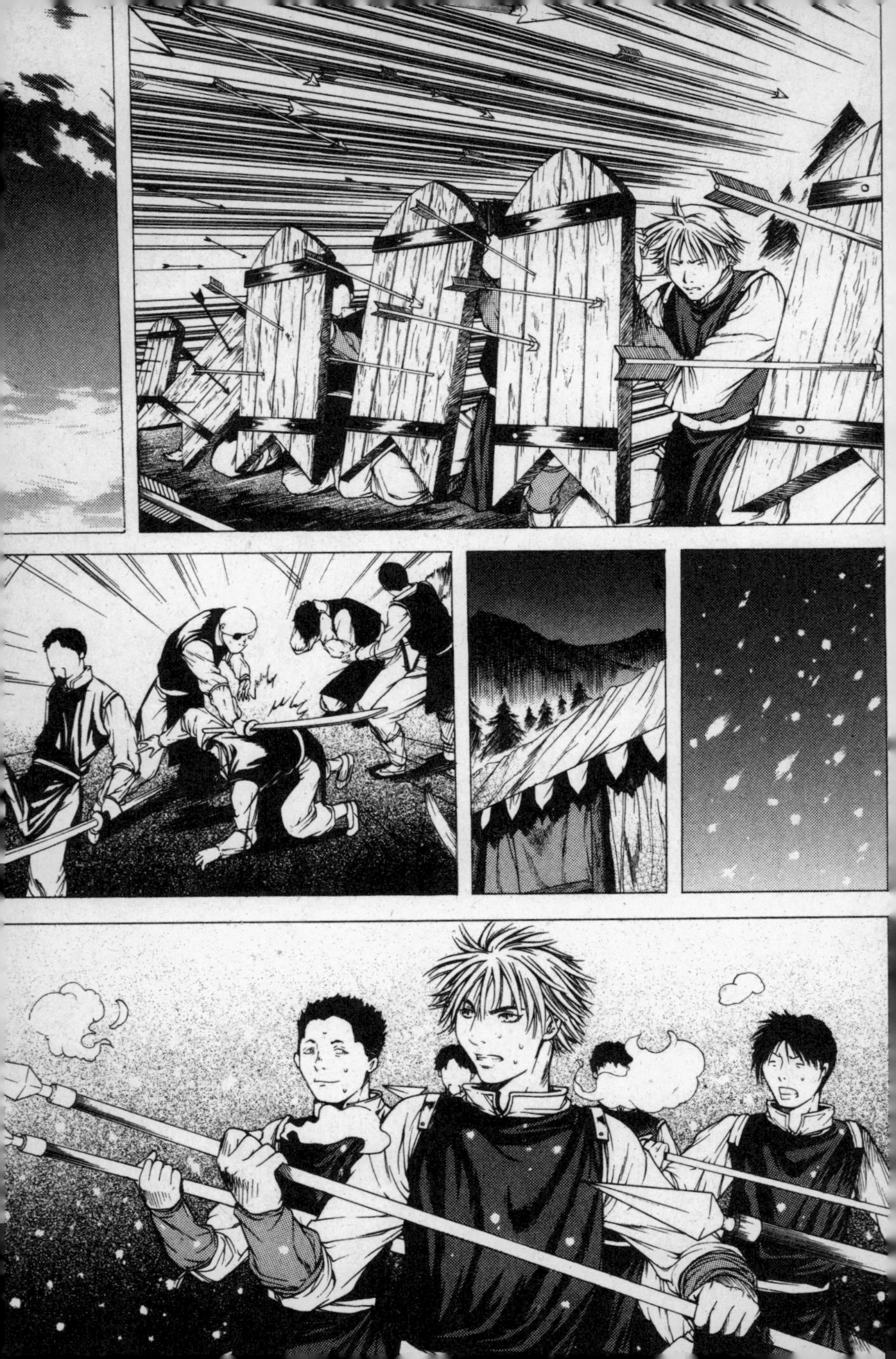

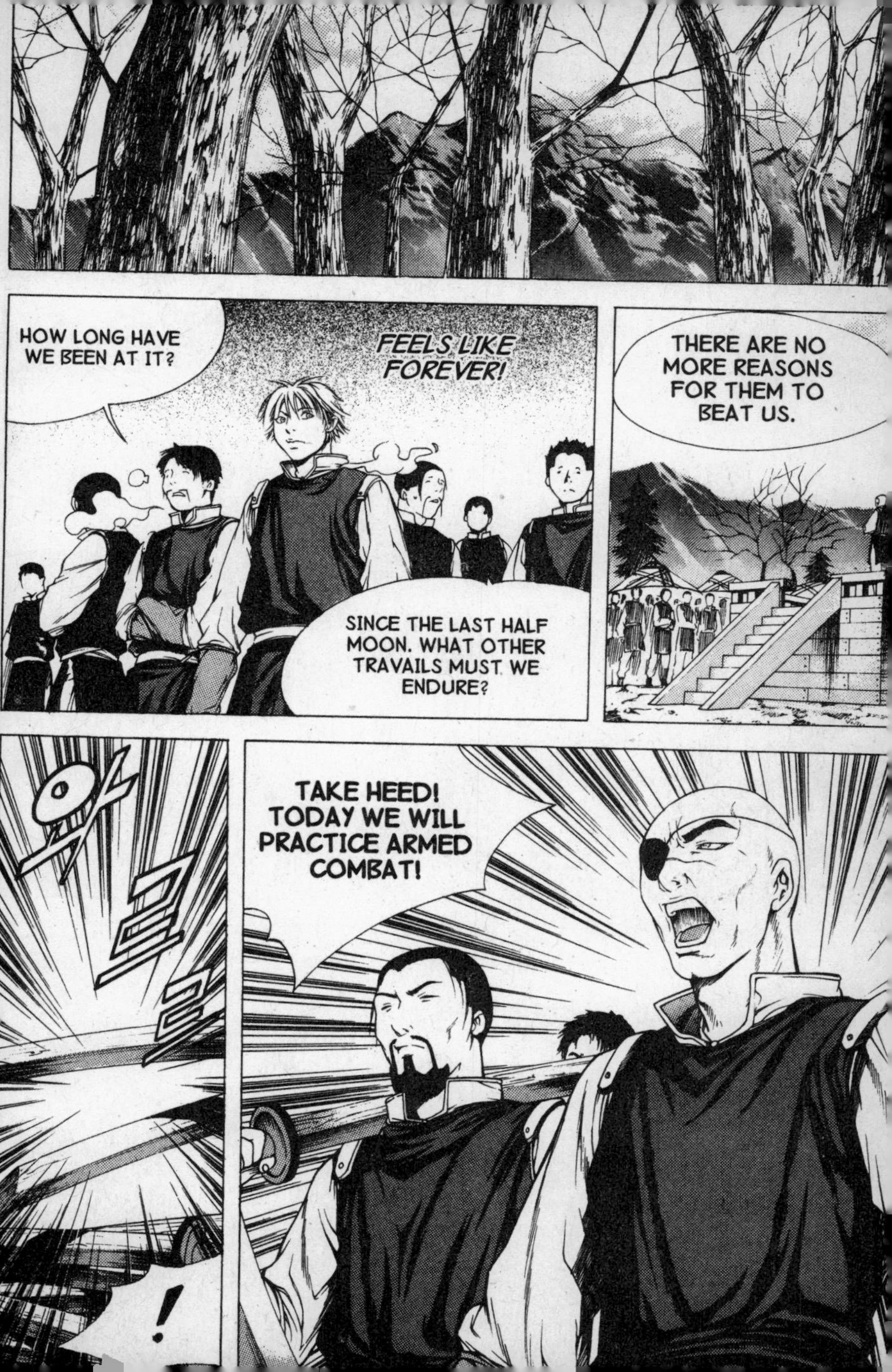
HOW LONG HAVE WE BEEN AT IT?
FEELS LIKE FOREVER!
SINCE THE LAST HALF MOON. WHAT OTHER TRAVAILS MUST WE ENDURE?
THERE ARE NO MORE REASONS FOR THEM TO BEAT US.
!
TAKE HEED! TODAY WE WILL PRACTICE ARMED COMBAT!

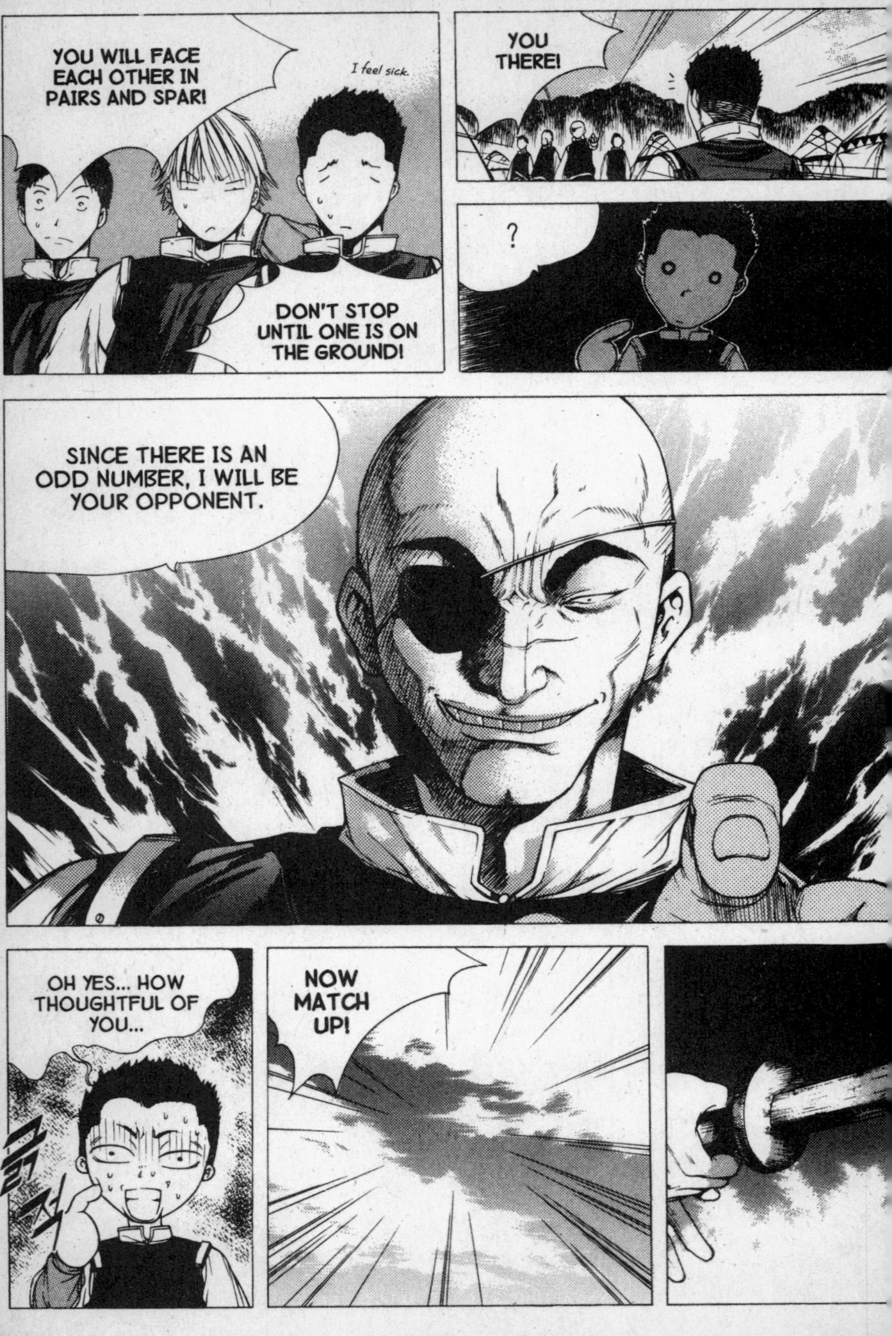
YOU WILL FACE EACH OTHER IN PAIRS AND SPAR!
I feel sick.
DON'T STOP UNTIL ONE IS ON THE GROUND!
YOU THERE!
?
SINCE THERE IS AN ODD NUMBER, I WILL BE YOUR OPPONENT.
OH YES... HOW THOUGHTFUL OF YOU...
NOW MATCH UP!

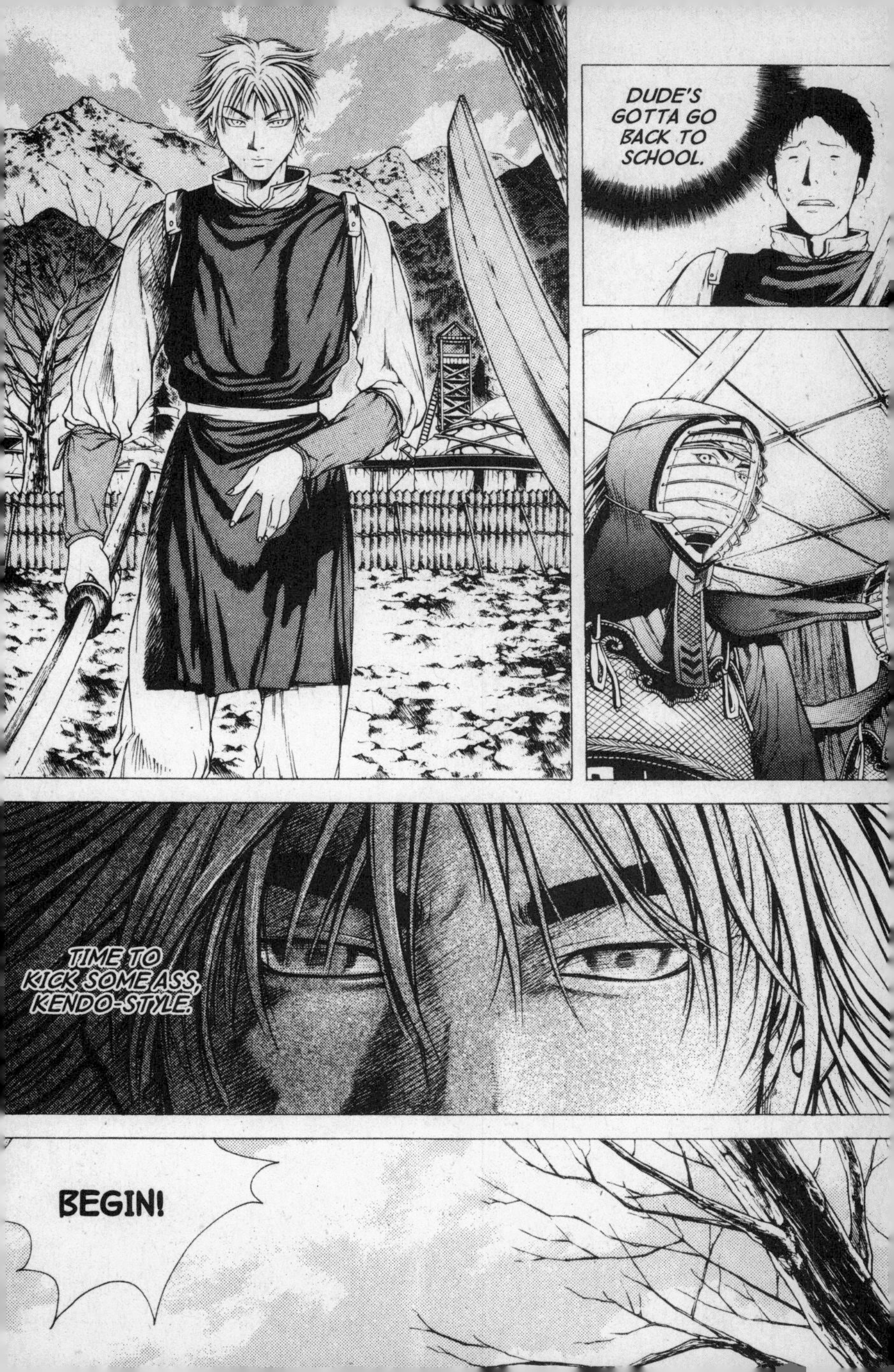
DUDE'S GOTTA GO BACK TO SCHOOL.
TIME TO KICK SOME ASS, KENDO-STYLE.
BEGIN!

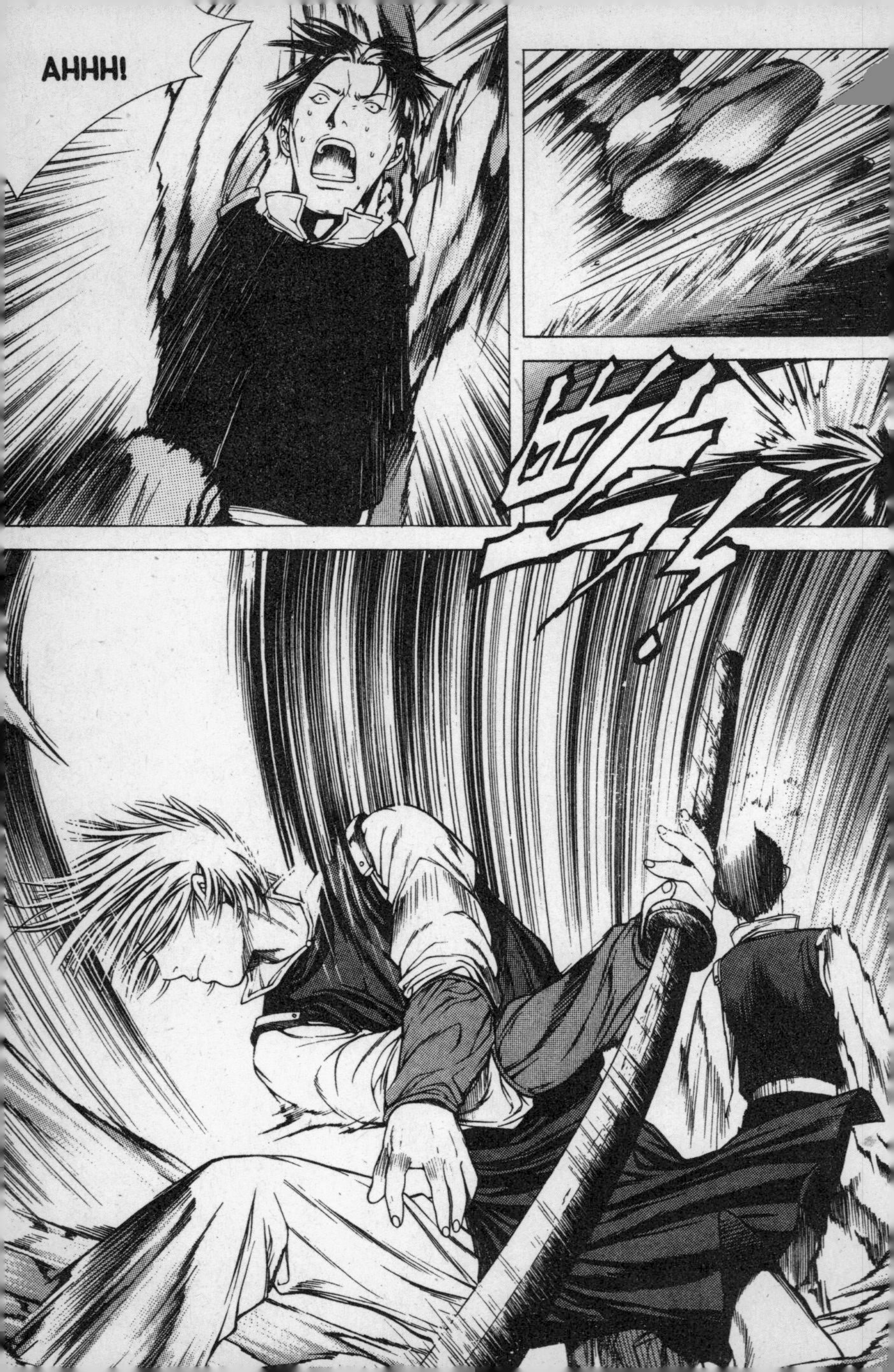
AHHH!

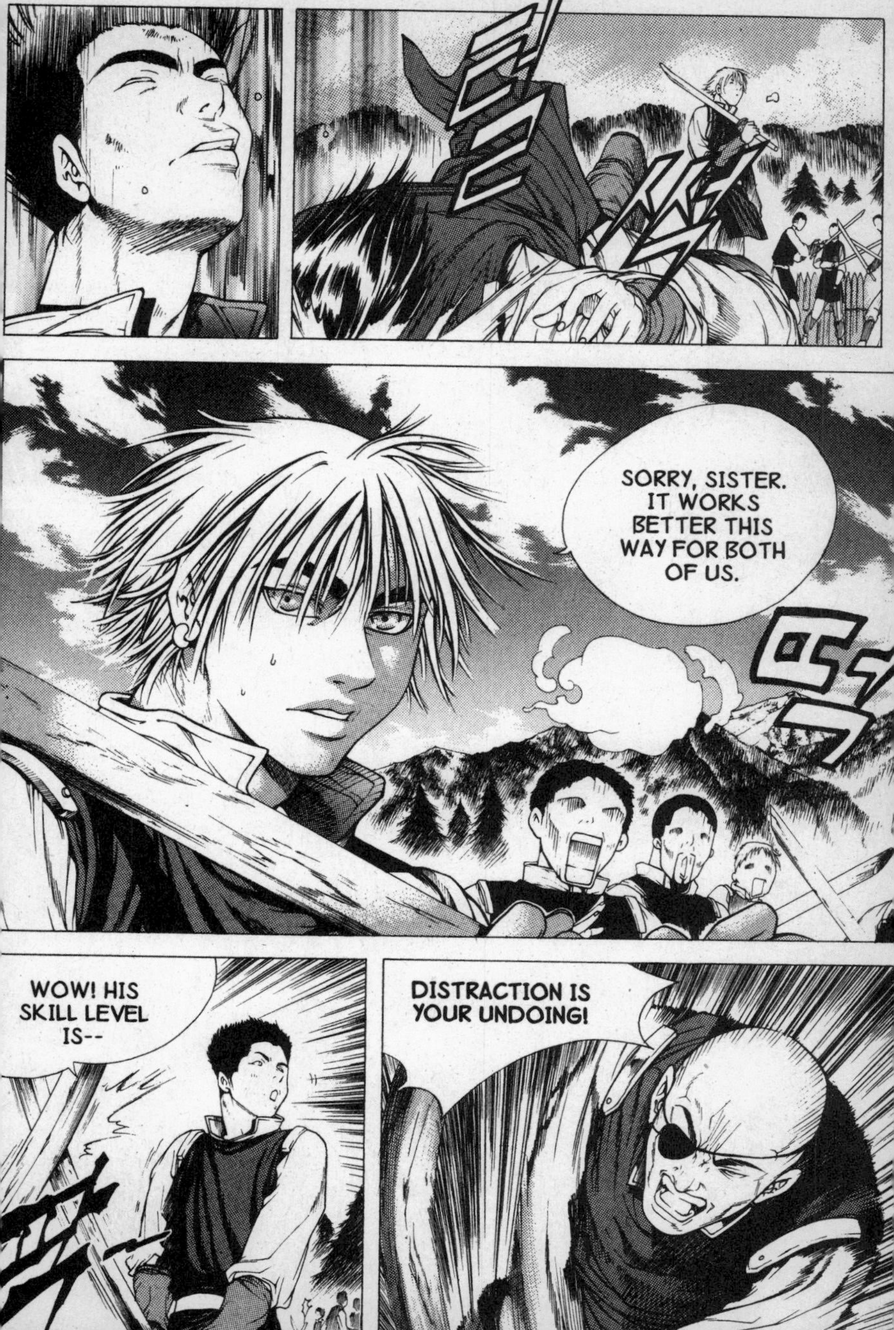
SORRY, SISTER. IT WORKS BETTER THIS WAY FOR BOTH OF US.
WOW! HIS SKILL LEVEL IS--
DISTRACTION IS YOUR UNDOING!

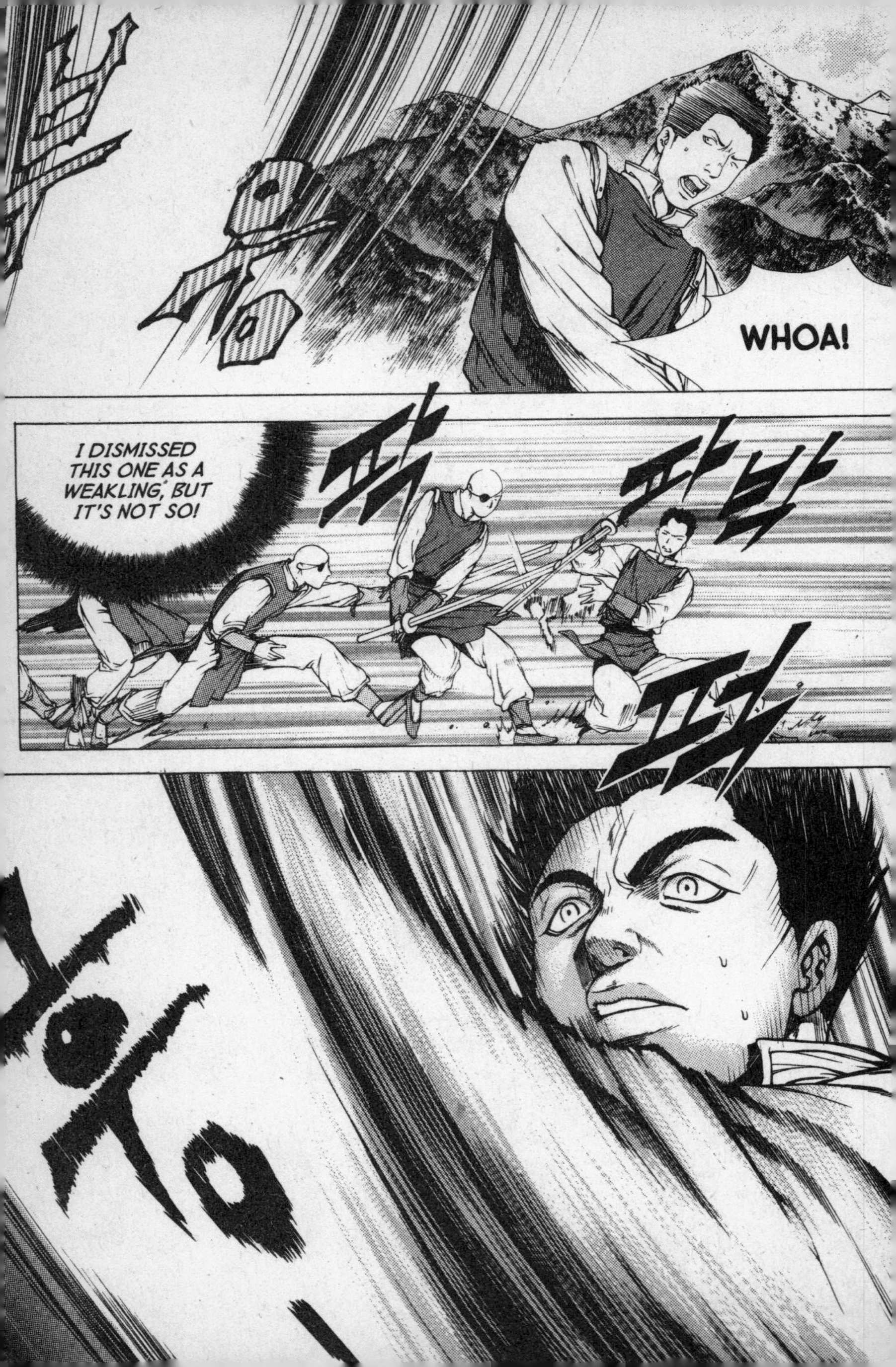
WHOA!
I DISMISSED THIS ONE AS A WEAKLING, BUT IT'S NOT SO!

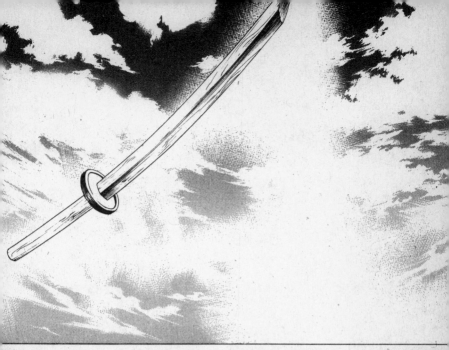

PHEW!

BOY, YOU ARE A STRONG ONE.

Ouch!

......

OUR SURVIVAL RATE IS MINIMAL--GOOD IGHTERS CAN BECOME LIKE GODS.

ARROGANT JESTERS WHO DON'T RECOGNIZE THIS MUST BE TAUGHT A LESSON.

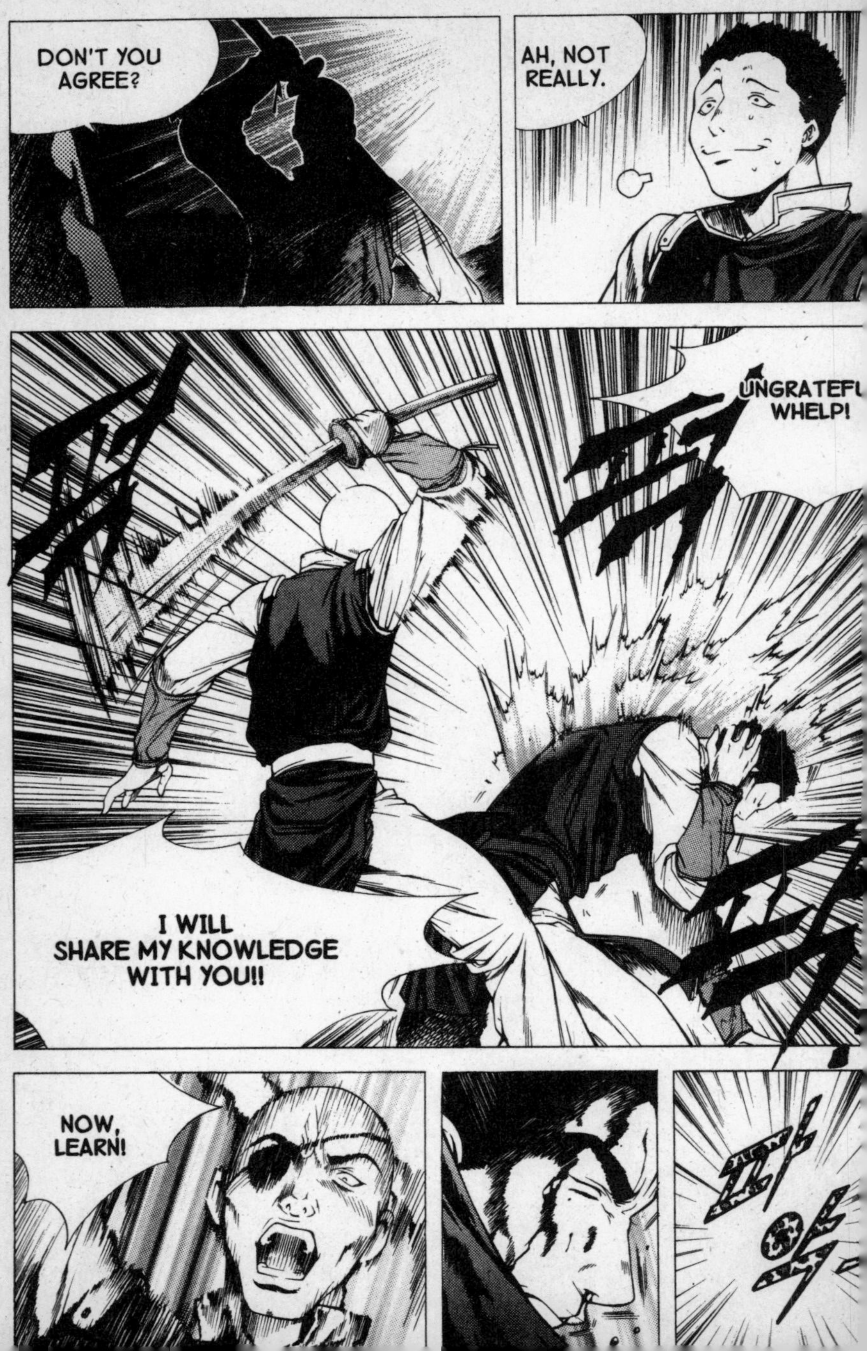
DON'T YOU AGREE?
AH, NOT REALLY.
UNGRATEFU WHELP!
I WILL SHARE MY KNOWLEDGE WITH YOU!!
NOW, LEARN!

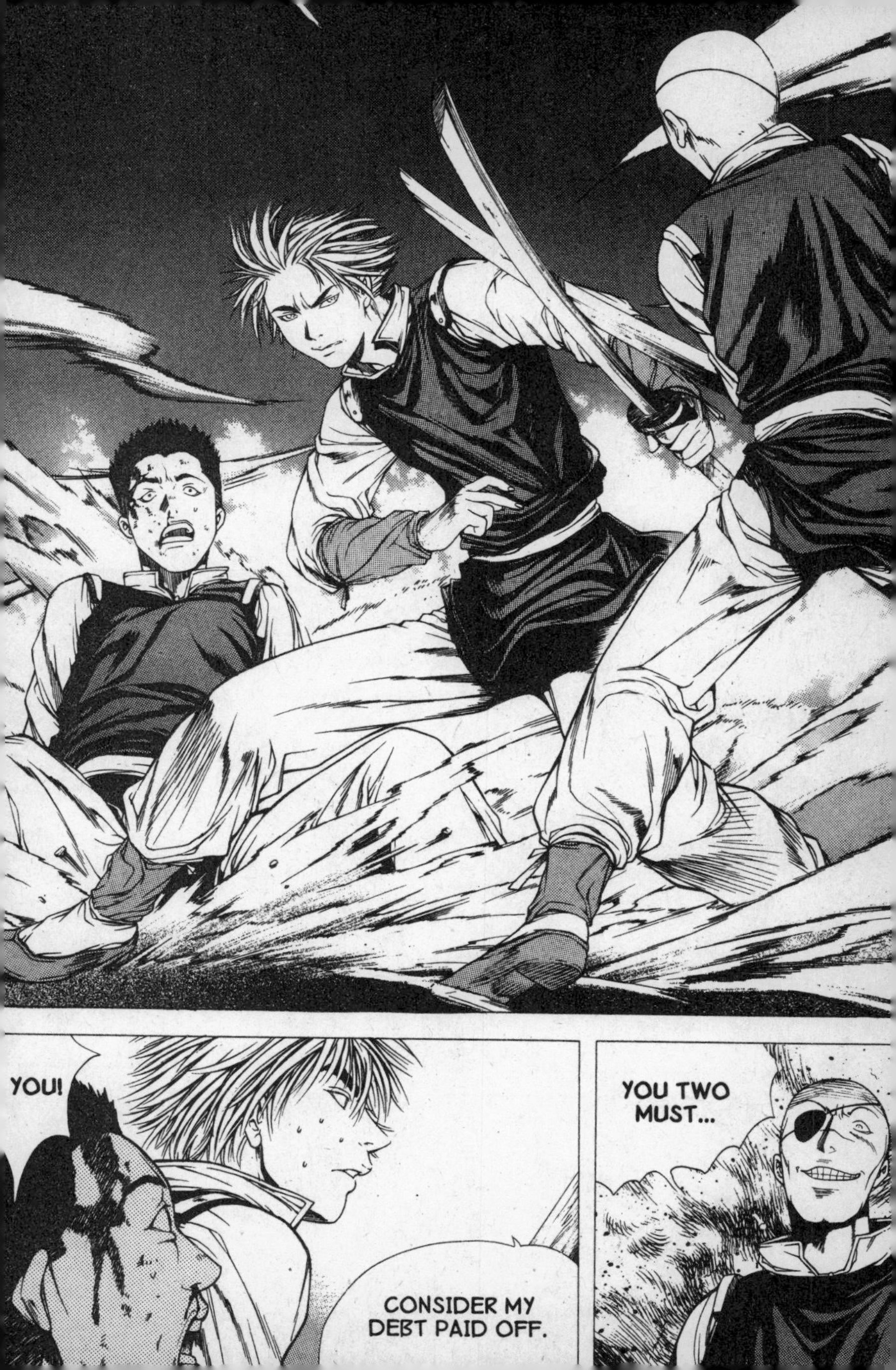
YOU!
CONSIDER MY DEBT PAID OFF.
YOU TWO MUST...

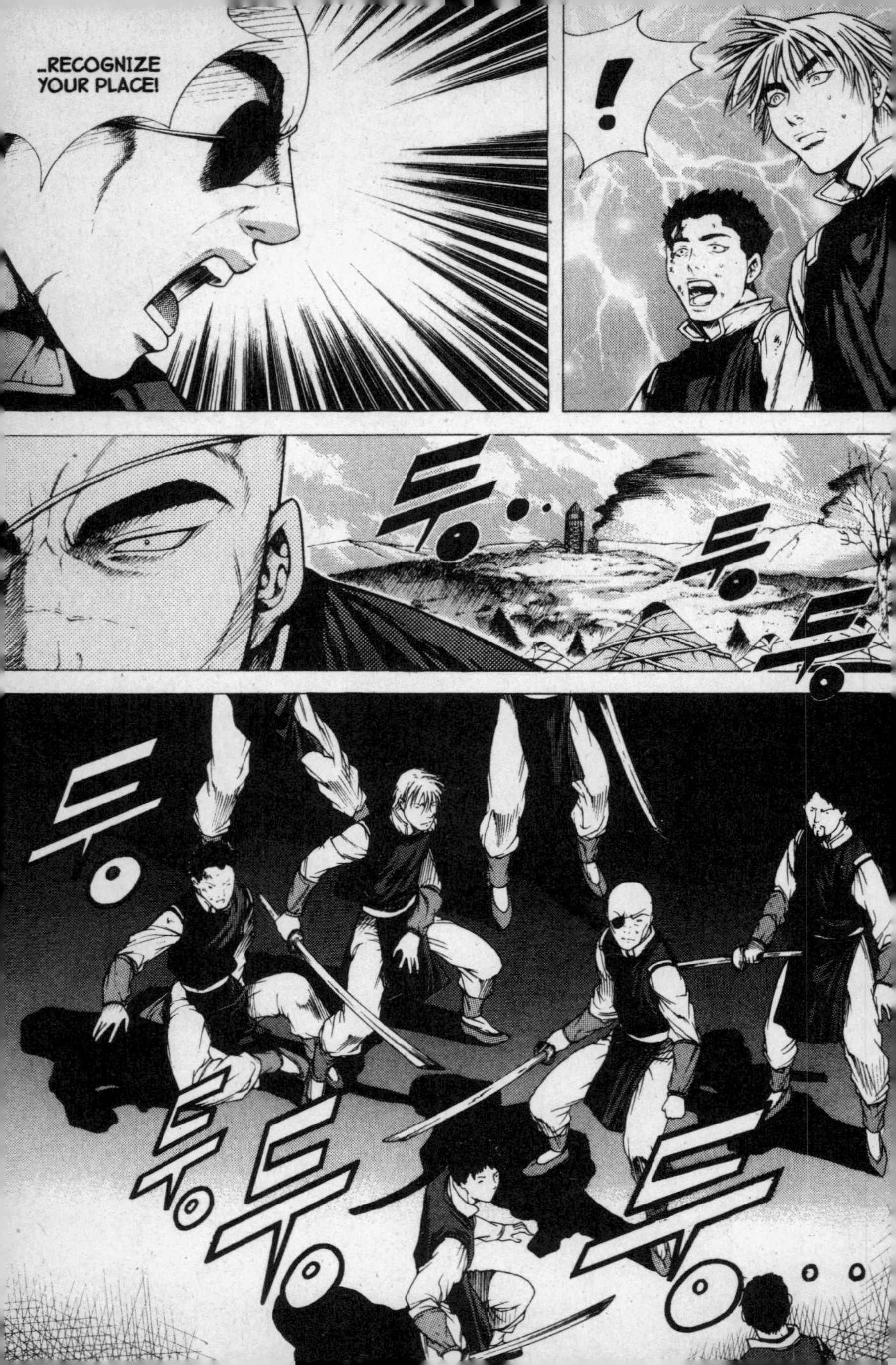
...RECOGNIZE YOUR PLACE!
!
둥...
둥
둥
둥
둥
둥
둥...

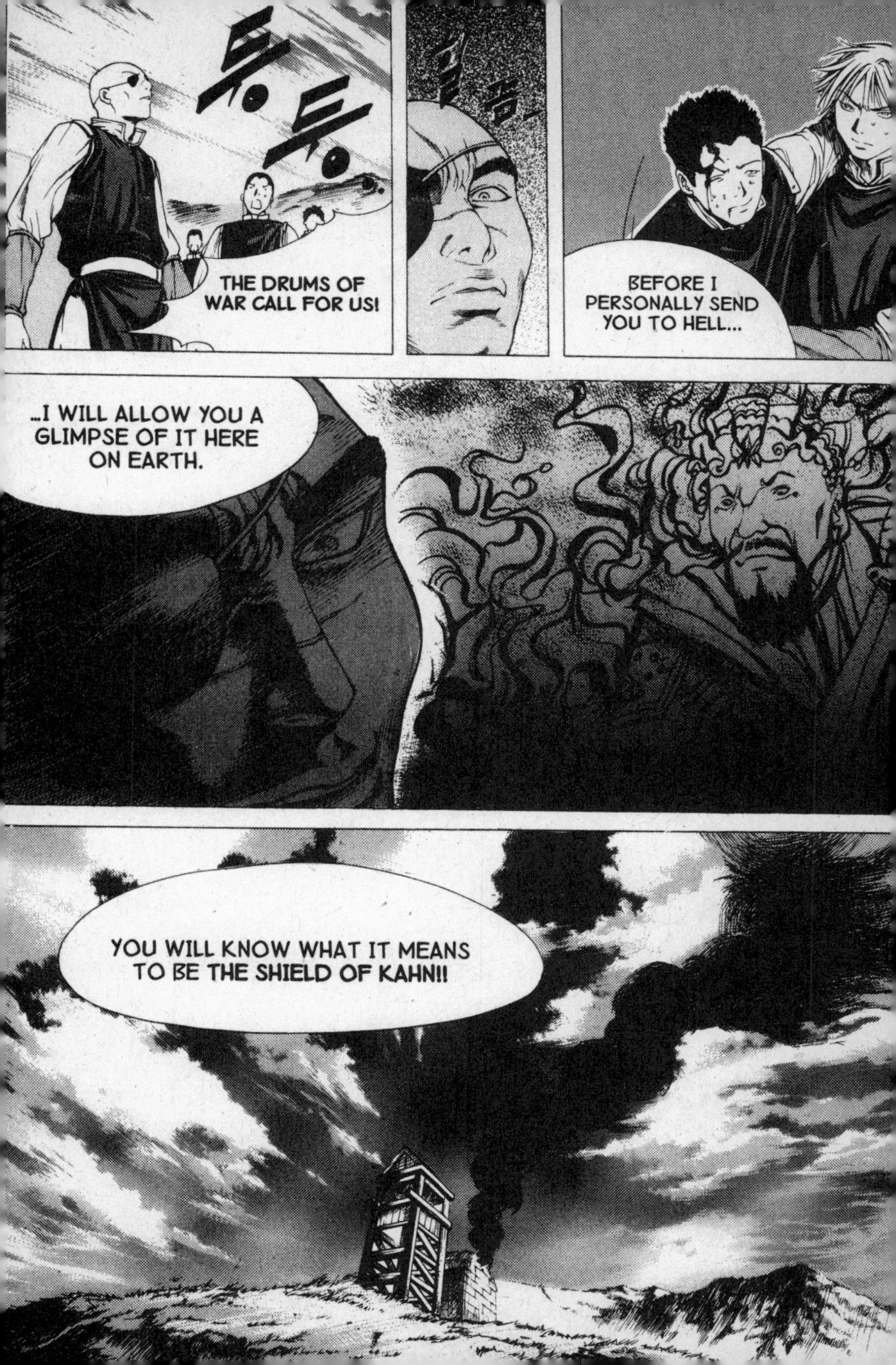
THE DRUMS OF WAR CALL FOR US!
BEFORE I PERSONALLY SEND YOU TO HELL...
...I WILL ALLOW YOU A GLIMPSE OF IT HERE ON EARTH.
YOU WILL KNOW WHAT IT MEANS TO BE THE SHIELD OF KAHN!!

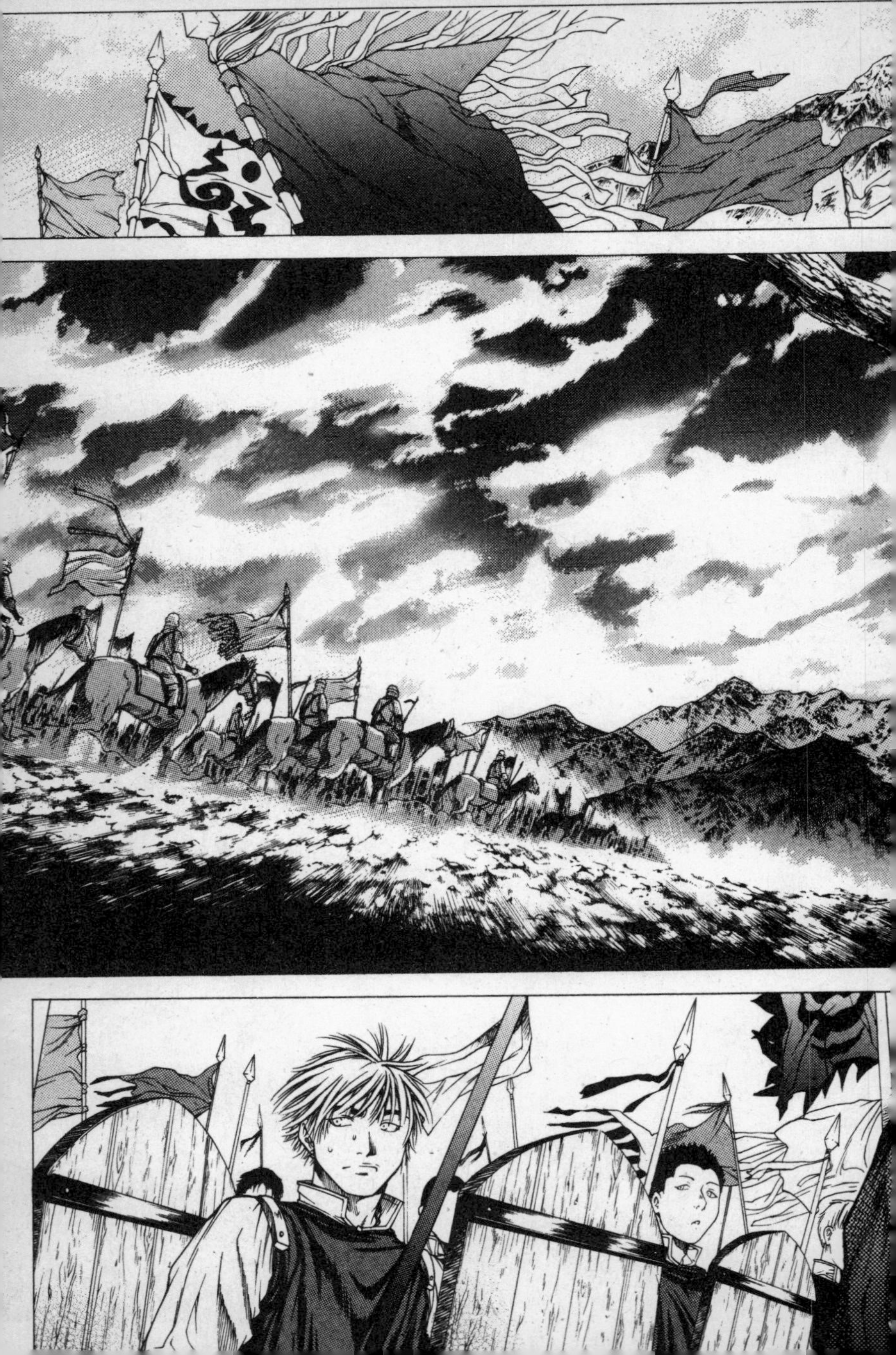

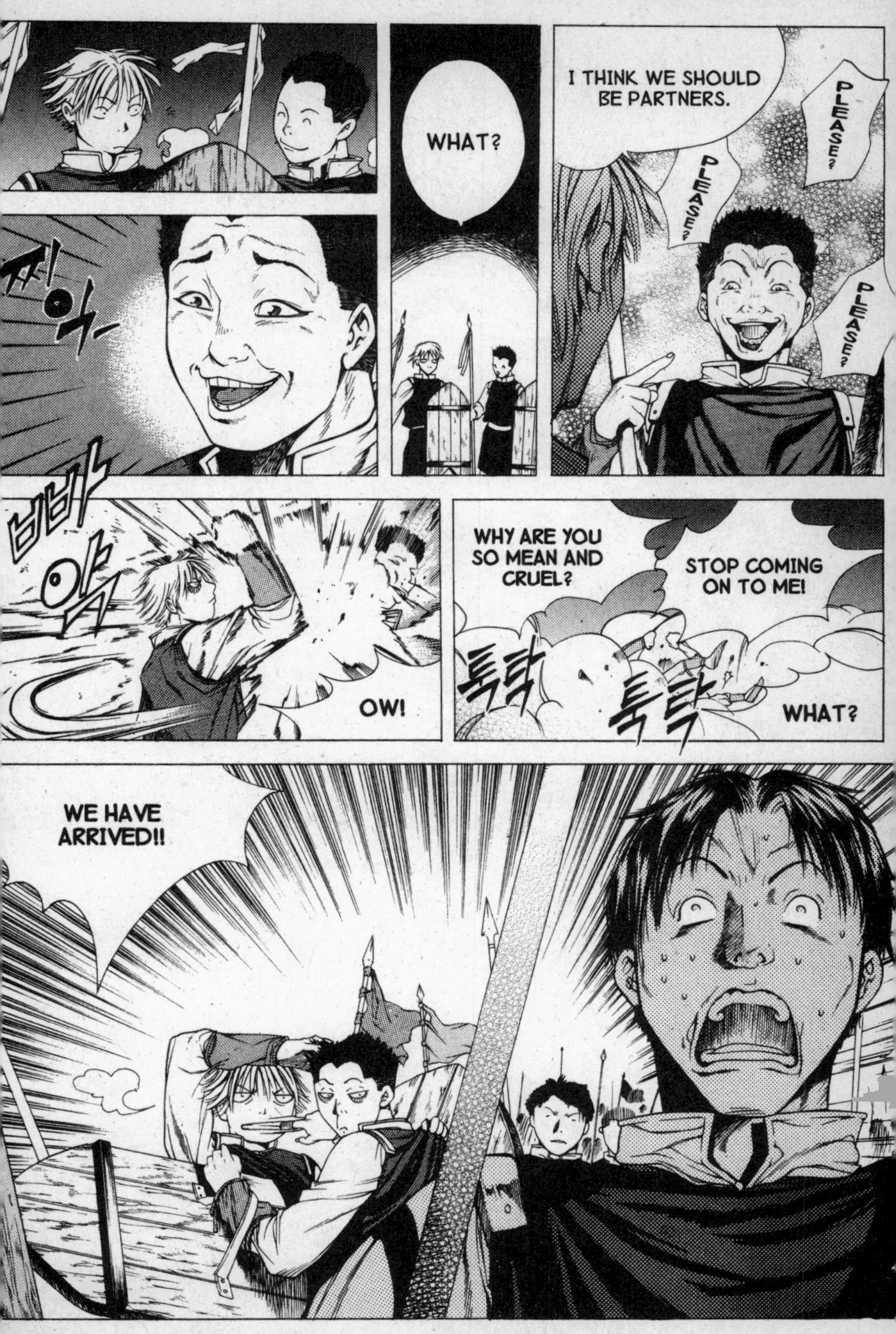
WHAT?
I THINK WE SHOULD BE PARTNERS.
PLEASE?
PLEASE?
PLEASE?
OW!
WHY ARE YOU SO MEAN AND CRUEL?
STOP COMING ON TO ME!
WHAT?
WE HAVE ARRIVED!!

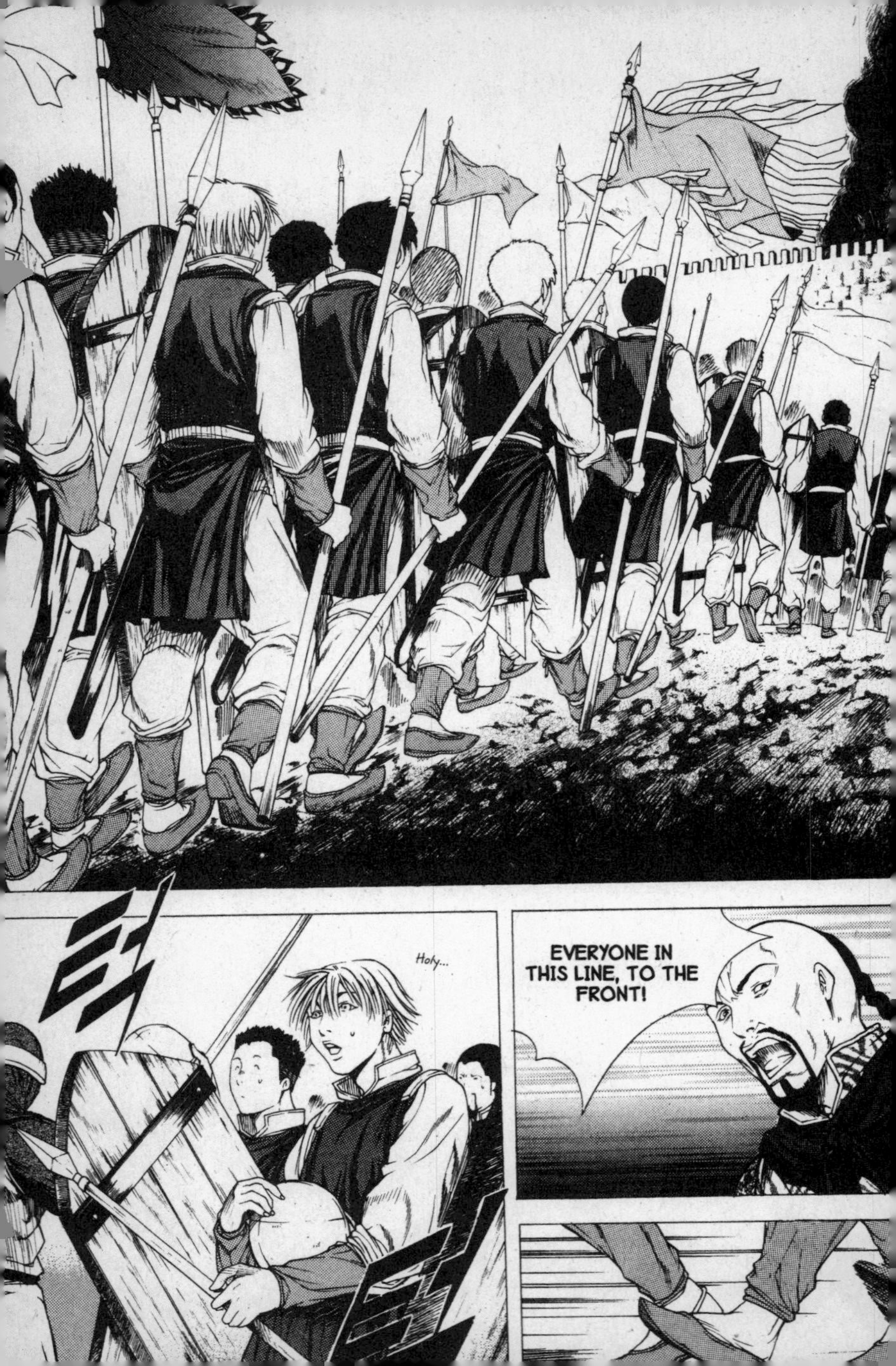
Holy...
EVERYONE IN THIS LINE, TO THE FRONT!

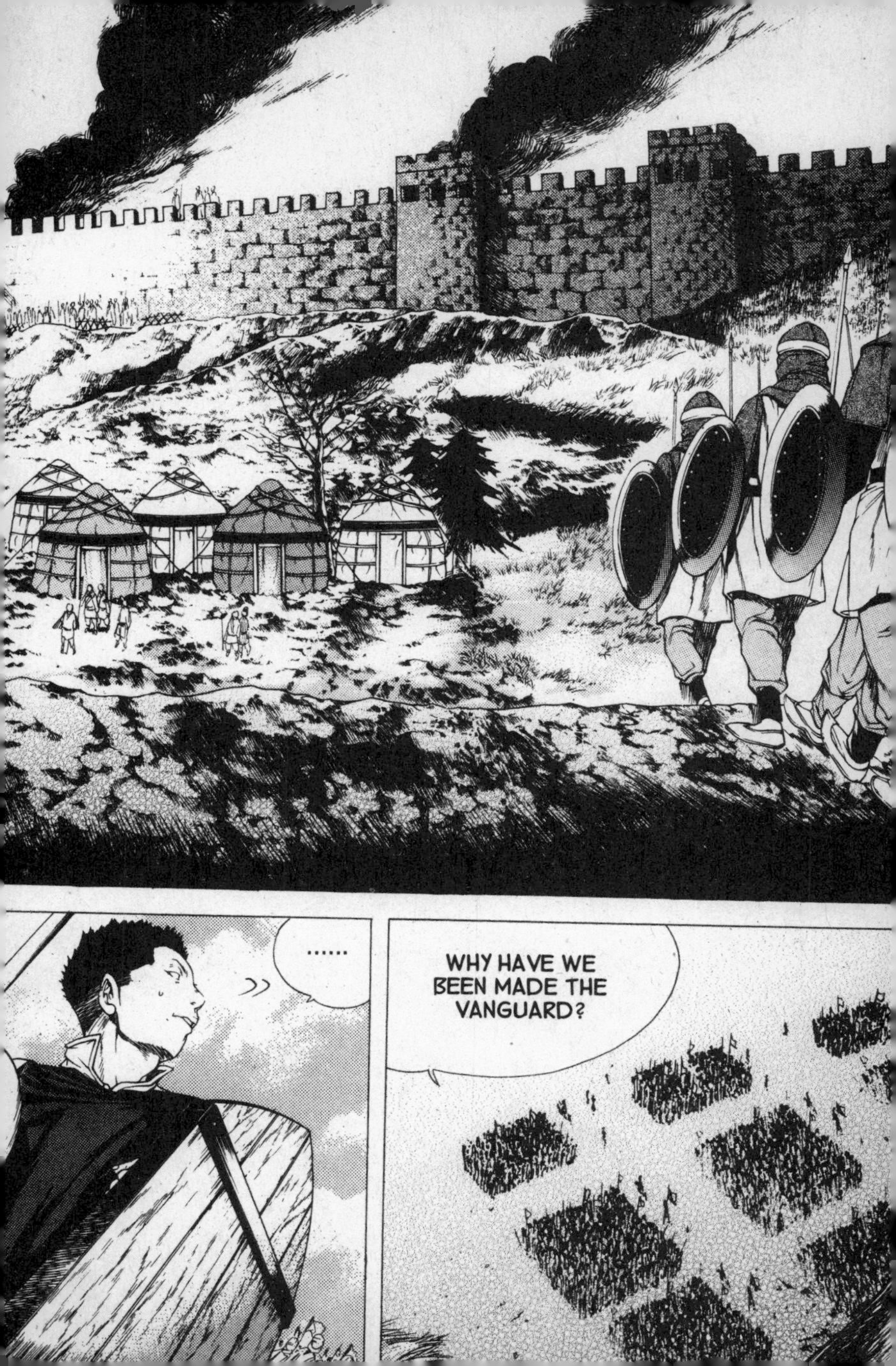
......
WHY HAVE WE BEEN MADE THE VANGUARD?

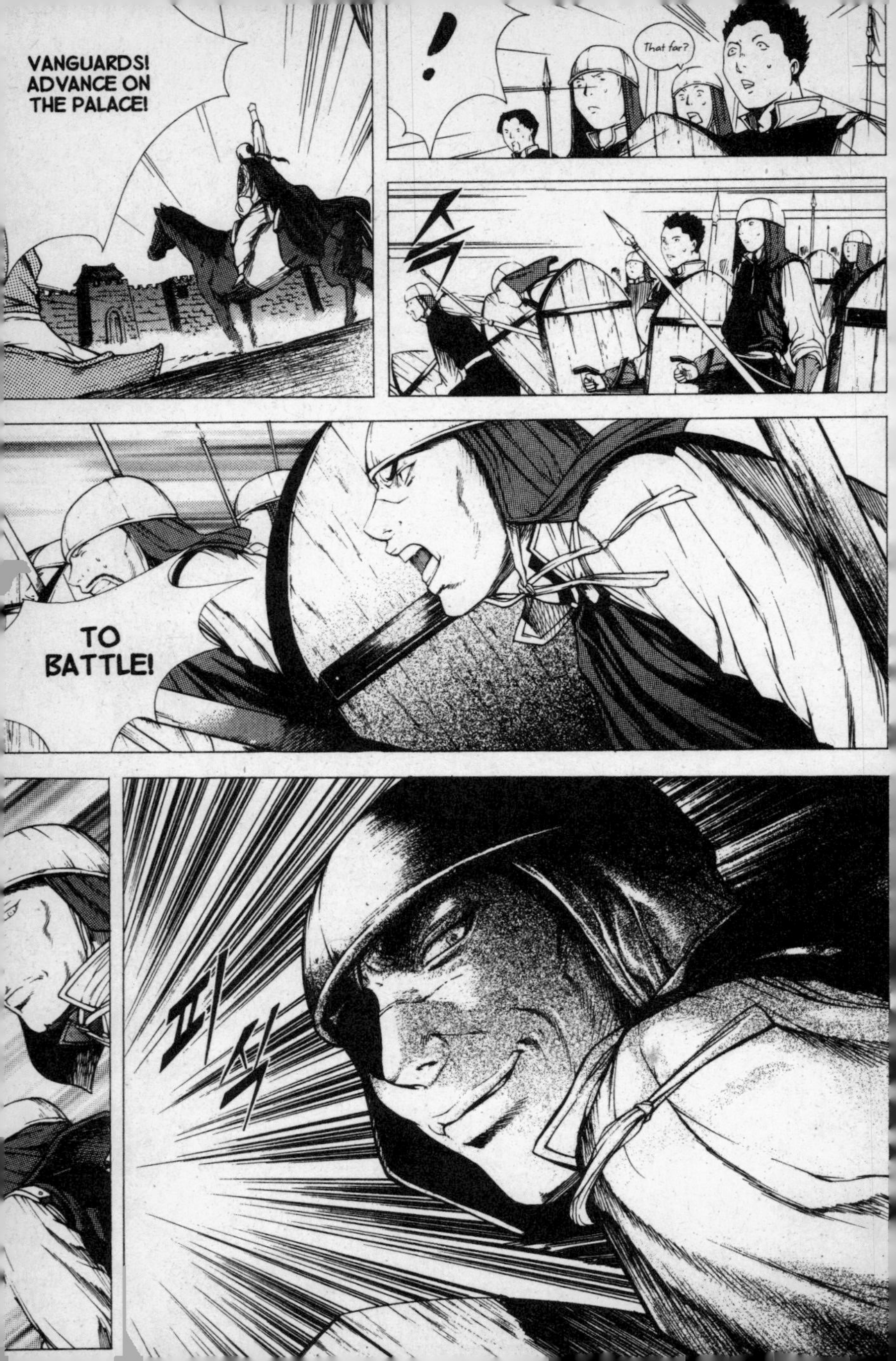
VANGUARDS! ADVANCE ON THE PALACE!
!
That far?
TO BATTLE!

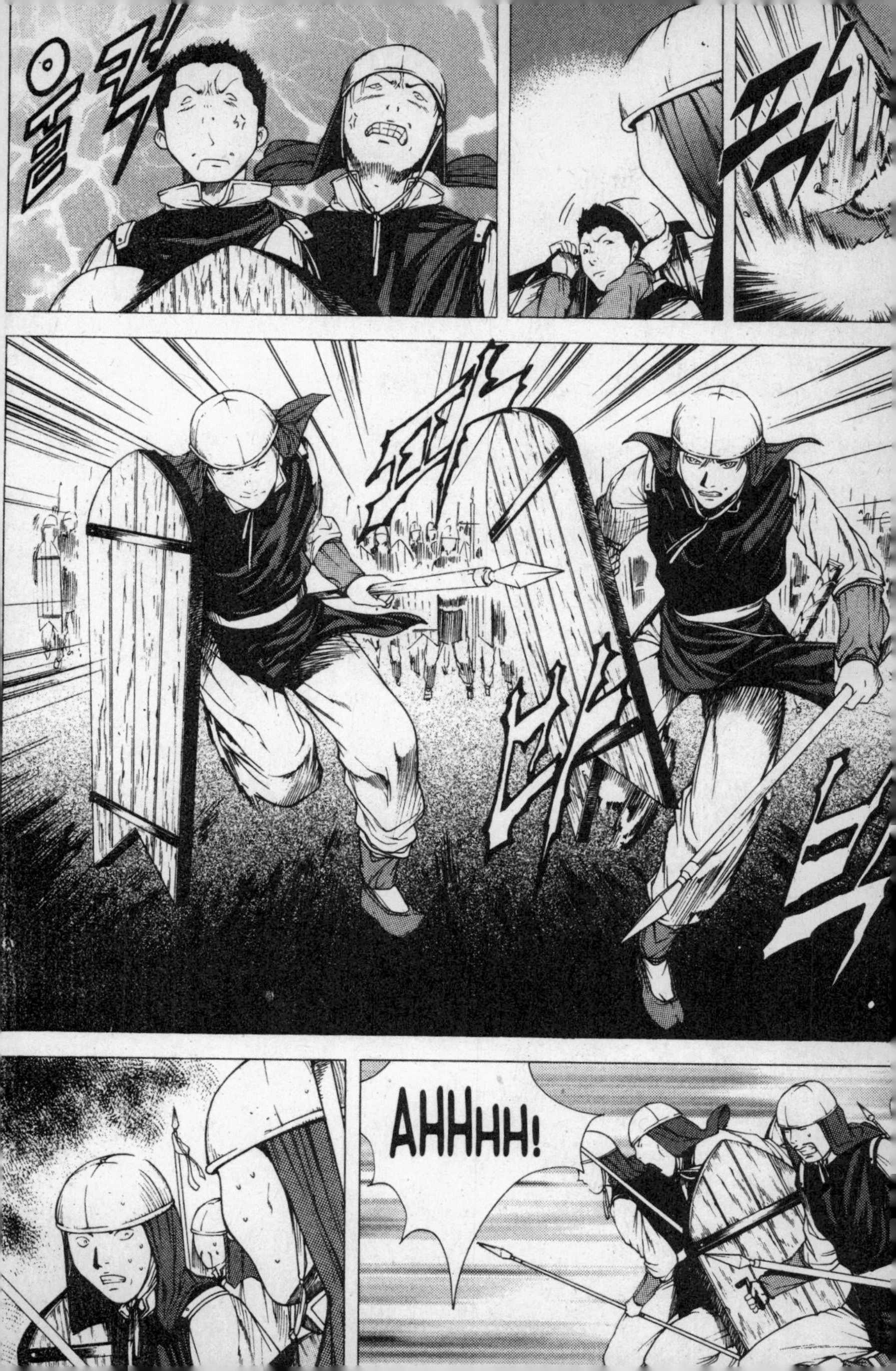
AHHHH!

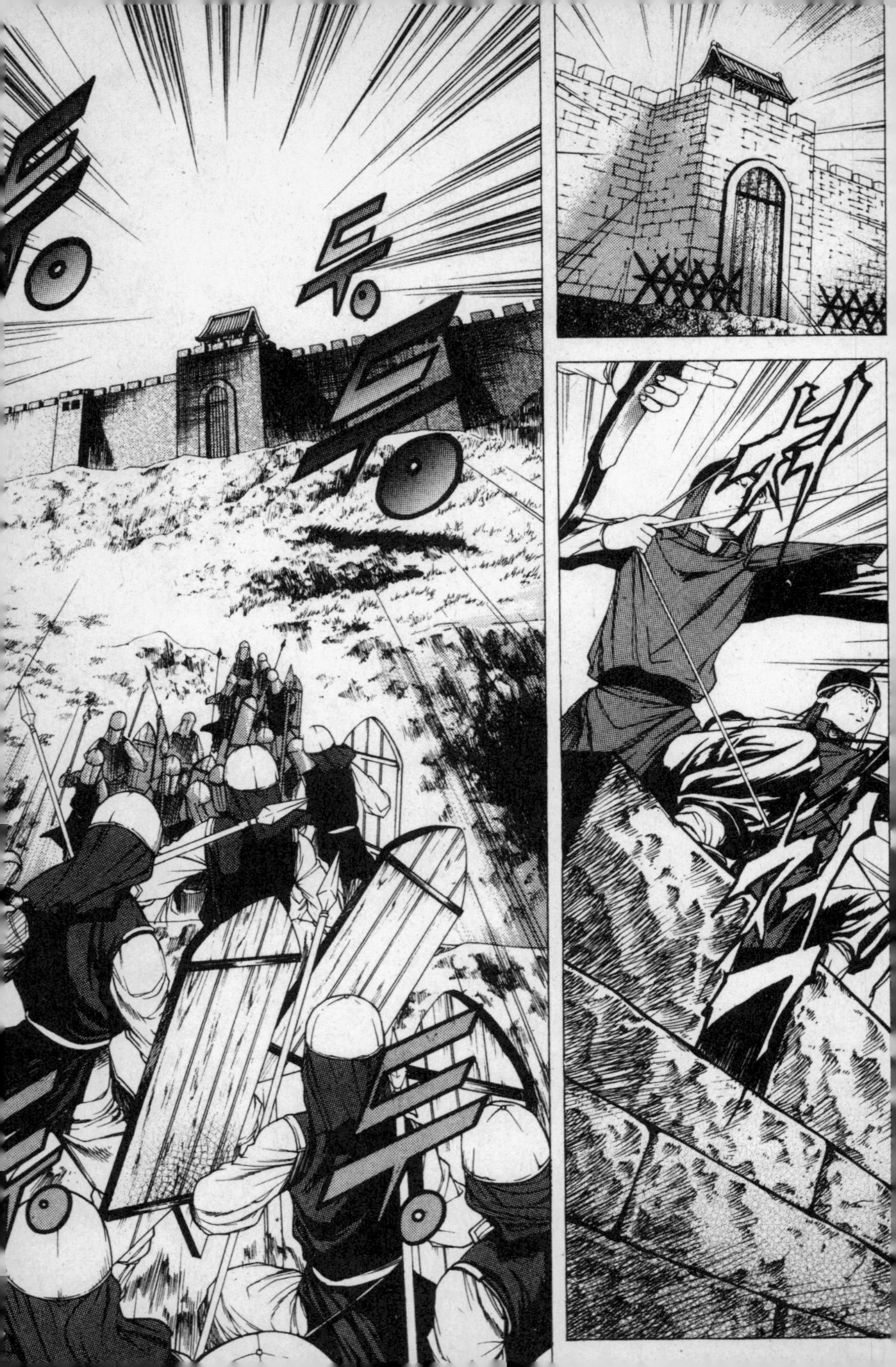
둥
둥
둥
둥

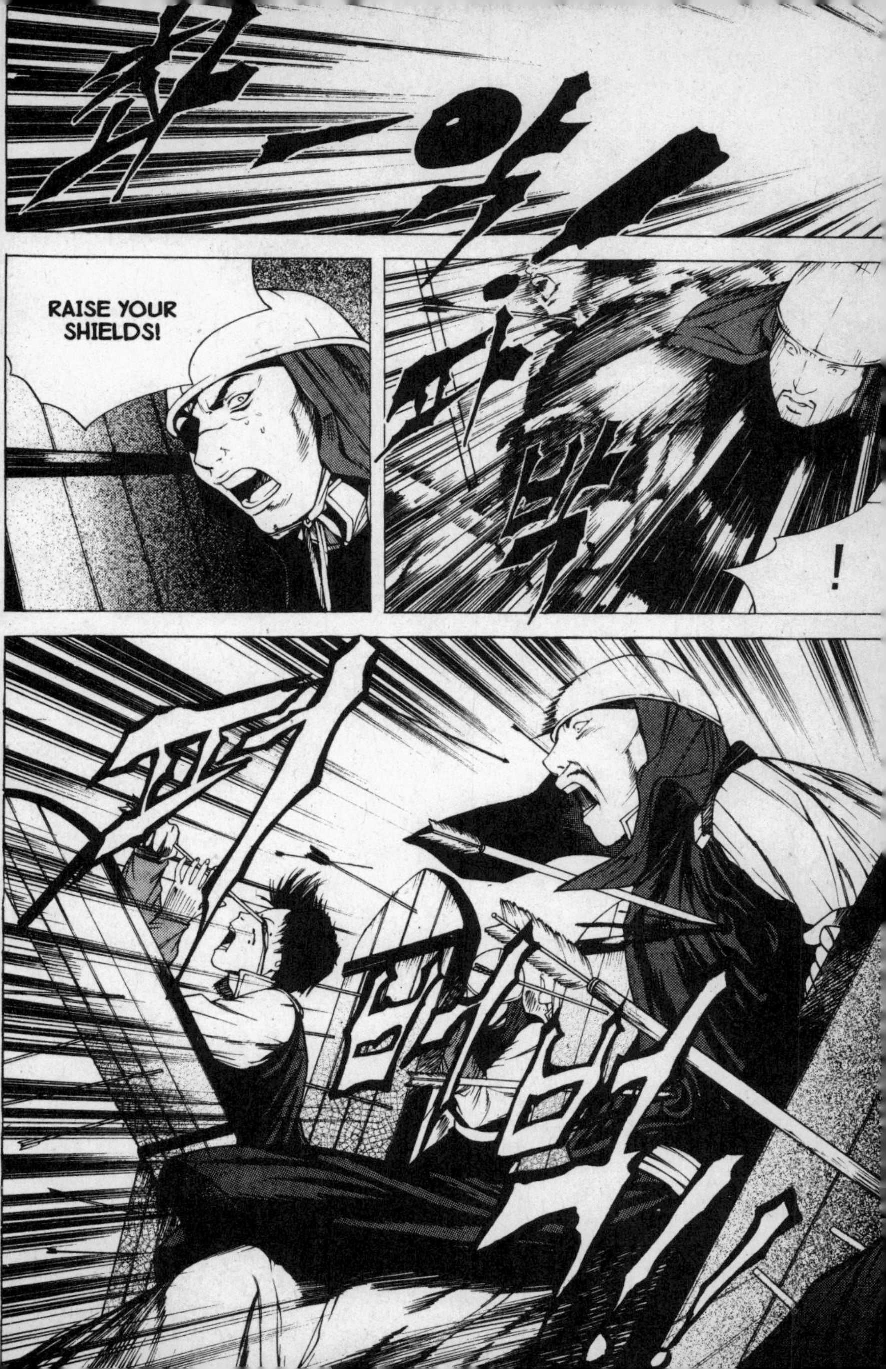
RAISE YOUR SHIELDS!
!

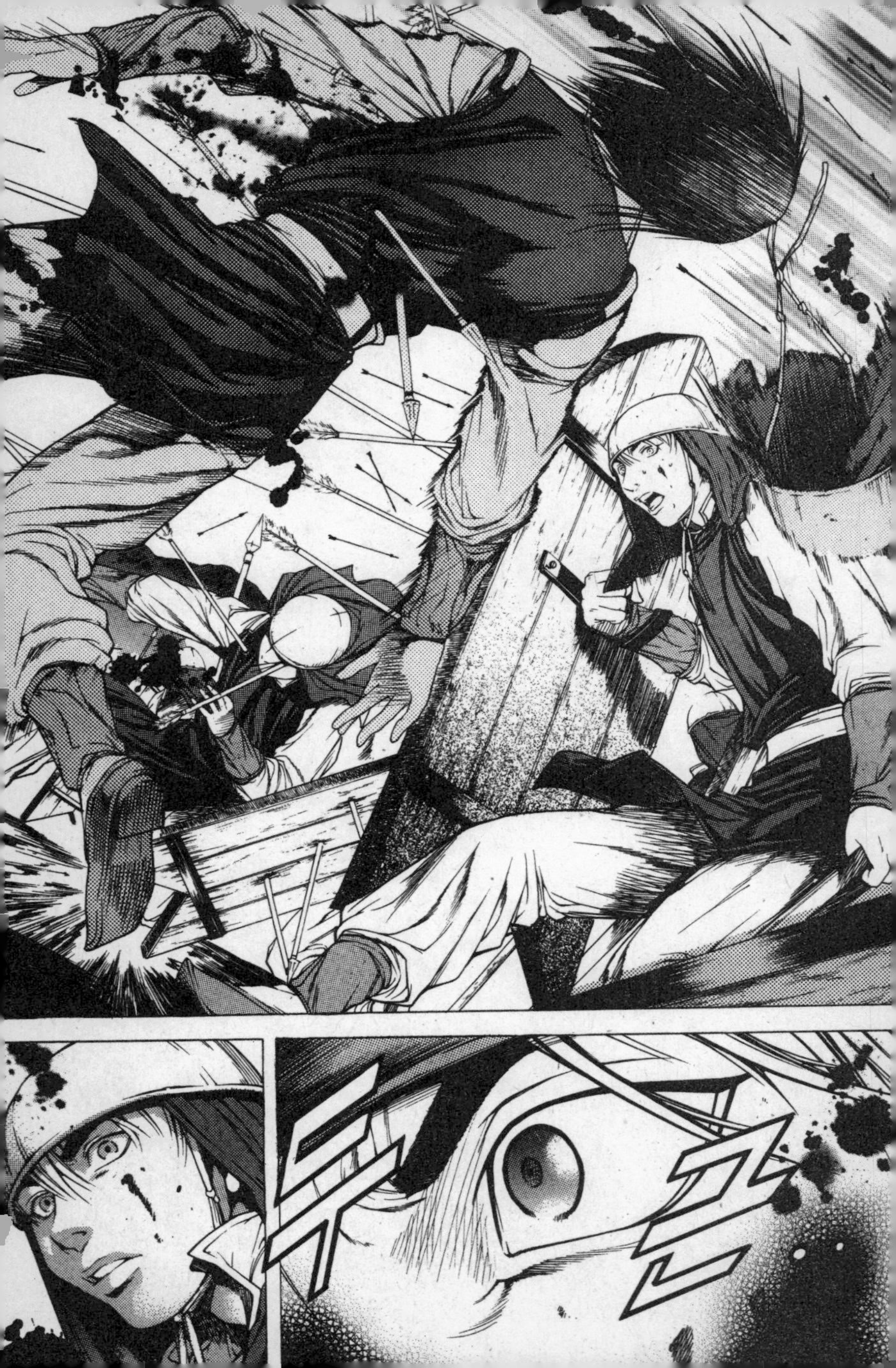

Chapter 29
Rules of Survival

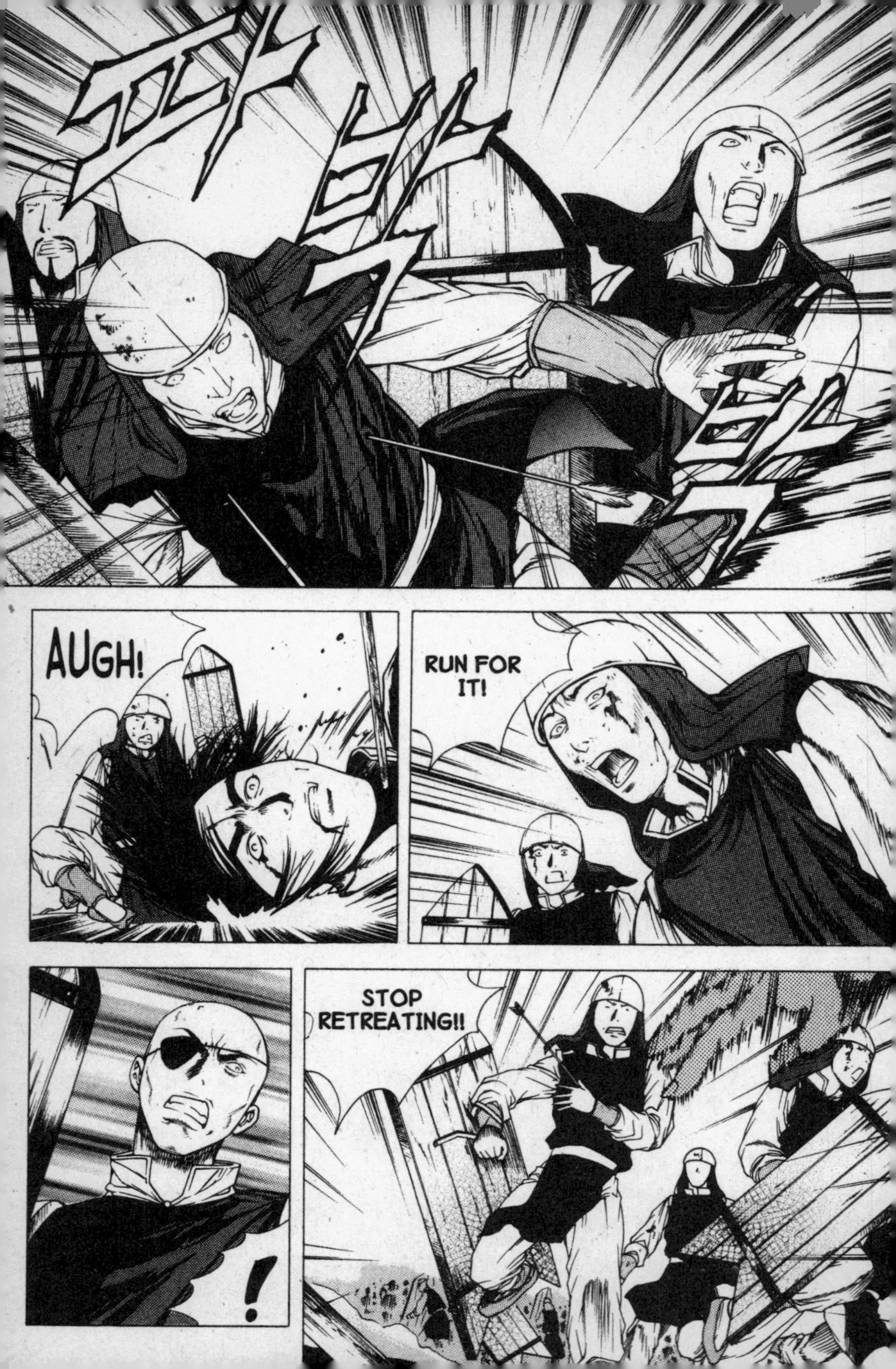
AUGH!
RUN FOR IT!
STOP RETREATING!!
!

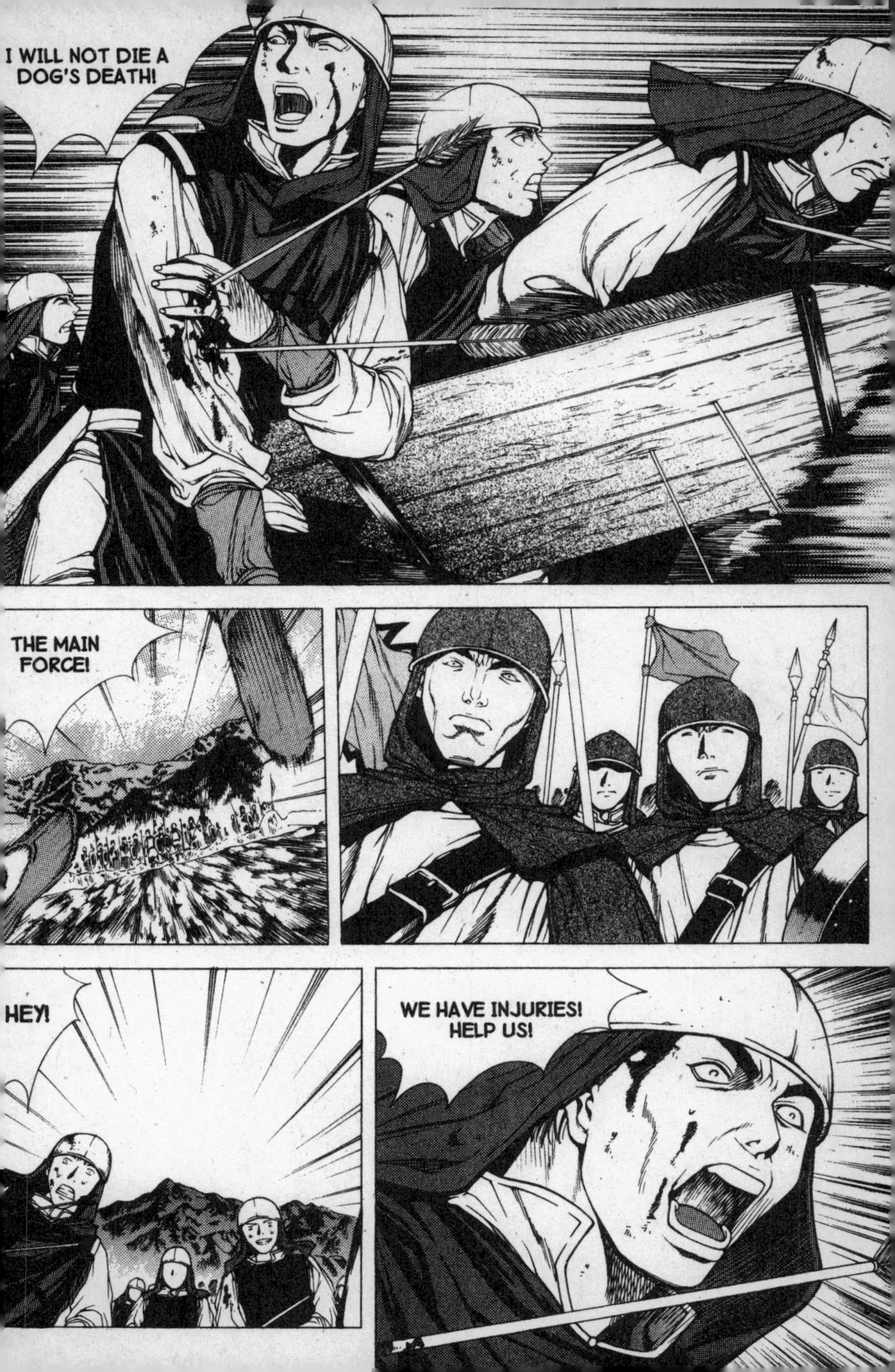
I WILL NOT DIE A DOG'S DEATH!
THE MAIN FORCE!
HEY!
WE HAVE INJURIES! HELP US!

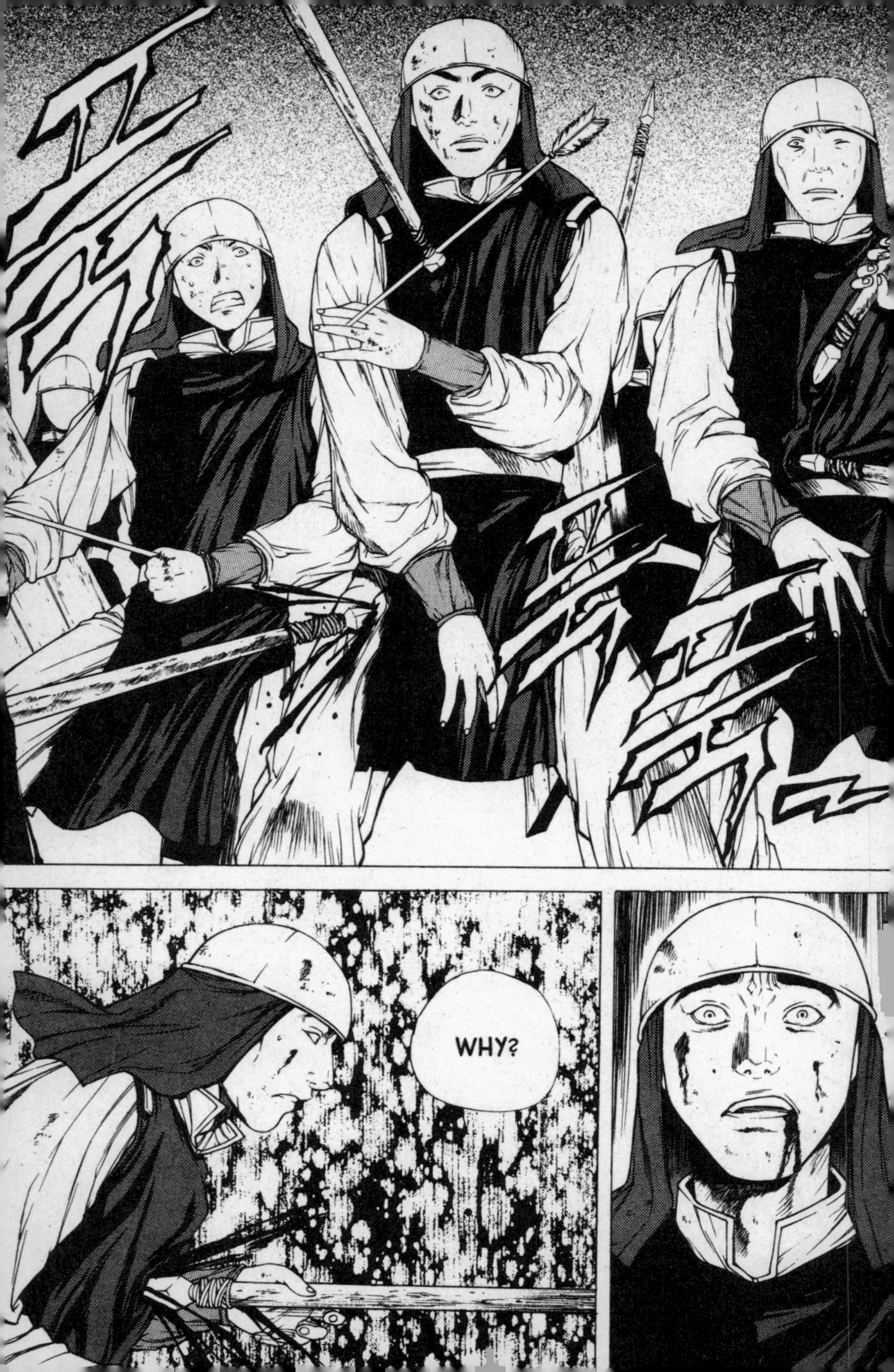
WHY?

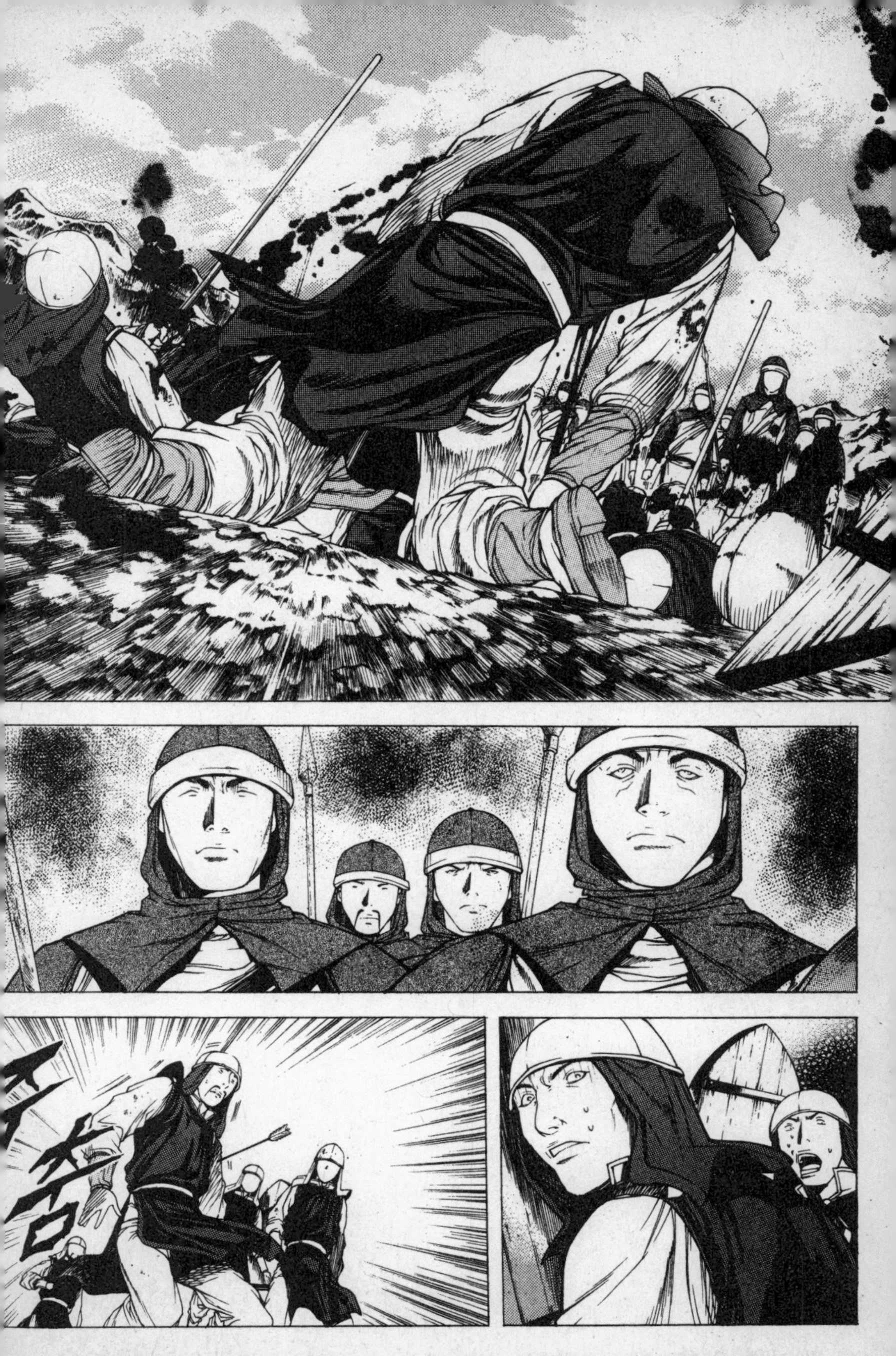

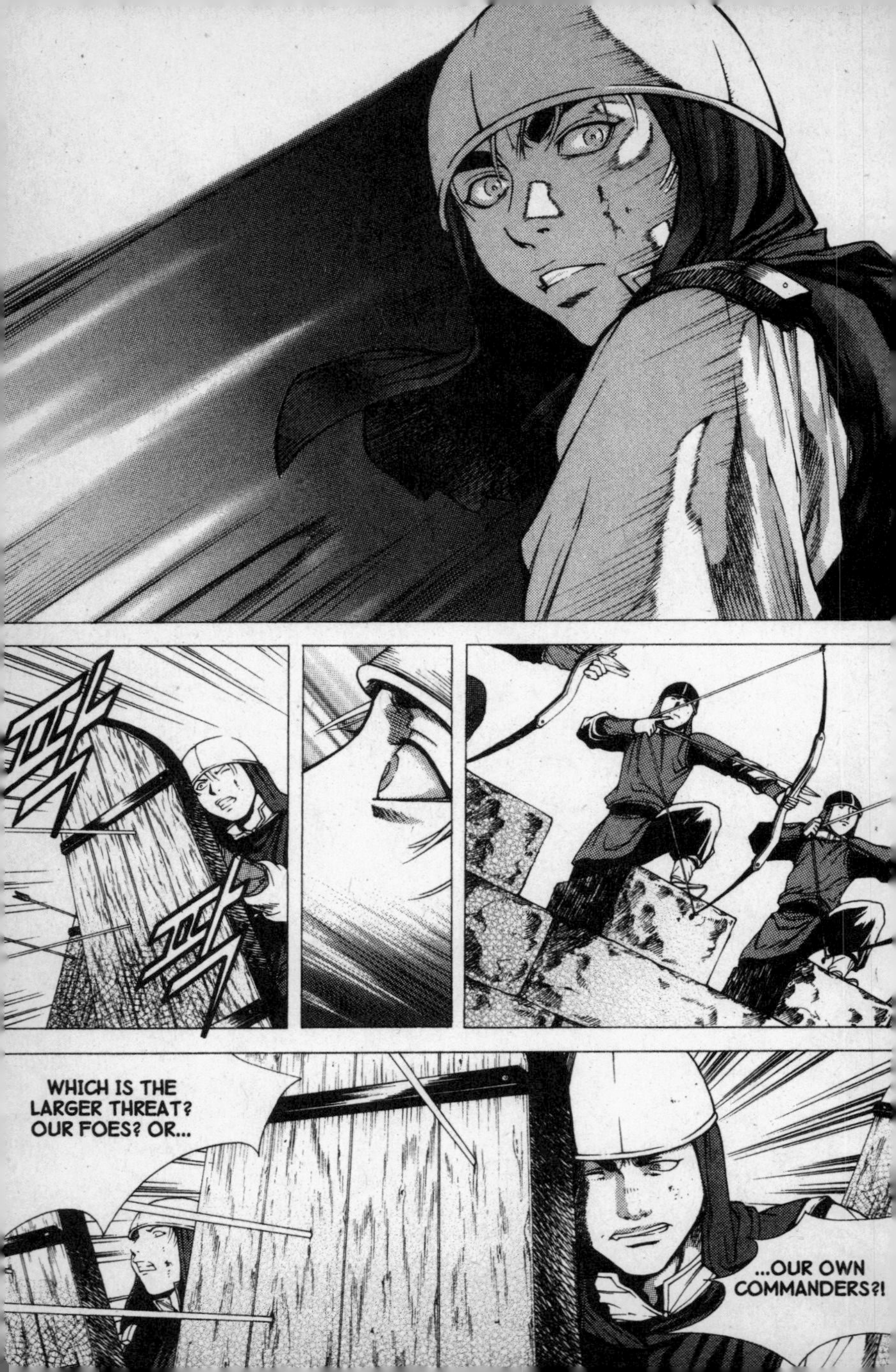
WHICH IS THE LARGER THREAT? OUR FOES? OR...
...OUR OWN COMMANDERS?!

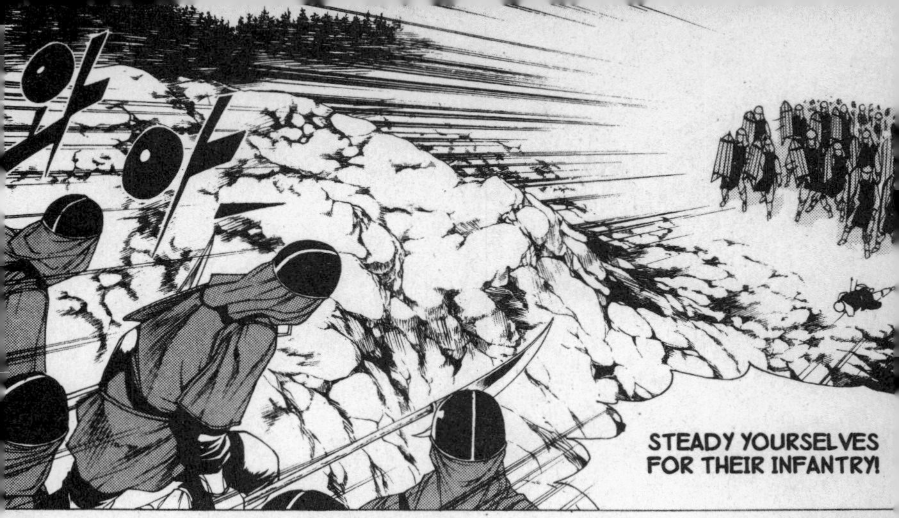
STEADY YOURSELVES FOR THEIR INFANTRY!
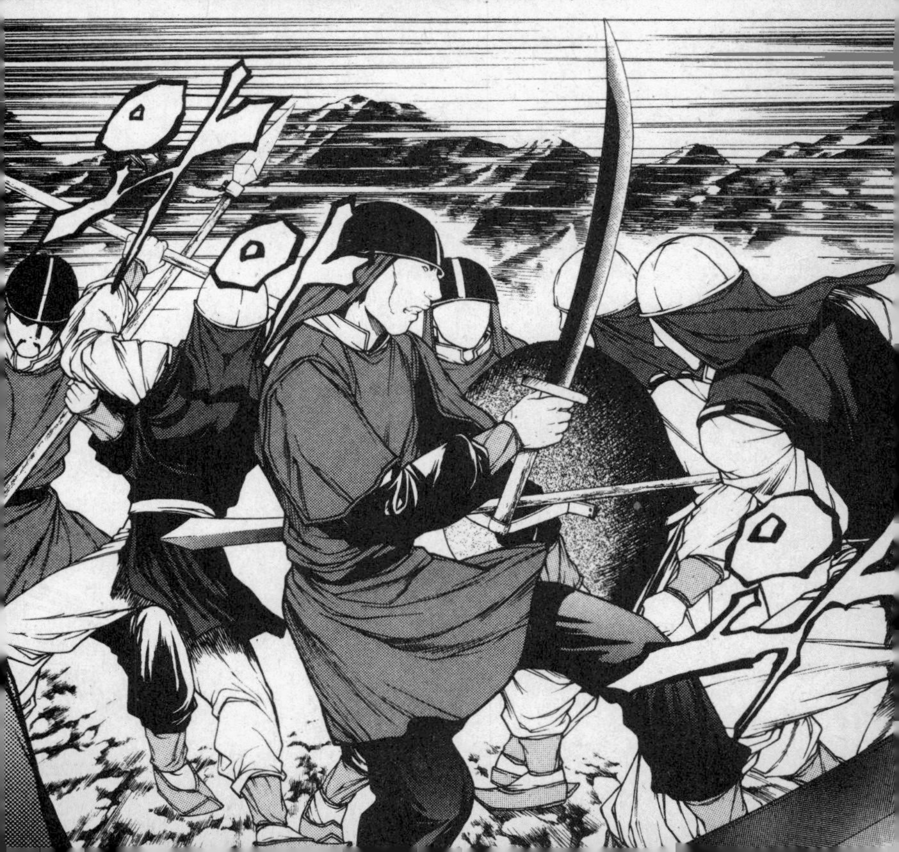

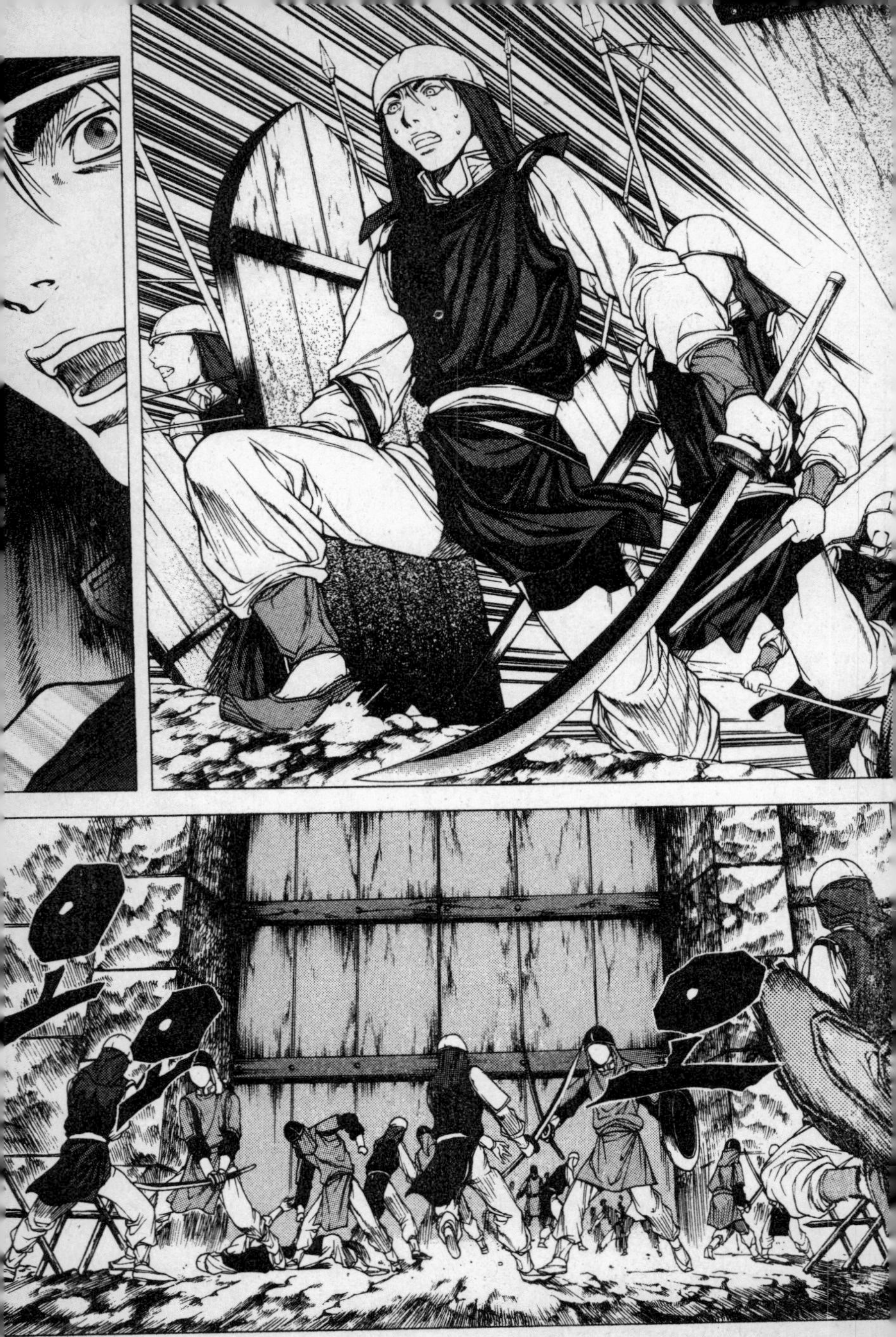

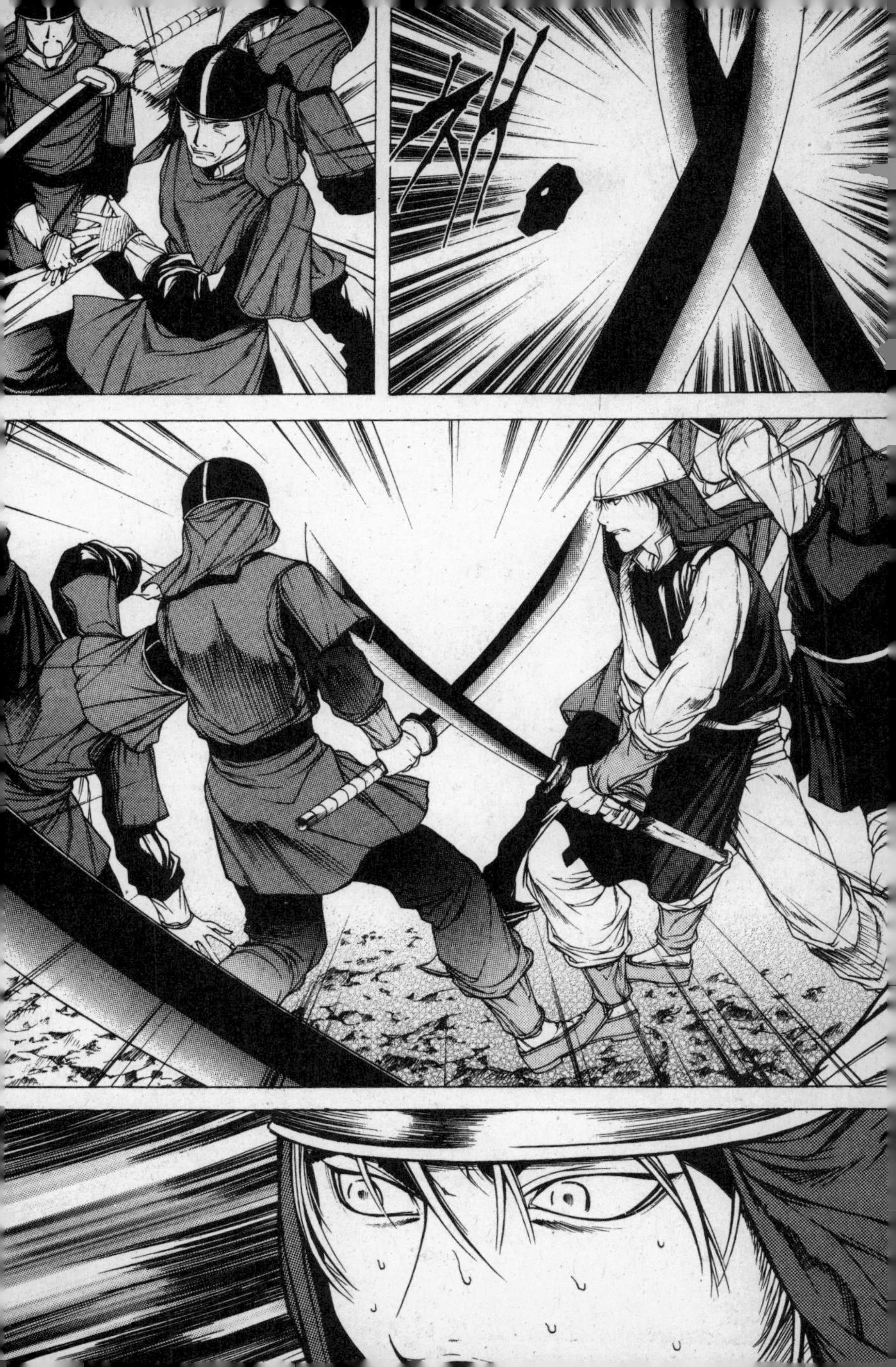

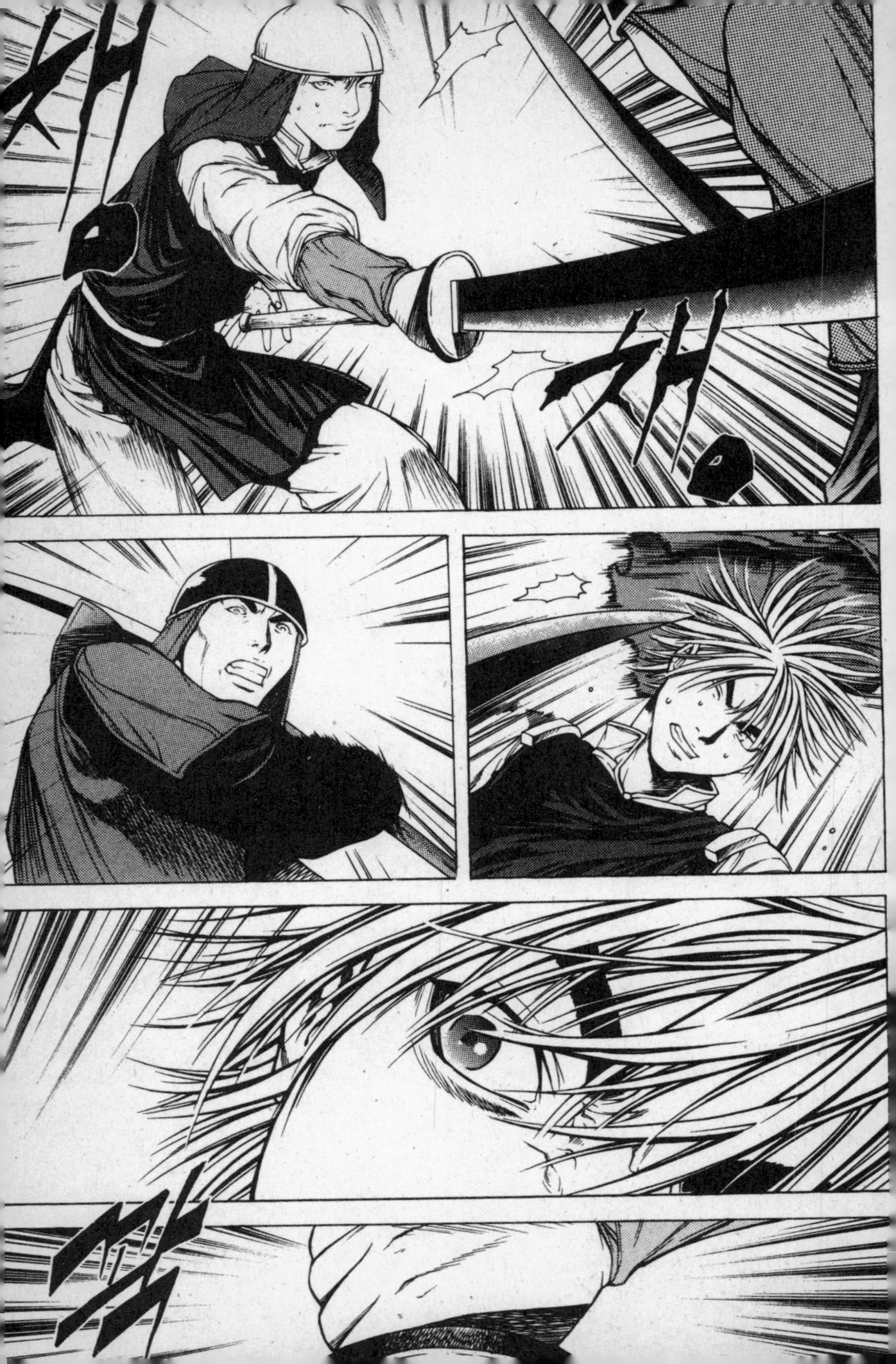

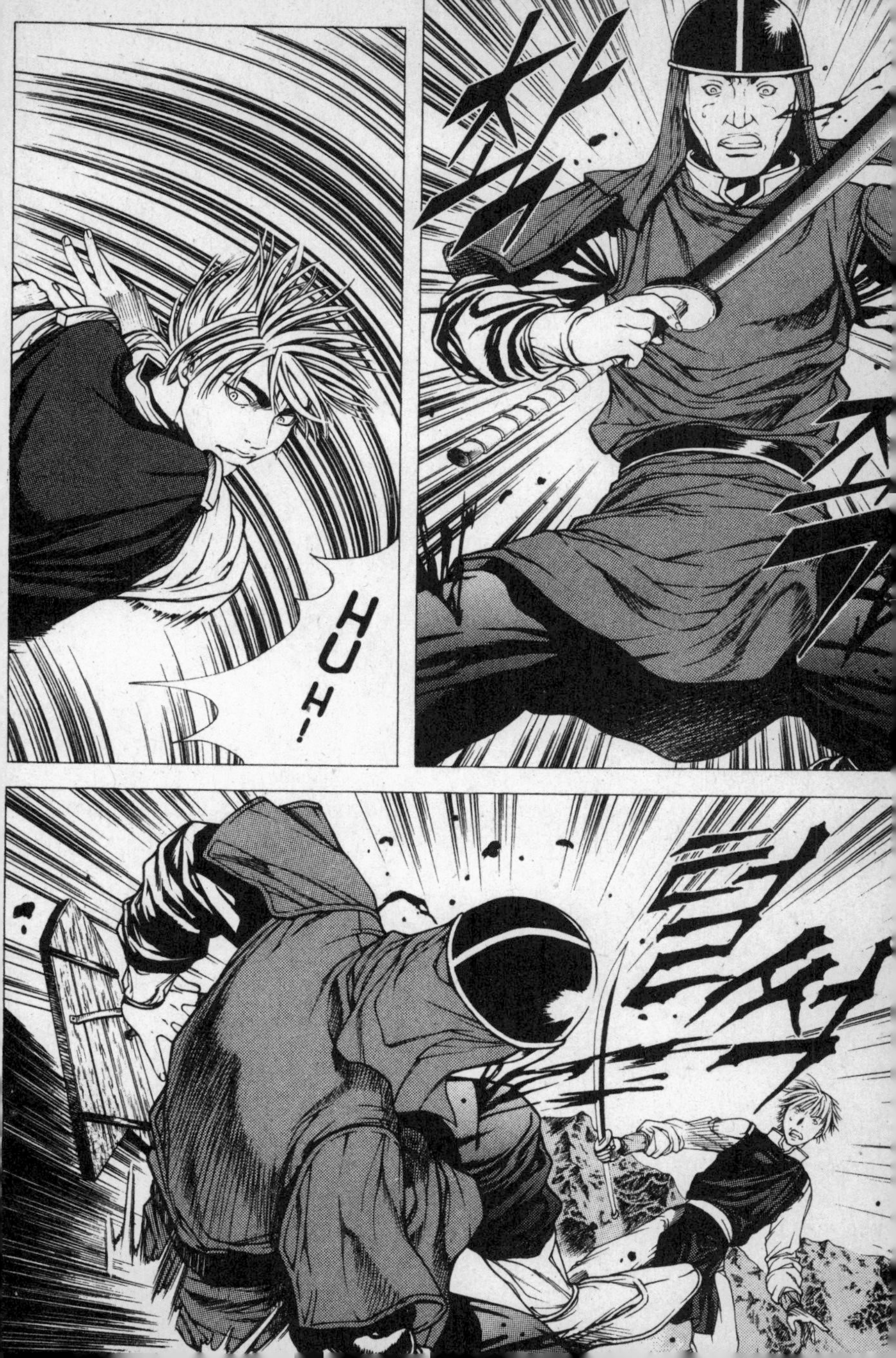
HUH!

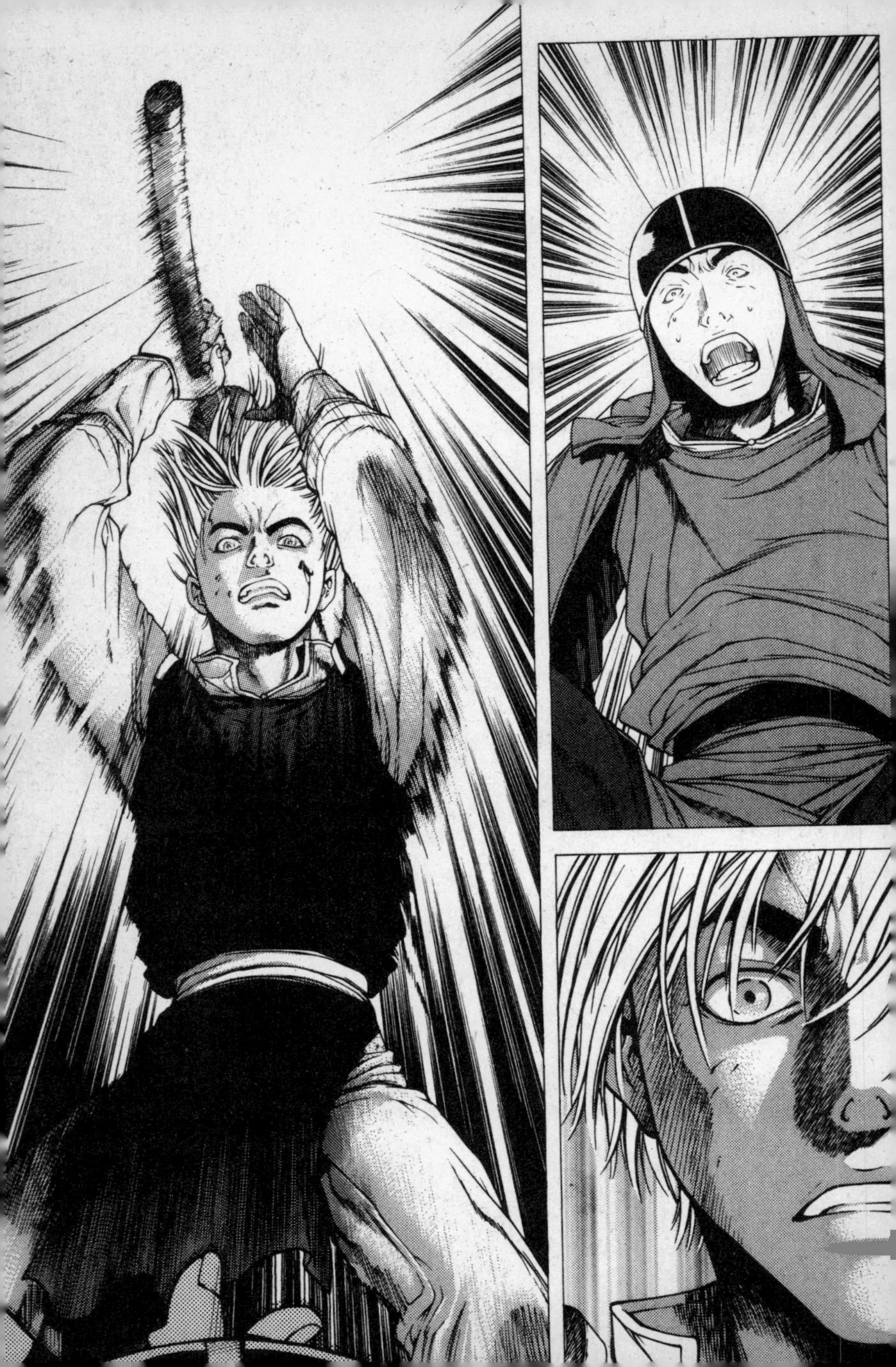

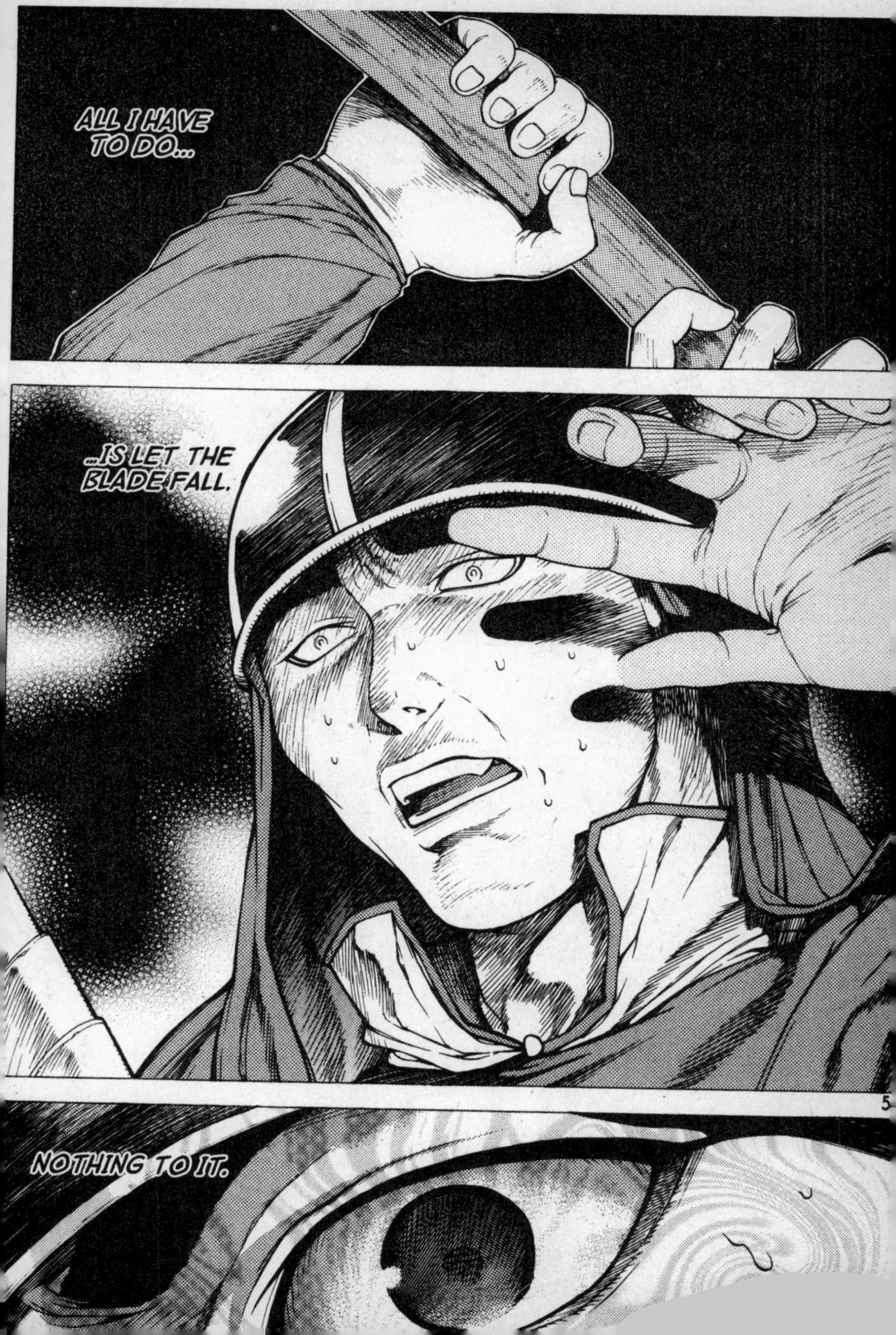
ALL I HAVE TO DO...
...IS LET THE BLADE FALL.
NOTHING TO IT.

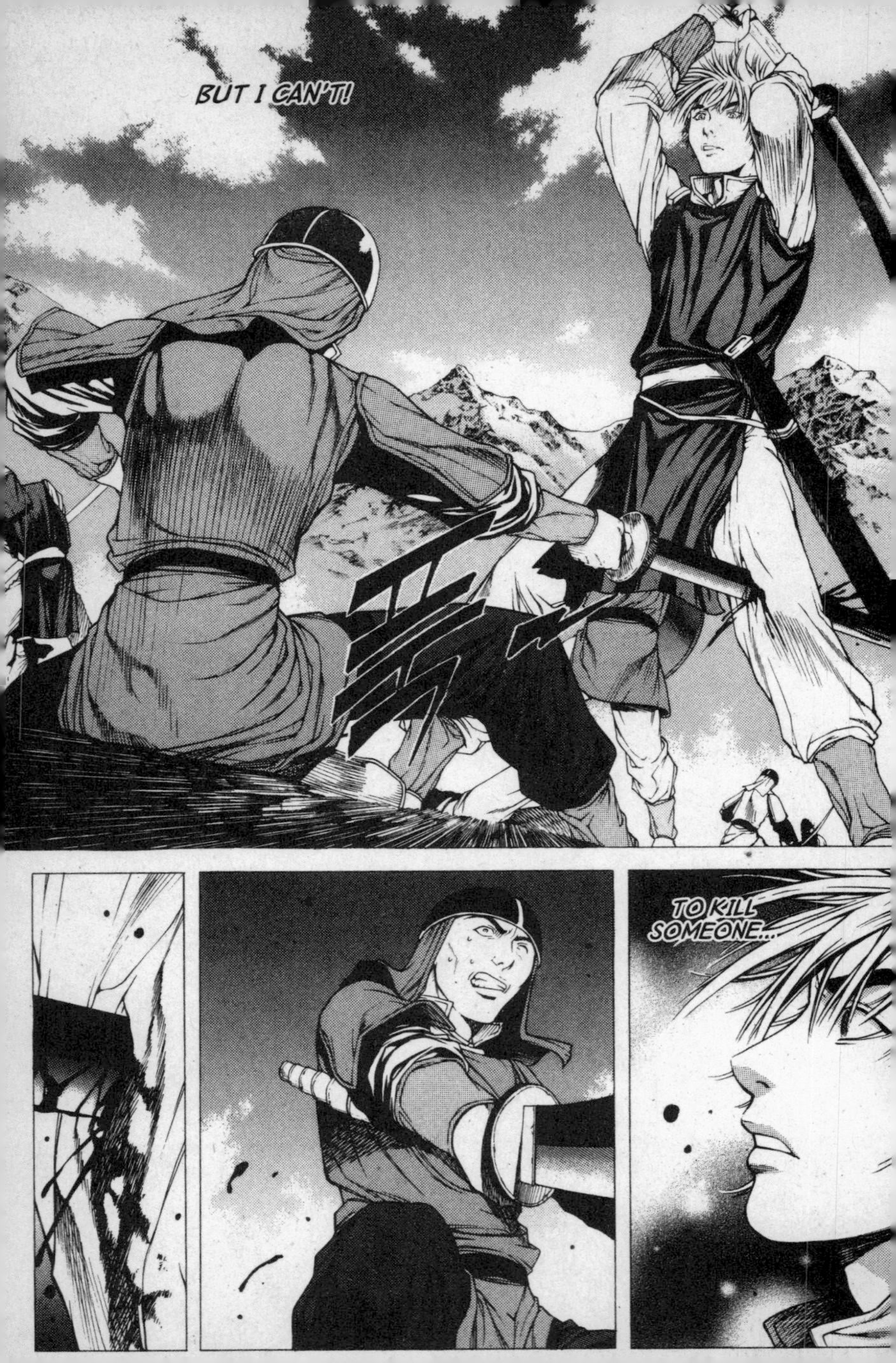
BUT I CAN'T!
TO KILL SOMEONE...

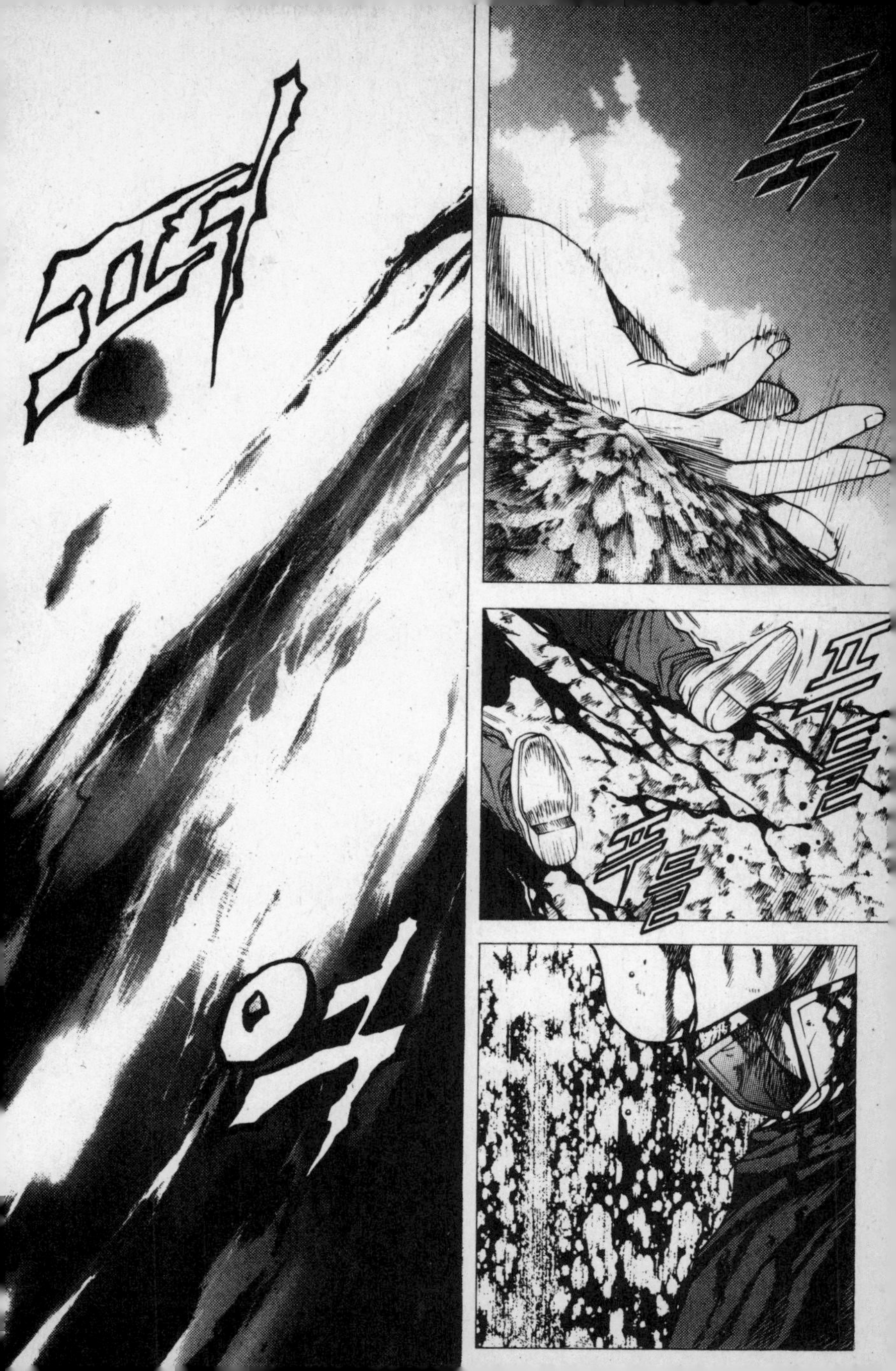
SOCK

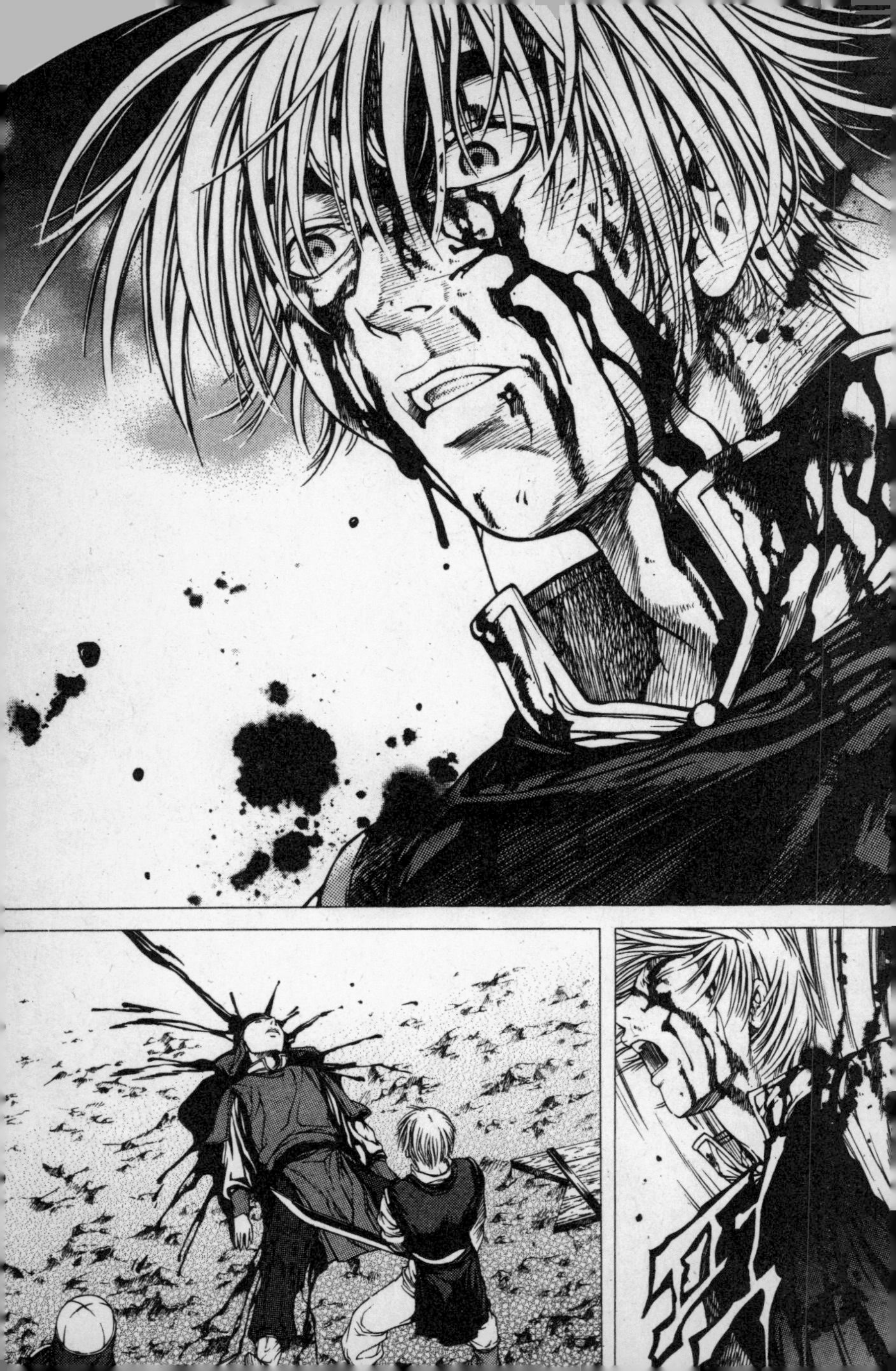

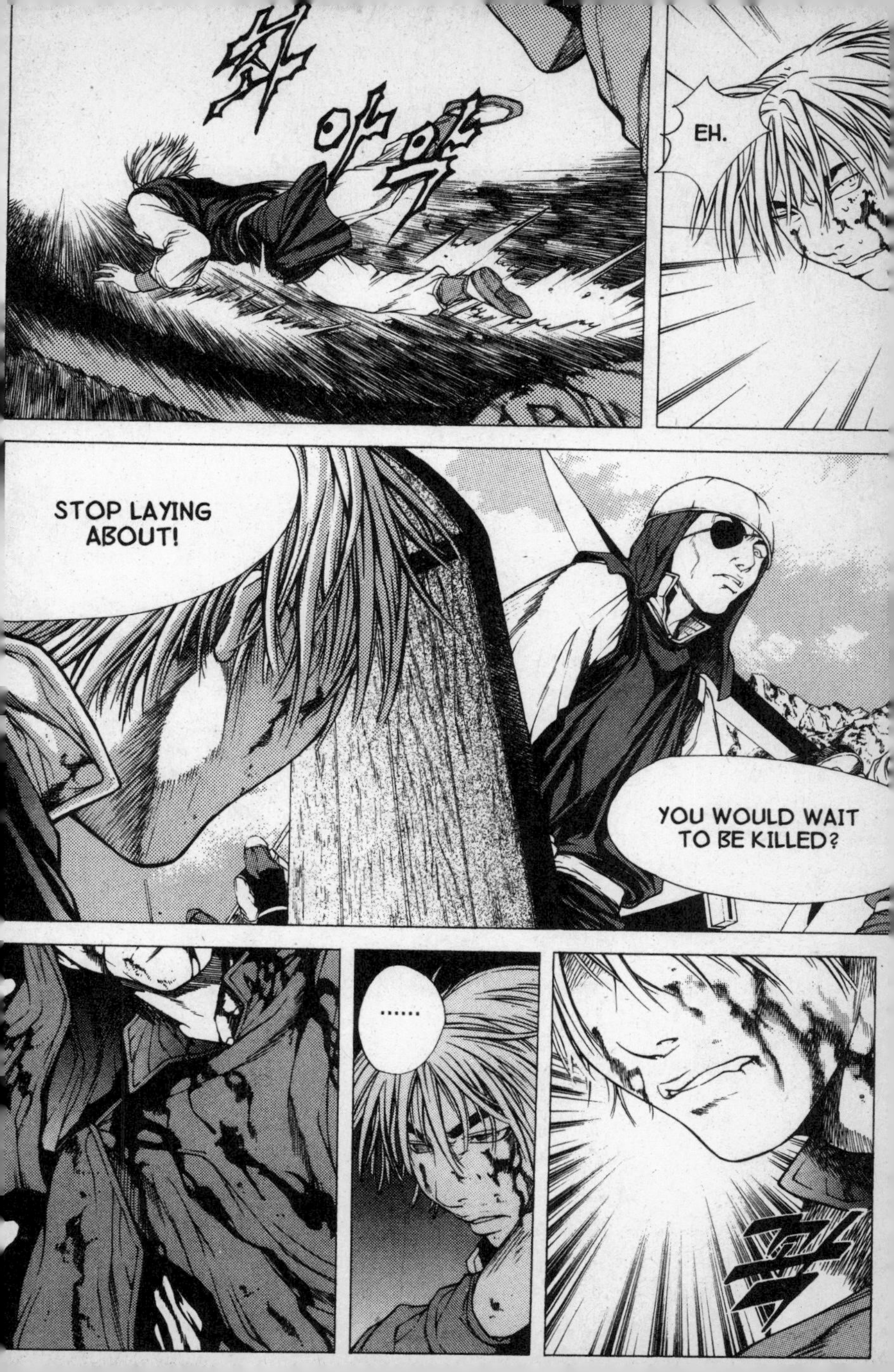
EH.
STOP LAYING ABOUT!
YOU WOULD WAIT TO BE KILLED?
......

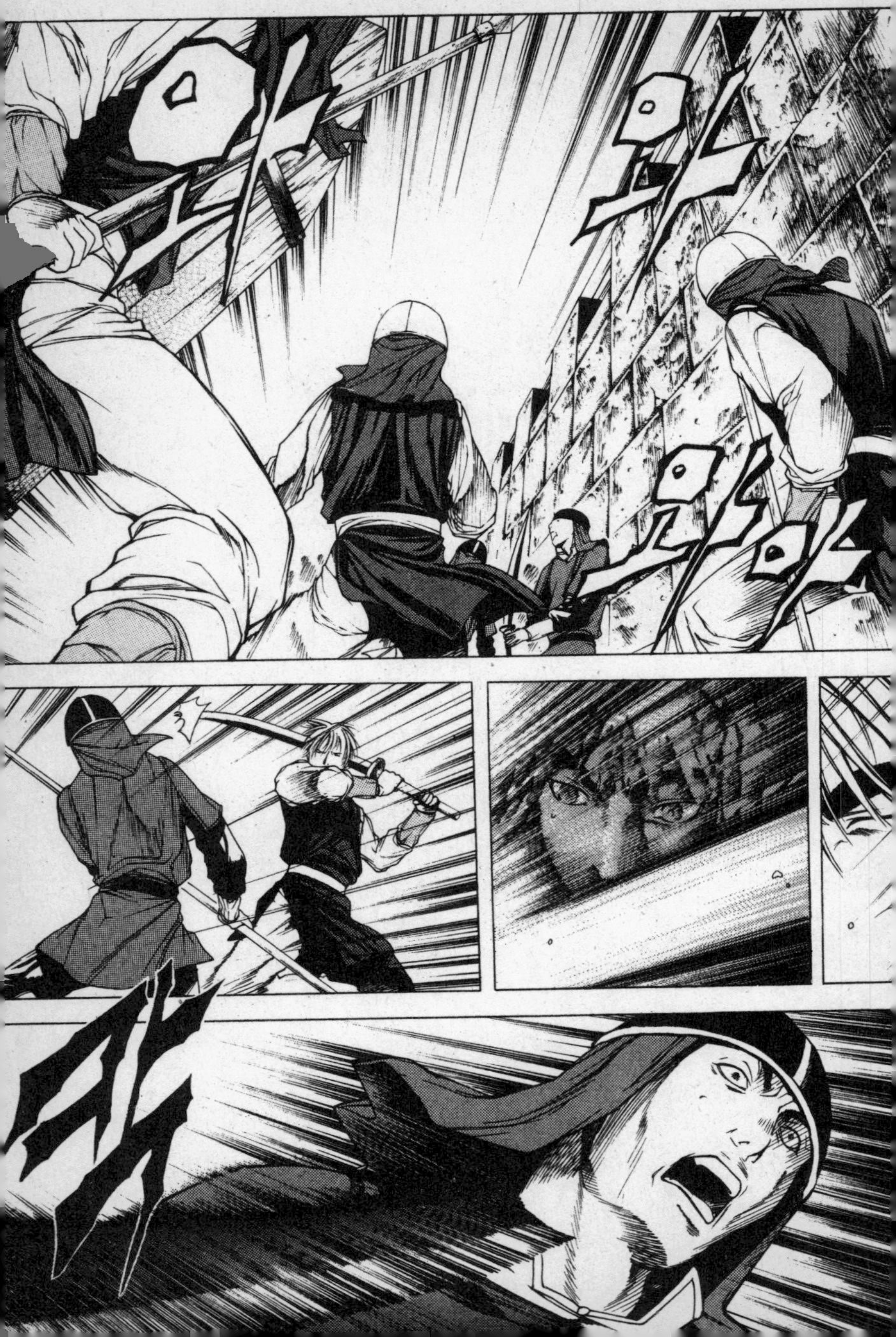

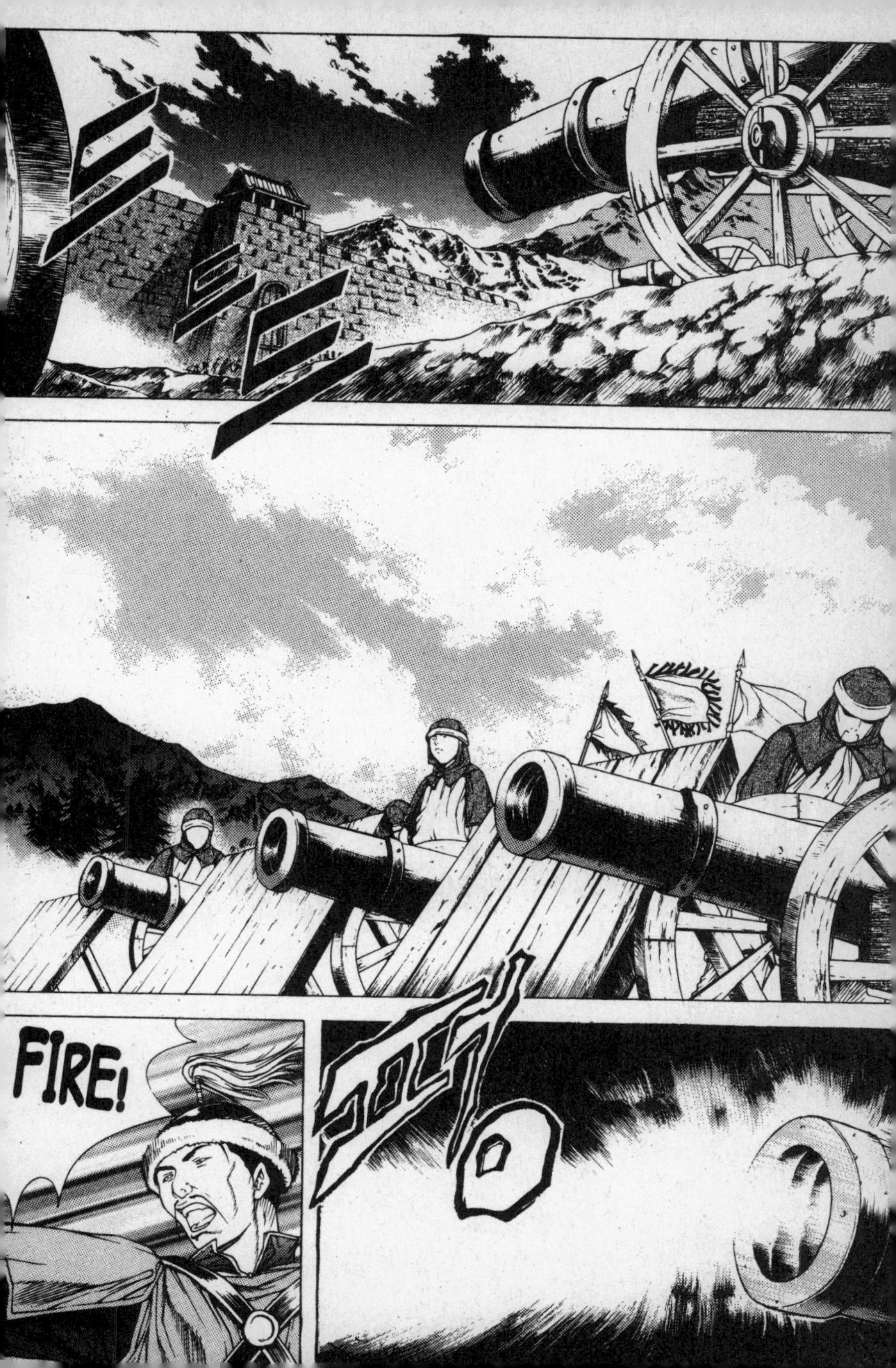
FIRE!

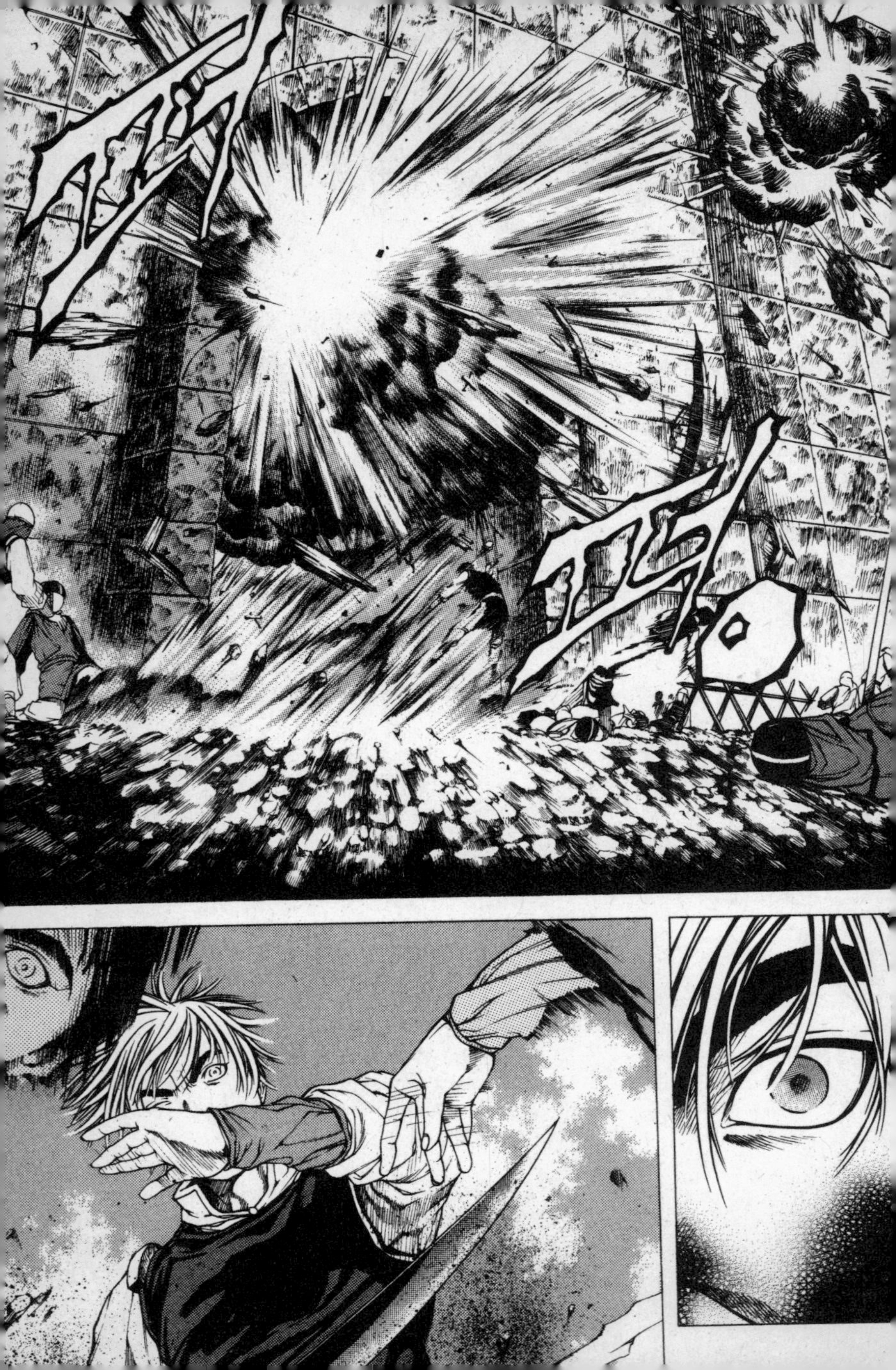

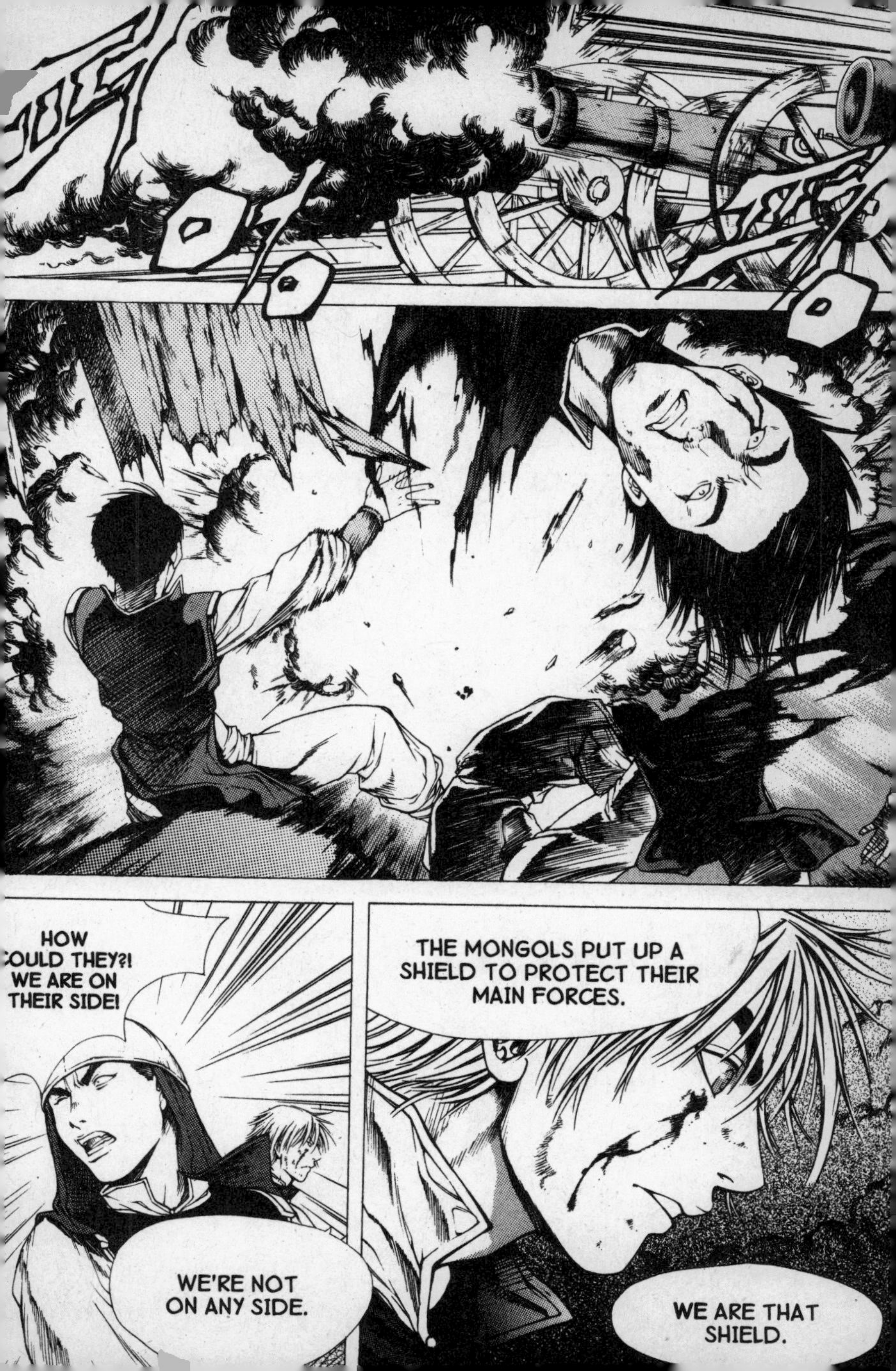
HOW COULD THEY?! WE ARE ON THEIR SIDE!
WE'RE NOT ON ANY SIDE.
THE MONGOLS PUT UP A SHIELD TO PROTECT THEIR MAIN FORCES.
WE ARE THAT SHIELD.

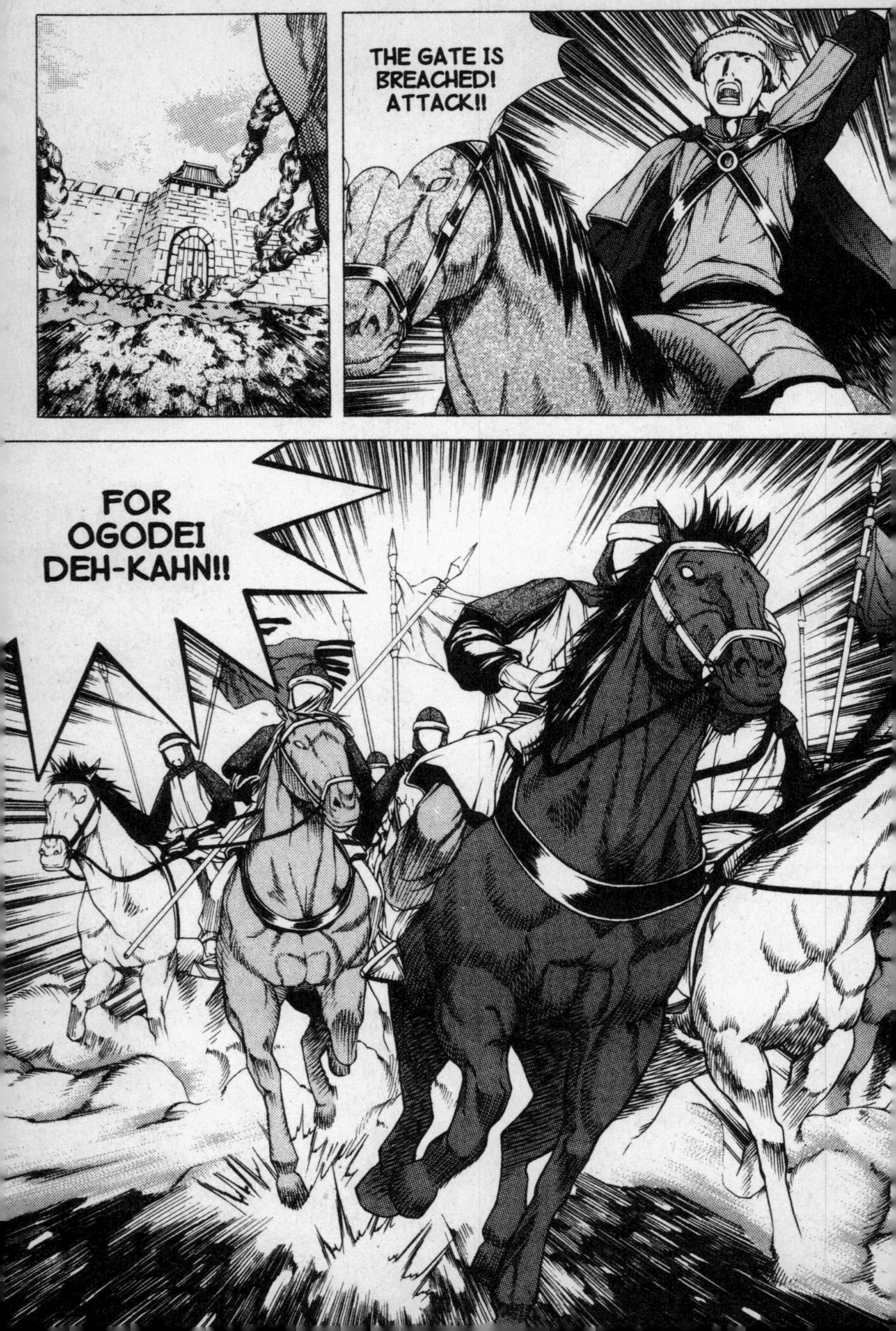
THE GATE IS BREACHED! ATTACK!!
FOR OGODEI DEH-KAHN!!

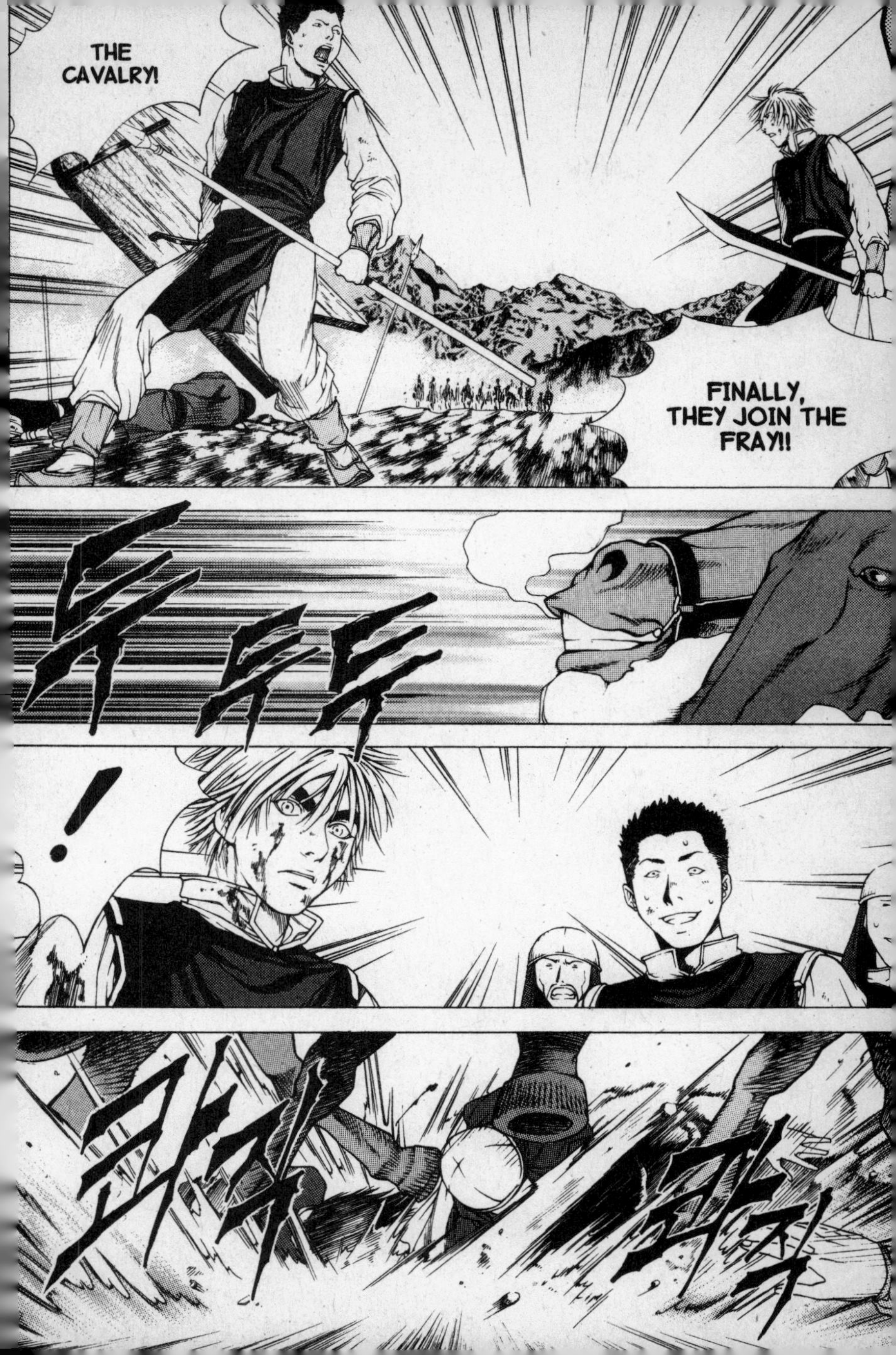
THE CAVALRY!
FINALLY, THEY JOIN THE FRAY!!
!

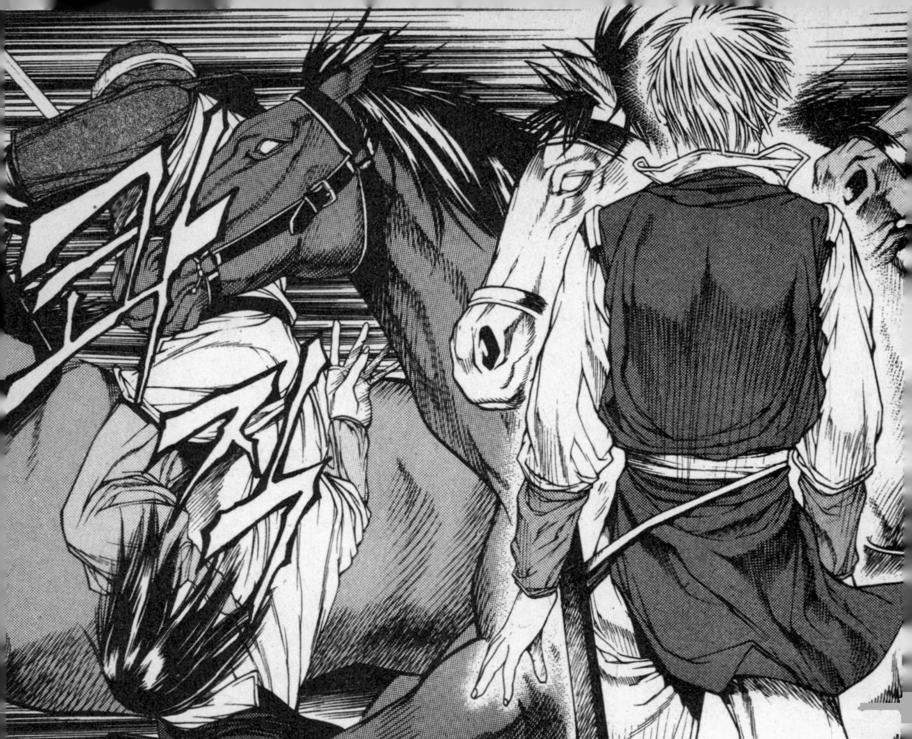

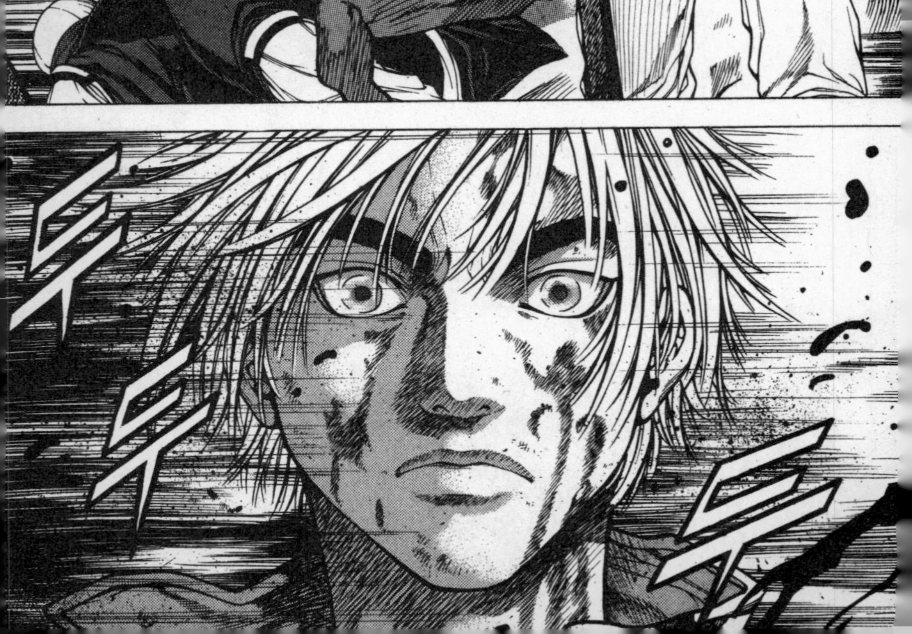

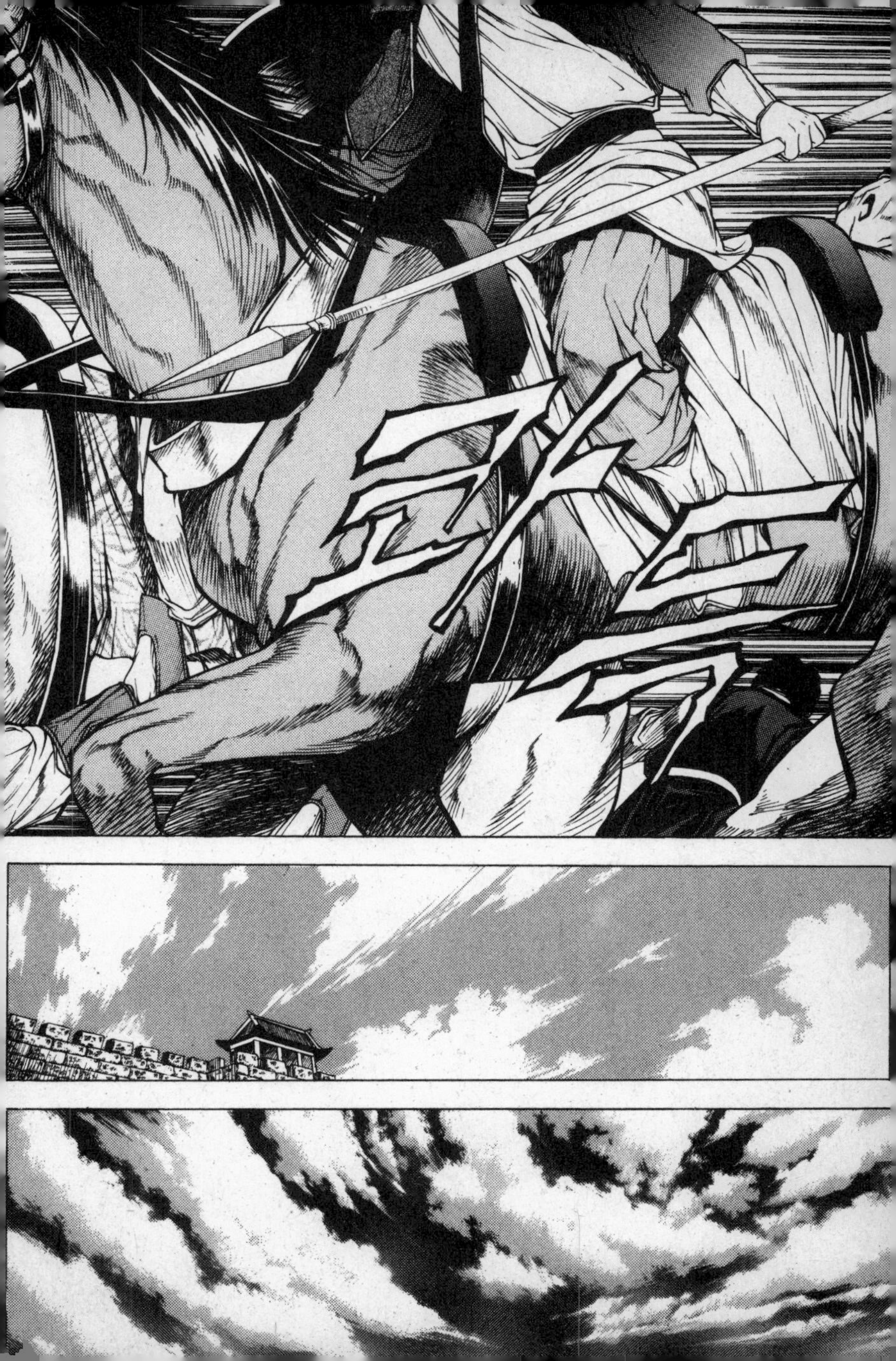

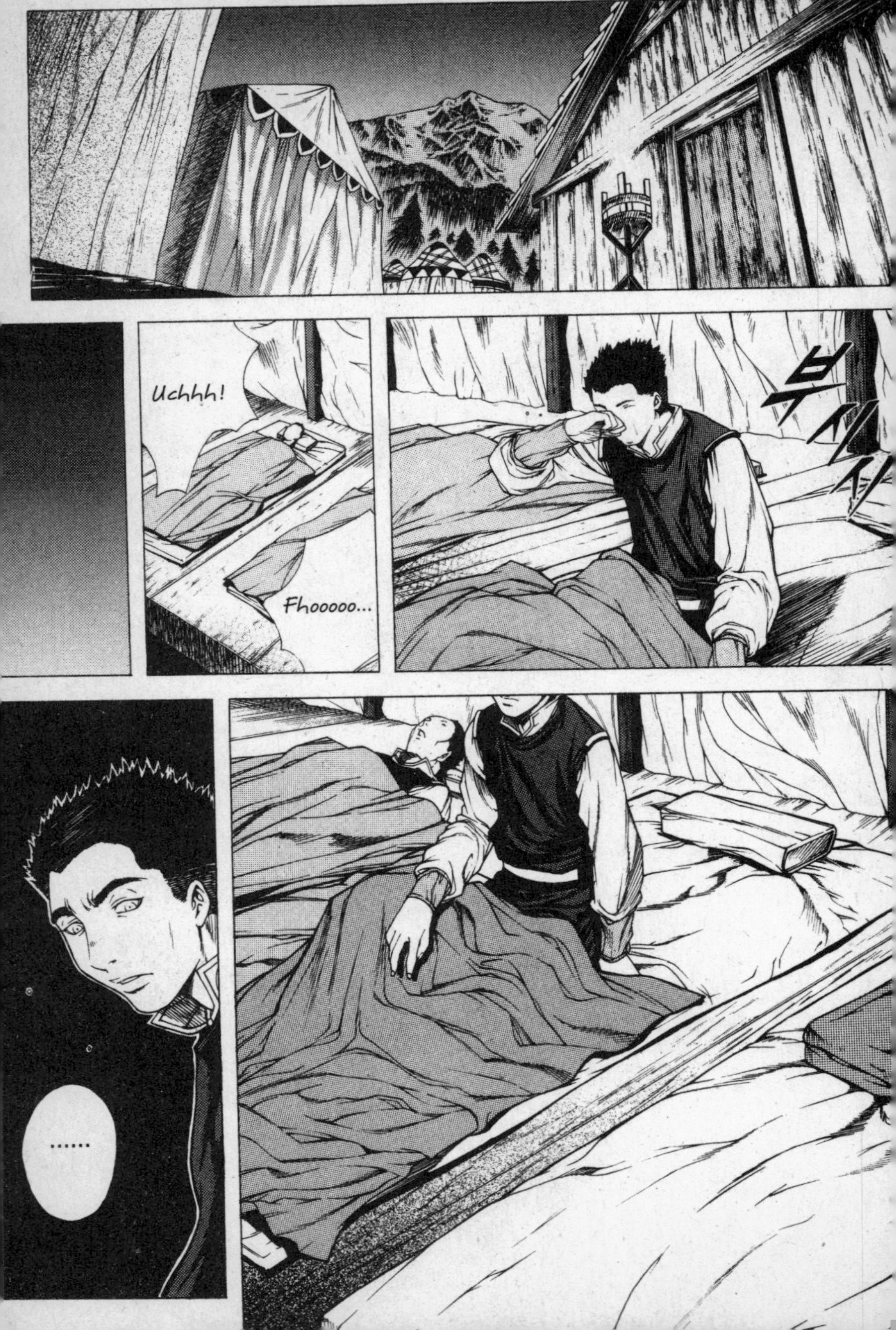
Uchhh!
Fhooooo...
부시시
......

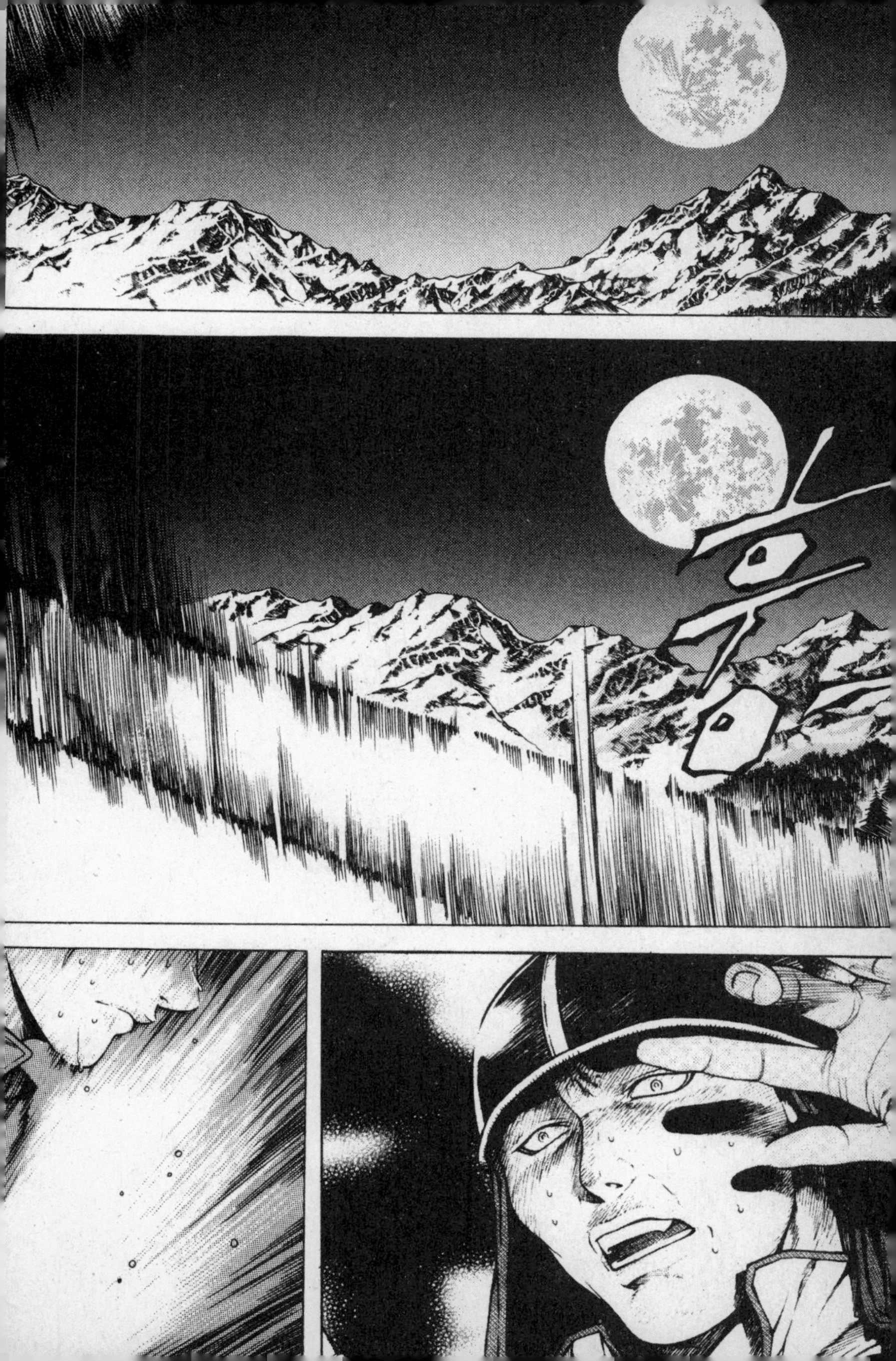

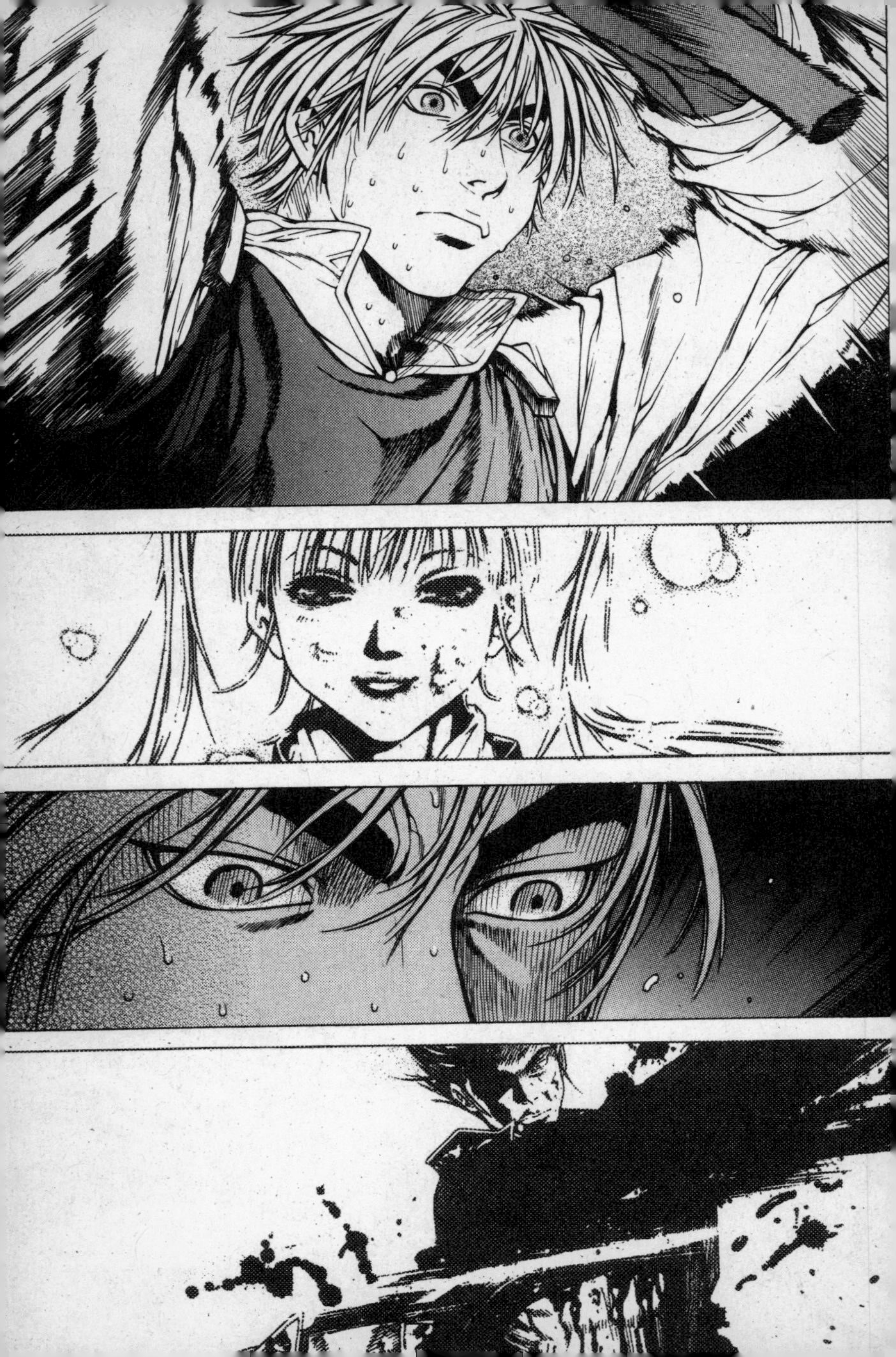

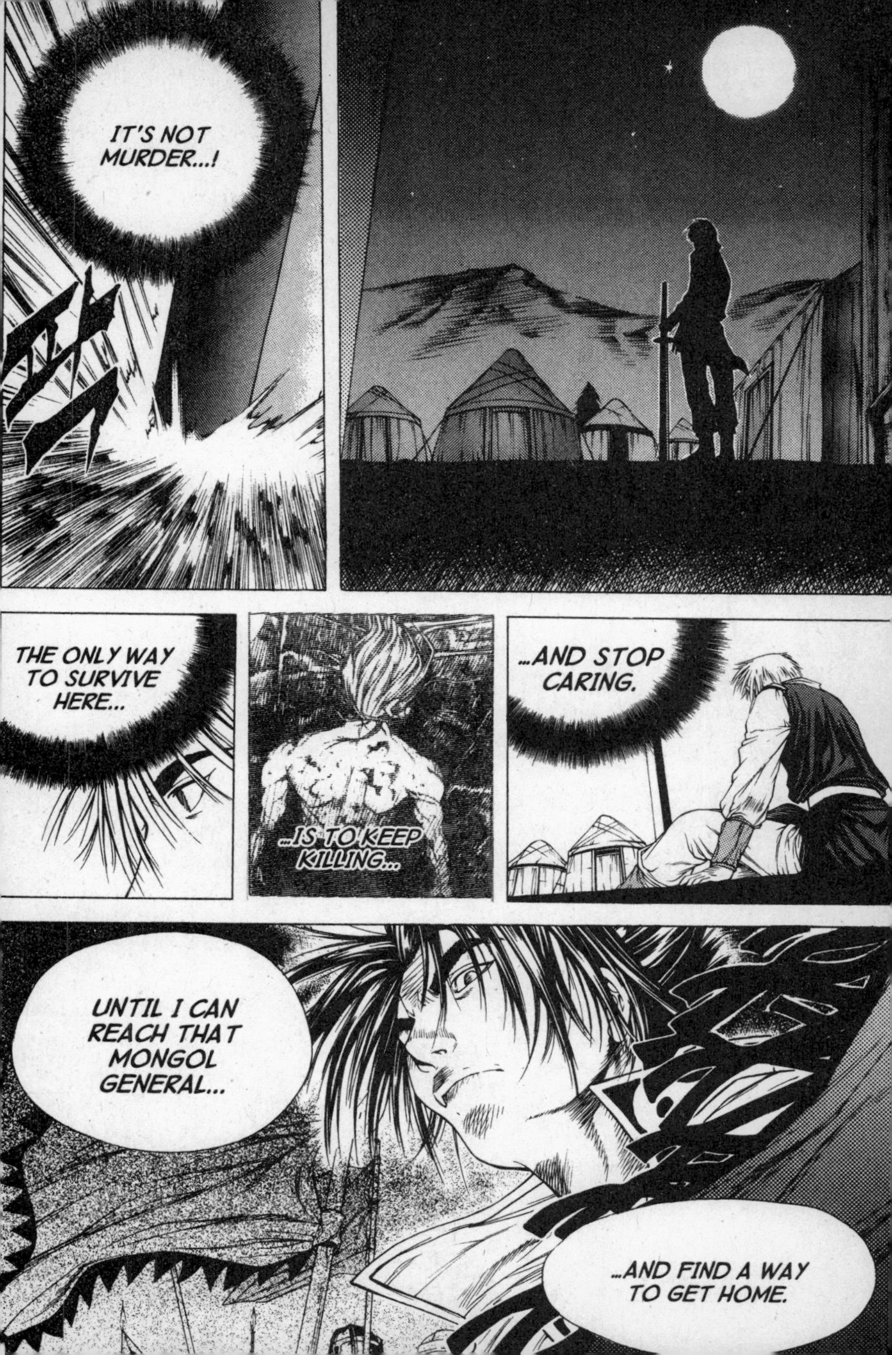
IT'S NOT MURDER...!
THE ONLY WAY TO SURVIVE HERE...
...IS TO KEEP KILLING...
...AND STOP CARING.
UNTIL I CAN REACH THAT MONGOL GENERAL...
...AND FIND A WAY TO GET HOME.

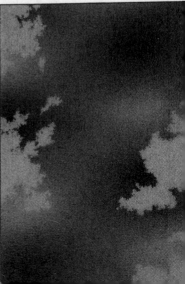

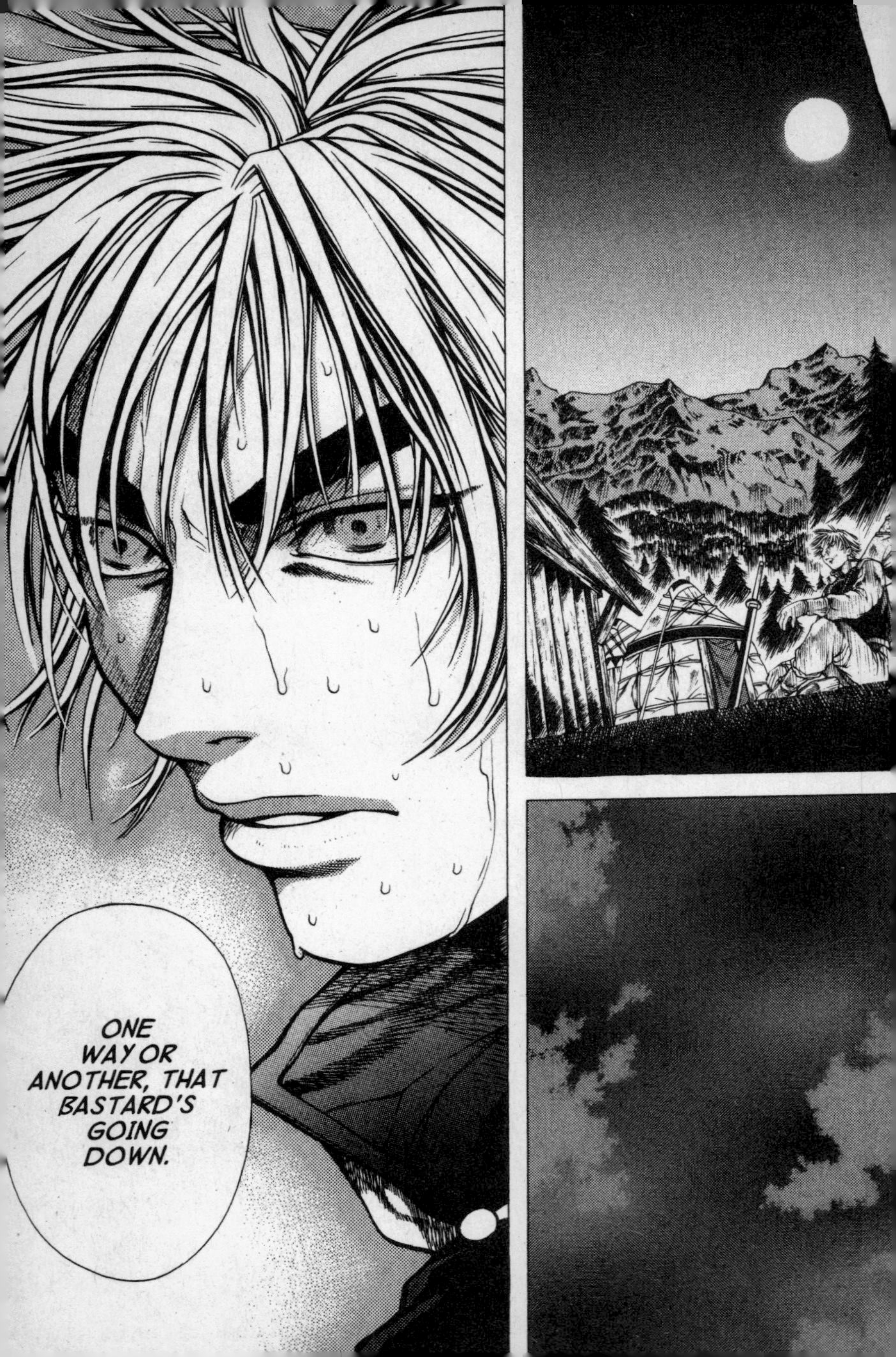
ONE WAY OR ANOTHER, THAT BASTARD'S GOING DOWN.

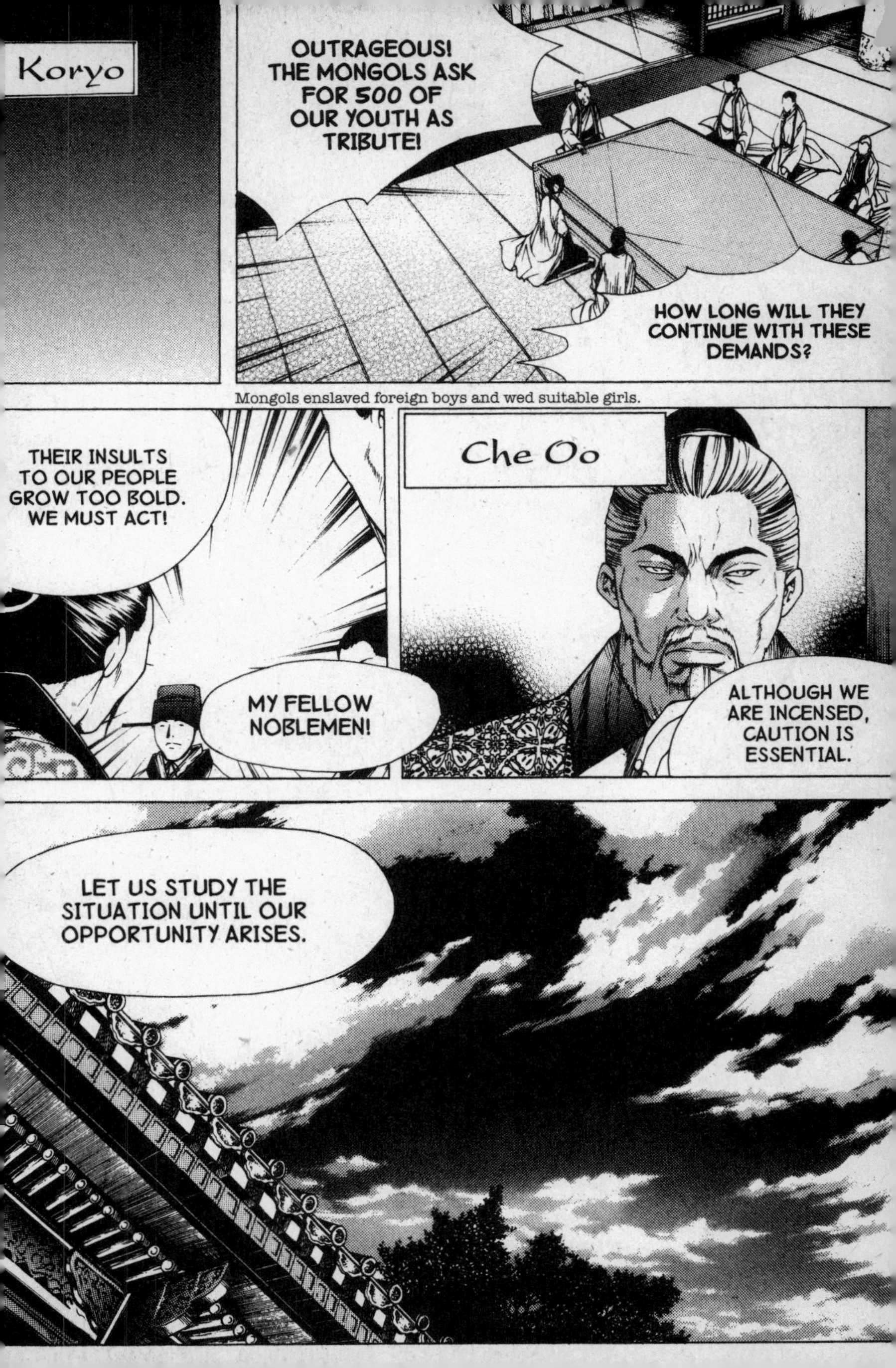
Koryo
OUTRAGEOUS! THE MONGOLS ASK FOR 500 OF OUR YOUTH AS TRIBUTE!
HOW LONG WILL THEY CONTINUE WITH THESE DEMANDS?
Mongols enslaved foreign boys and wed suitable girls.
THEIR INSULTS TO OUR PEOPLE GROW TOO BOLD. WE MUST ACT!
MY FELLOW NOBLEMEN!
Che Oo
ALTHOUGH WE ARE INCENSED, CAUTION IS ESSENTIAL.
LET US STUDY THE SITUATION UNTIL OUR OPPORTUNITY ARISES.

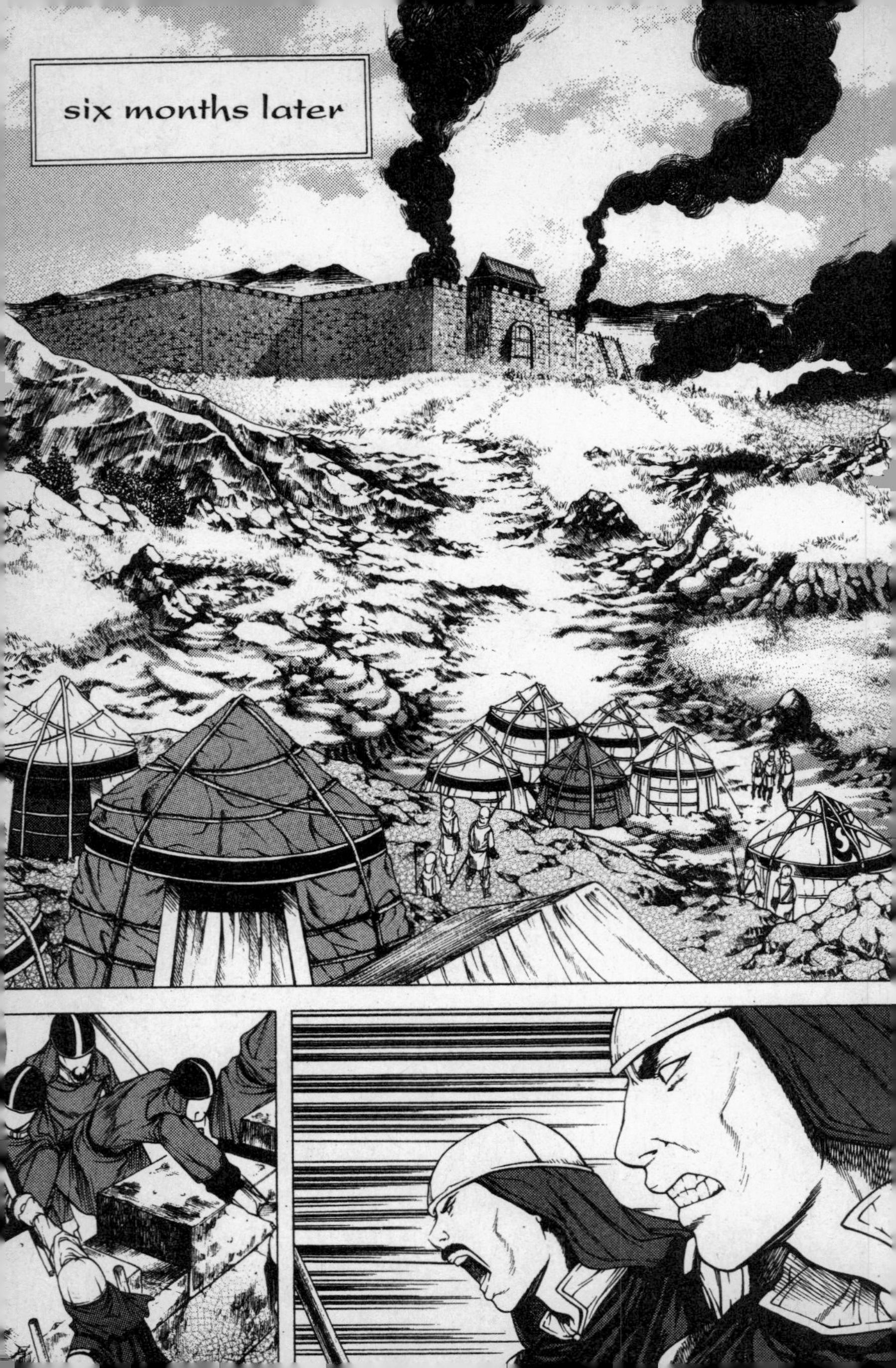
six months later

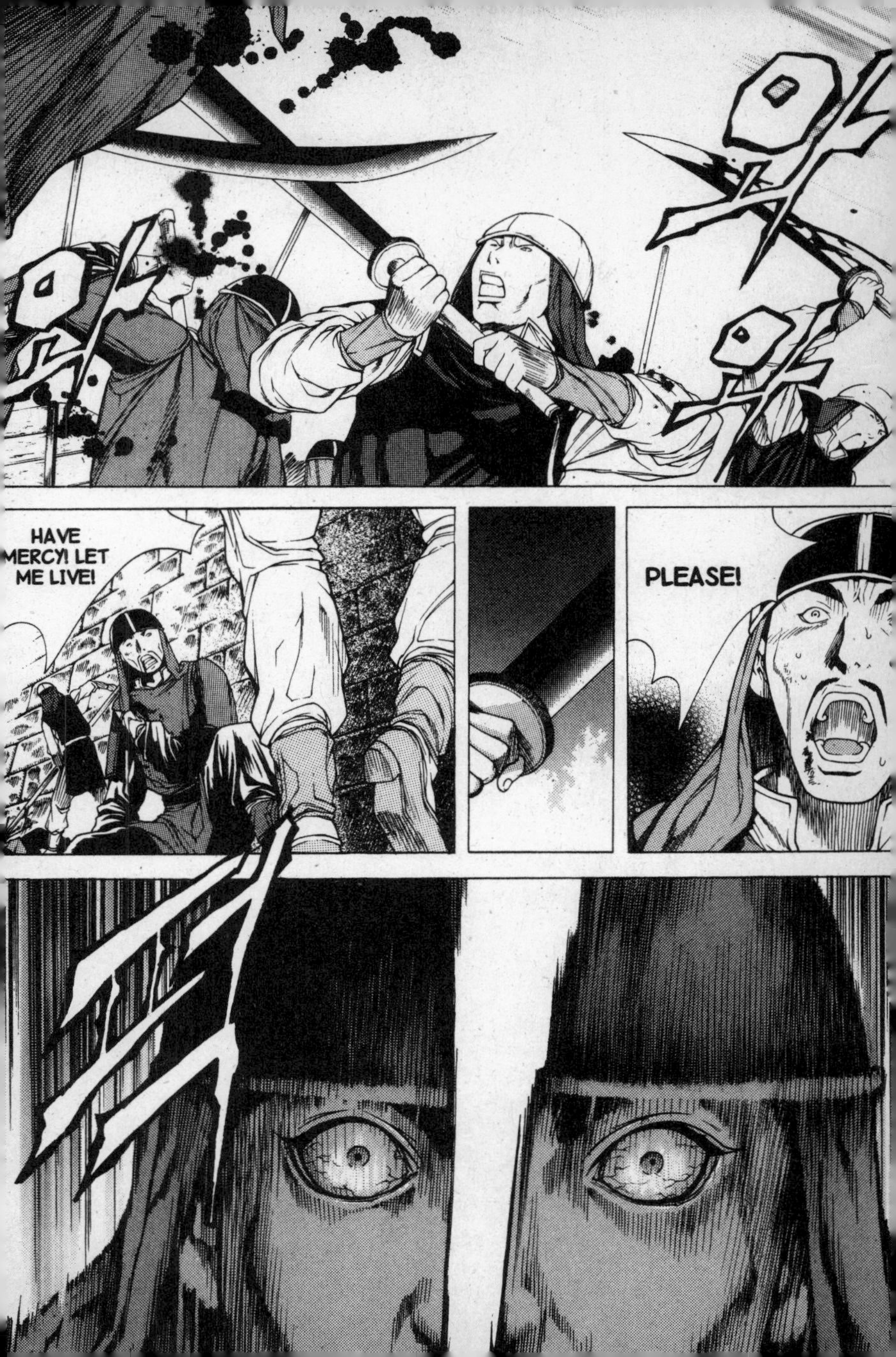
HAVE MERCY! LET ME LIVE!
PLEASE!

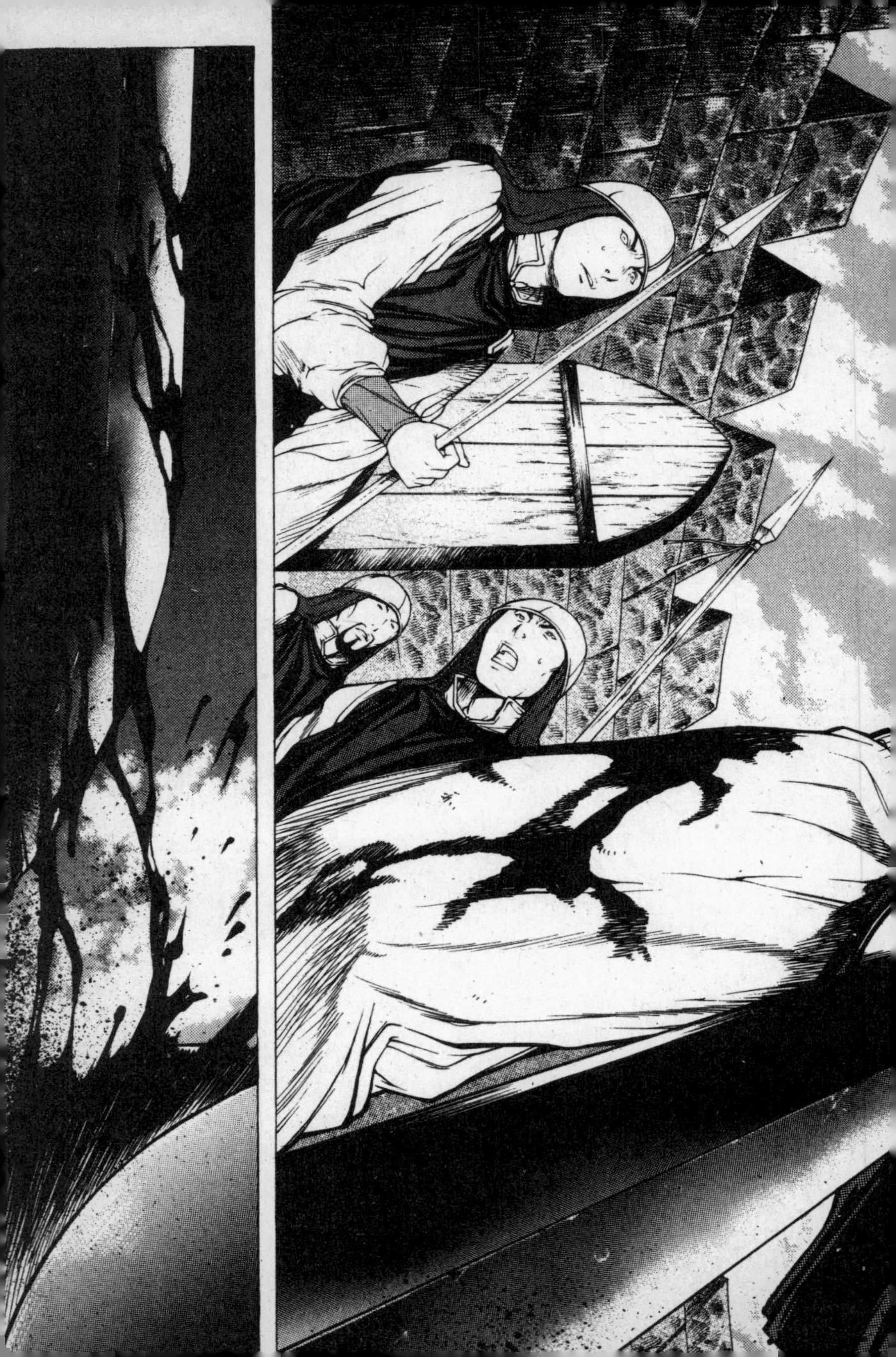

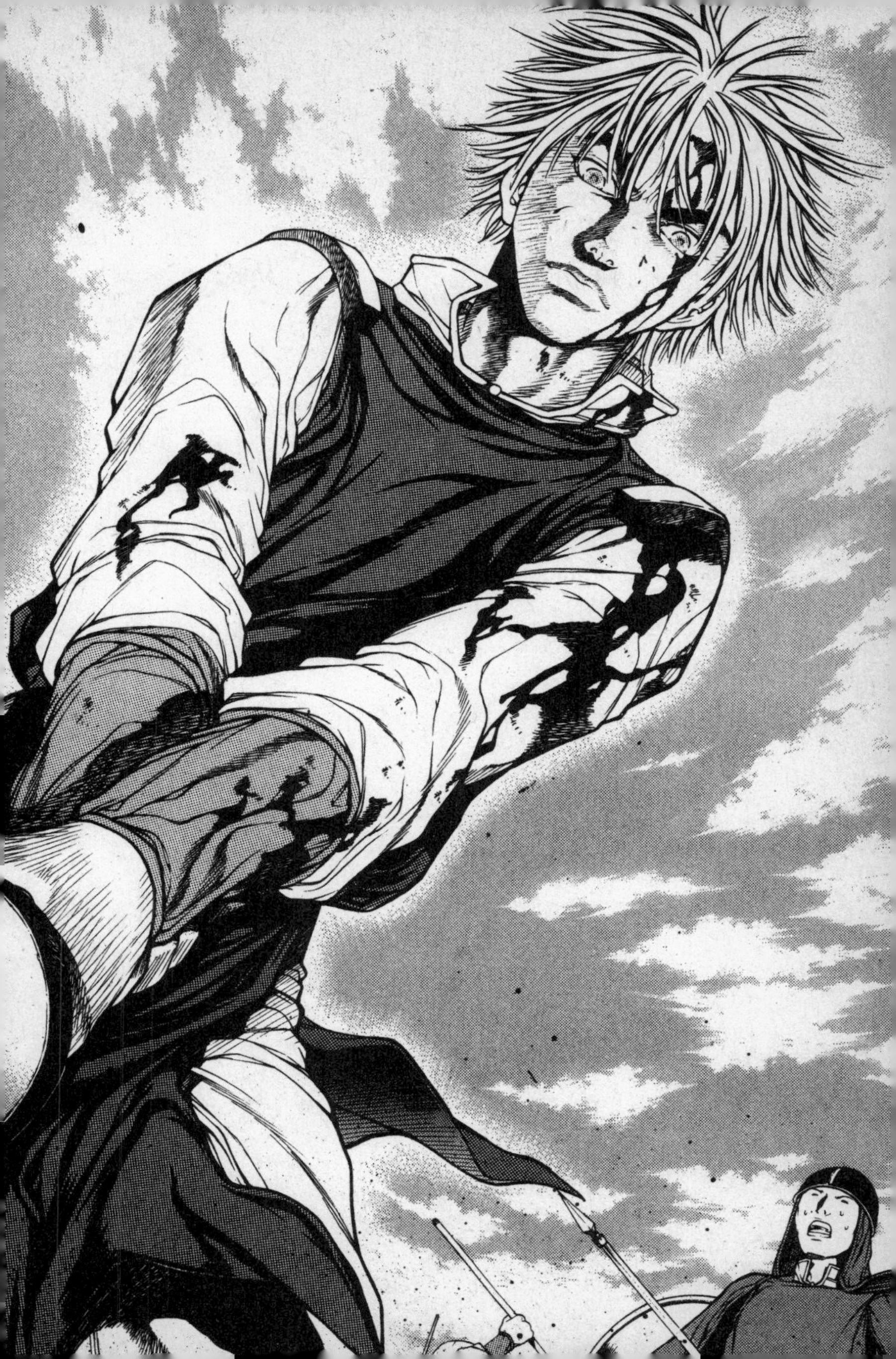

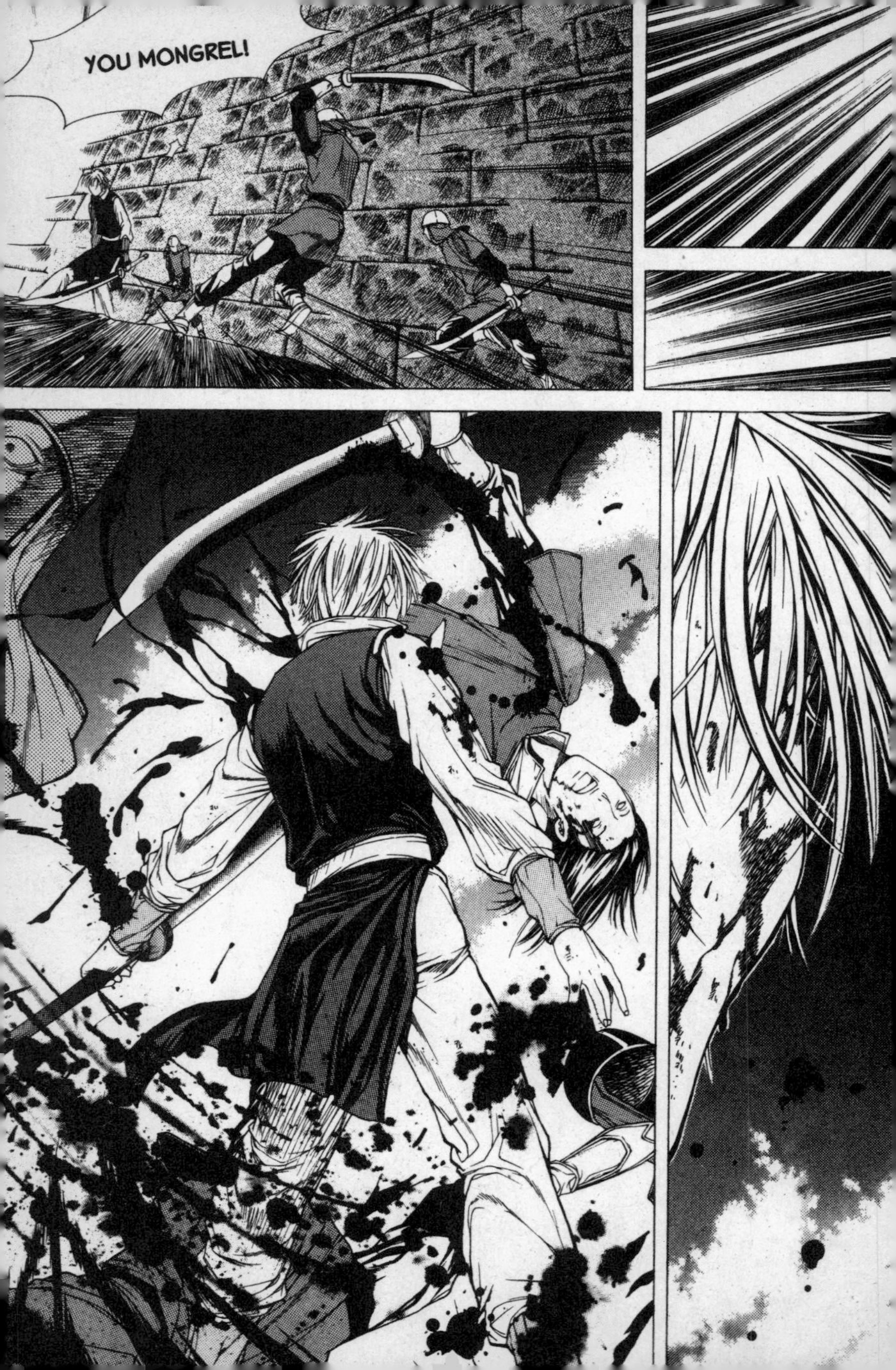
YOU MONGREL!

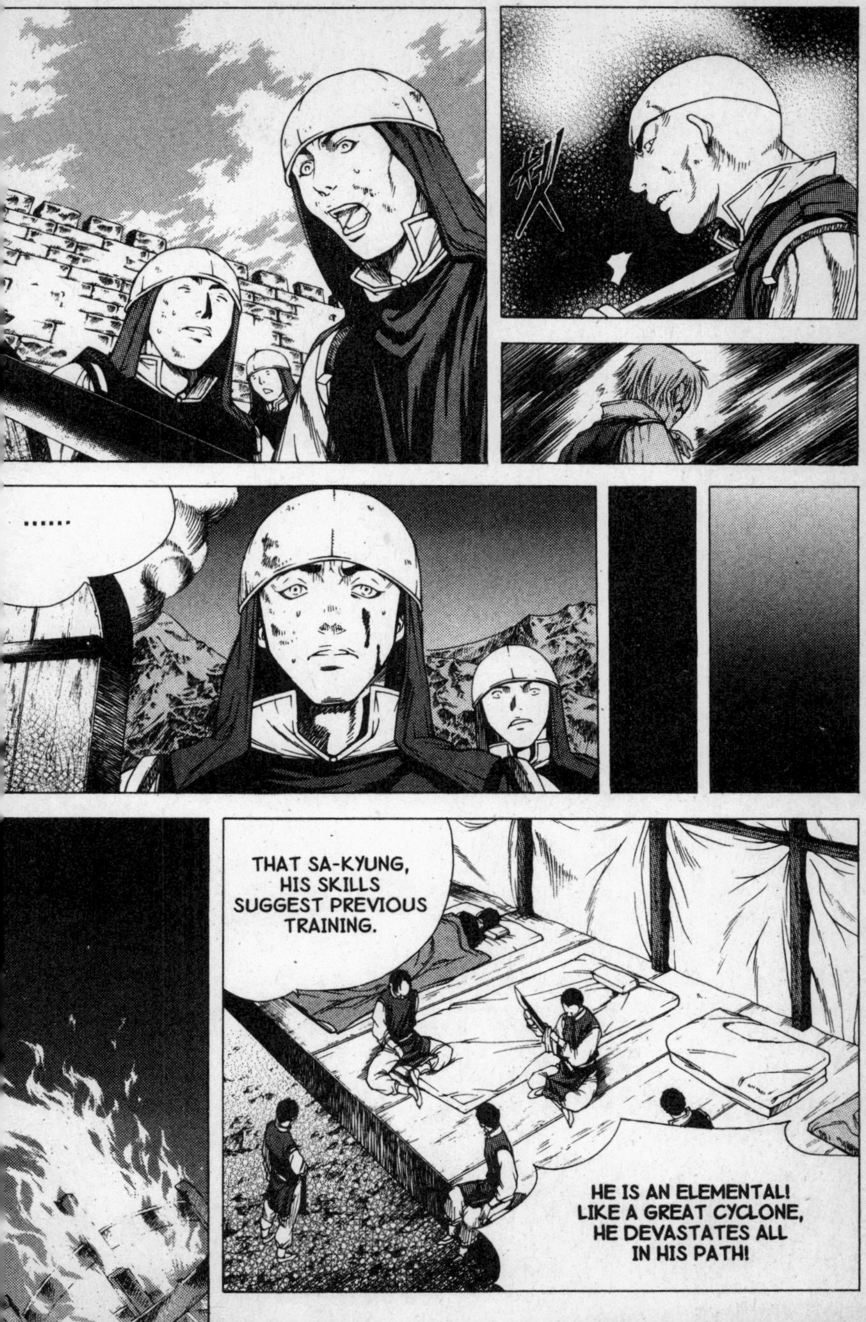
......
THAT SA-KYUNG, HIS SKILLS SUGGEST PREVIOUS TRAINING.
HE IS AN ELEMENTAL! LIKE A GREAT CYCLONE, HE DEVASTATES ALL IN HIS PATH!

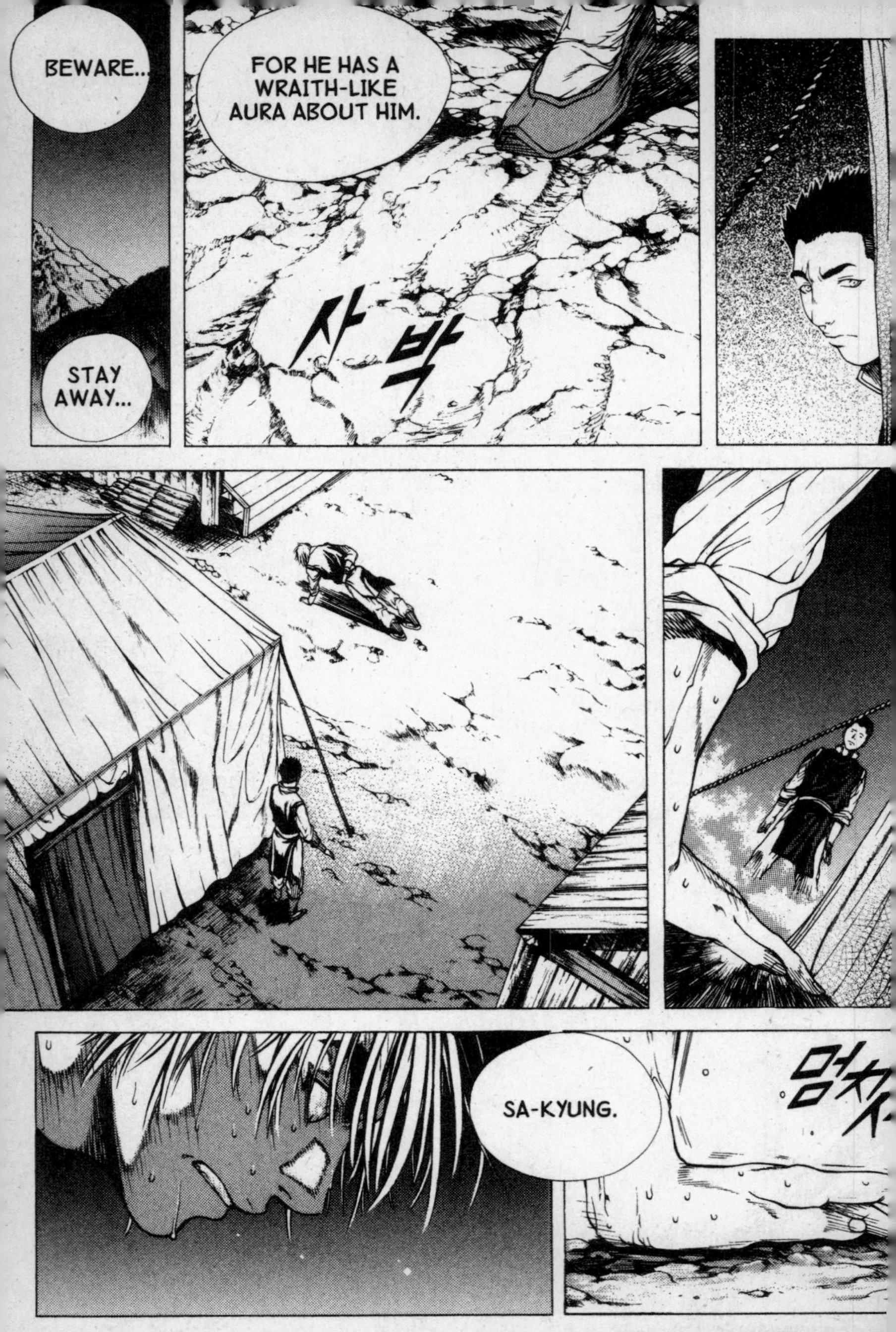
BEWARE...
STAY AWAY...
FOR HE HAS A WRAITH-LIKE AURA ABOUT HIM.
사박
SA-KYUNG.
멈칫

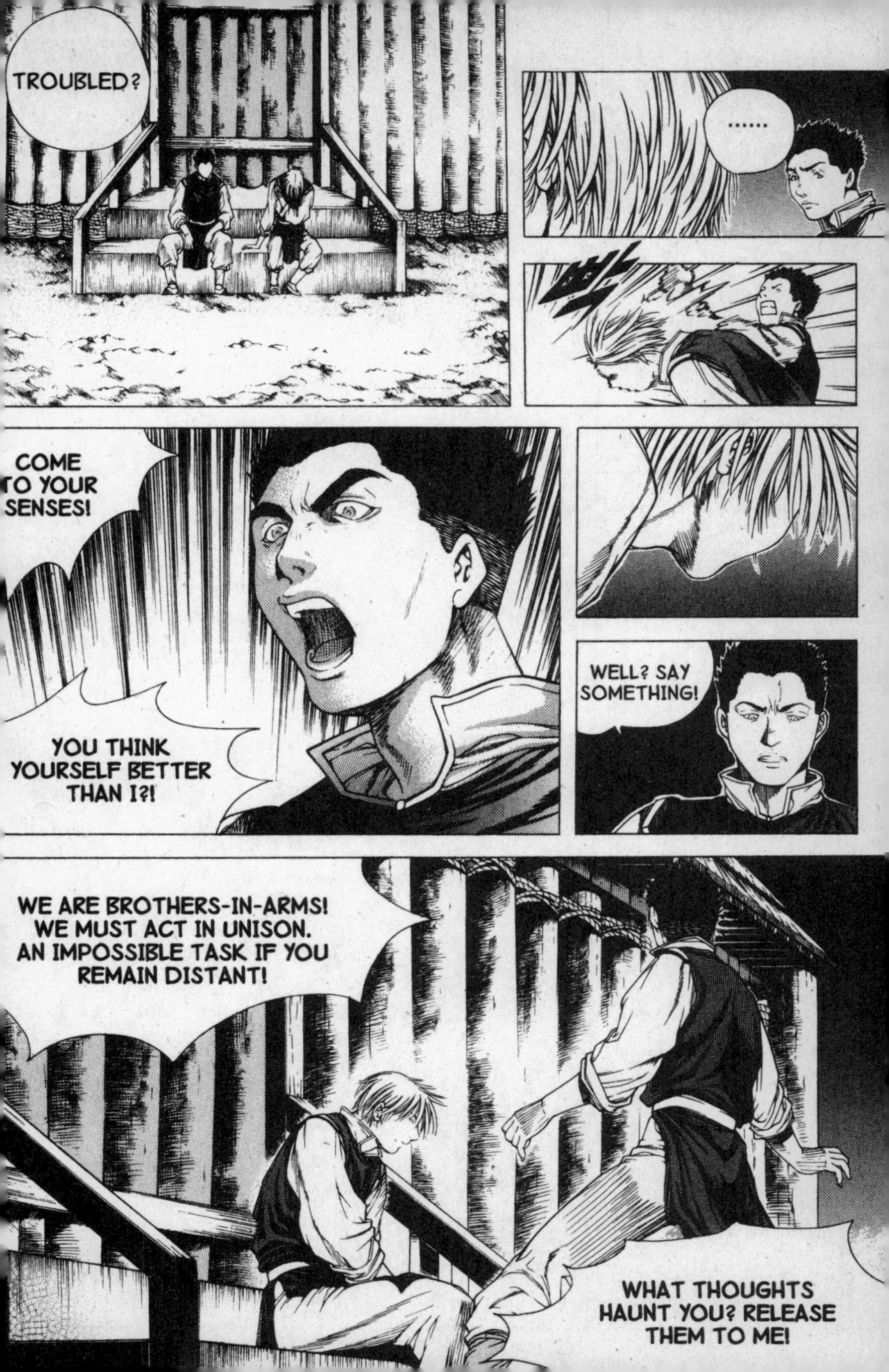
TROUBLED?
......
COME TO YOUR SENSES!
YOU THINK YOURSELF BETTER THAN I?!
WELL? SAY SOMETHING!
WE ARE BROTHERS-IN-ARMS! WE MUST ACT IN UNISON. AN IMPOSSIBLE TASK IF YOU REMAIN DISTANT!
WHAT THOUGHTS HAUNT YOU? RELEASE THEM TO ME!

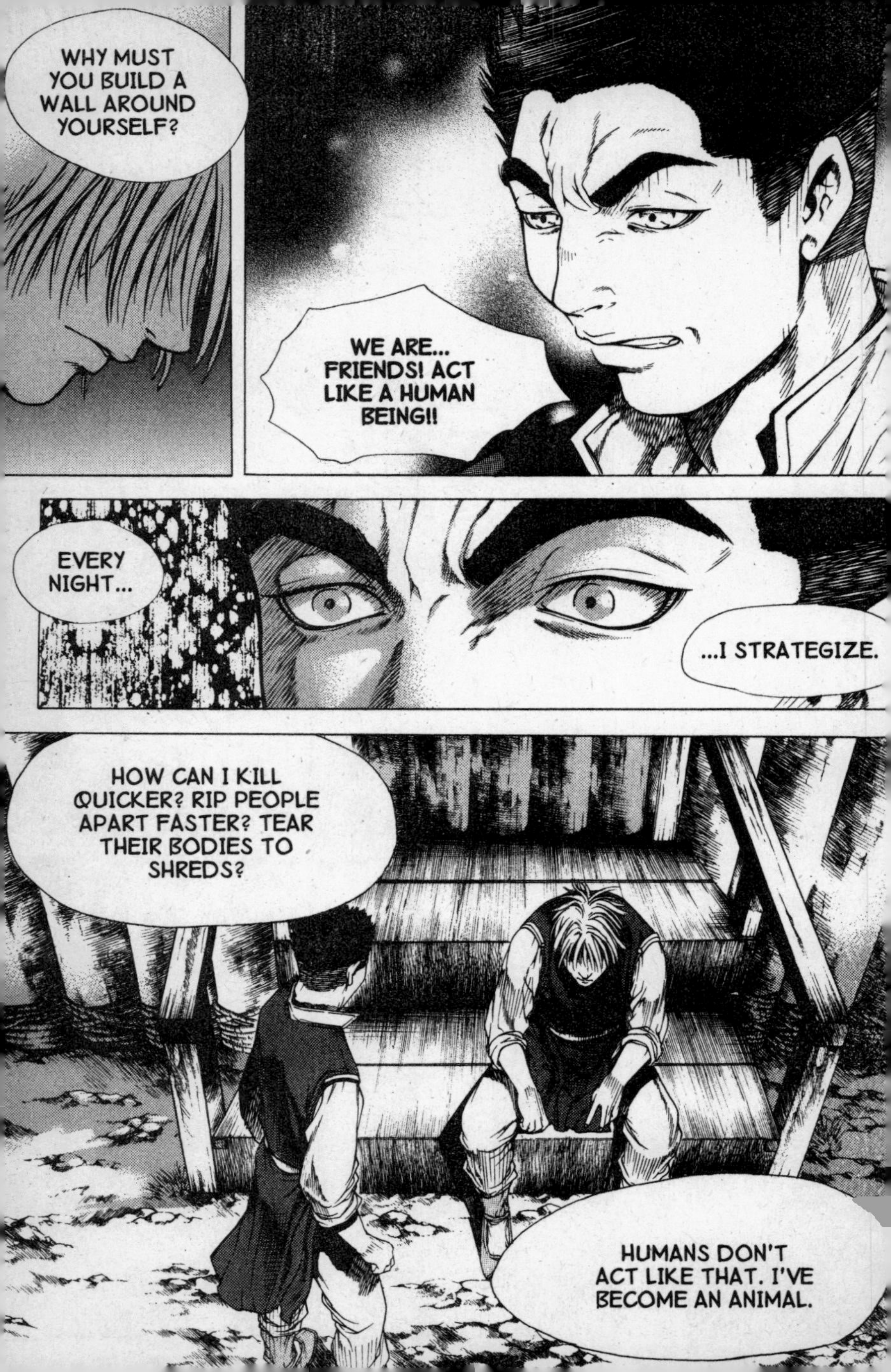
WHY MUST YOU BUILD A WALL AROUND YOURSELF?
WE ARE... FRIENDS! ACT LIKE A HUMAN BEING!!
EVERY NIGHT...
...I STRATEGIZE.
HOW CAN I KILL QUICKER? RIP PEOPLE APART FASTER? TEAR THEIR BODIES TO SHREDS?
HUMANS DON'T ACT LIKE THAT. I'VE BECOME AN ANIMAL.

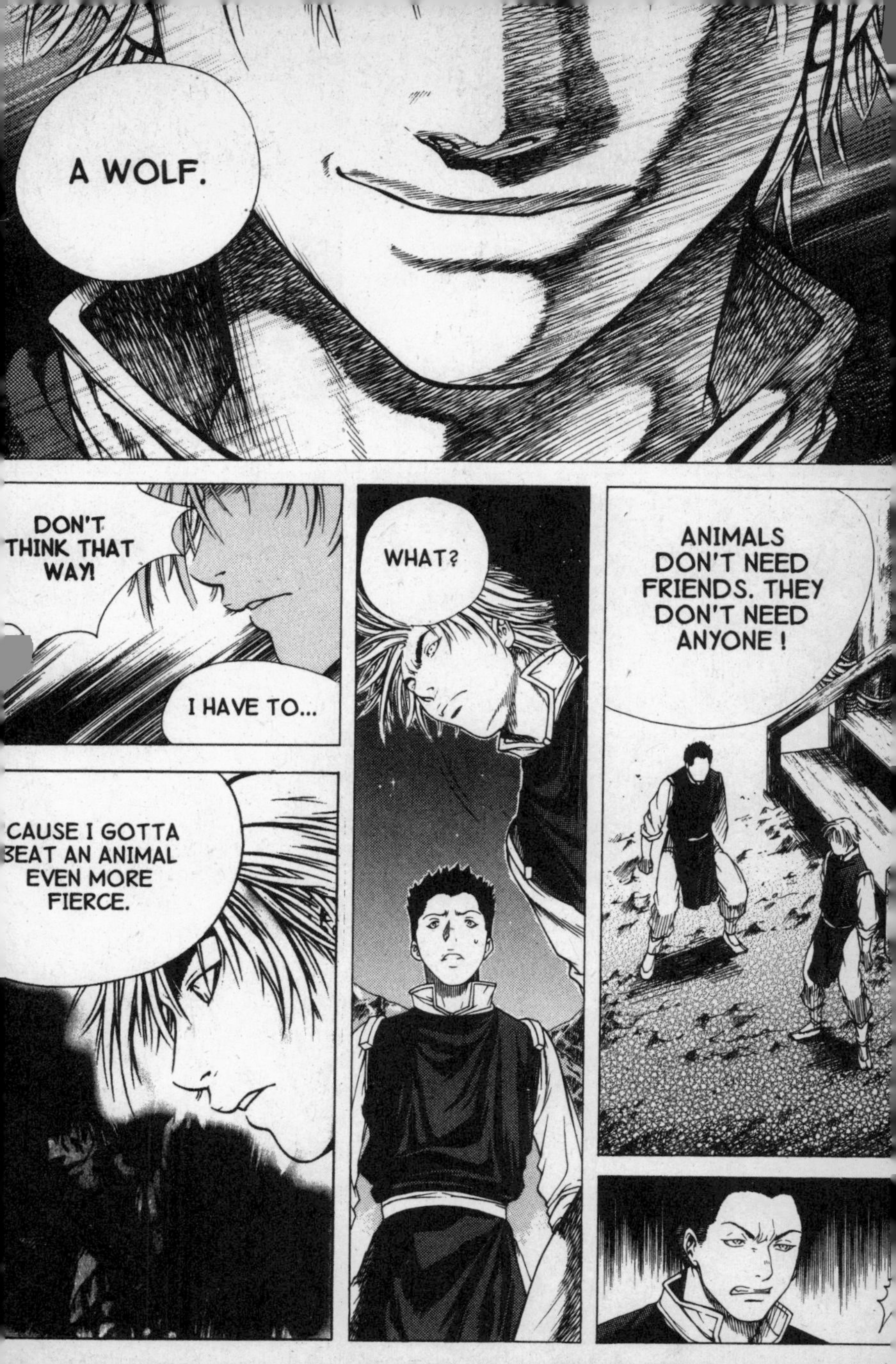
A WOLF.
DON'T THINK THAT WAY!
I HAVE TO...
CAUSE I GOTTA BEAT AN ANIMAL EVEN MORE FIERCE.
WHAT?
ANIMALS DON'T NEED FRIENDS. THEY DON'T NEED ANYONE !

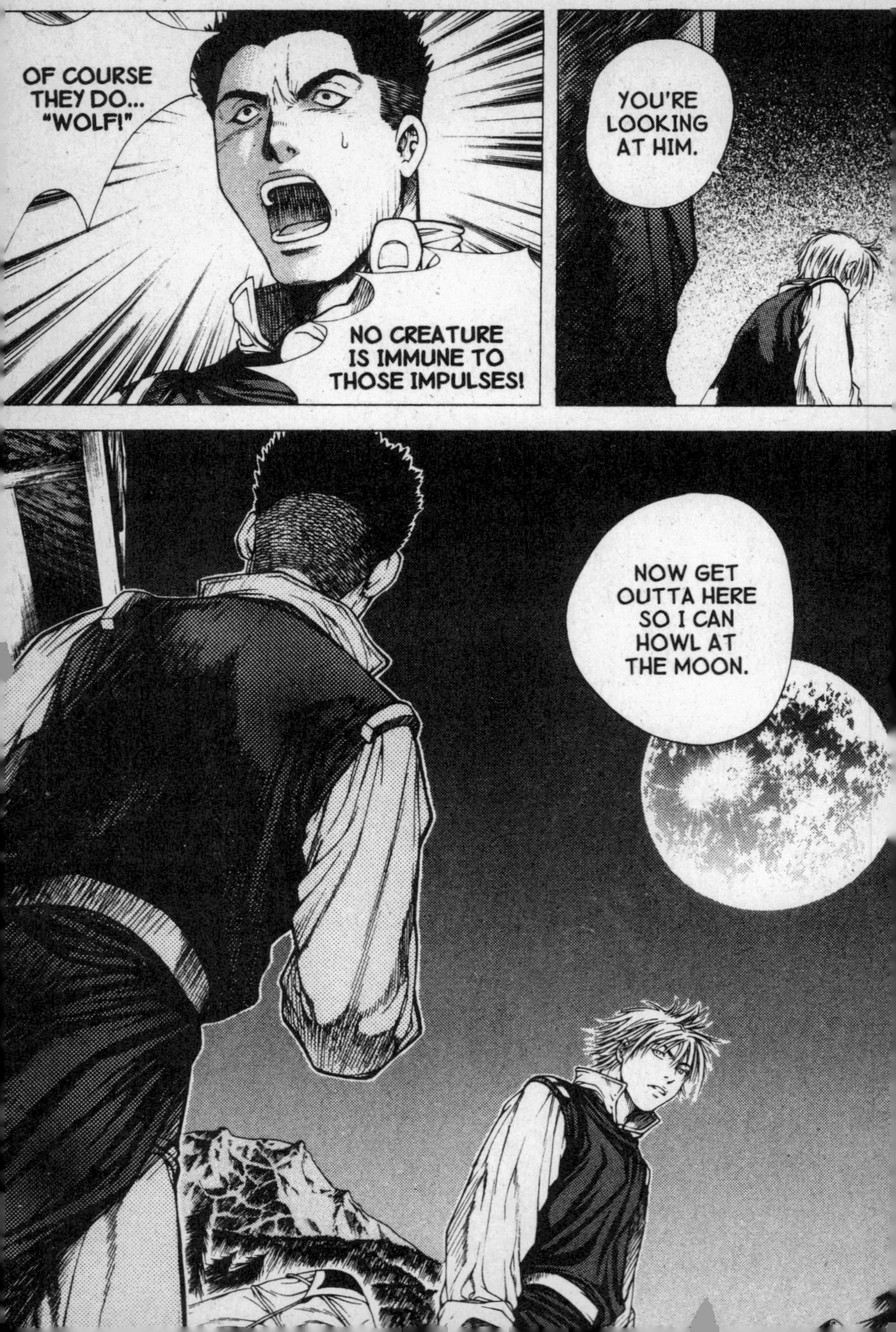
OF COURSE THEY DO... "WOLF!"
NO CREATURE IS IMMUNE TO THOSE IMPULSES!
YOU'RE LOOKING AT HIM.
NOW GET OUTTA HERE SO I CAN HOWL AT THE MOON.

Chapter 30
The Wolf

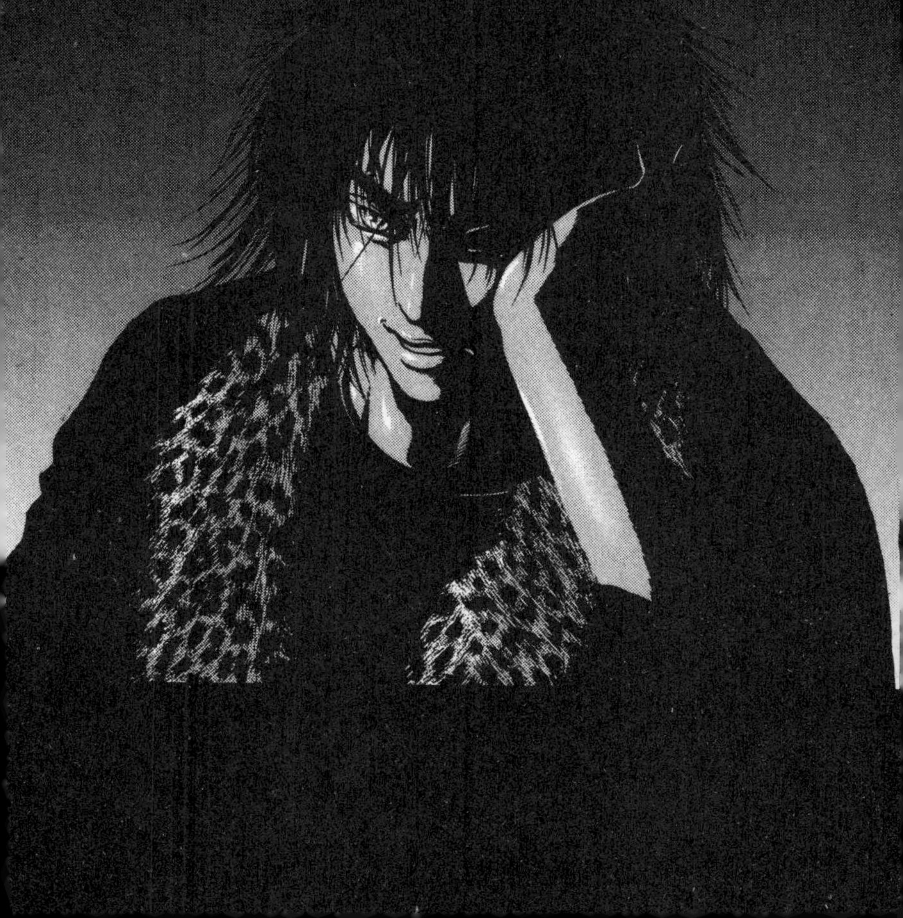

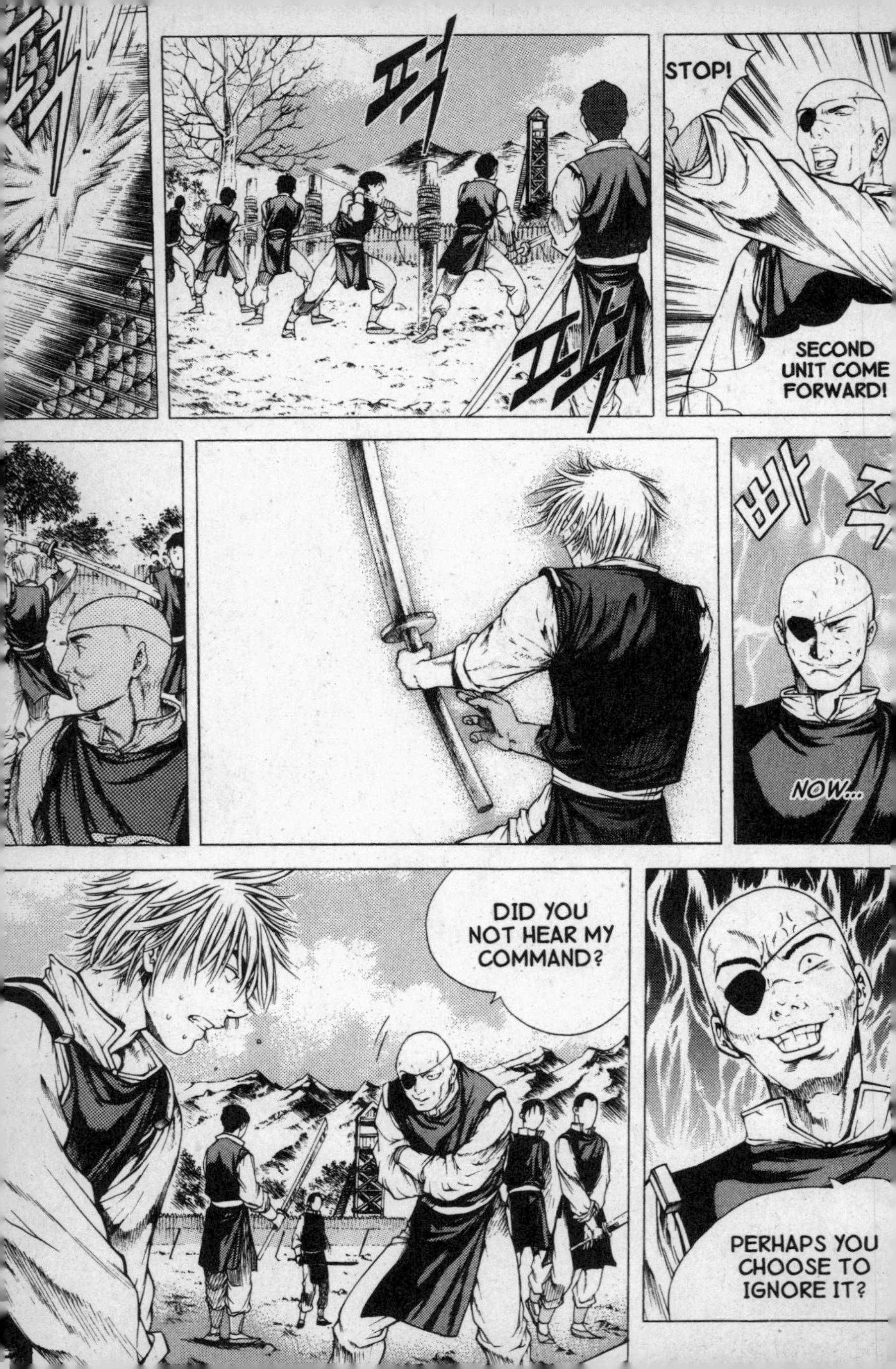
STOP!
SECOND UNIT COME FORWARD!
NOW...
DID YOU NOT HEAR MY COMMAND?
PERHAPS YOU CHOOSE TO IGNORE IT?

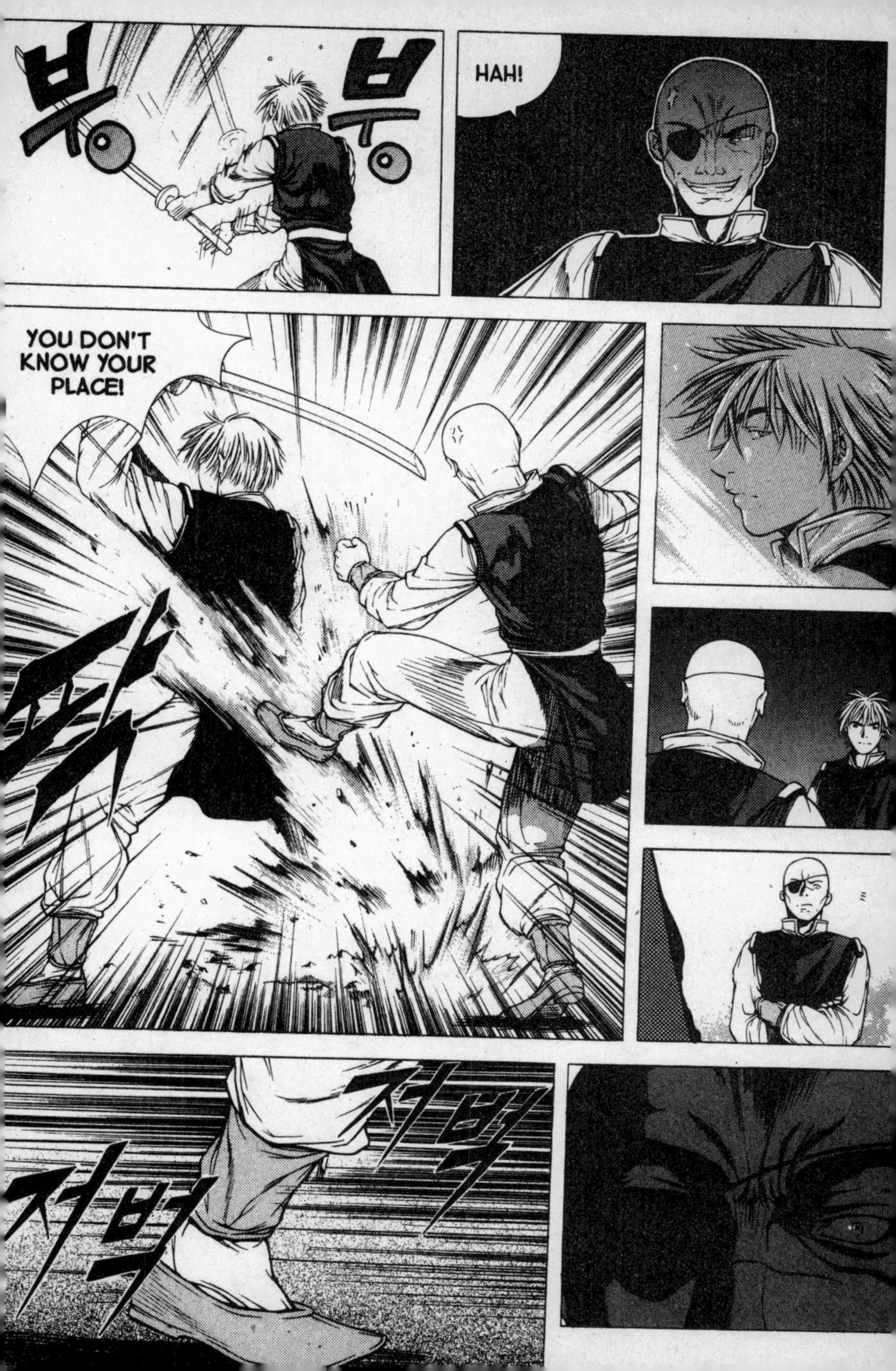
붕
붕
HAH!
YOU DON'T KNOW YOUR PLACE!
퍽
저벅
저벅

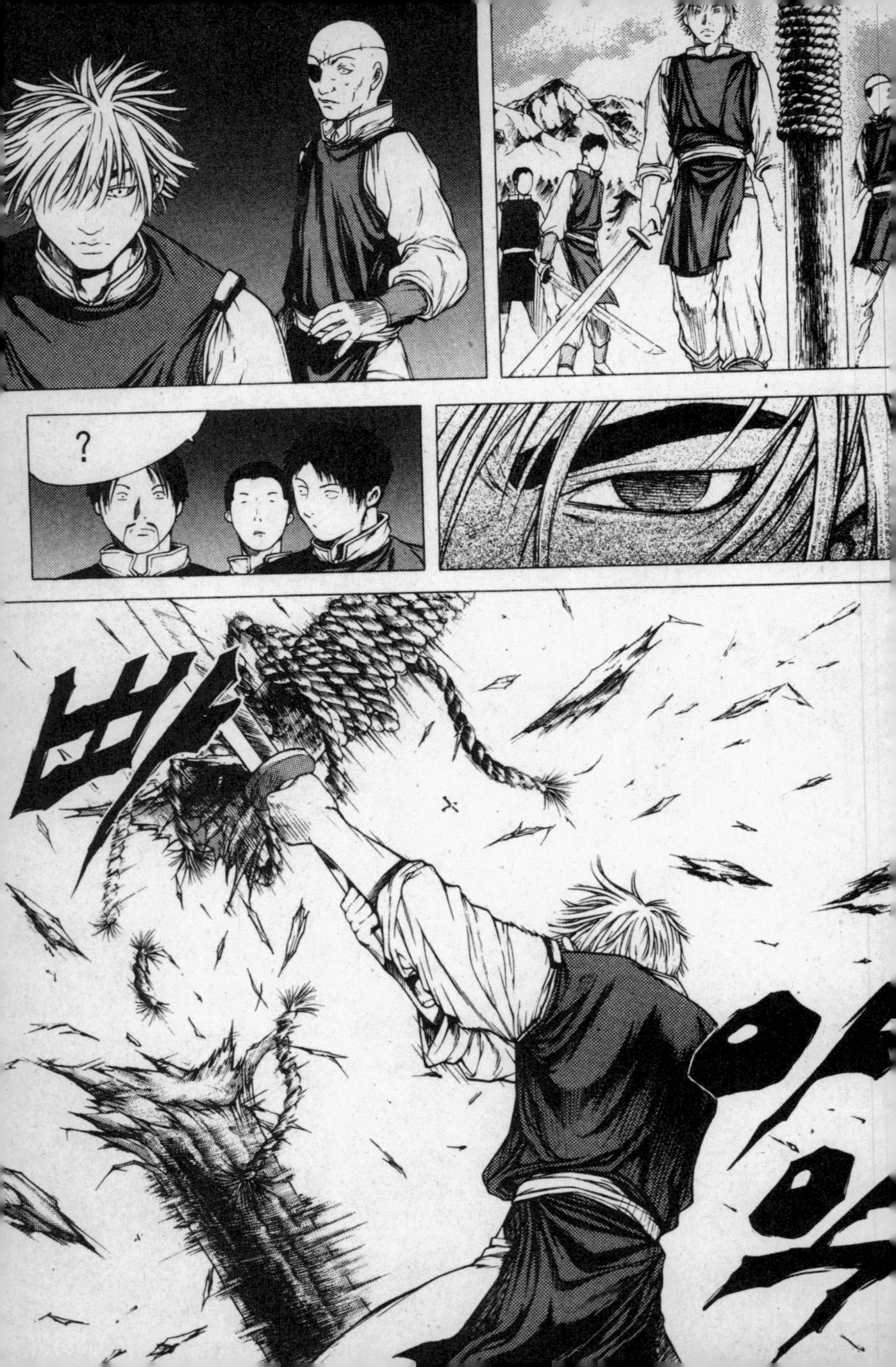
?

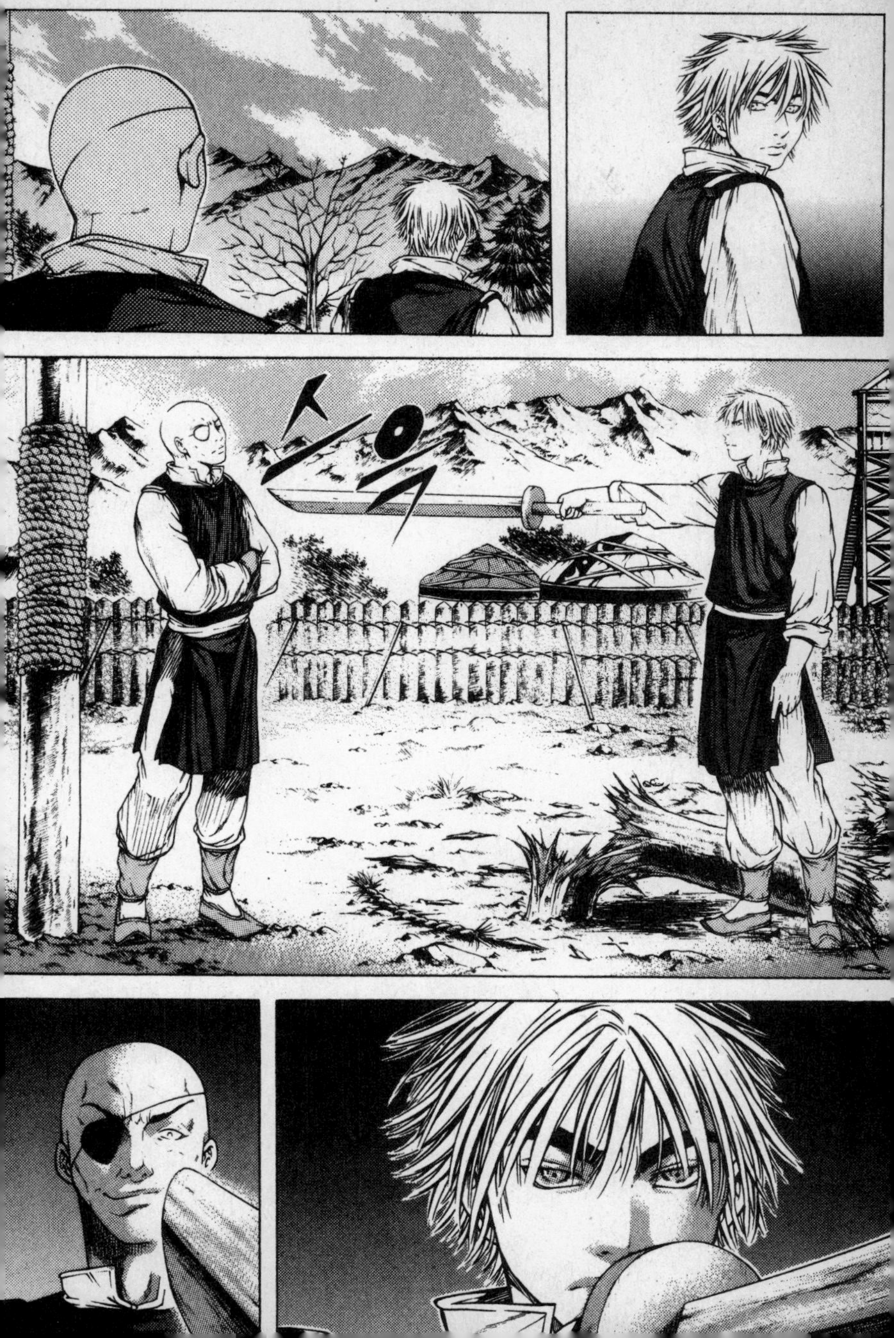

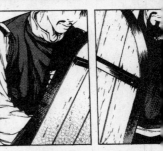

SO, YOU WANT TO TRY YOUR SKILLS.

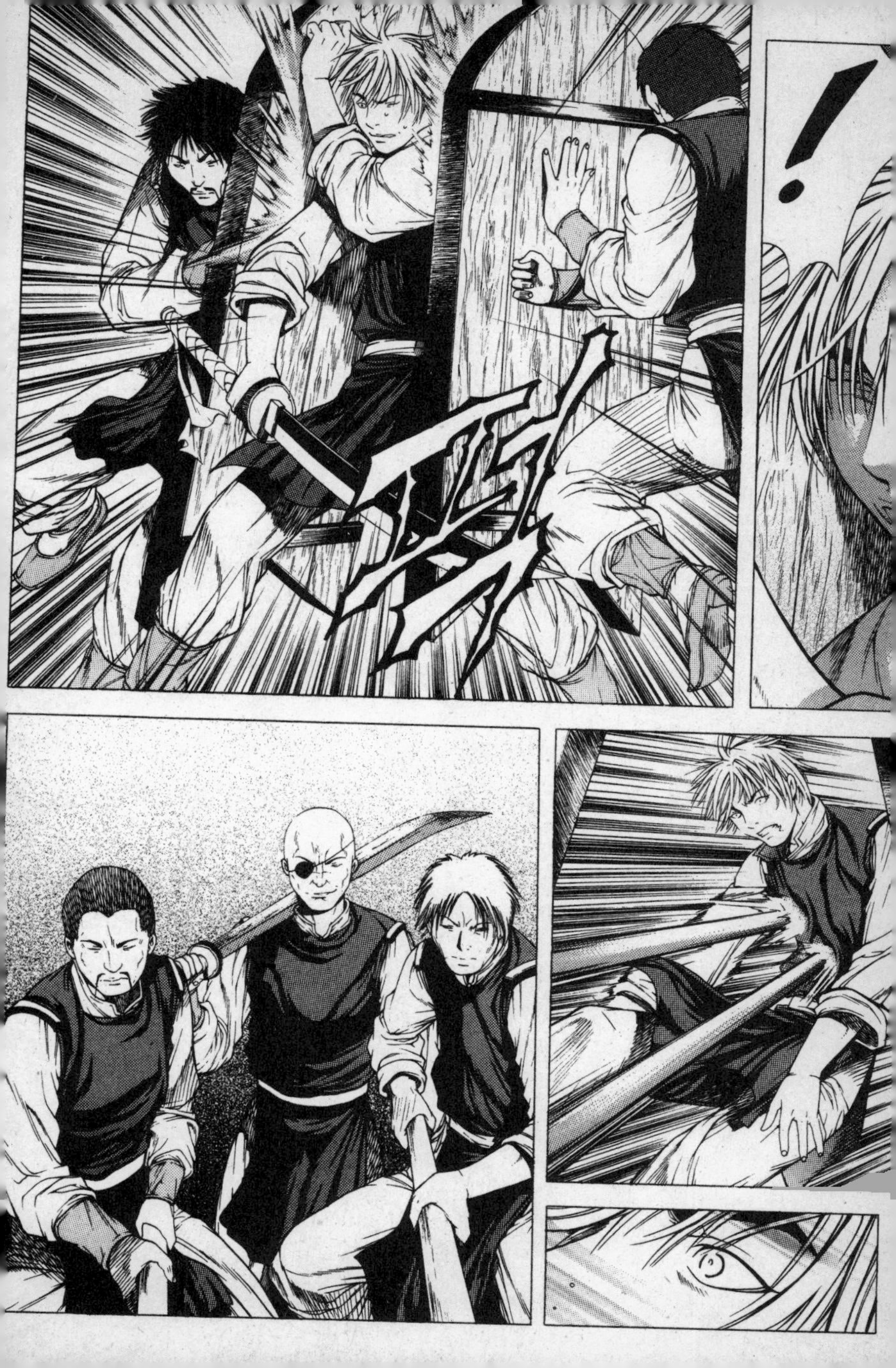
!

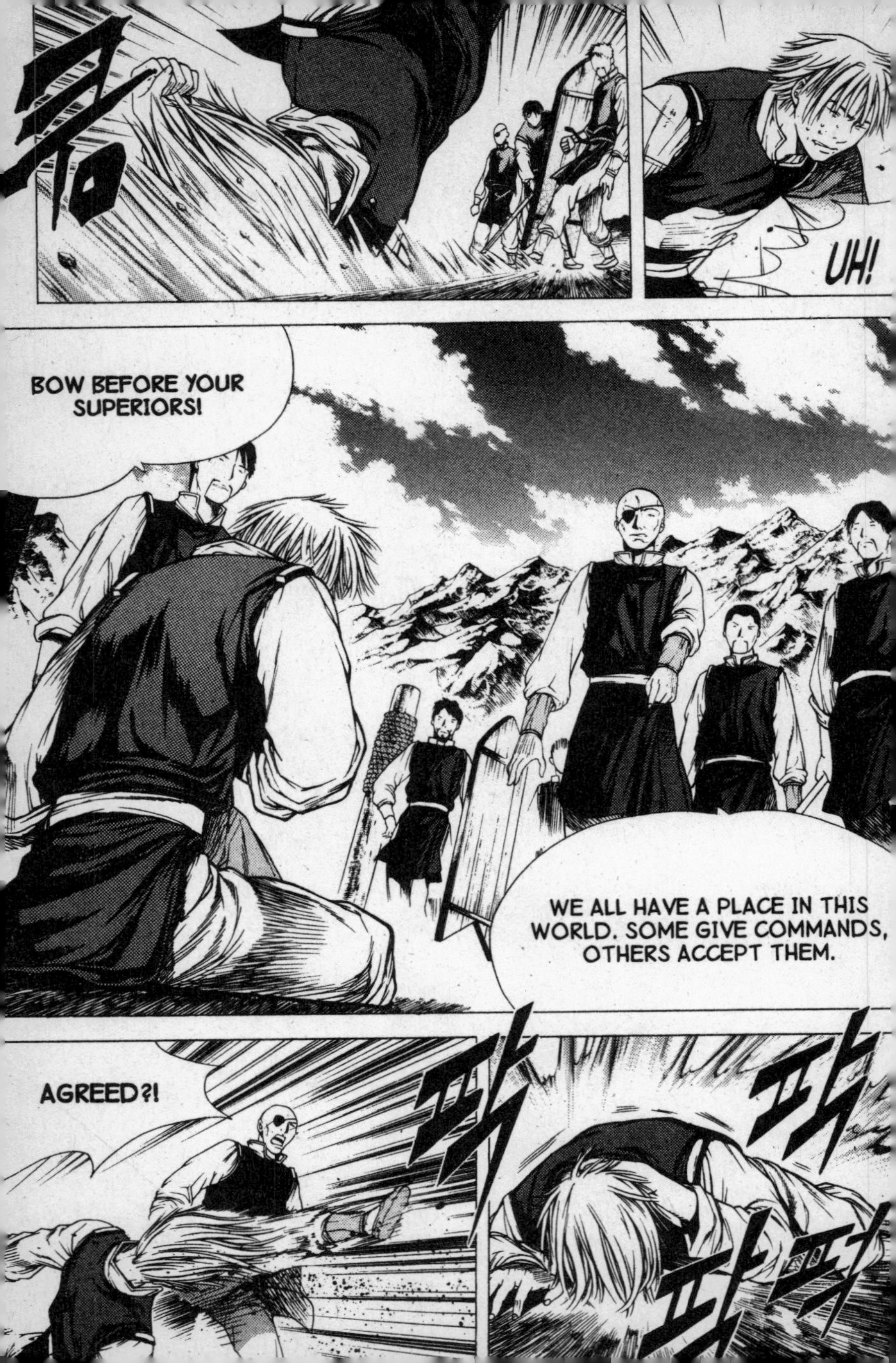
UH!
BOW BEFORE YOUR SUPERIORS!
WE ALL HAVE A PLACE IN THIS WORLD. SOME GIVE COMMANDS, OTHERS ACCEPT THEM.
AGREED?!

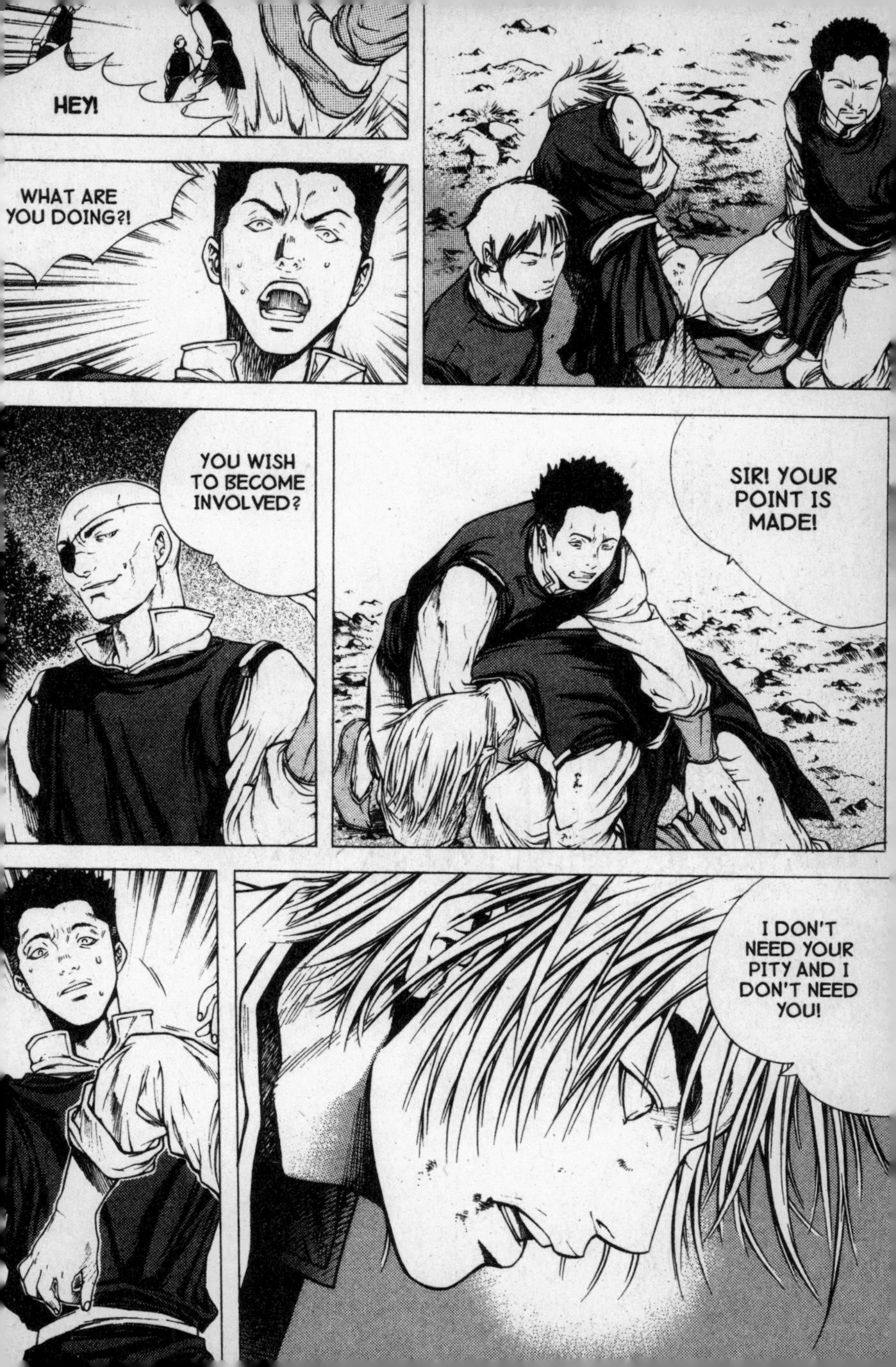
HEY!
WHAT ARE YOU DOING?!
YOU WISH TO BECOME INVOLVED?
SIR! YOUR POINT IS MADE!
I DON'T NEED YOUR PITY AND I DON'T NEED YOU!

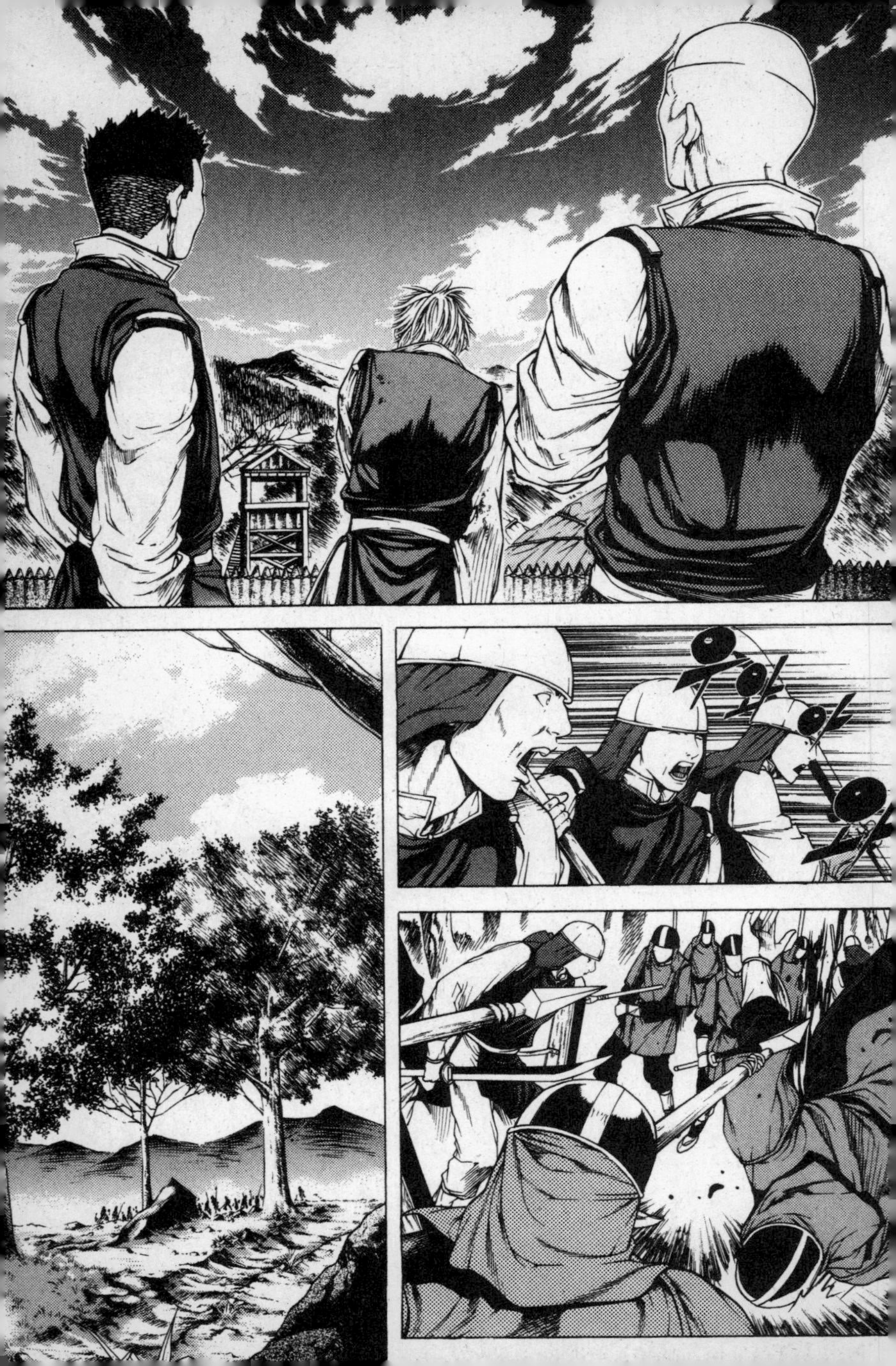

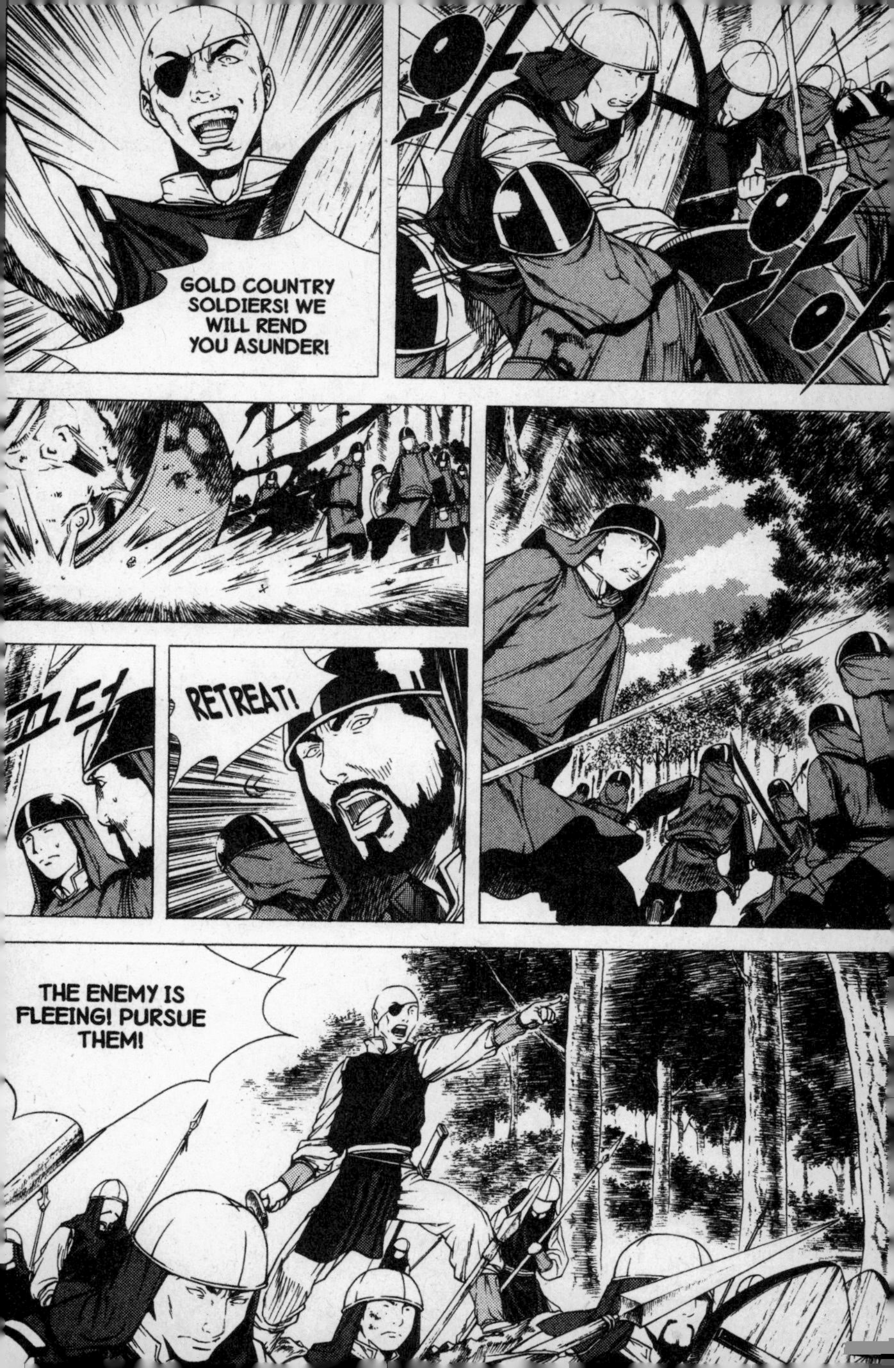
GOLD COUNTRY SOLDIERS! WE WILL REND YOU ASUNDER!
RETREAT!
THE ENEMY IS FLEEING! PURSUE THEM!

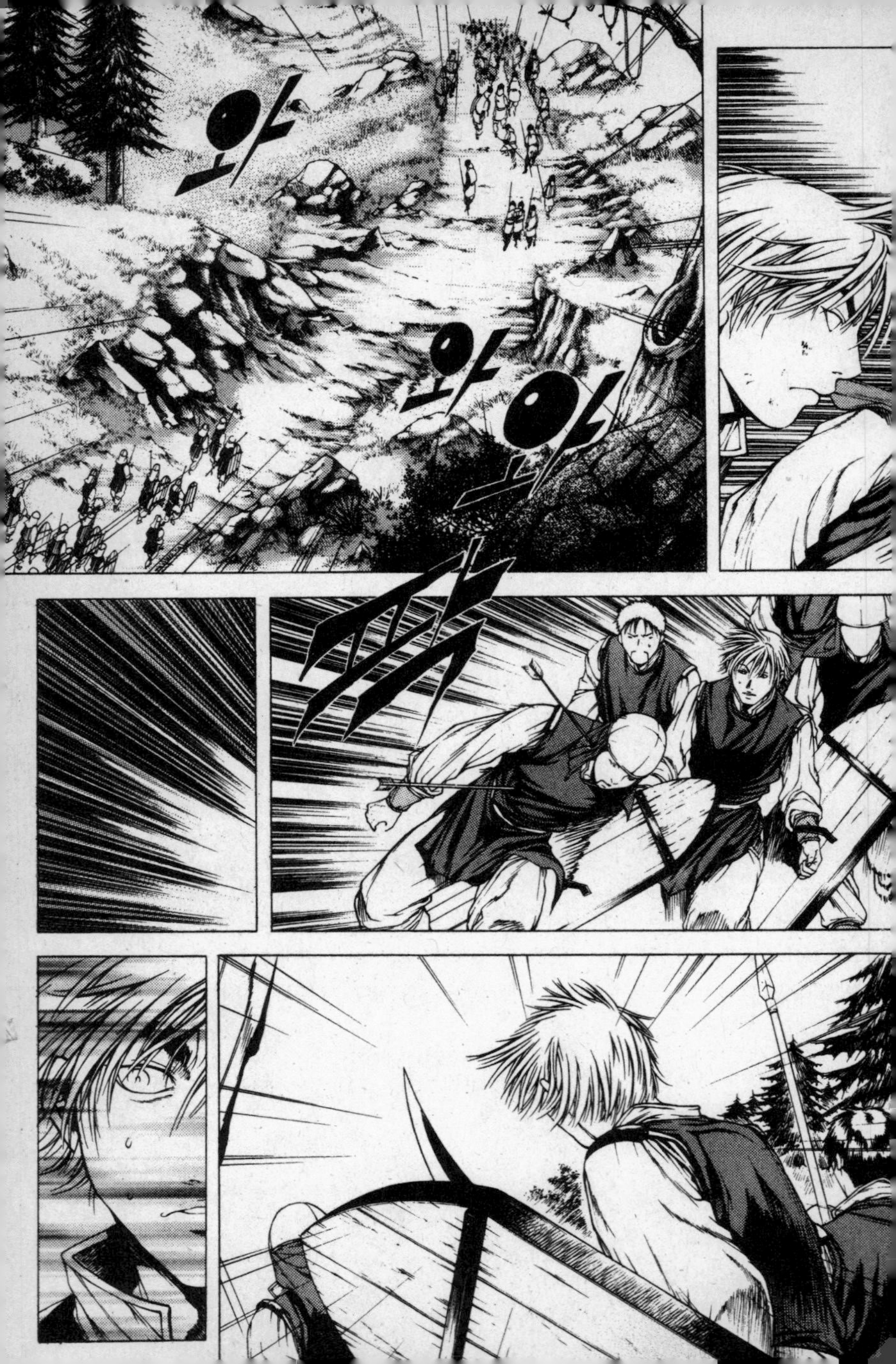
와
와
와

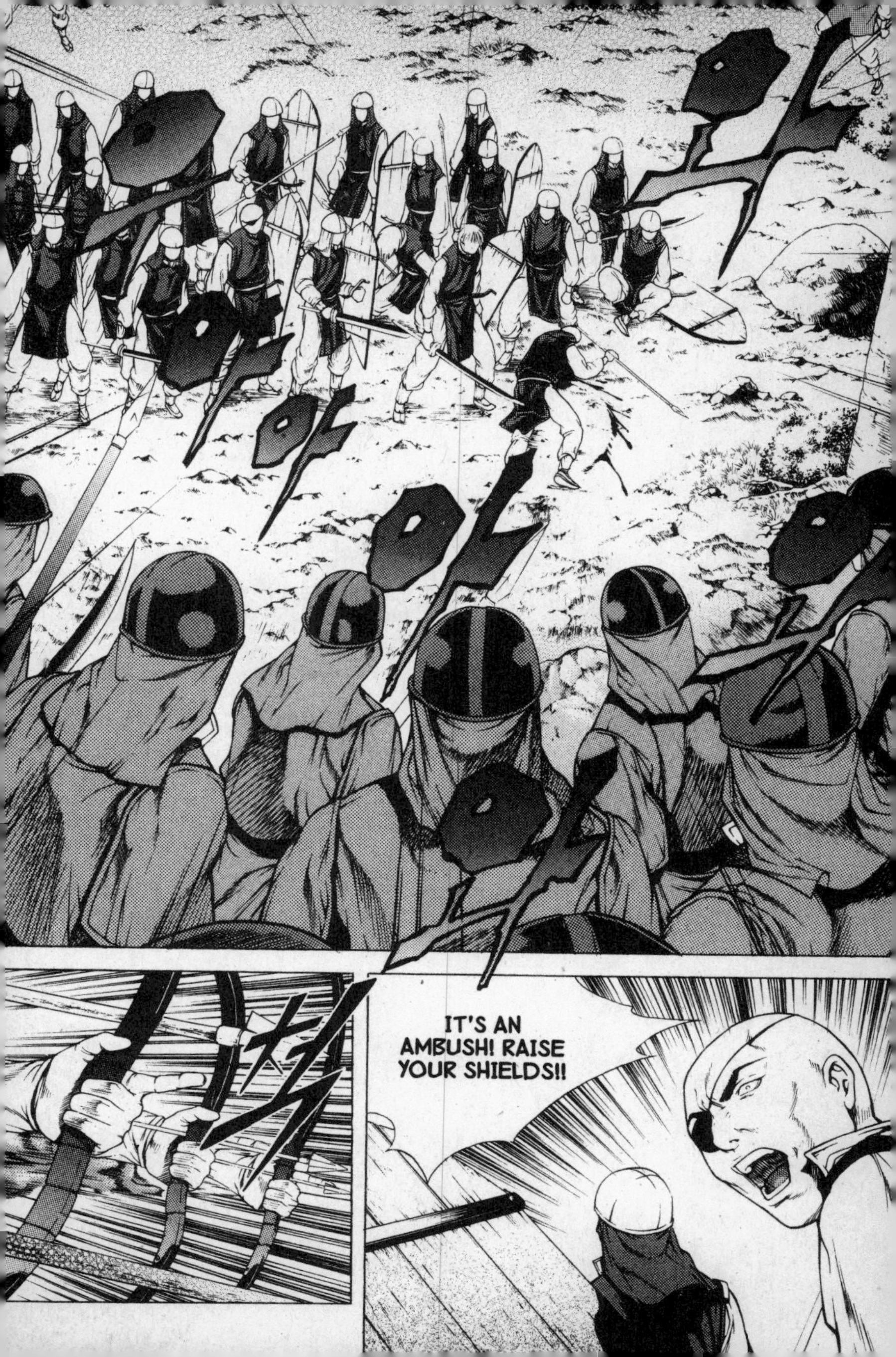
IT'S AN AMBUSH! RAISE YOUR SHIELDS!!

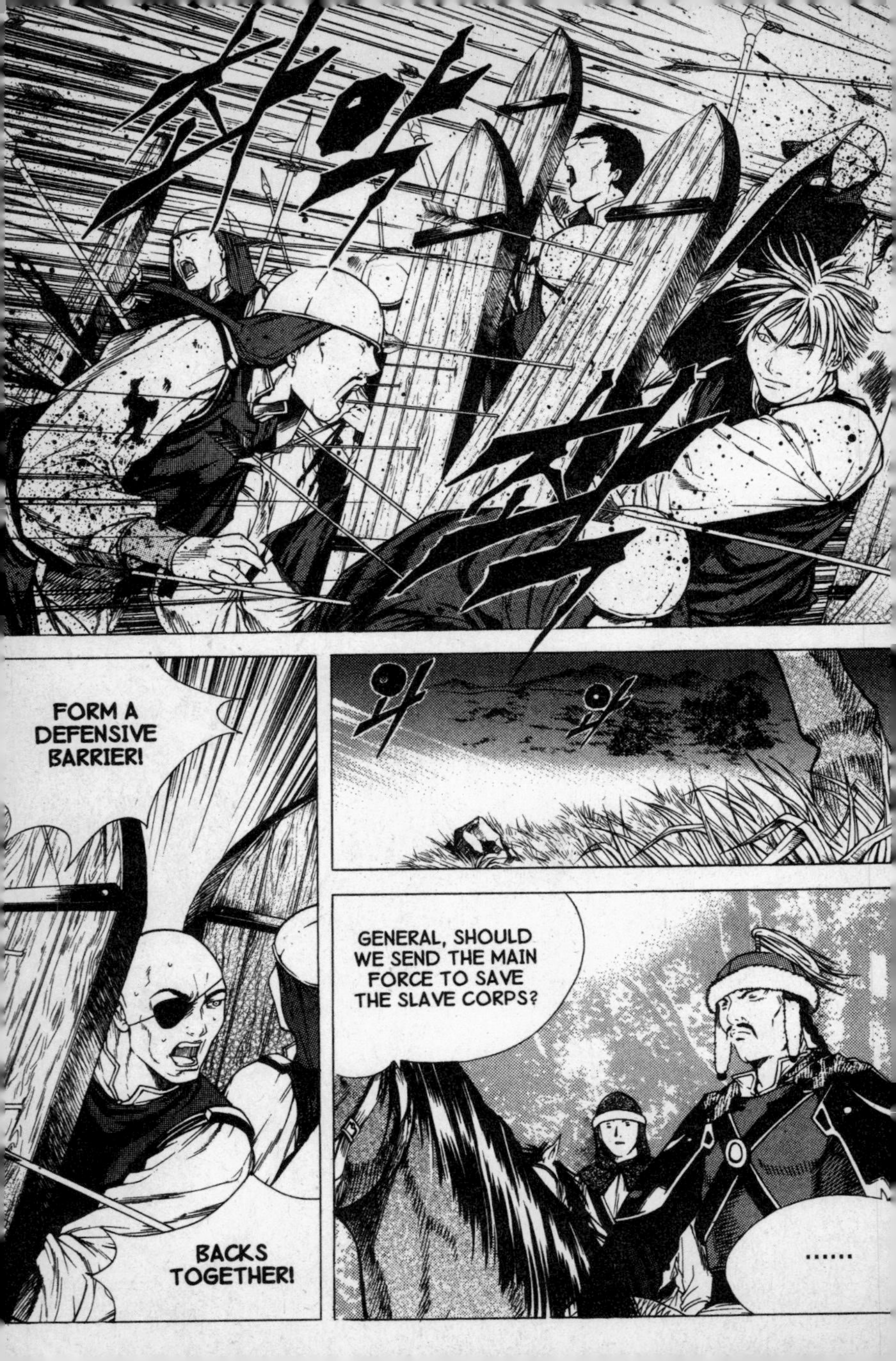
FORM A DEFENSIVE BARRIER!
BACKS TOGETHER!
와
와
GENERAL, SHOULD WE SEND THE MAIN FORCE TO SAVE THE SLAVE CORPS?
......

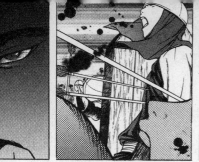

IF FATE HAS DECREED THEY FALL...IT WOULD BE UNWISE TO RISK THE REGULAR ARMY.

YES, SIR!

WAITAMINUTE!

LOOK!!

THEY'RE COMING WITH LANCERS! NOW'S OUR CHANCE!

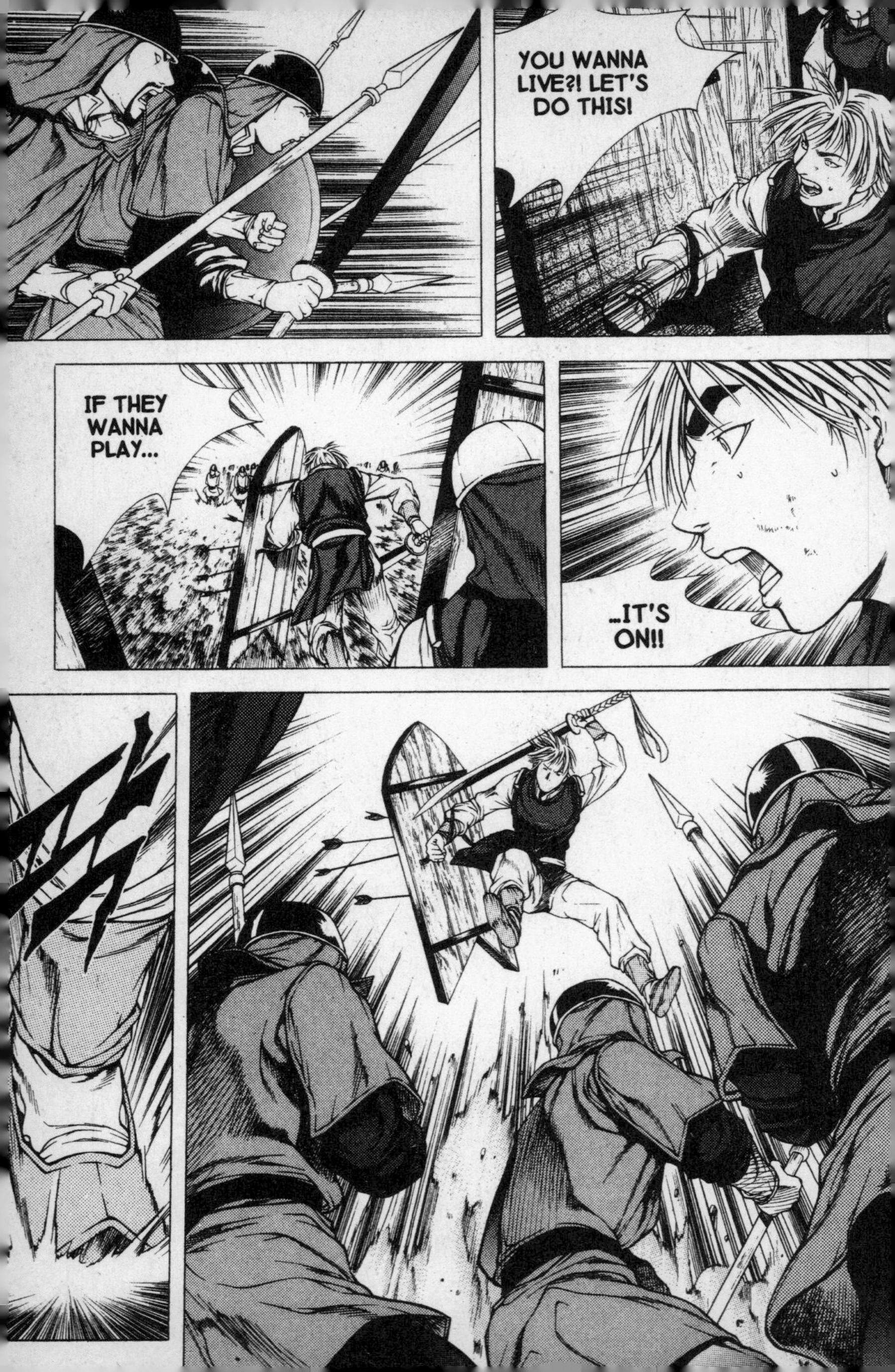
YOU WANNA LIVE?! LET'S DO THIS!
IF THEY WANNA PLAY...
...IT'S ON!!

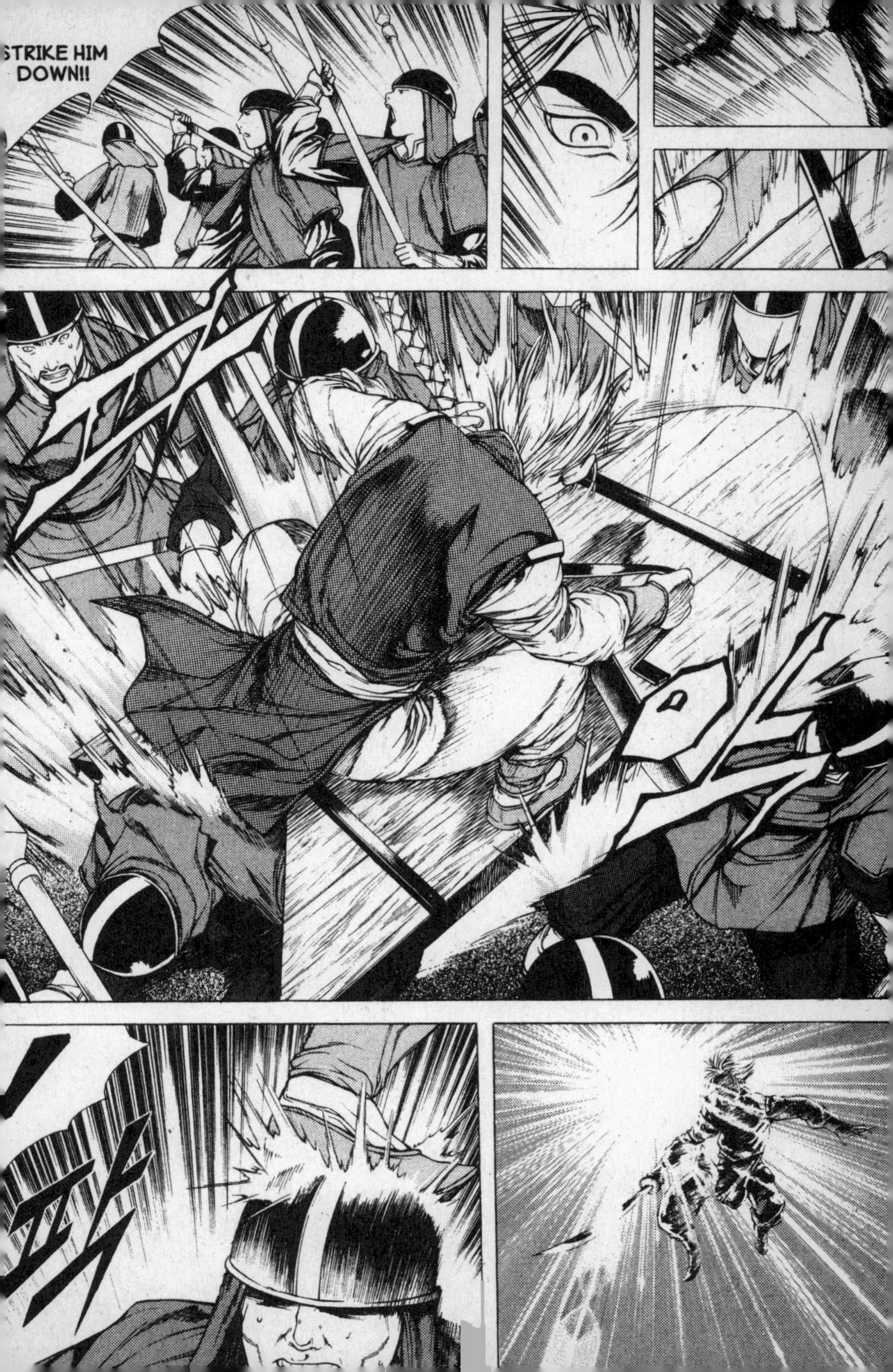
STRIKE HIM DOWN!!

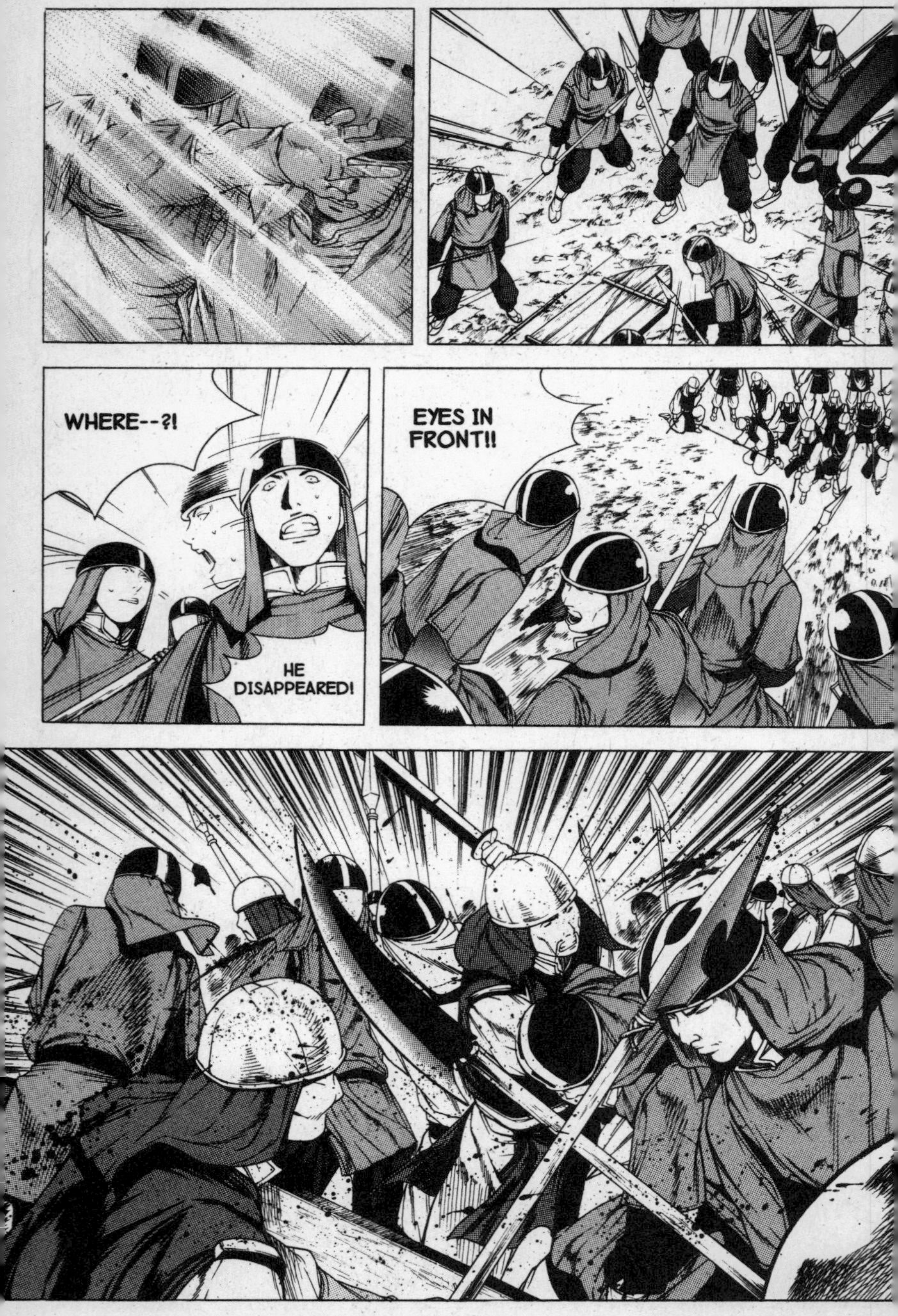
WHERE--?!
HE DISAPPEARED!
EYES IN FRONT!!

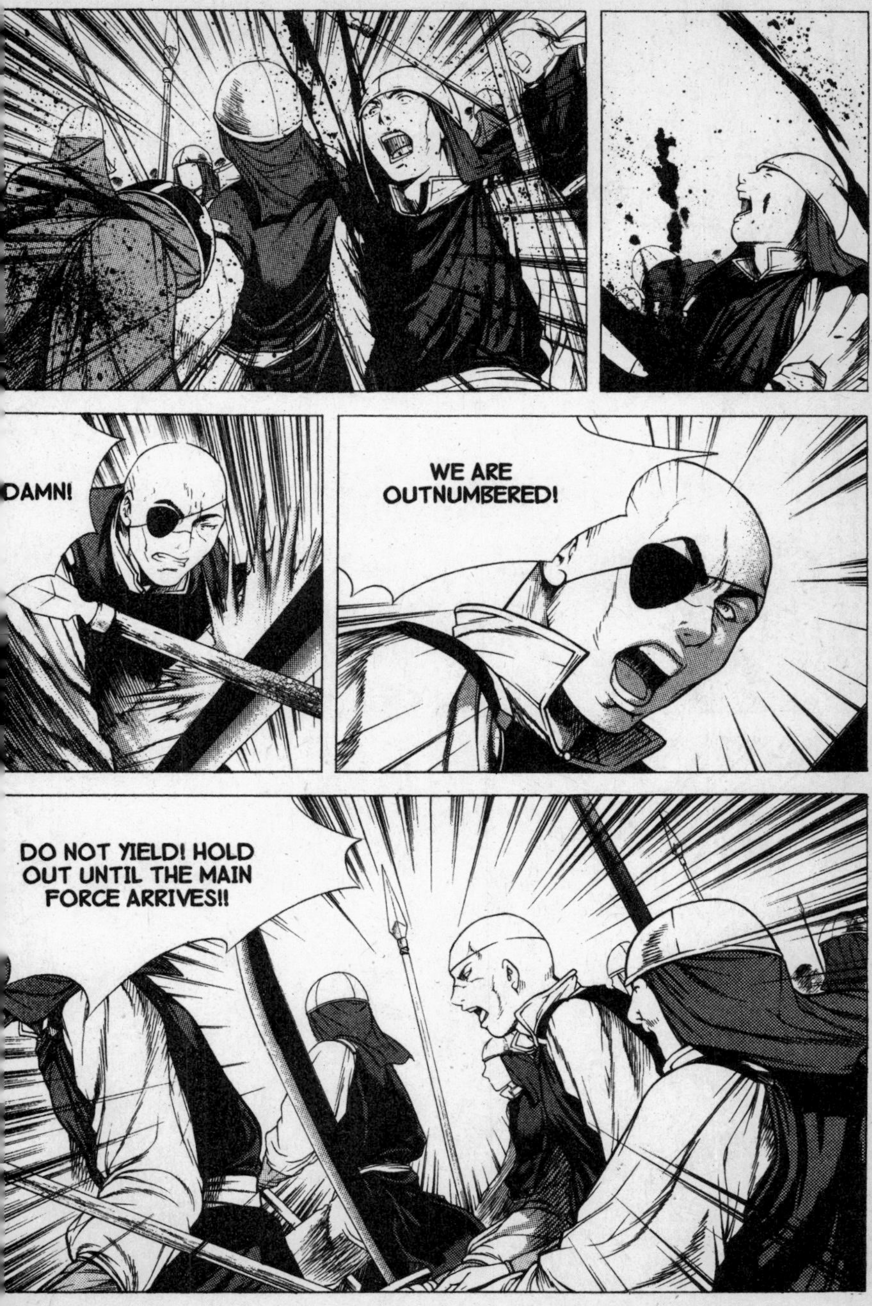
DAMN!
WE ARE OUTNUMBERED!
DO NOT YIELD! HOLD OUT UNTIL THE MAIN FORCE ARRIVES!!

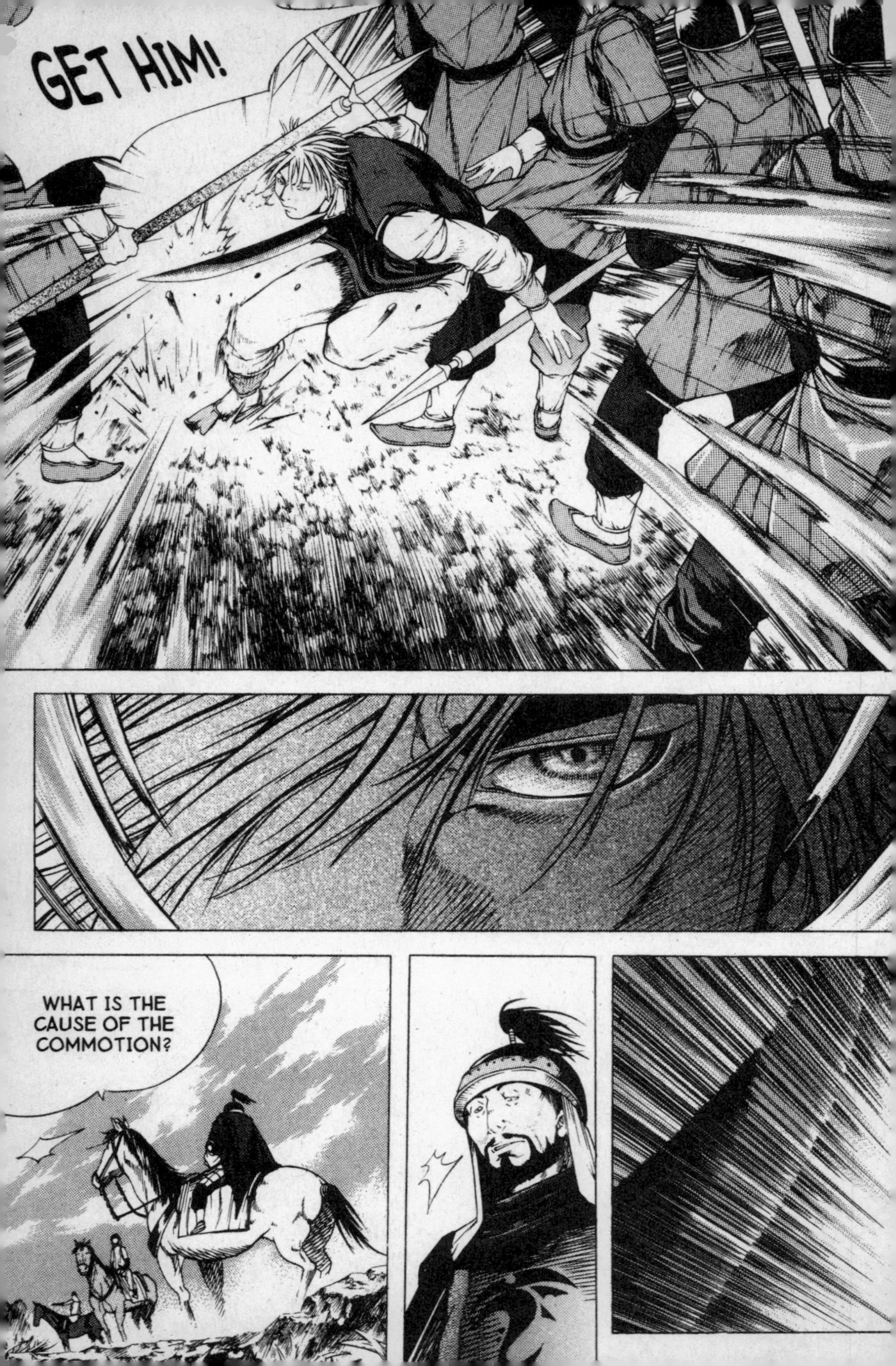
GET HIM!
WHAT IS THE CAUSE OF THE COMMOTION?

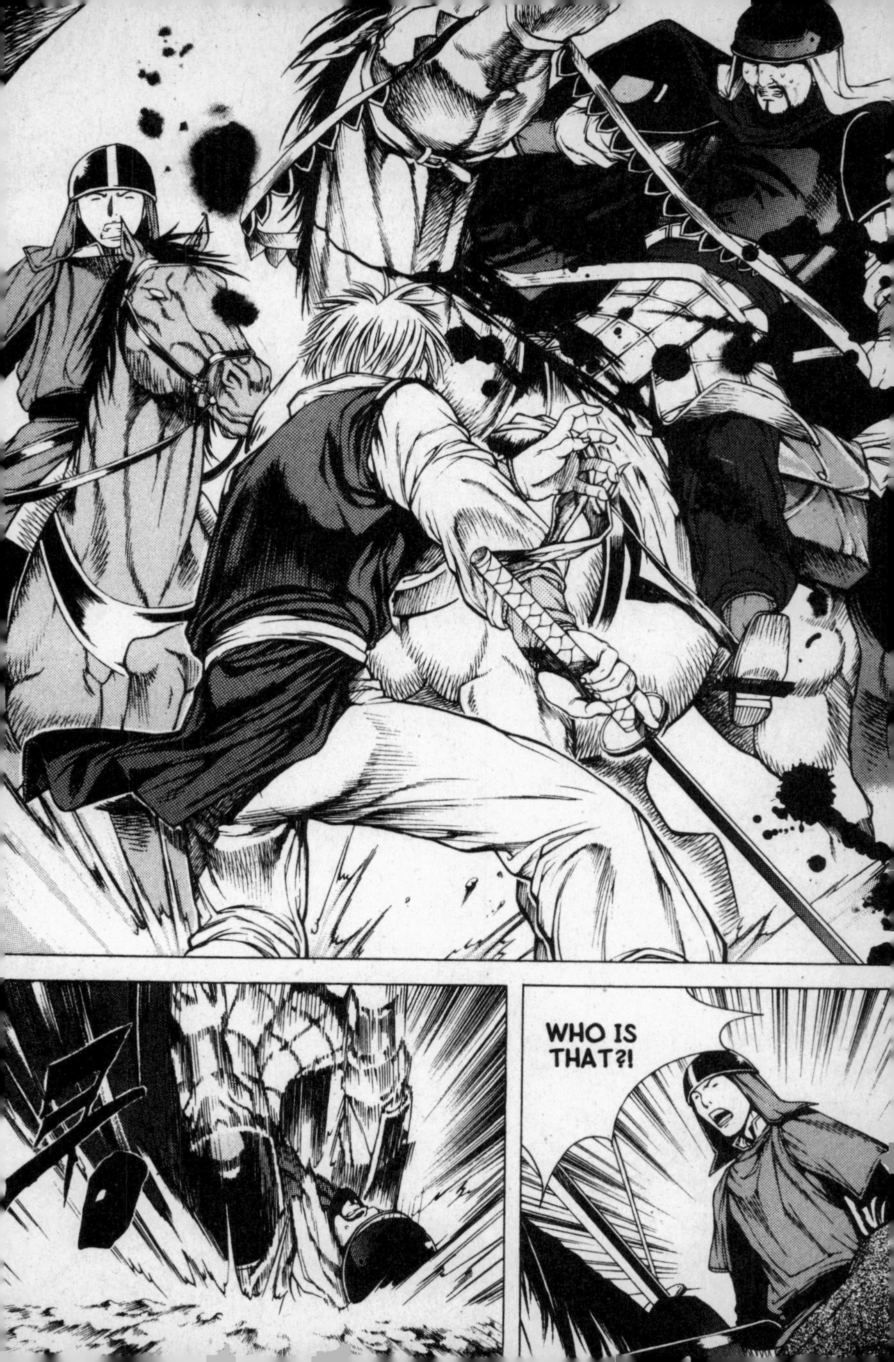
WHO IS
THAT?!

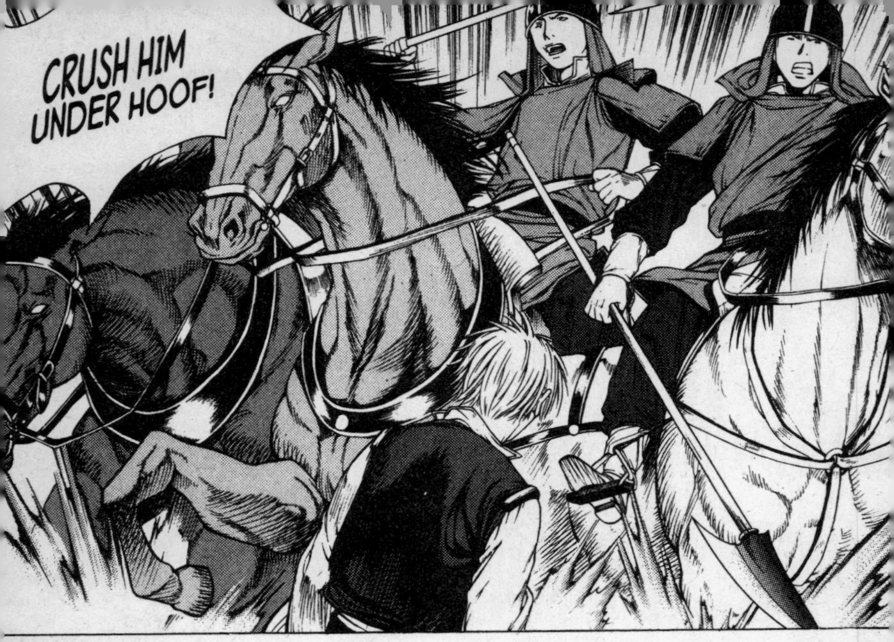
CRUSH HIM UNDER HOOF!
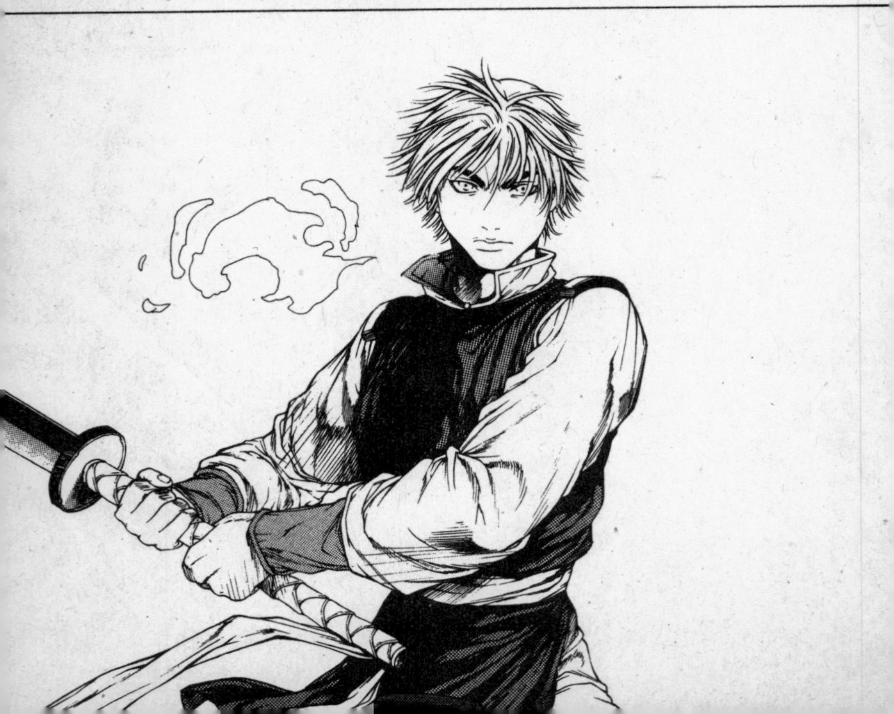

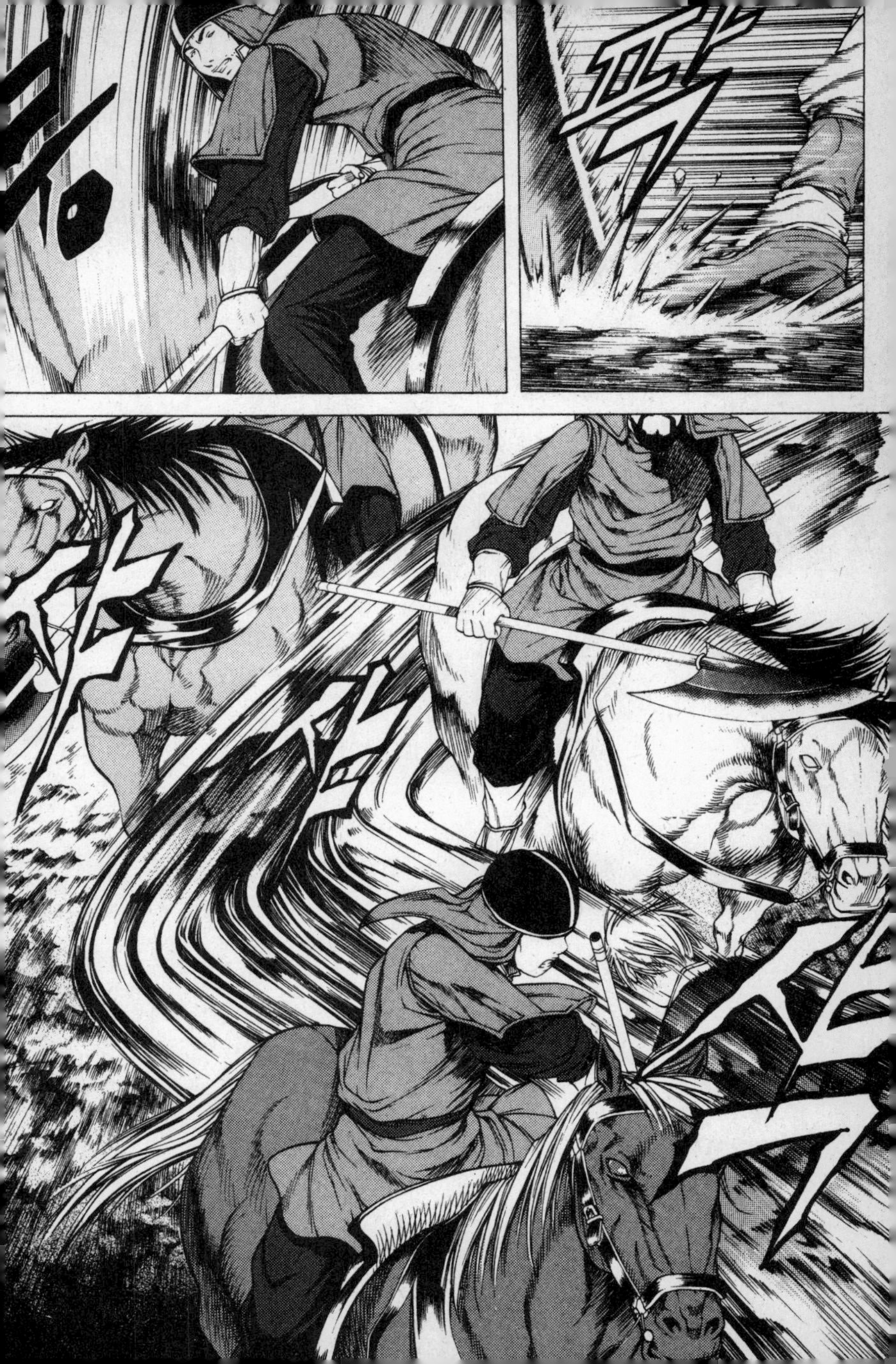

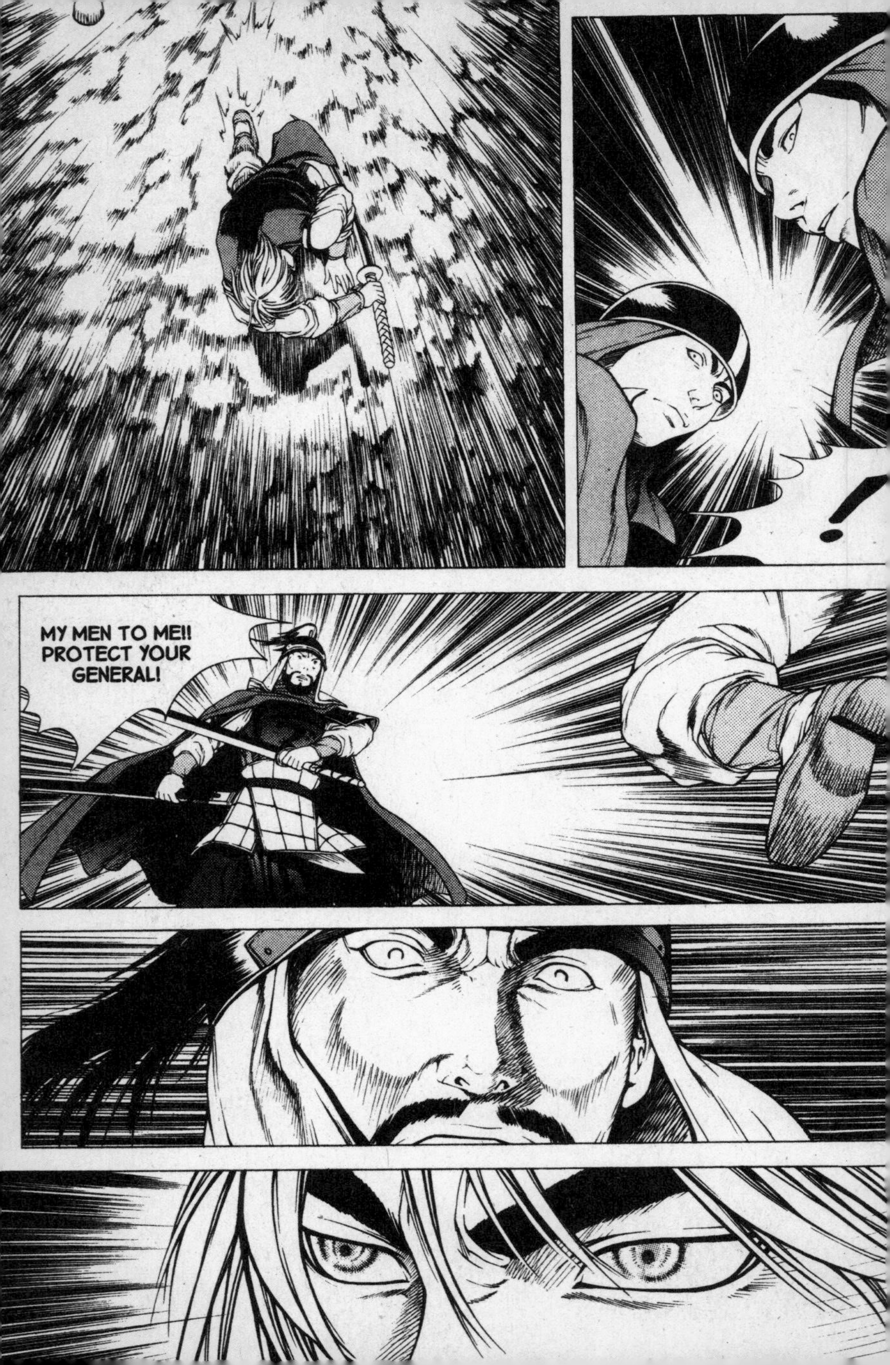
!
MY MEN TO ME!! PROTECT YOUR GENERAL!

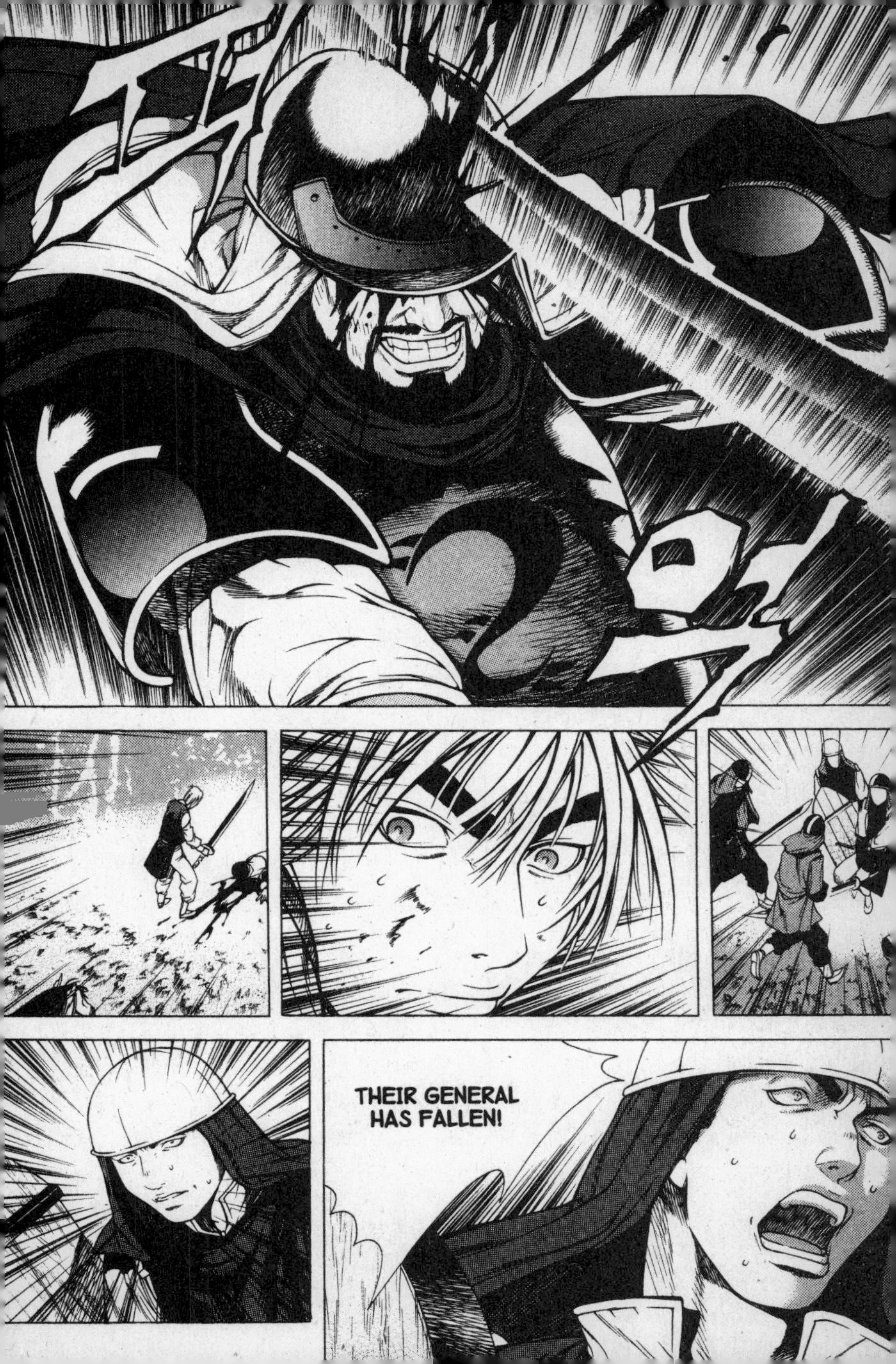
THEIR GENERAL HAS FALLEN!

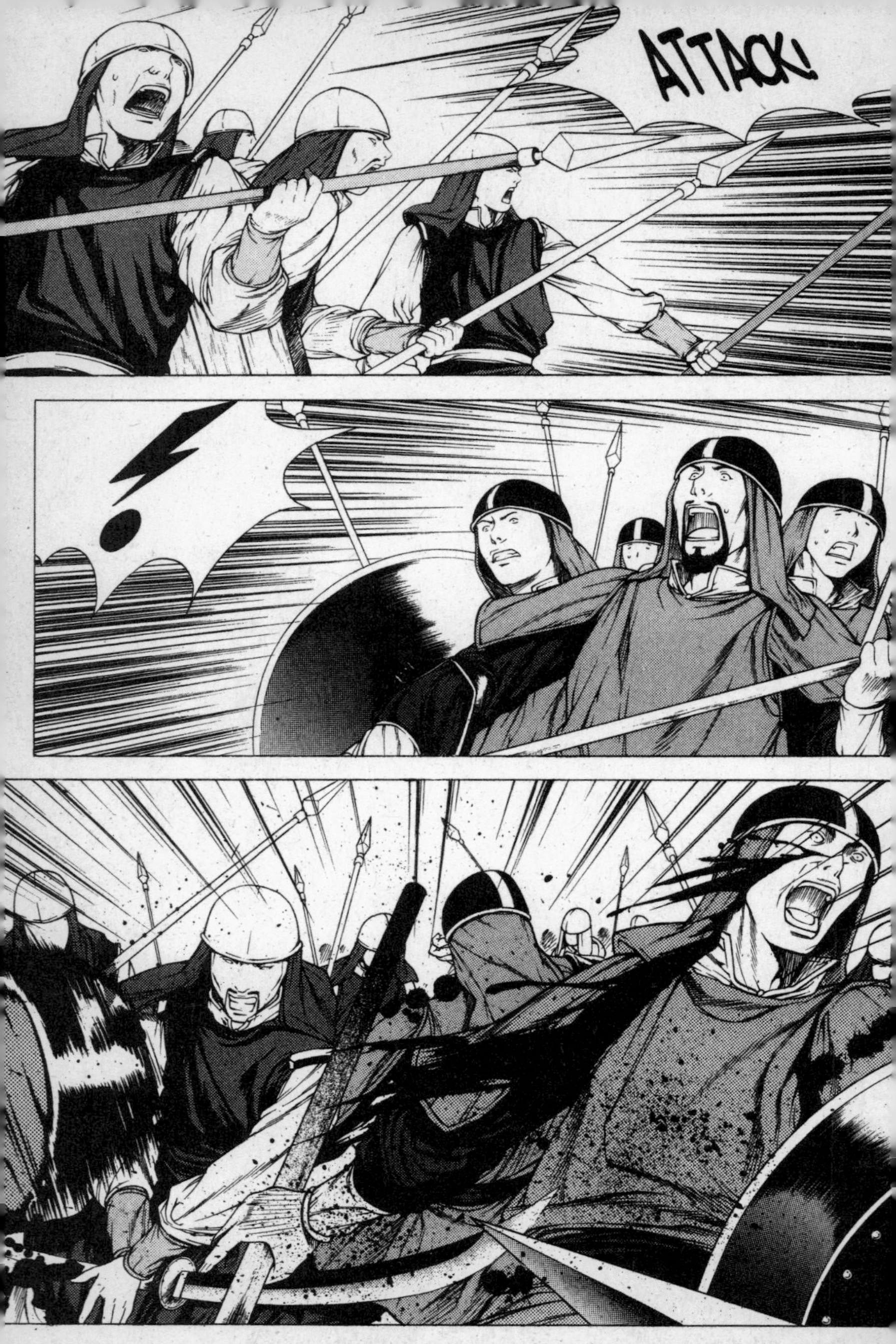
ATTACK!

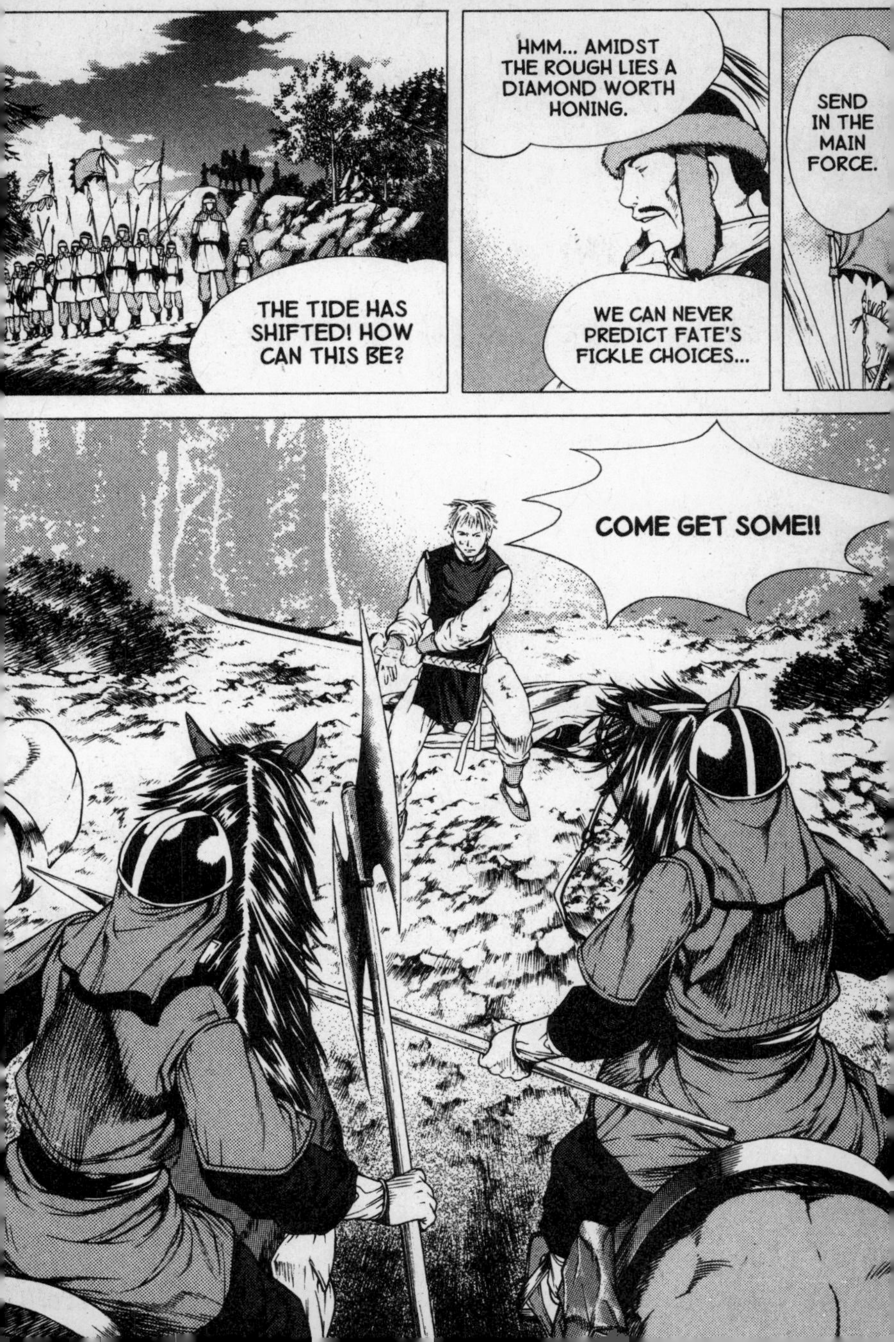
THE TIDE HAS SHIFTED! HOW CAN THIS BE?
HMM... AMIDST THE ROUGH LIES A DIAMOND WORTH HONING.
WE CAN NEVER PREDICT FATE'S FICKLE CHOICES...
SEND IN THE MAIN FORCE.
COME GET SOME!!

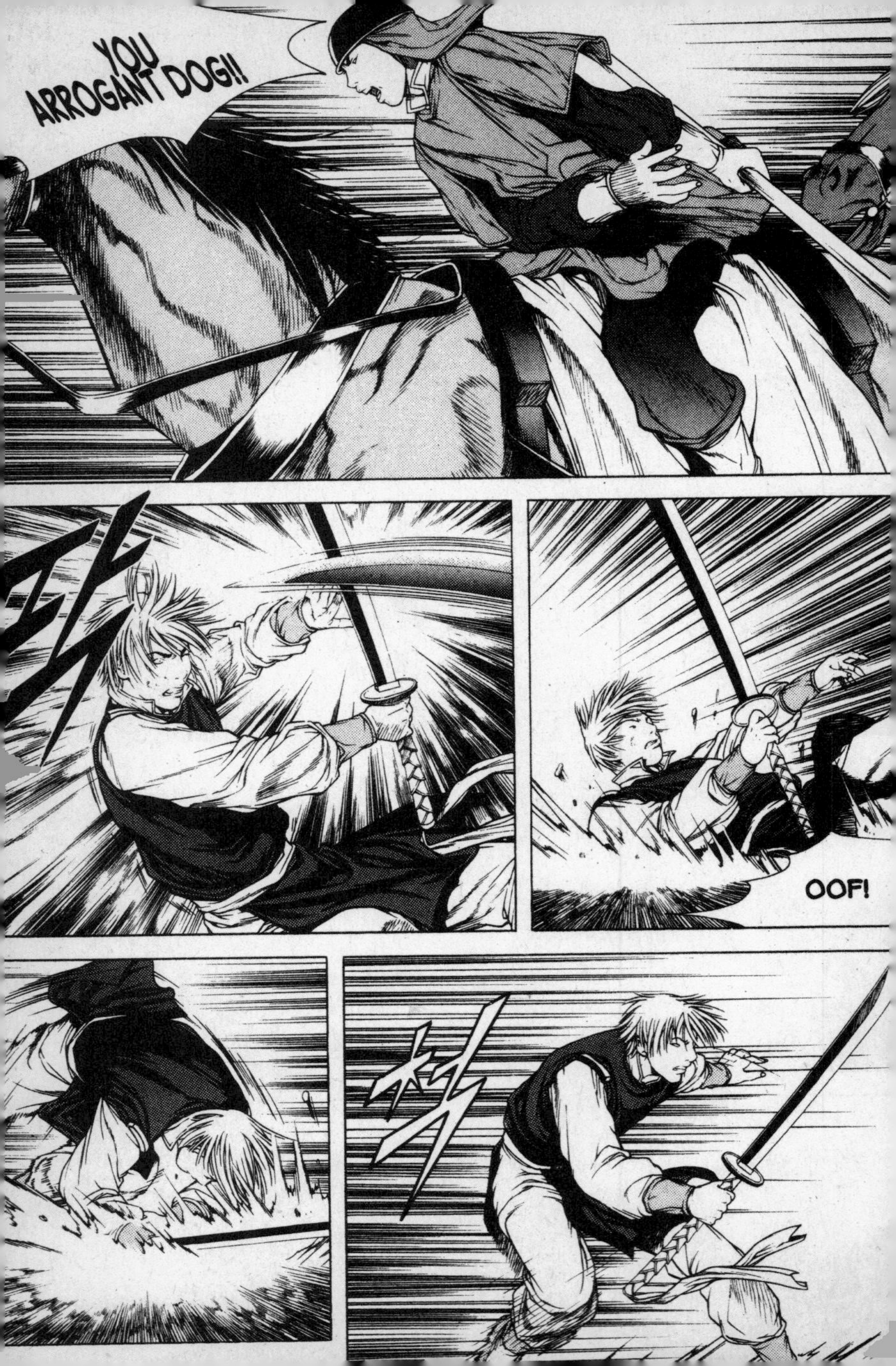
YOU ARROGANT DOG!!
OOF!

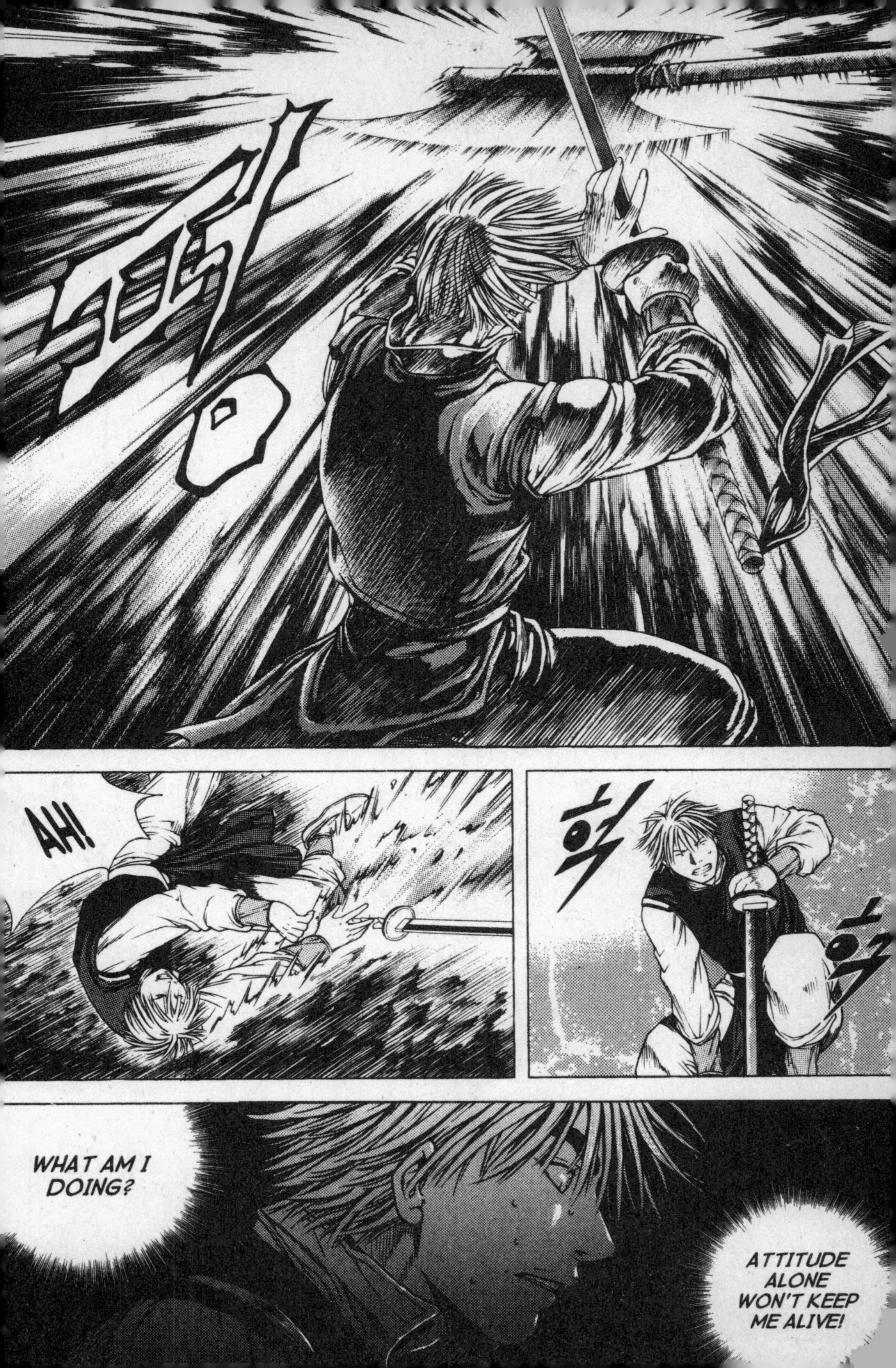
AH!
헉
헉
WHAT AM I DOING?
ATTITUDE ALONE WON'T KEEP ME ALIVE!

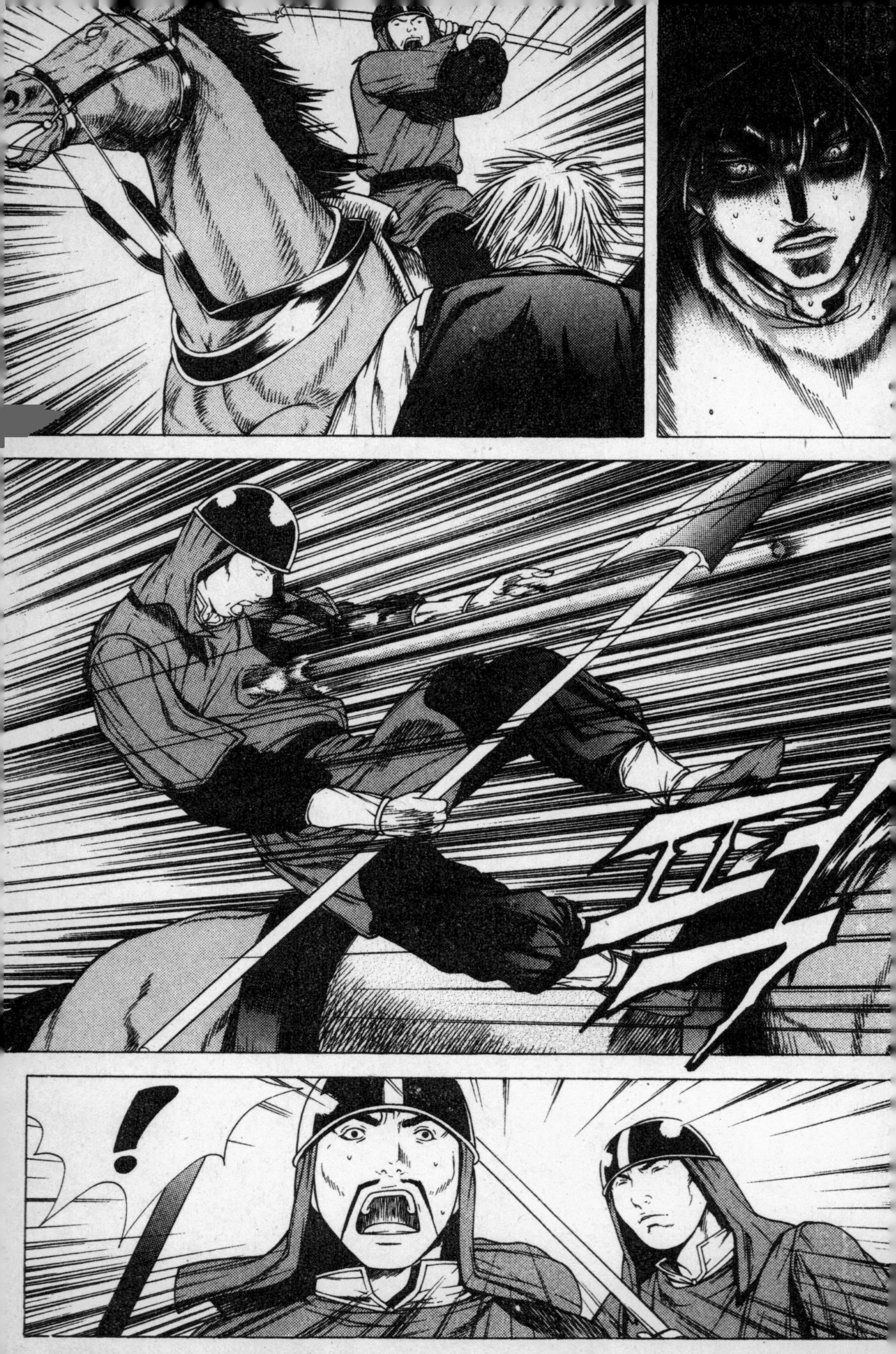
!

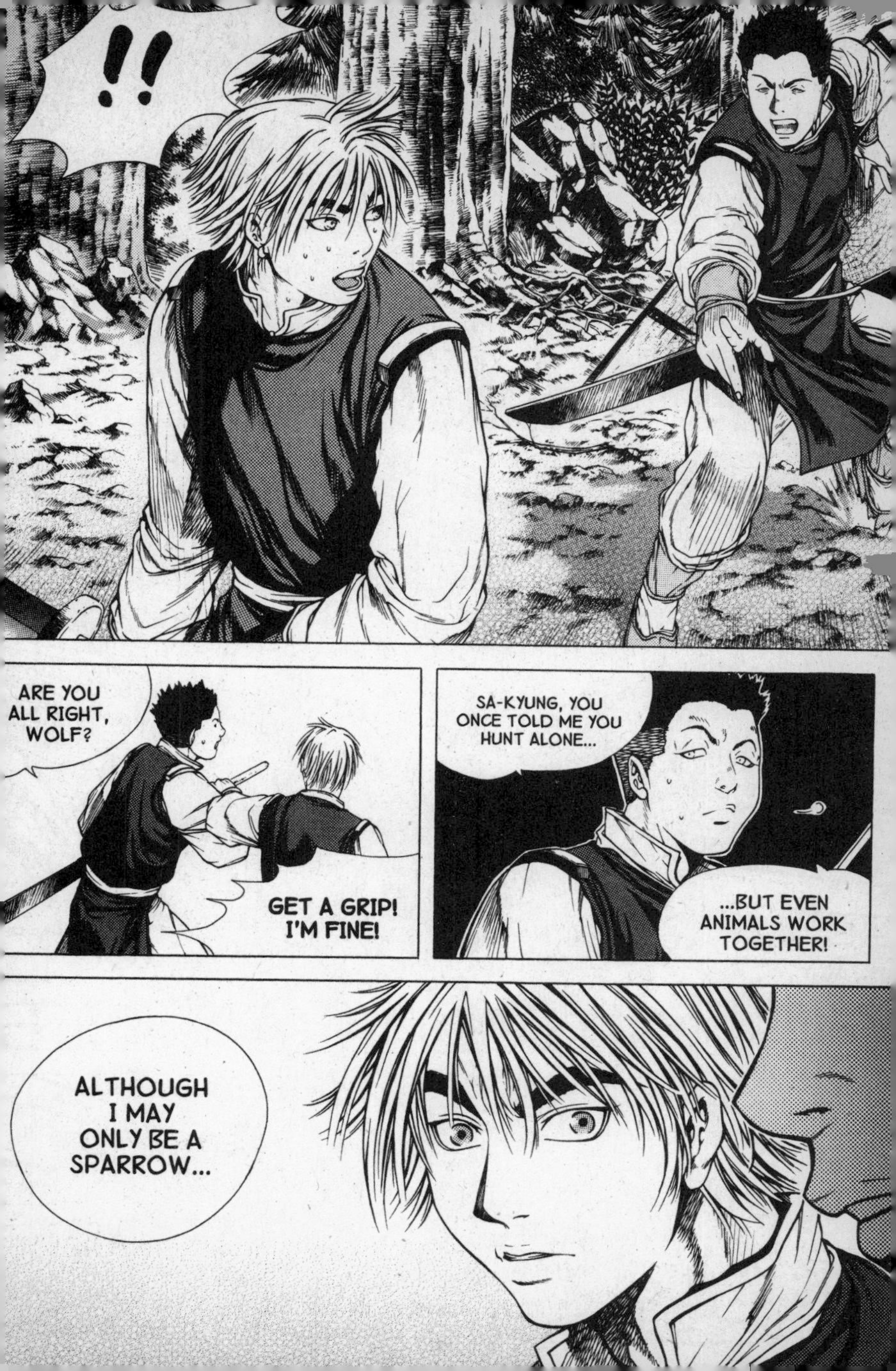
!!
ARE YOU ALL RIGHT, WOLF?
GET A GRIP! I'M FINE!
SA-KYUNG, YOU ONCE TOLD ME YOU HUNT ALONE...
...BUT EVEN ANIMALS WORK TOGETHER!
ALTHOUGH I MAY ONLY BE A SPARROW...

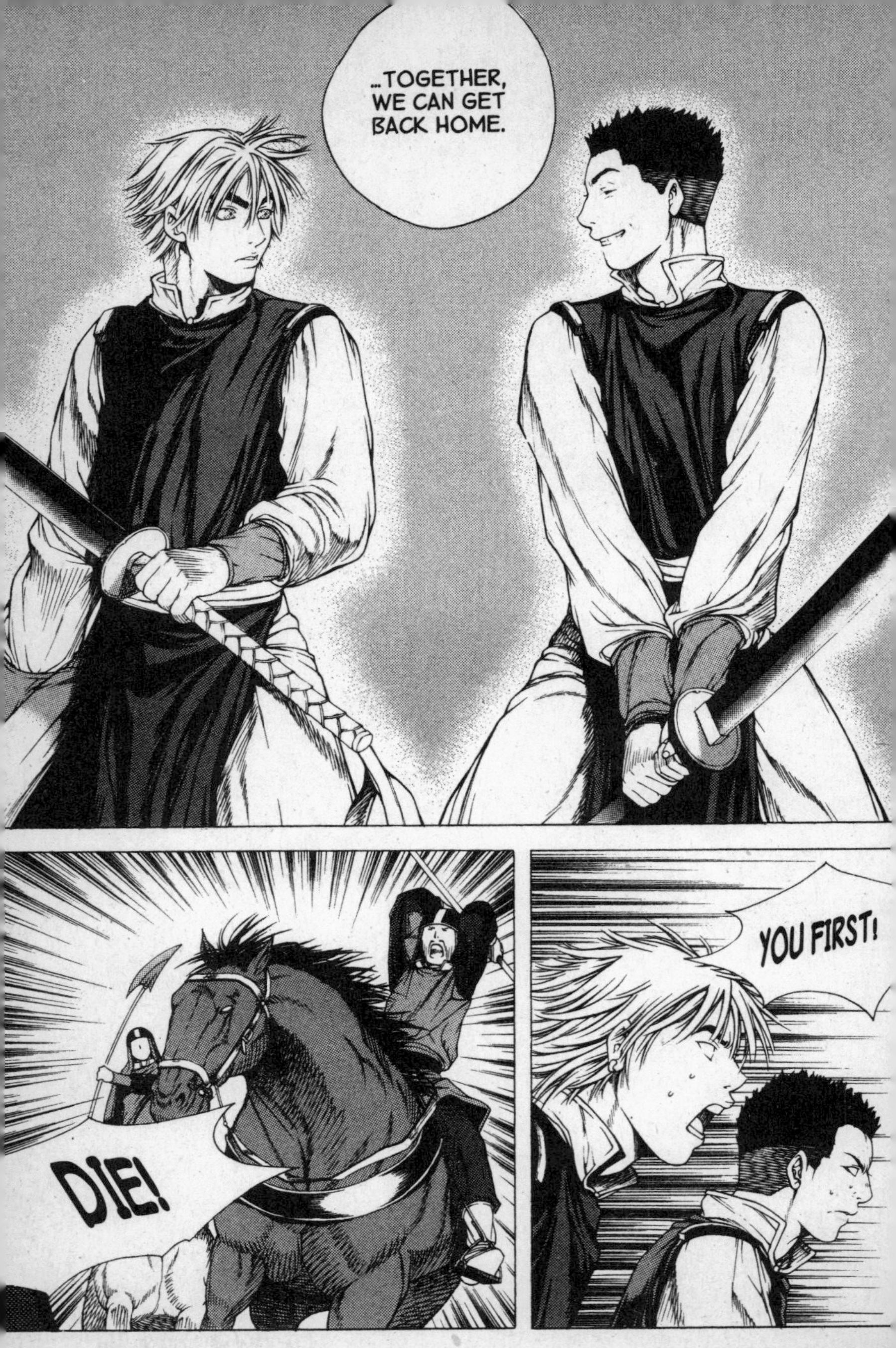
...TOGETHER, WE CAN GET BACK HOME.
DIE!
YOU FIRST!

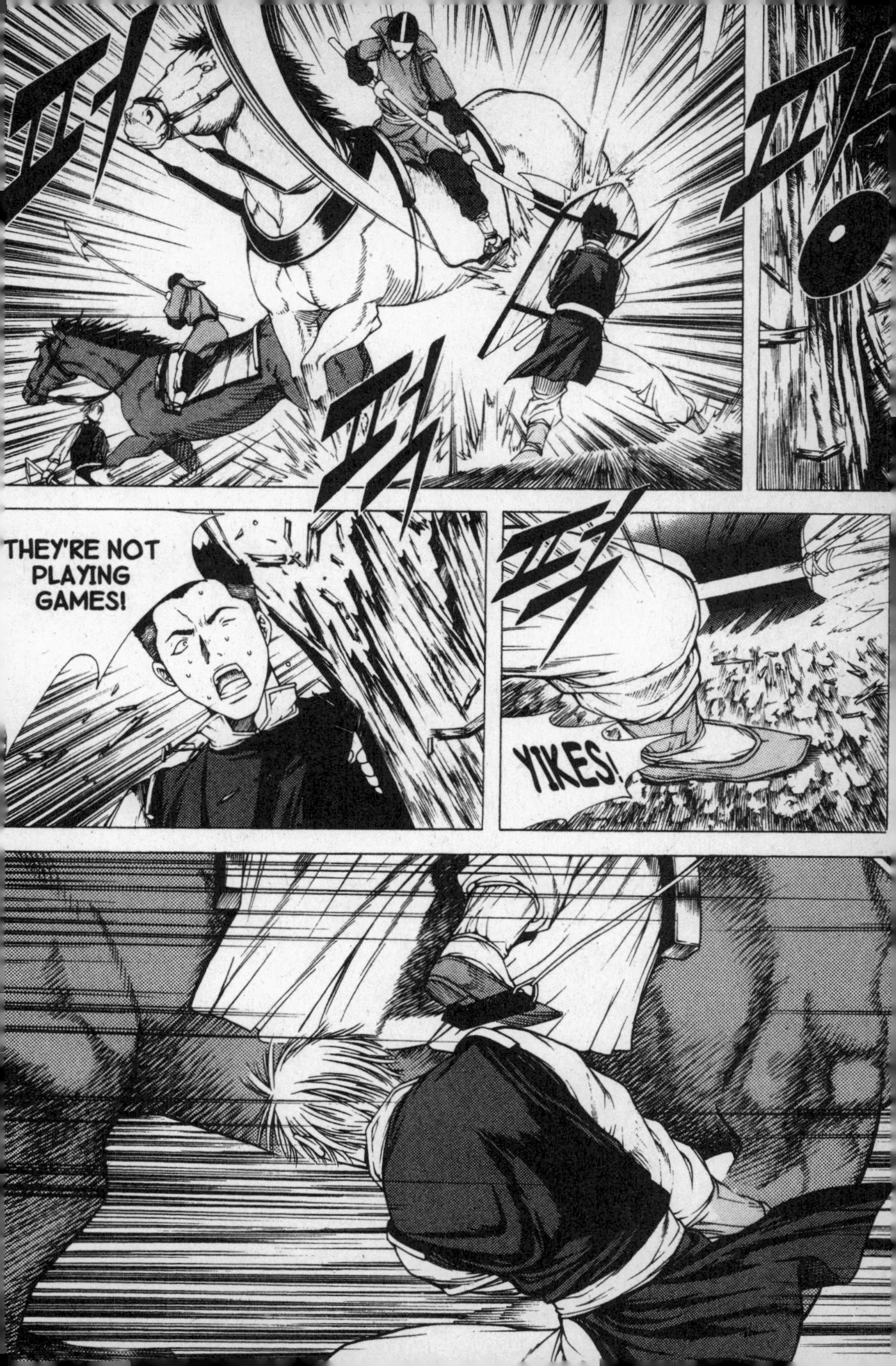
THEY'RE NOT PLAYING GAMES!
YIKES!

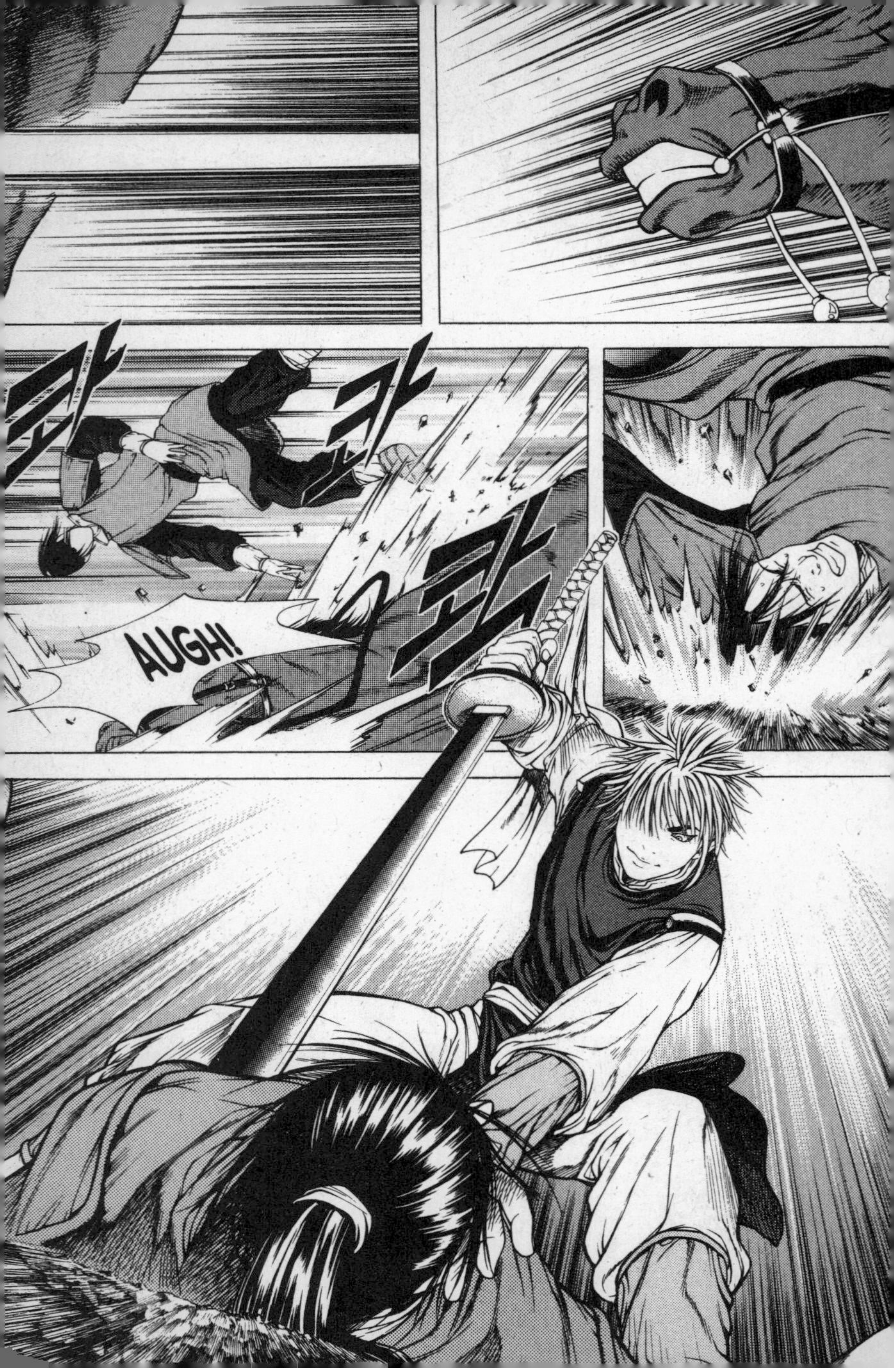
AUGH!

ONLY
ONE
LEFT!

OULD WE
OT HELP
THEM?

FIRST WE MUST
HELP OURSELVES!

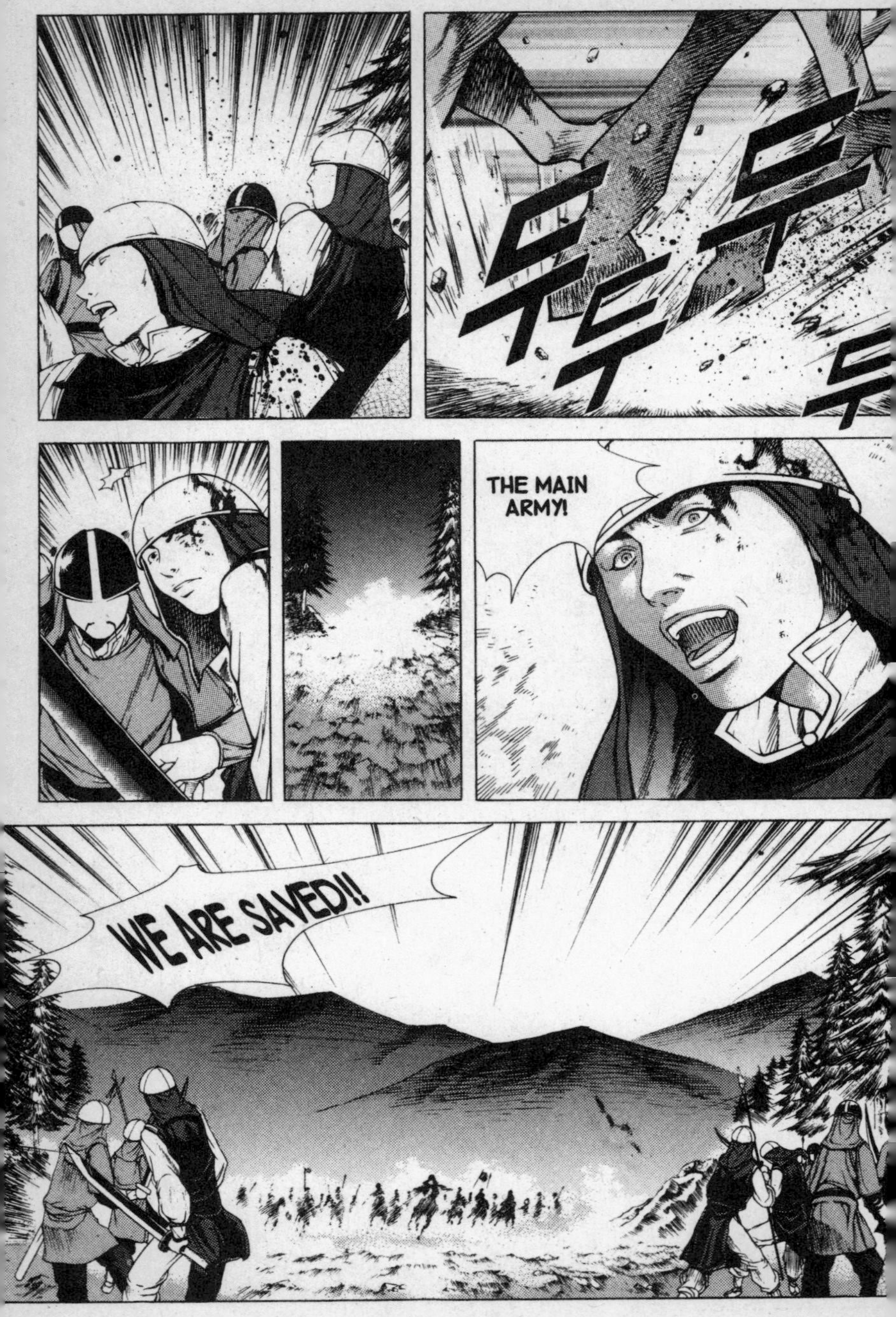
두두두두
THE MAIN ARMY!
WE ARE SAVED!!

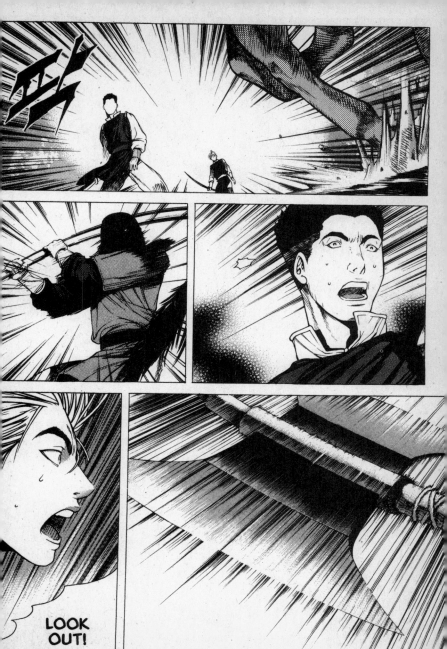

LOOK
OUT!

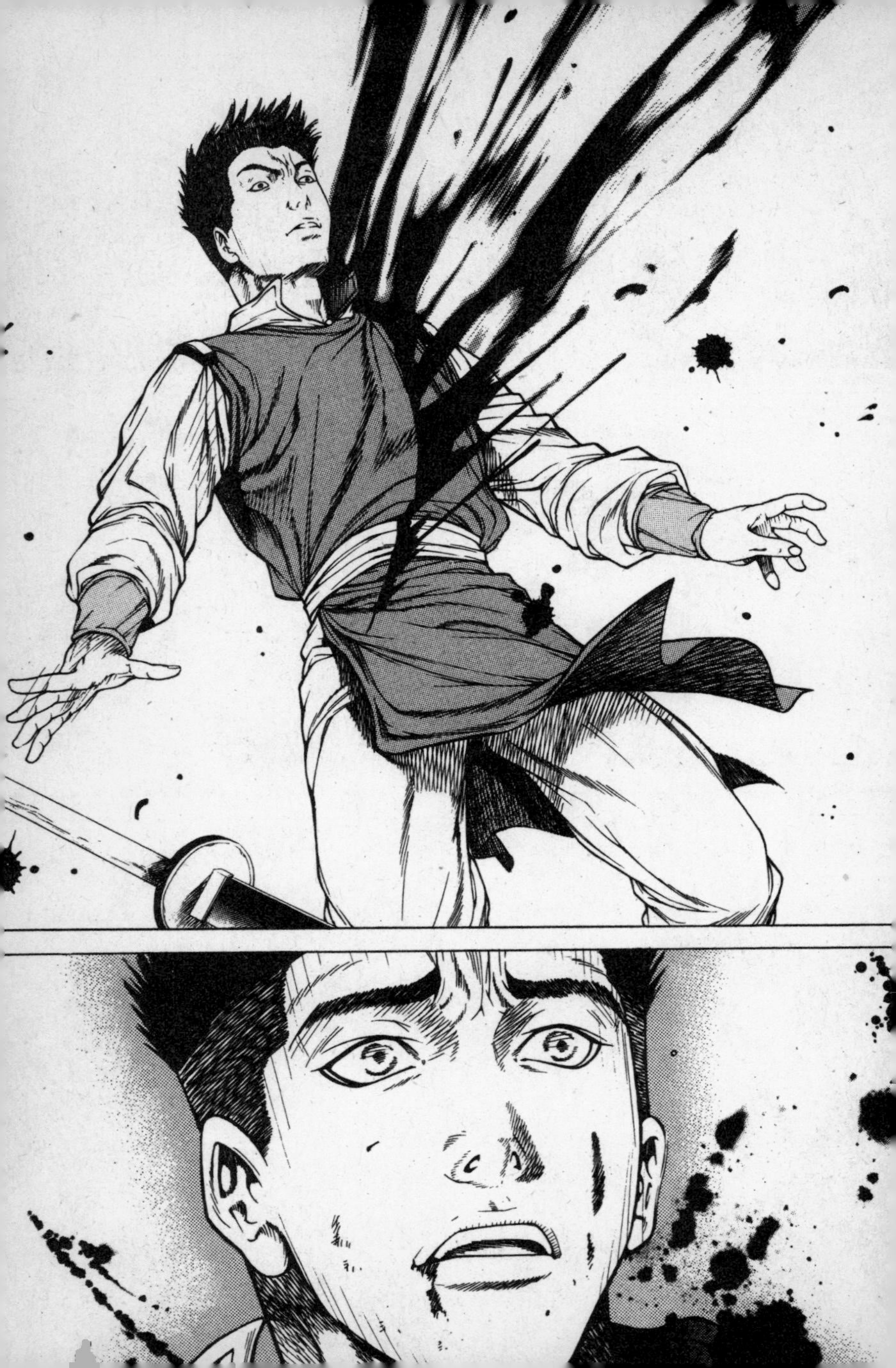

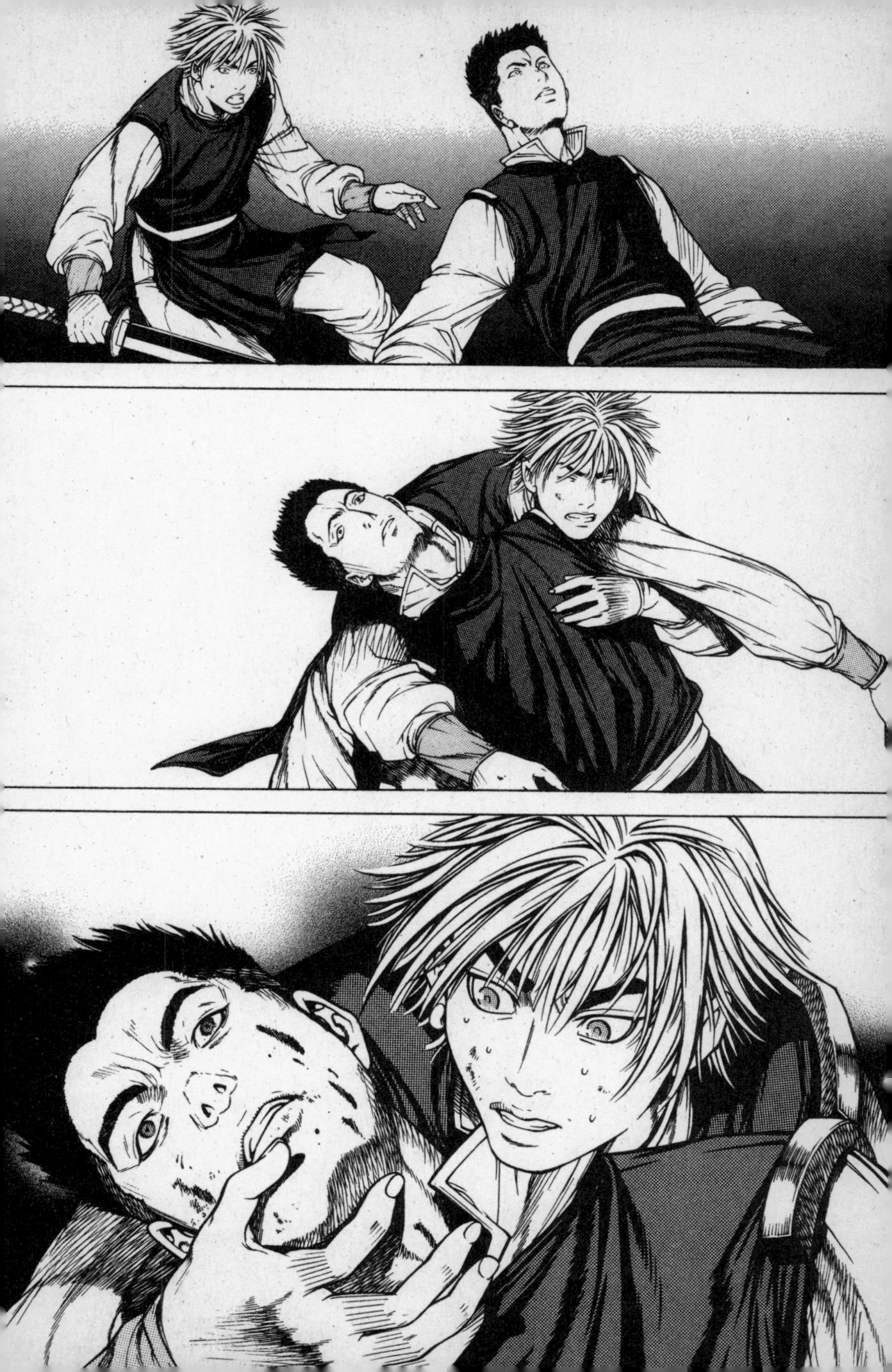

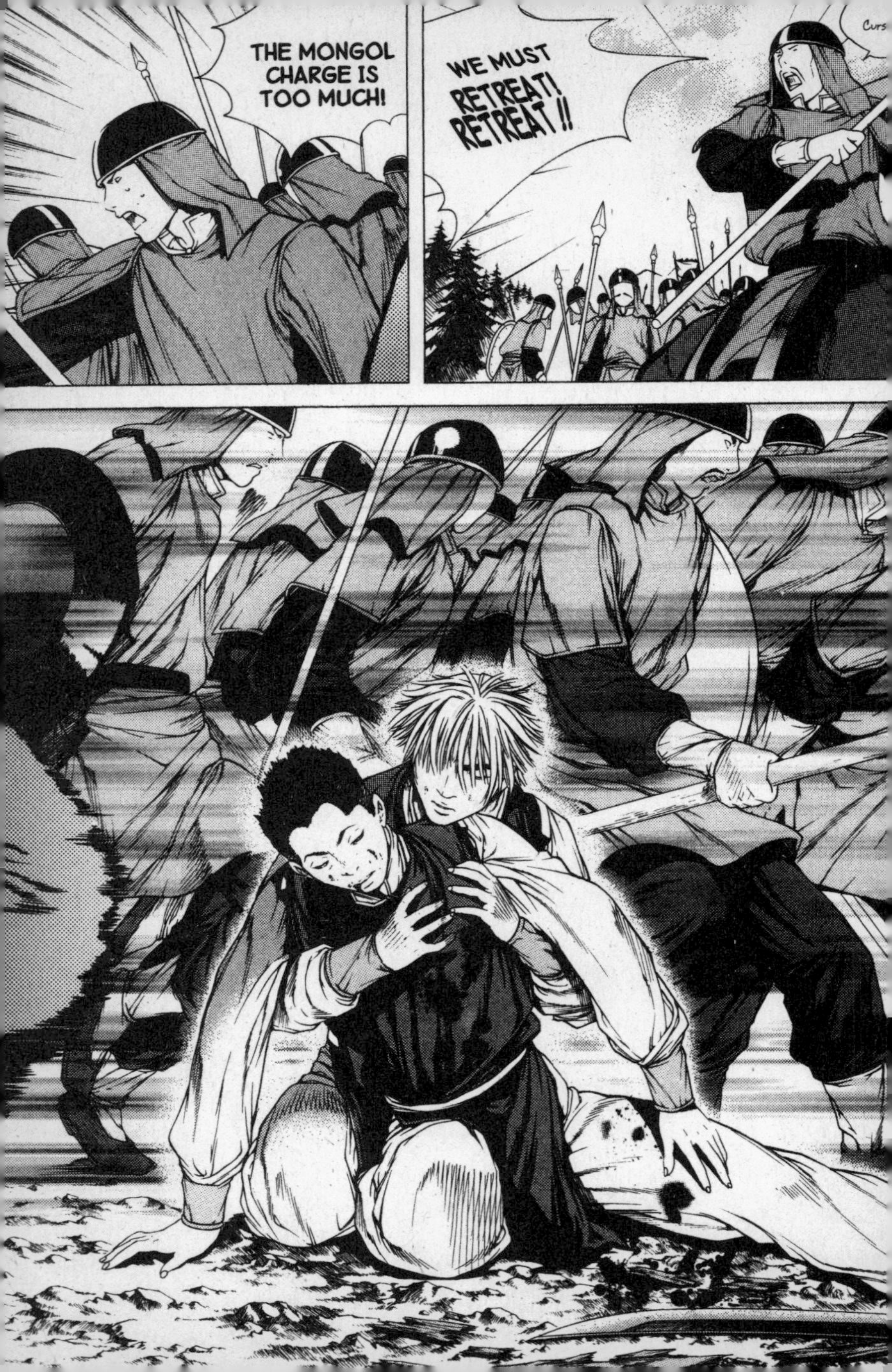
THE MONGOL CHARGE IS TOO MUCH!
WE MUST
RETREAT! RETREAT!!

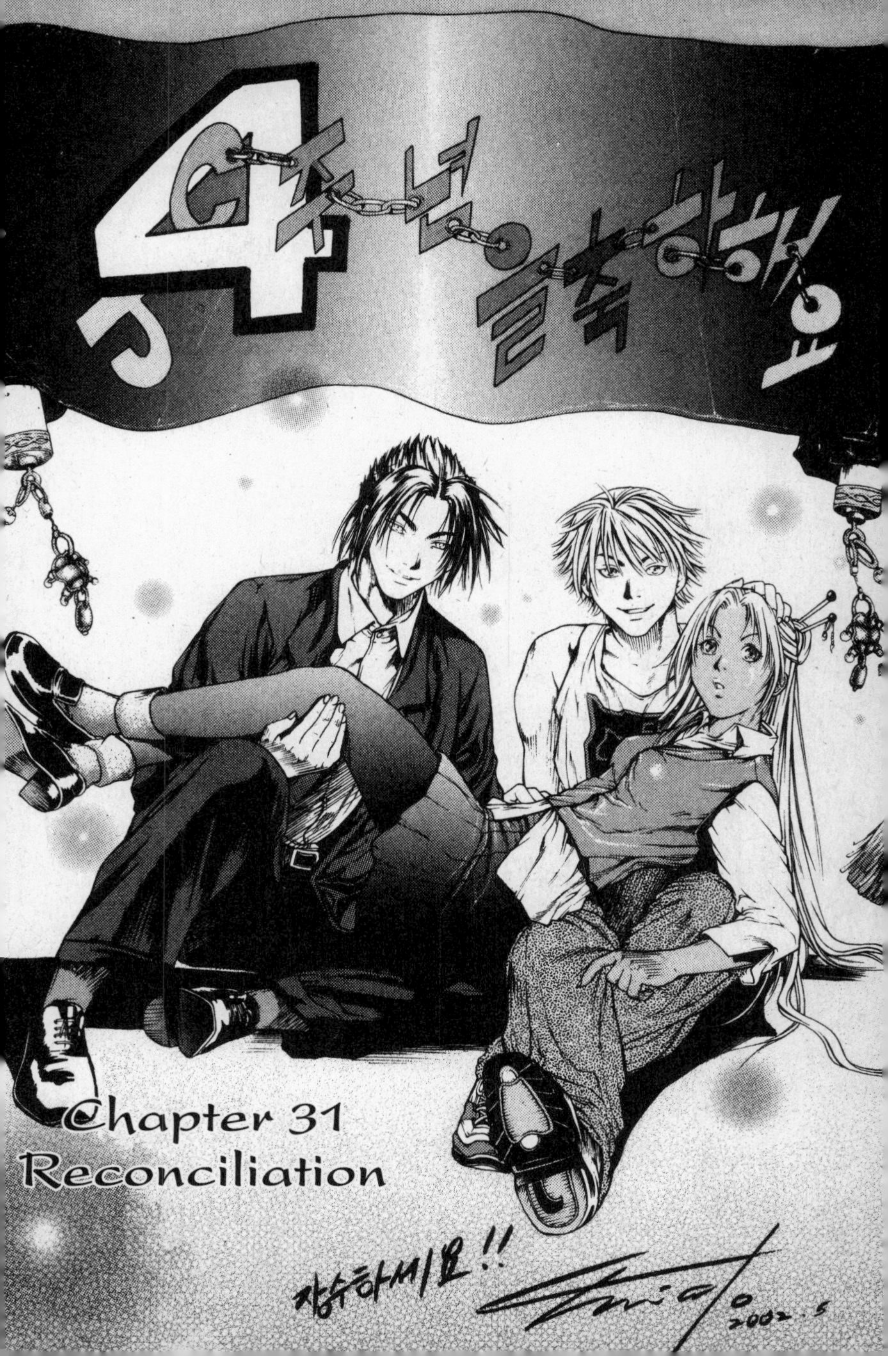
JC 4주년을 축하해요
Chapter 31
Reconciliation
장수하세요!!
2002. 5

THAT'S MINE! DON'T TOUCH!

GET YOUR HANDS OFF ME

SHH!

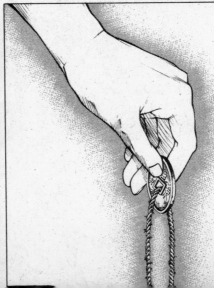

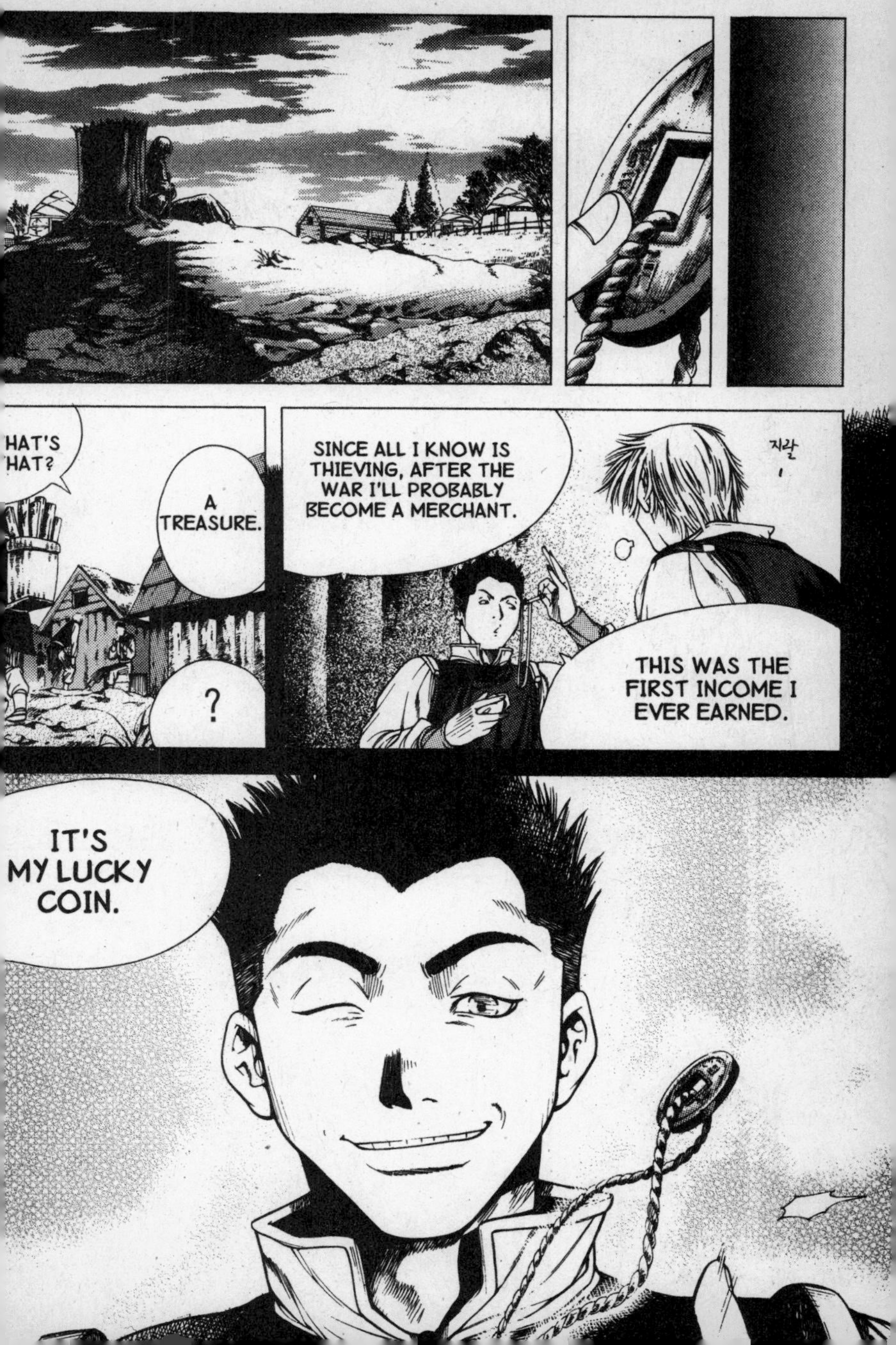
HAT'S
HAT?
A TREASURE.
?
SINCE ALL I KNOW IS THIEVING, AFTER THE WAR I'LL PROBABLY BECOME A MERCHANT.
지랄
THIS WAS THE FIRST INCOME I EVER EARNED.
IT'S MY LUCKY COIN.

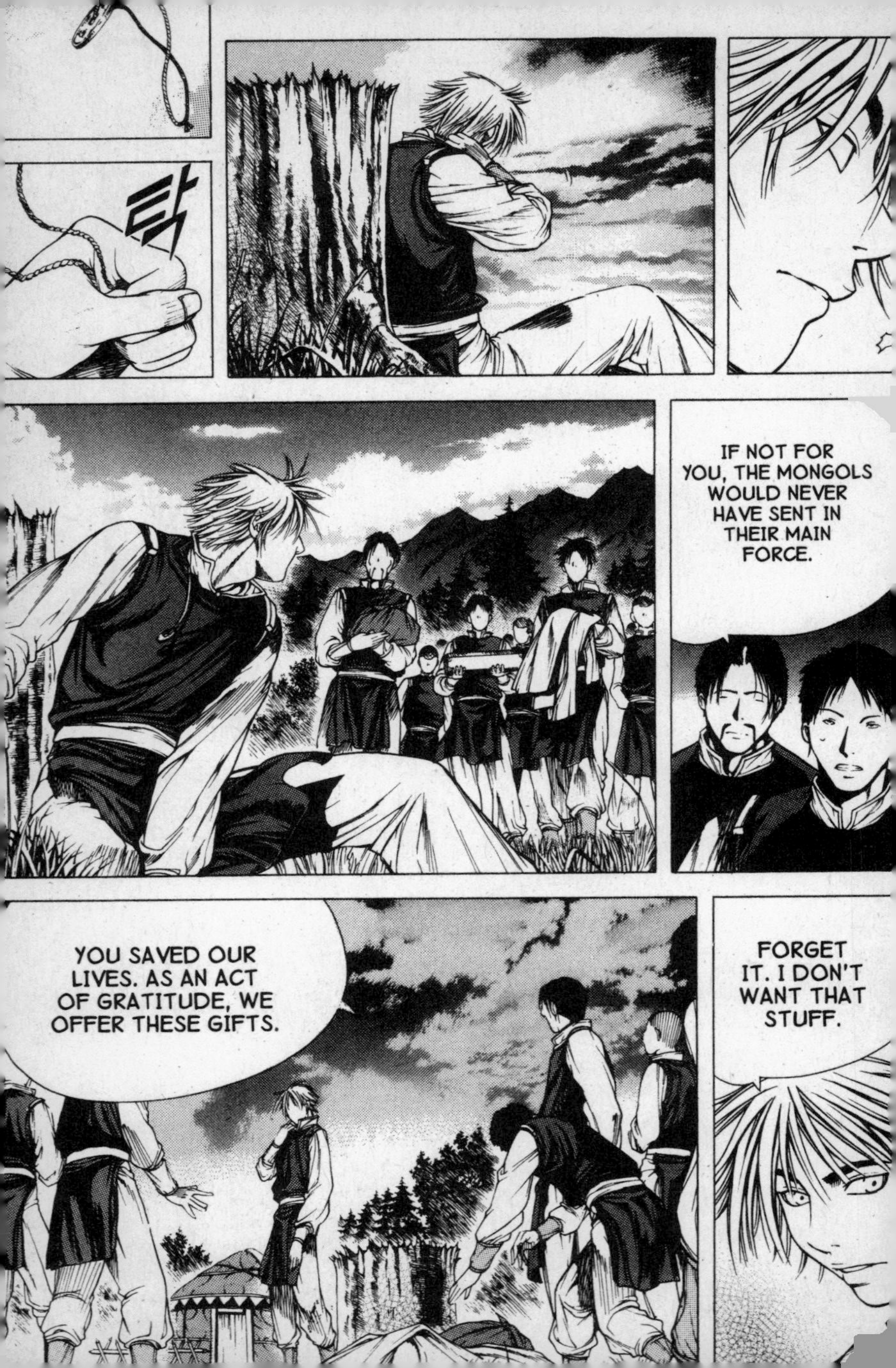
탁
IF NOT FOR YOU, THE MONGOLS WOULD NEVER HAVE SENT IN THEIR MAIN FORCE.
YOU SAVED OUR LIVES. AS AN ACT OF GRATITUDE, WE OFFER THESE GIFTS.
FORGET IT. I DON'T WANT THAT STUFF.

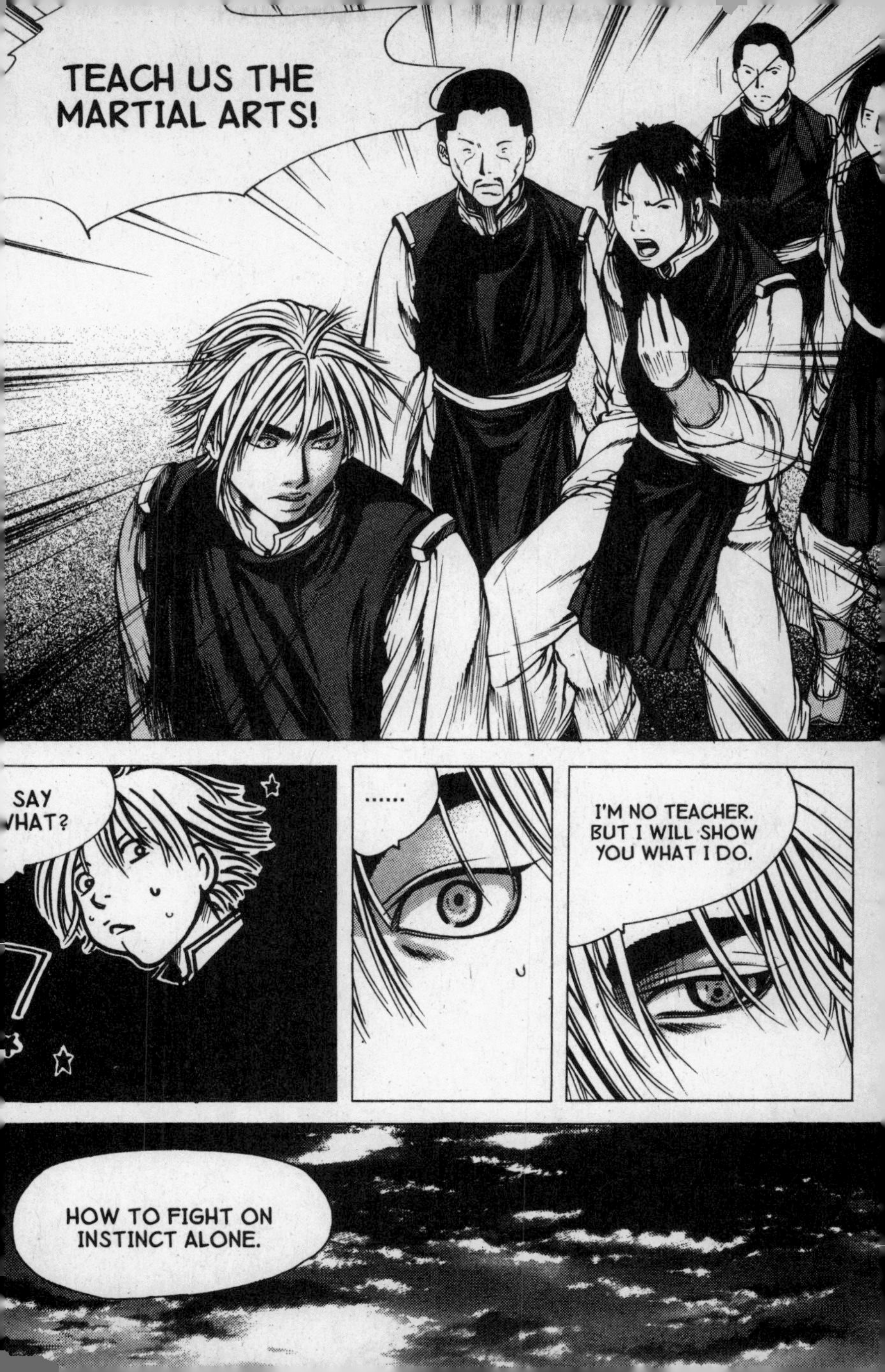
TEACH US THE MARTIAL ARTS!
SAY WHAT?
......
I'M NO TEACHER. BUT I WILL SHOW YOU WHAT I DO.
HOW TO FIGHT ON INSTINCT ALONE.

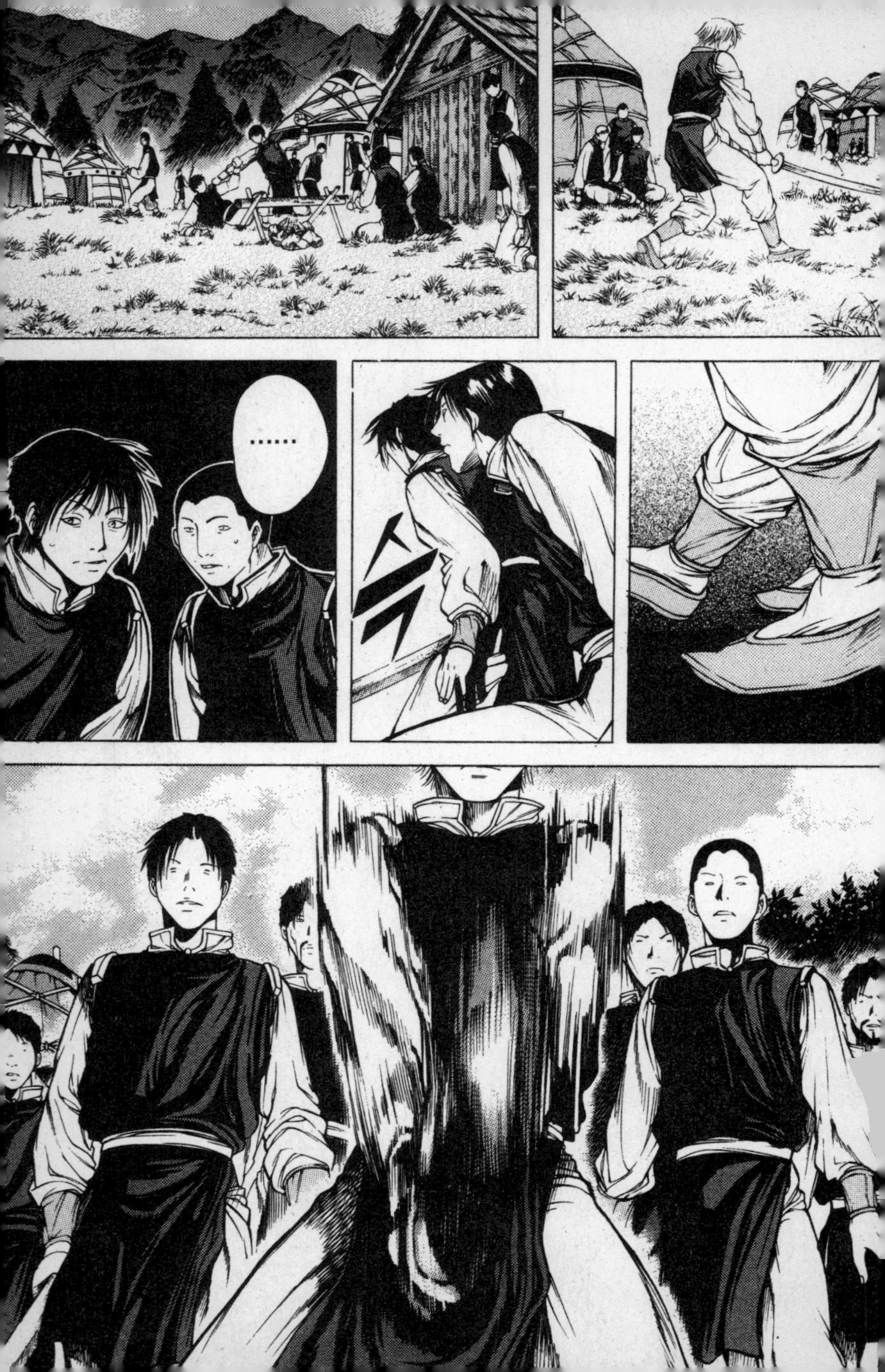
......

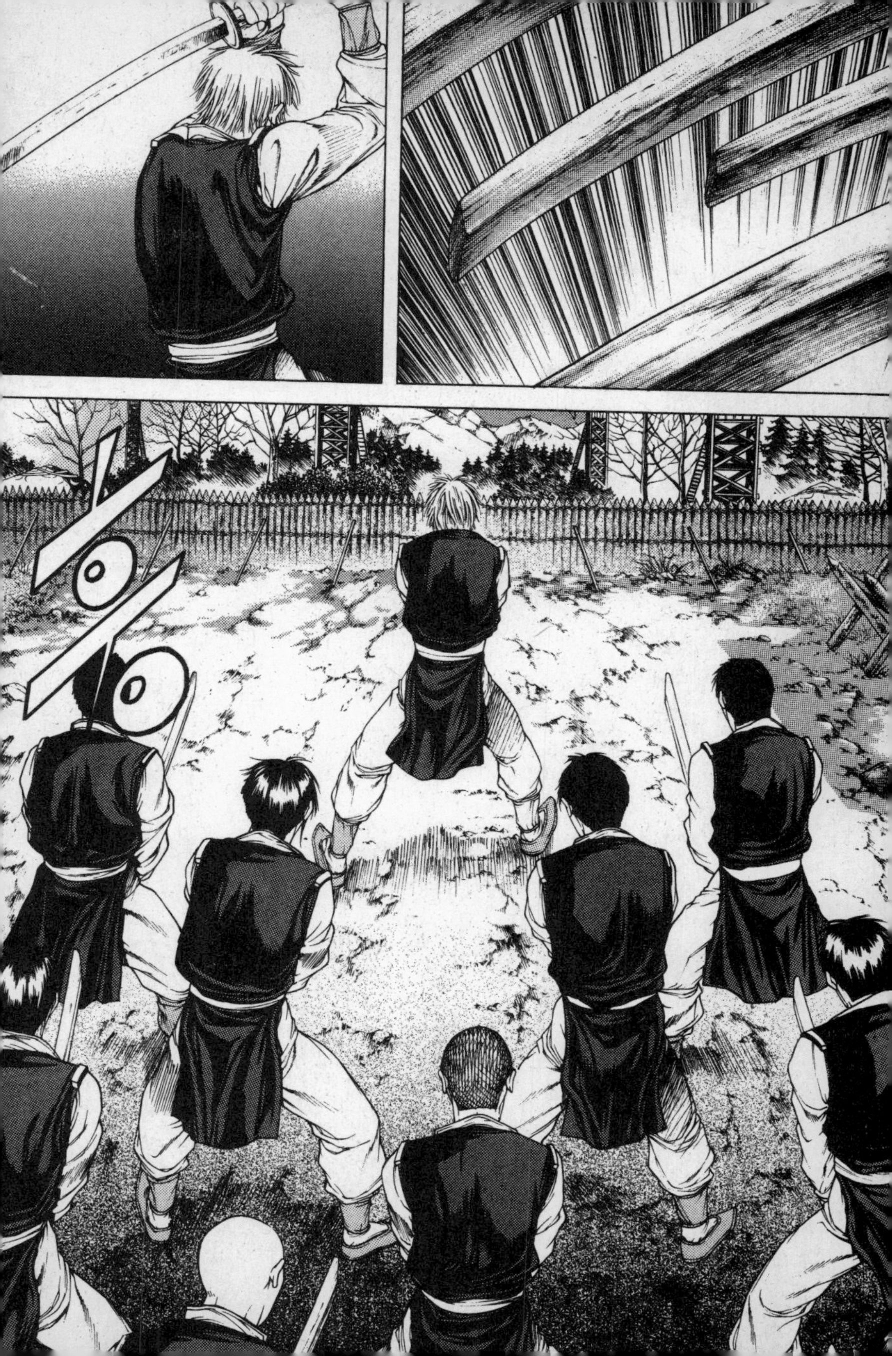

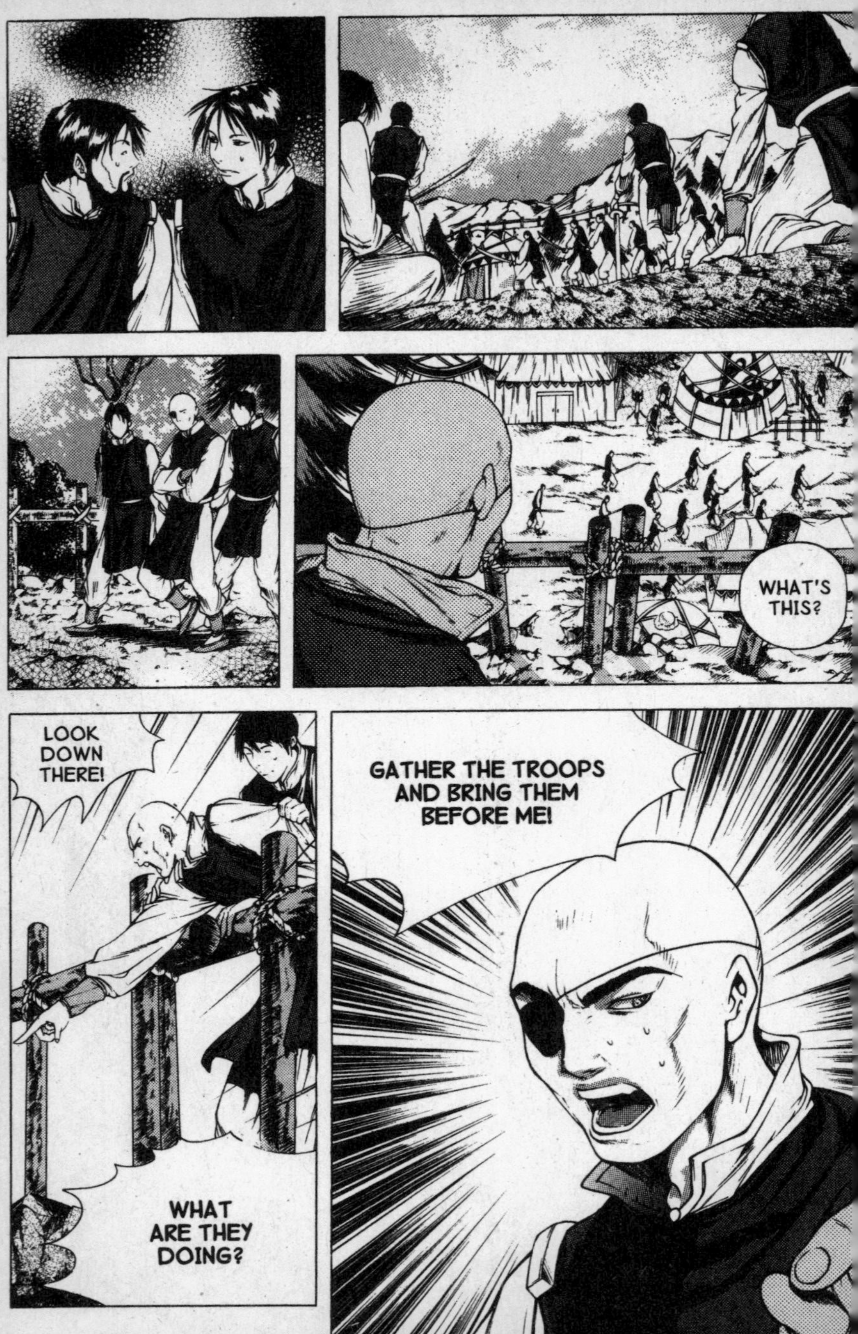
WHAT'S THIS?
LOOK DOWN THERE!
WHAT ARE THEY DOING?
GATHER THE TROOPS AND BRING THEM BEFORE ME!

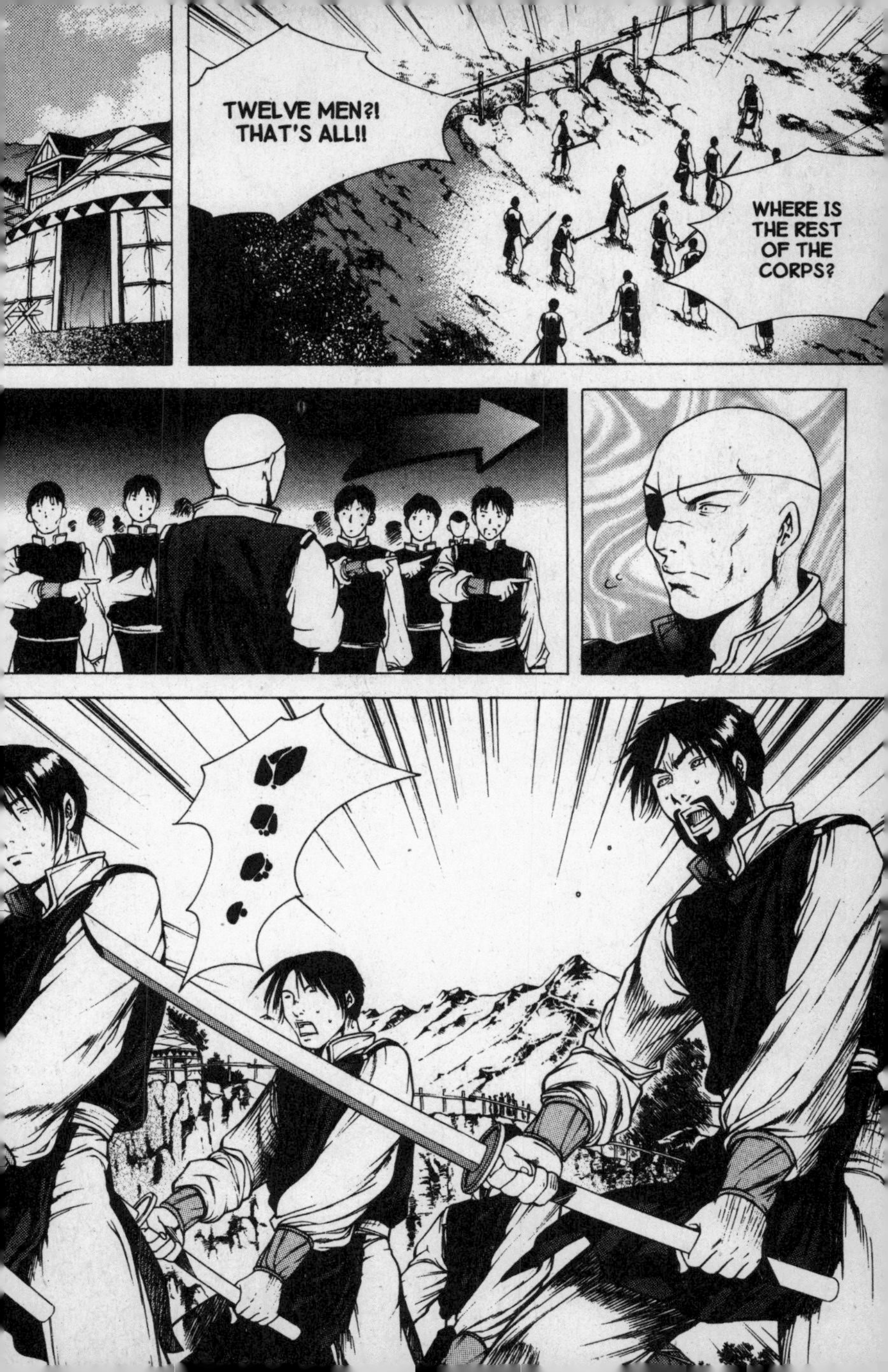
TWELVE MEN?! THAT'S ALL!!
WHERE IS THE REST OF THE CORPS?

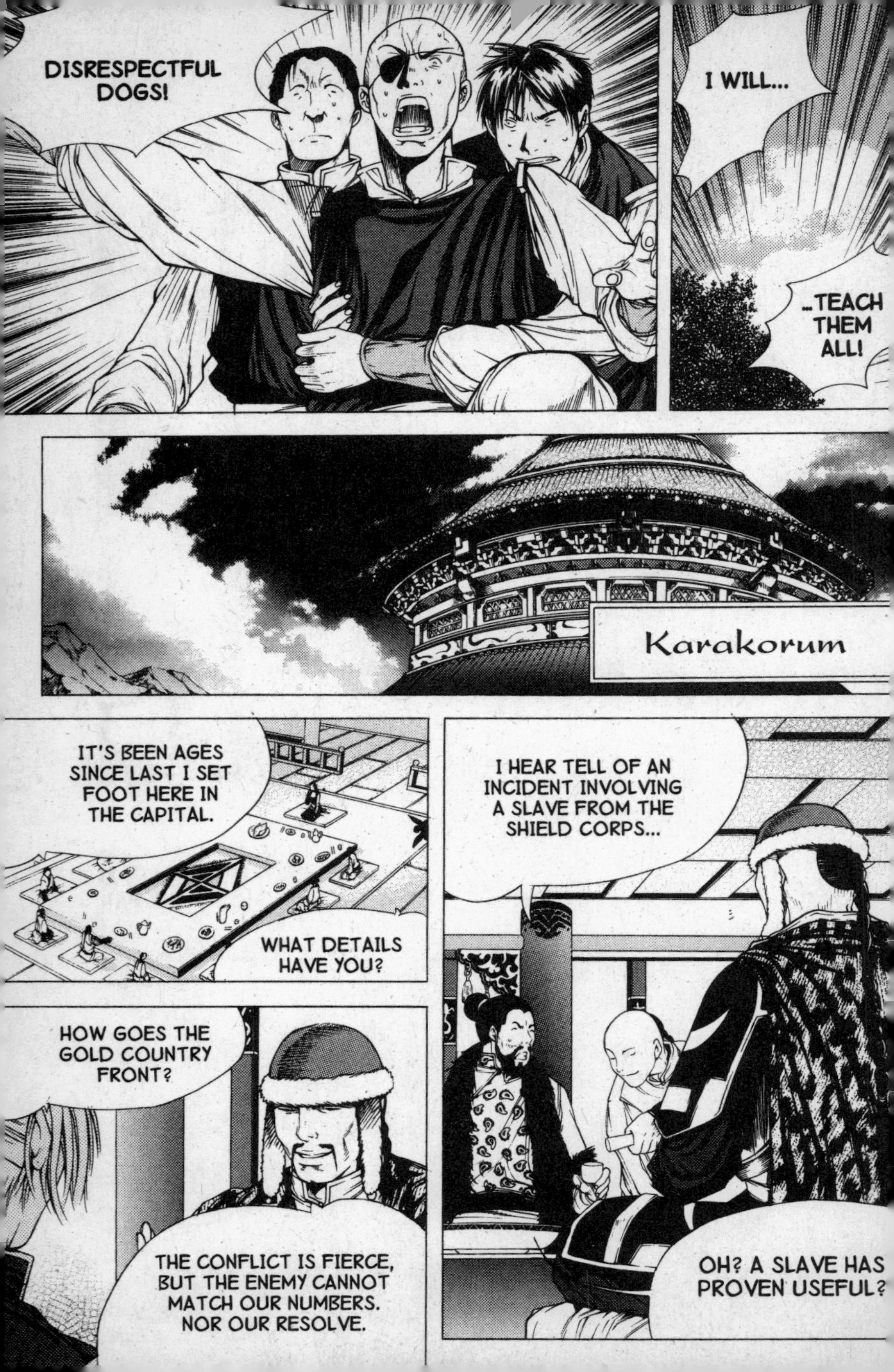
DISRESPECTFUL DOGS!
I WILL...
..TEACH THEM ALL!
Karakorum
IT'S BEEN AGES SINCE LAST I SET FOOT HERE IN THE CAPITAL.
WHAT DETAILS HAVE YOU?
HOW GOES THE GOLD COUNTRY FRONT?
THE CONFLICT IS FIERCE, BUT THE ENEMY CANNOT MATCH OUR NUMBERS. NOR OUR RESOLVE.
I HEAR TELL OF AN INCIDENT INVOLVING A SLAVE FROM THE SHIELD CORPS...
OH? A SLAVE HAS PROVEN USEFUL?

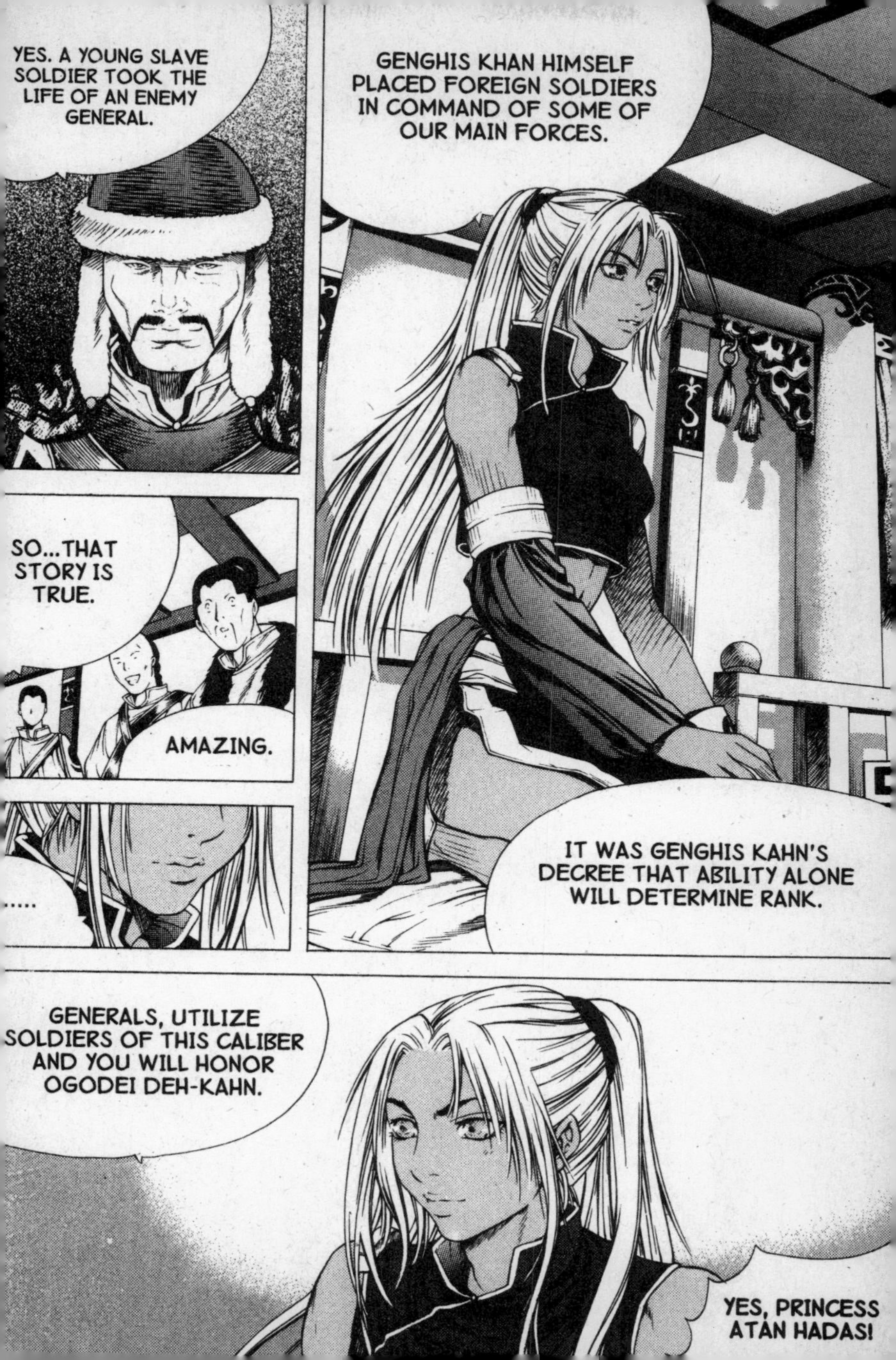
YES. A YOUNG SLAVE SOLDIER TOOK THE LIFE OF AN ENEMY GENERAL.
SO...THAT STORY IS TRUE.
AMAZING.
.....
GENGHIS KHAN HIMSELF PLACED FOREIGN SOLDIERS IN COMMAND OF SOME OF OUR MAIN FORCES.
IT WAS GENGHIS KAHN'S DECREE THAT ABILITY ALONE WILL DETERMINE RANK.
GENERALS, UTILIZE SOLDIERS OF THIS CALIBER AND YOU WILL HONOR OGODEI DEH-KAHN.
YES, PRINCESS ATAN HADAS!

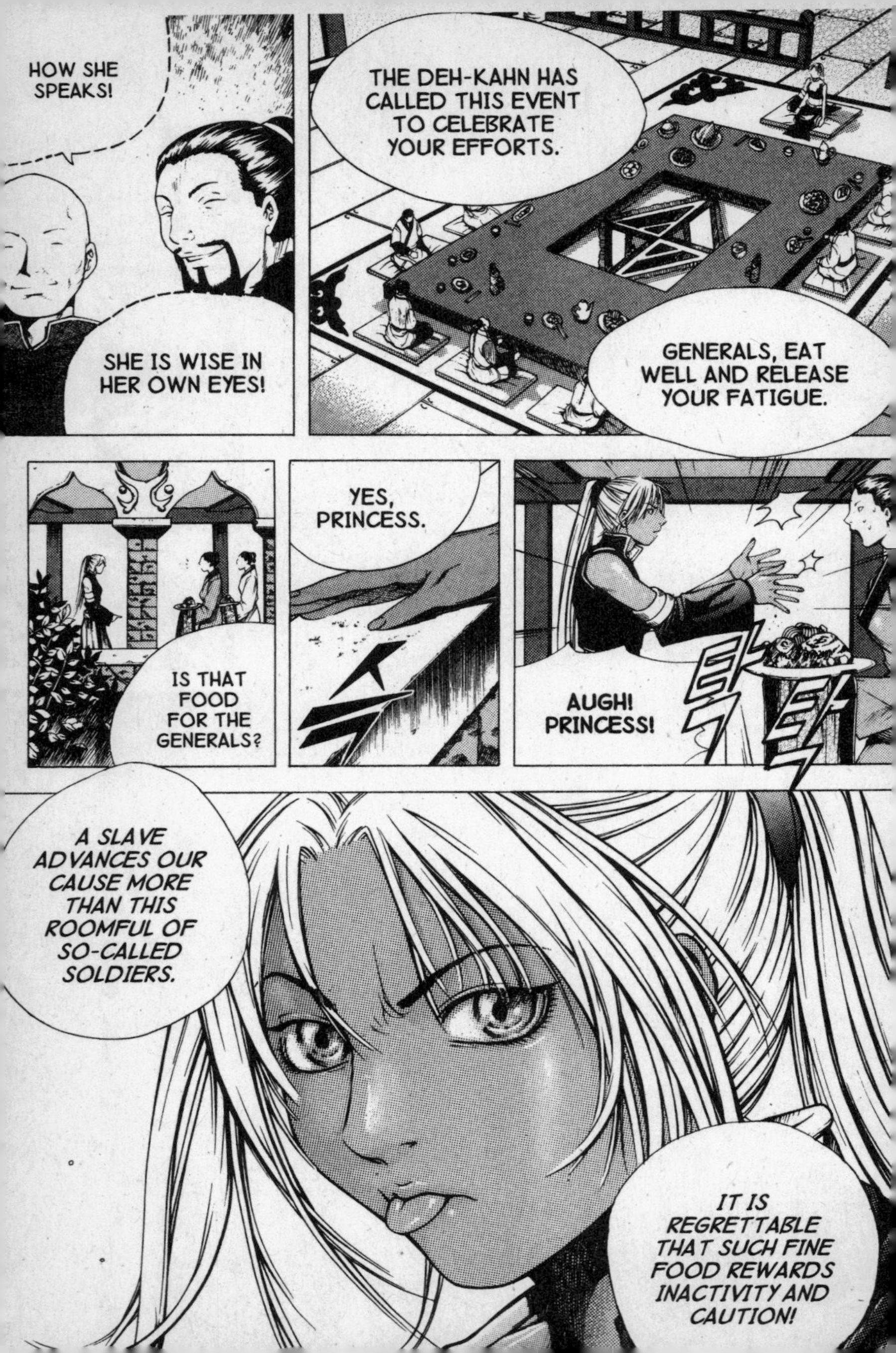
HOW SHE SPEAKS!
SHE IS WISE IN HER OWN EYES!
THE DEH-KAHN HAS CALLED THIS EVENT TO CELEBRATE YOUR EFFORTS.
GENERALS, EAT WELL AND RELEASE YOUR FATIGUE.
IS THAT FOOD FOR THE GENERALS?
YES, PRINCESS.
AUGH! PRINCESS!
A SLAVE ADVANCES OUR CAUSE MORE THAN THIS ROOMFUL OF SO-CALLED SOLDIERS.
IT IS REGRETTABLE THAT SUCH FINE FOOD REWARDS INACTIVITY AND CAUTION!

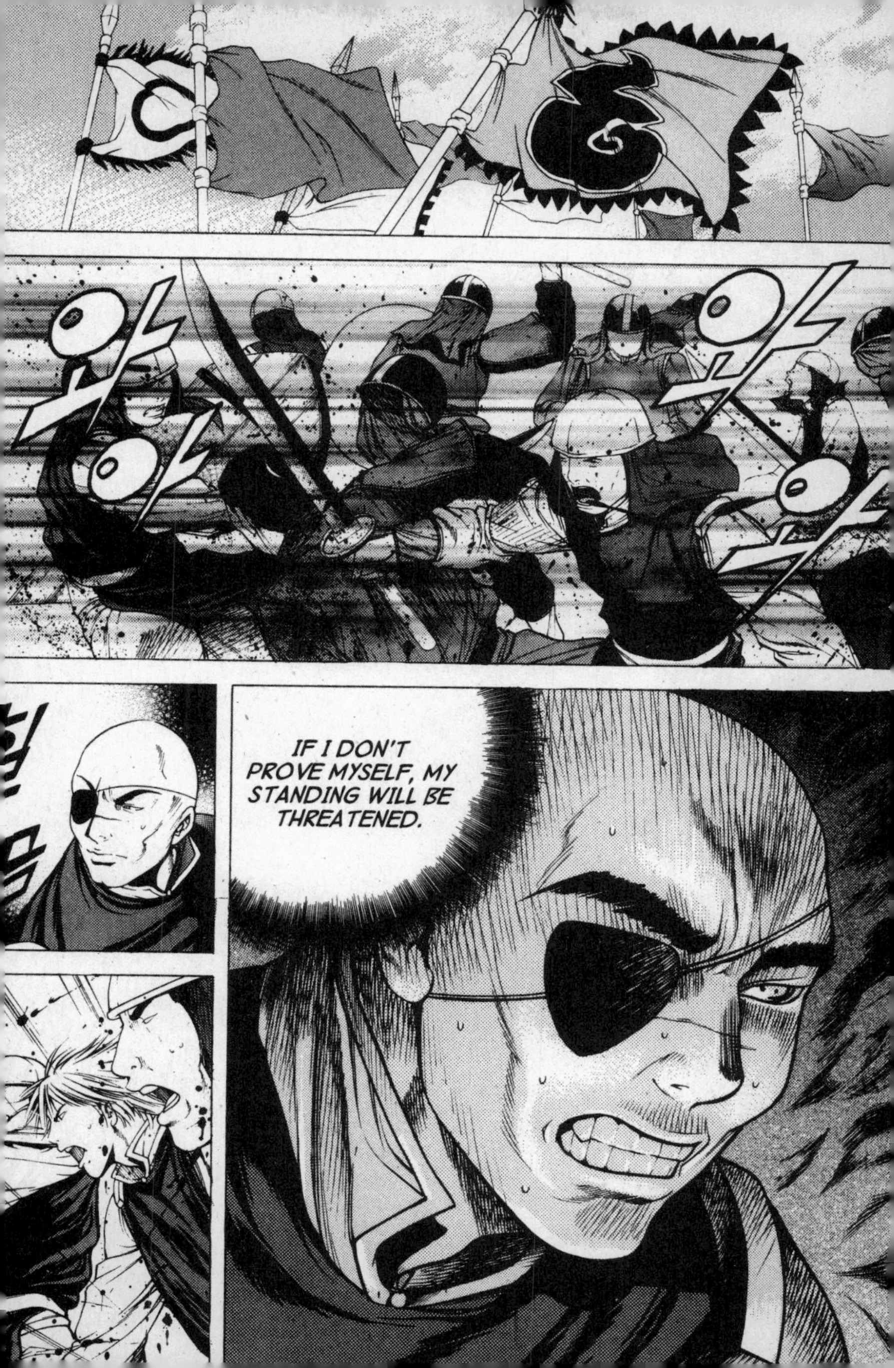
IF I DON'T PROVE MYSELF, MY STANDING WILL BE THREATENED.

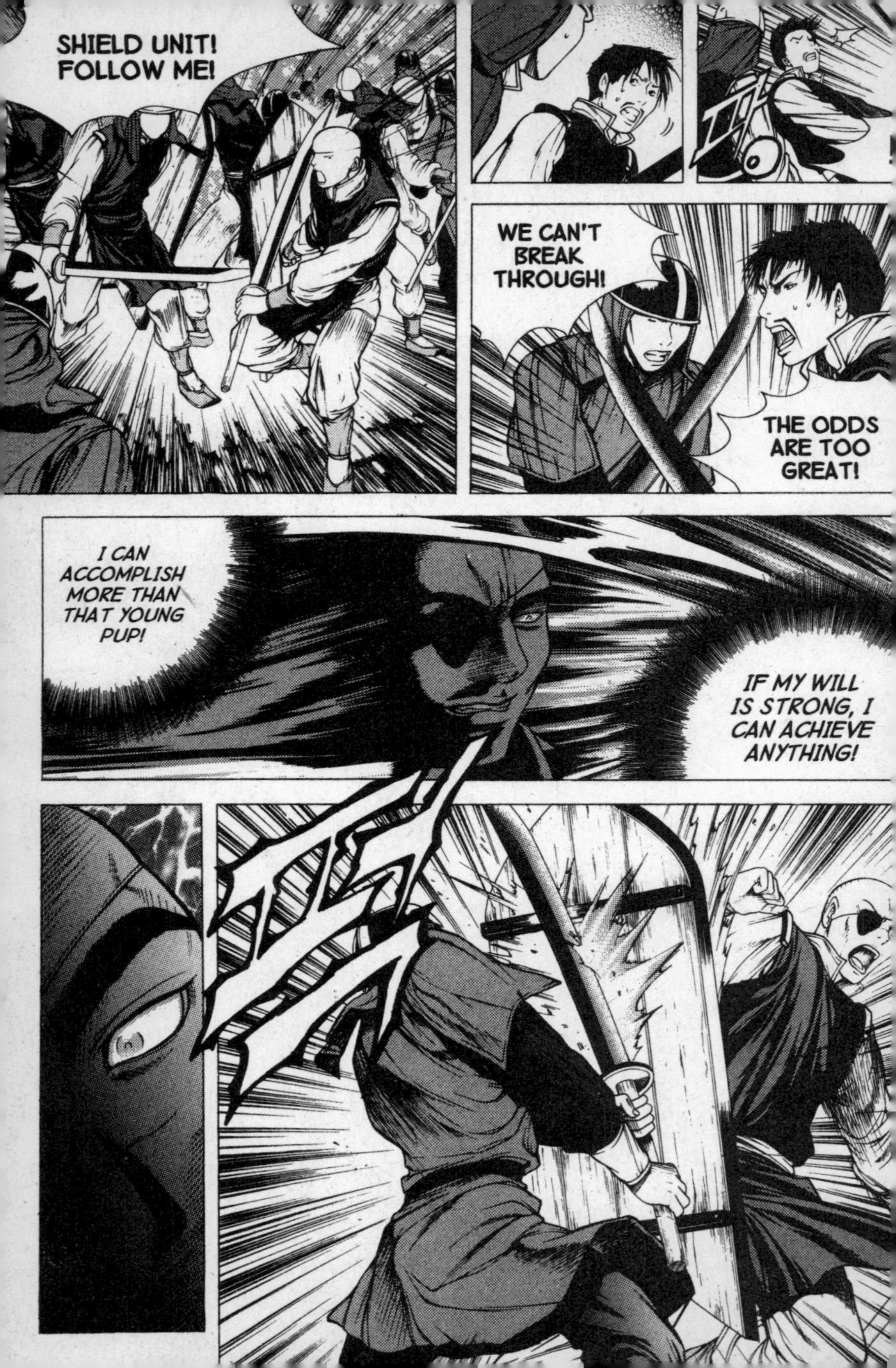
SHIELD UNIT! FOLLOW ME!
WE CAN'T BREAK THROUGH!
THE ODDS ARE TOO GREAT!
I CAN ACCOMPLISH MORE THAN THAT YOUNG PUP!
IF MY WILL IS STRONG, I CAN ACHIEVE ANYTHING!

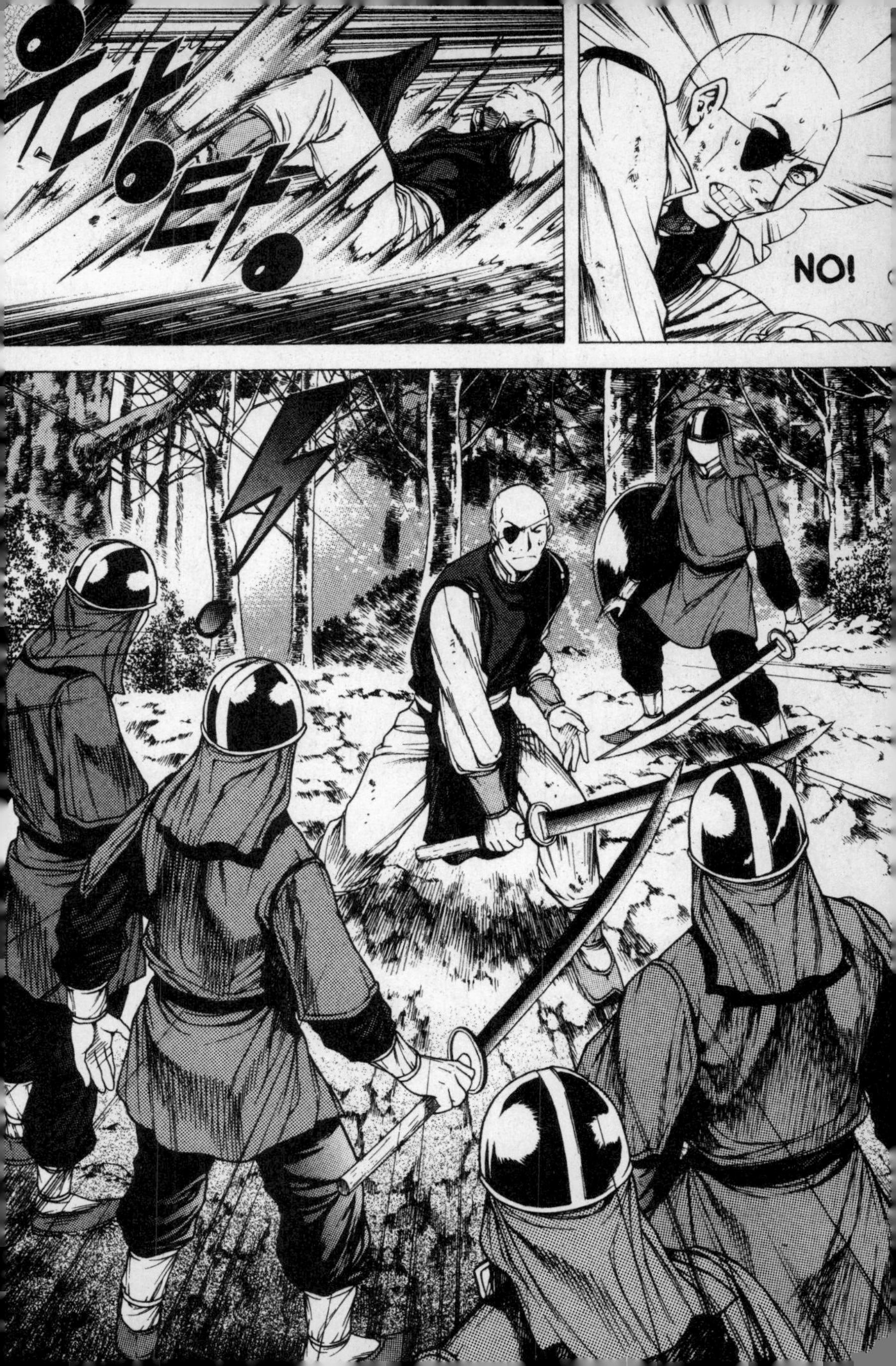
NO!

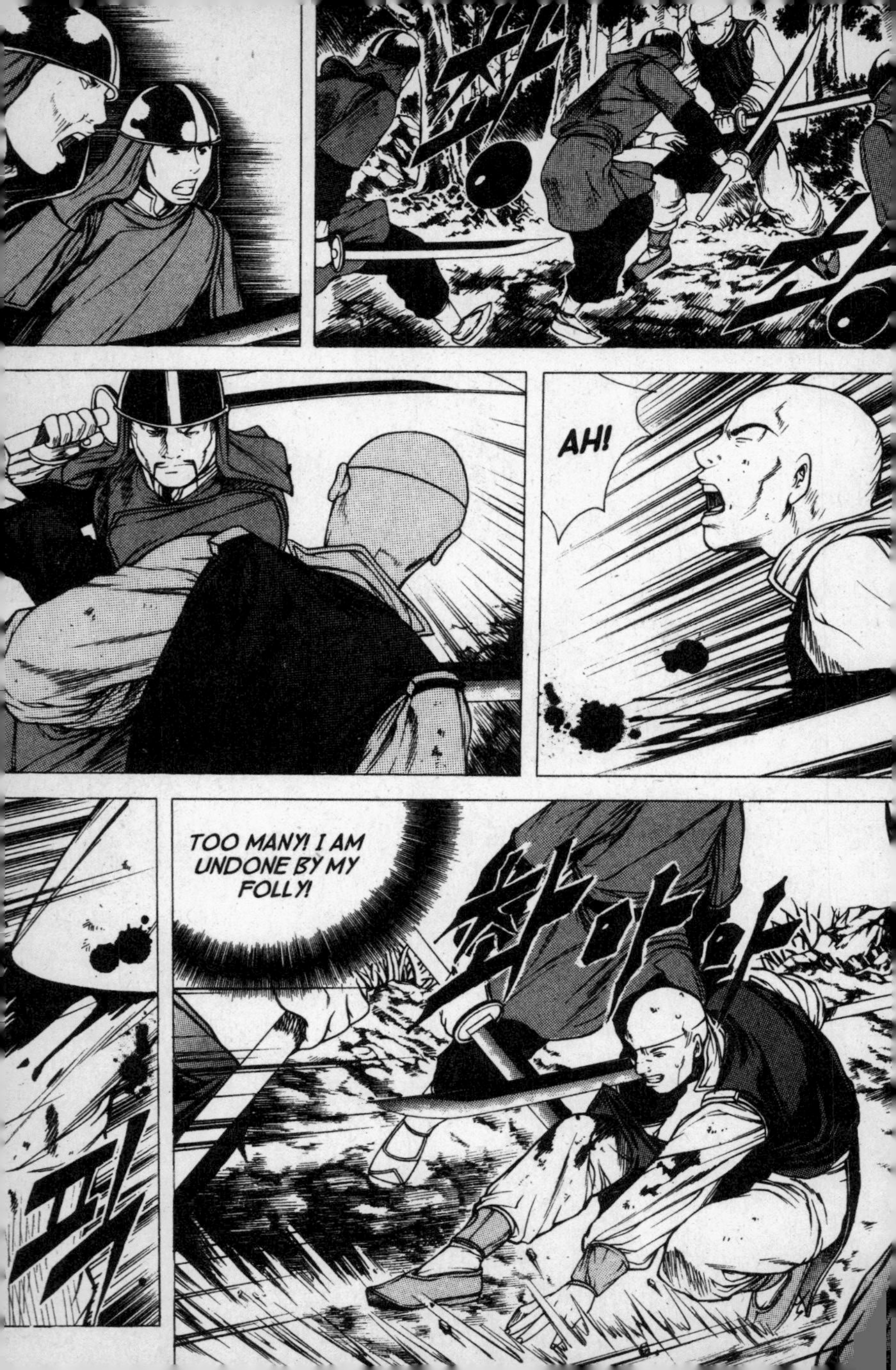
AH!
TOO MANY! I AM UNDONE BY MY FOLLY!

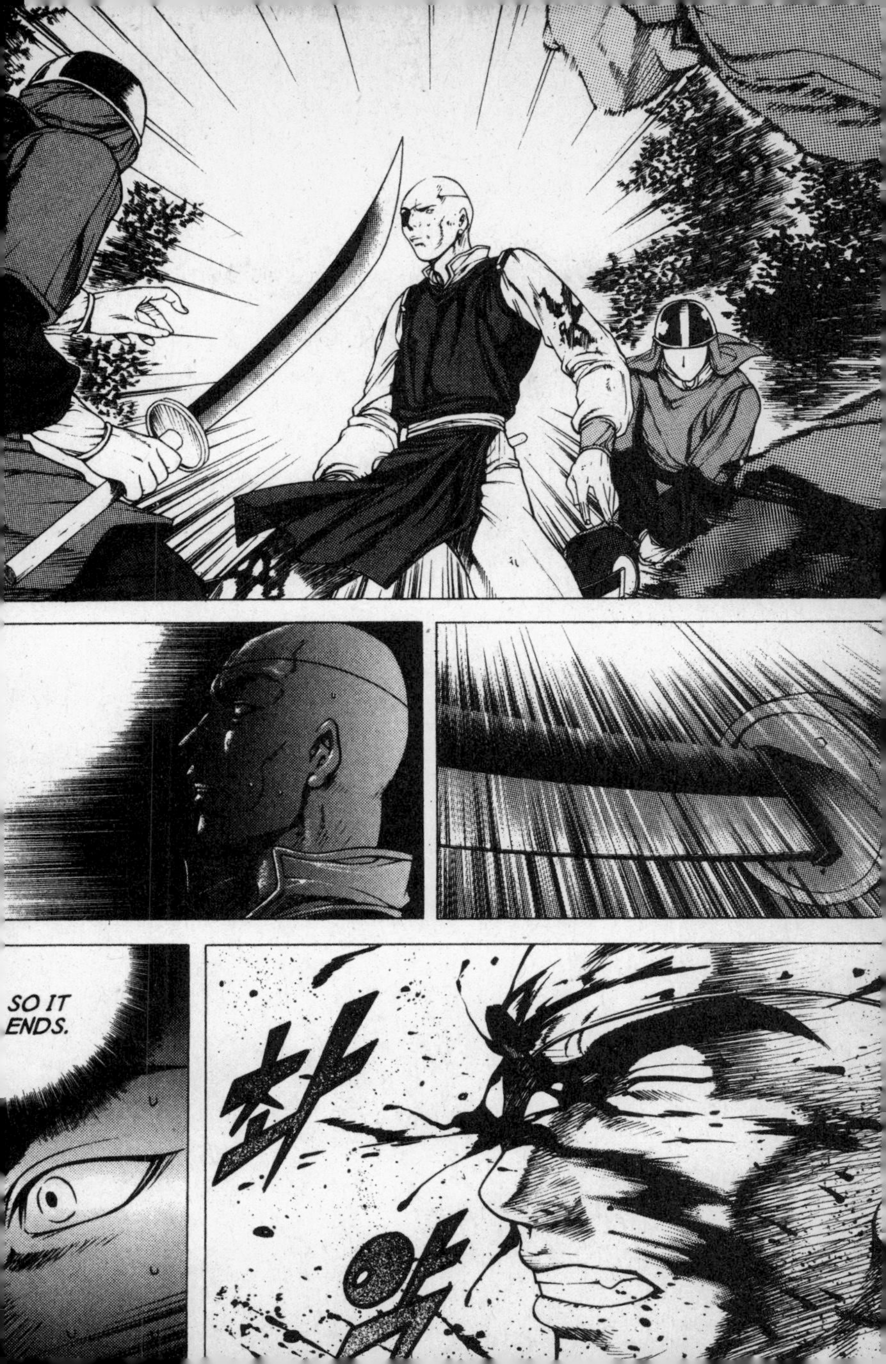
SO IT ENDS.

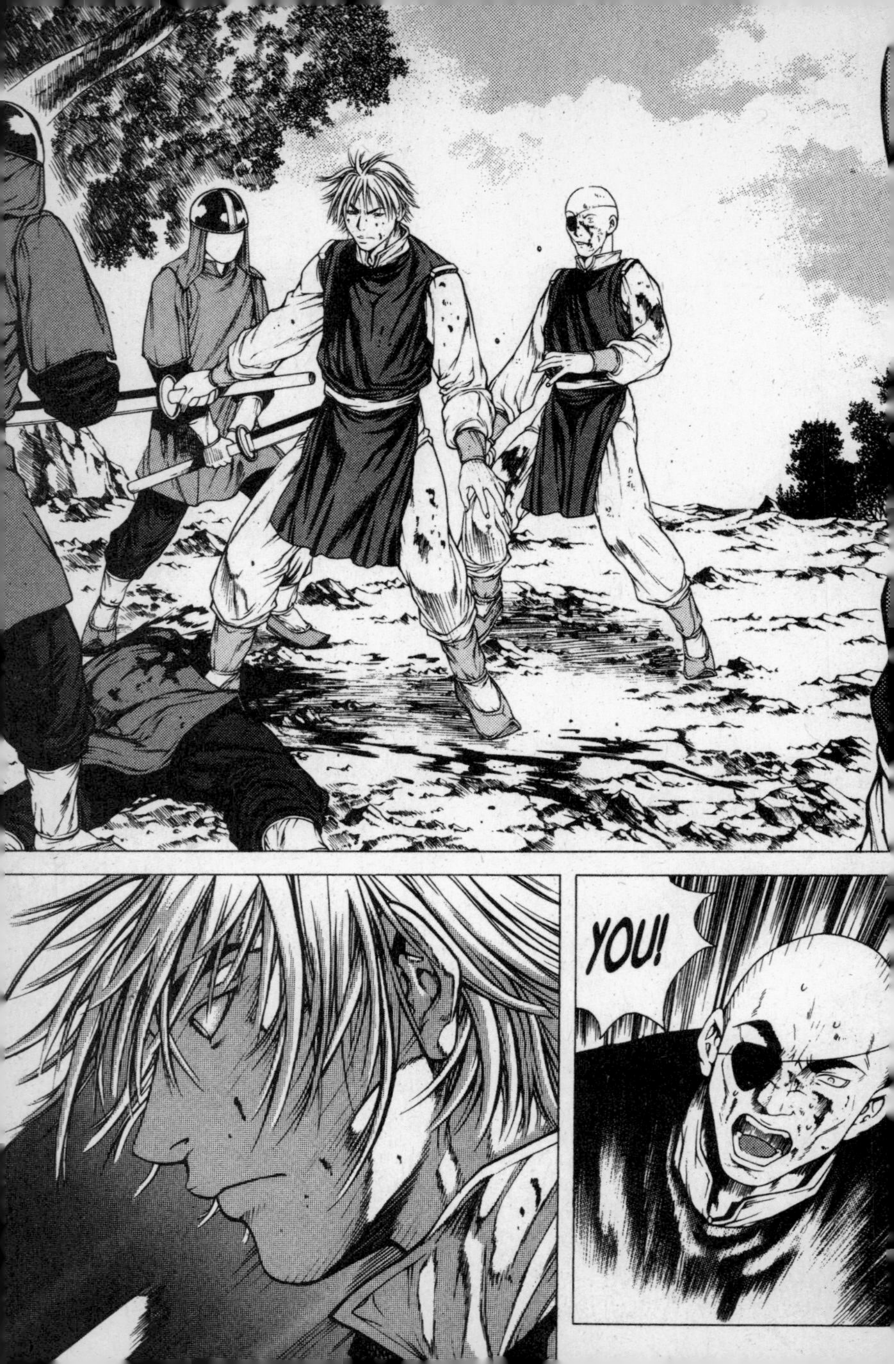
YOU!

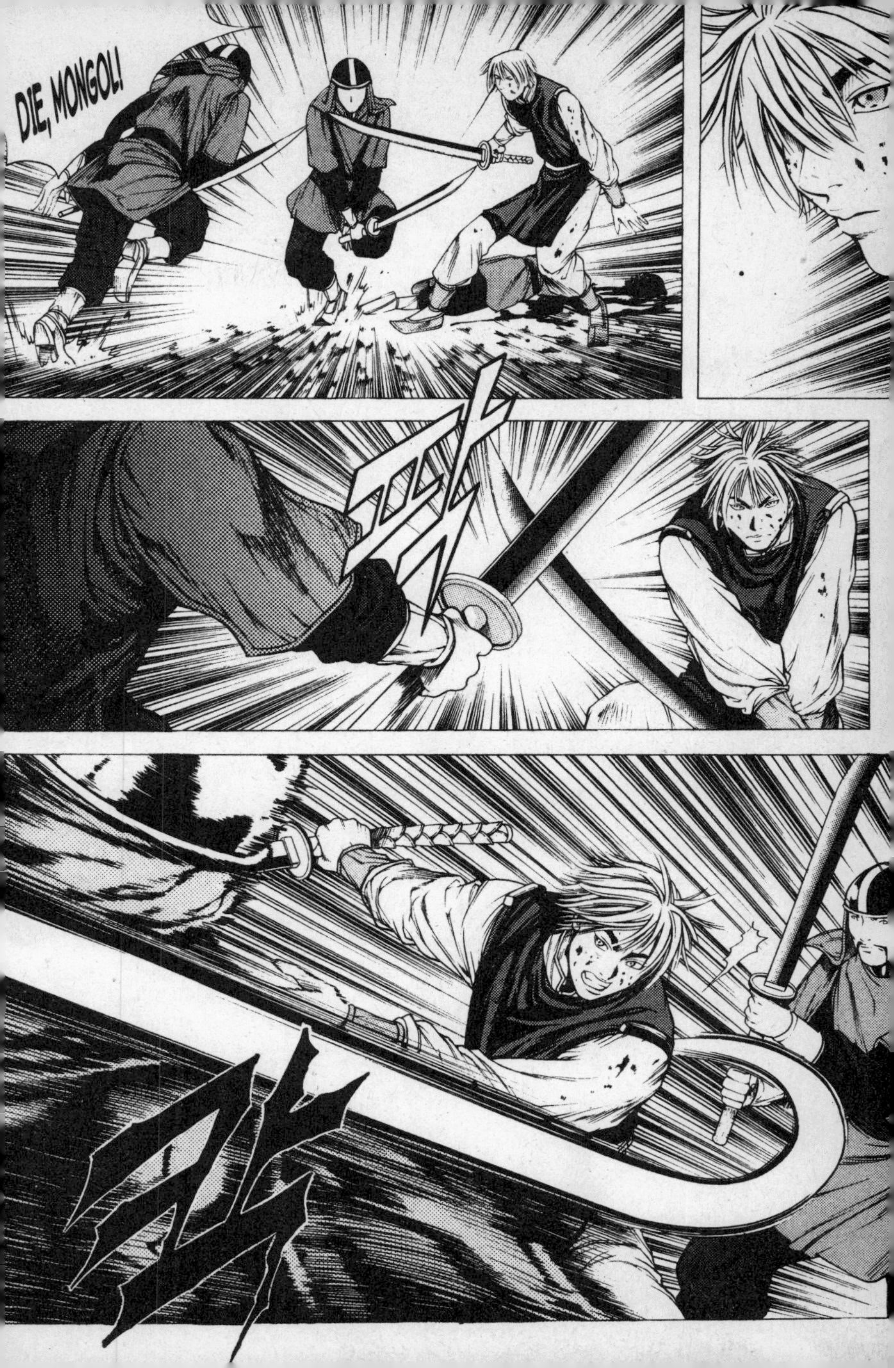
DIE, MONGOL!
SOCK

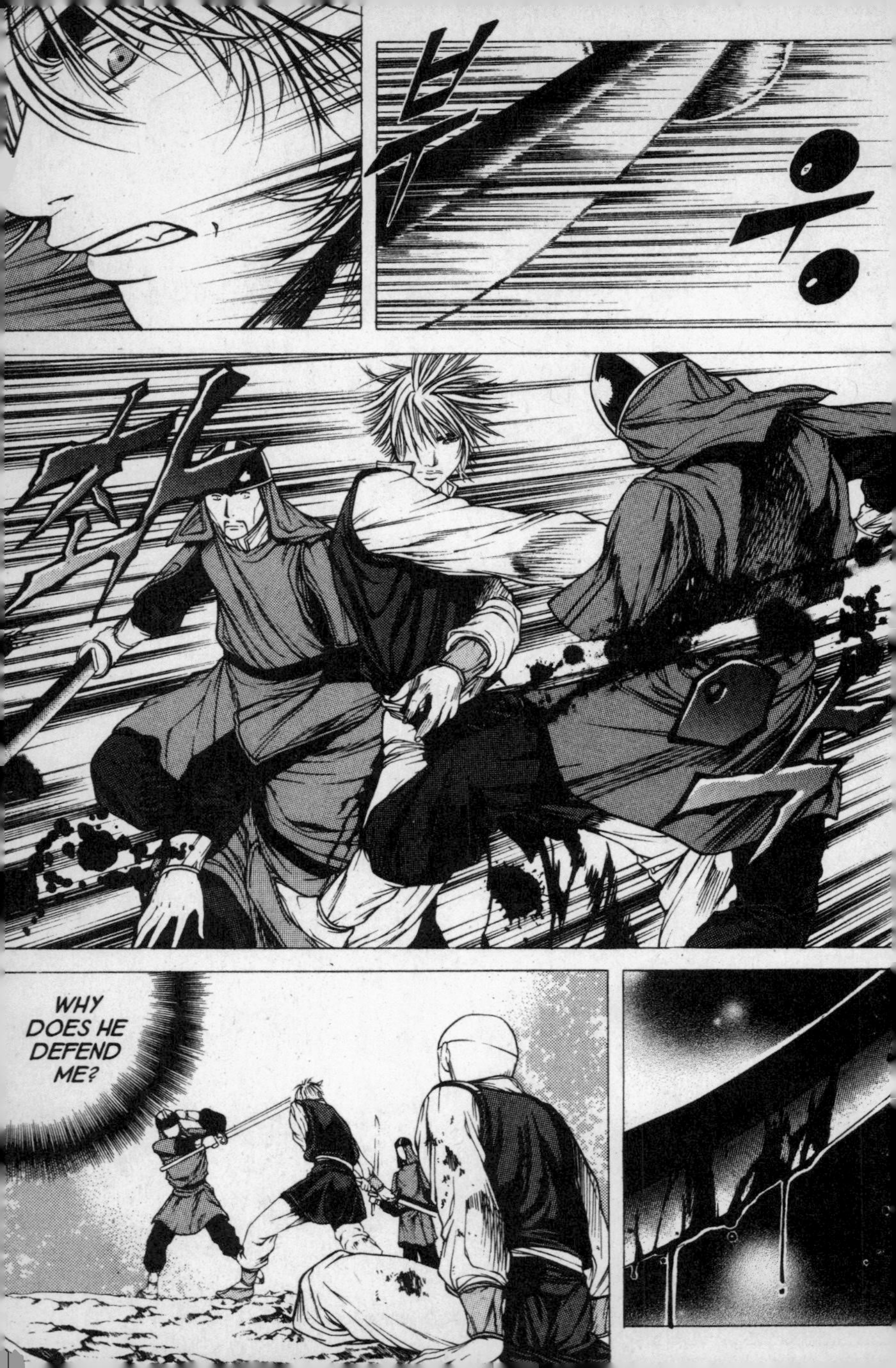
WHY DOES HE DEFEND ME?

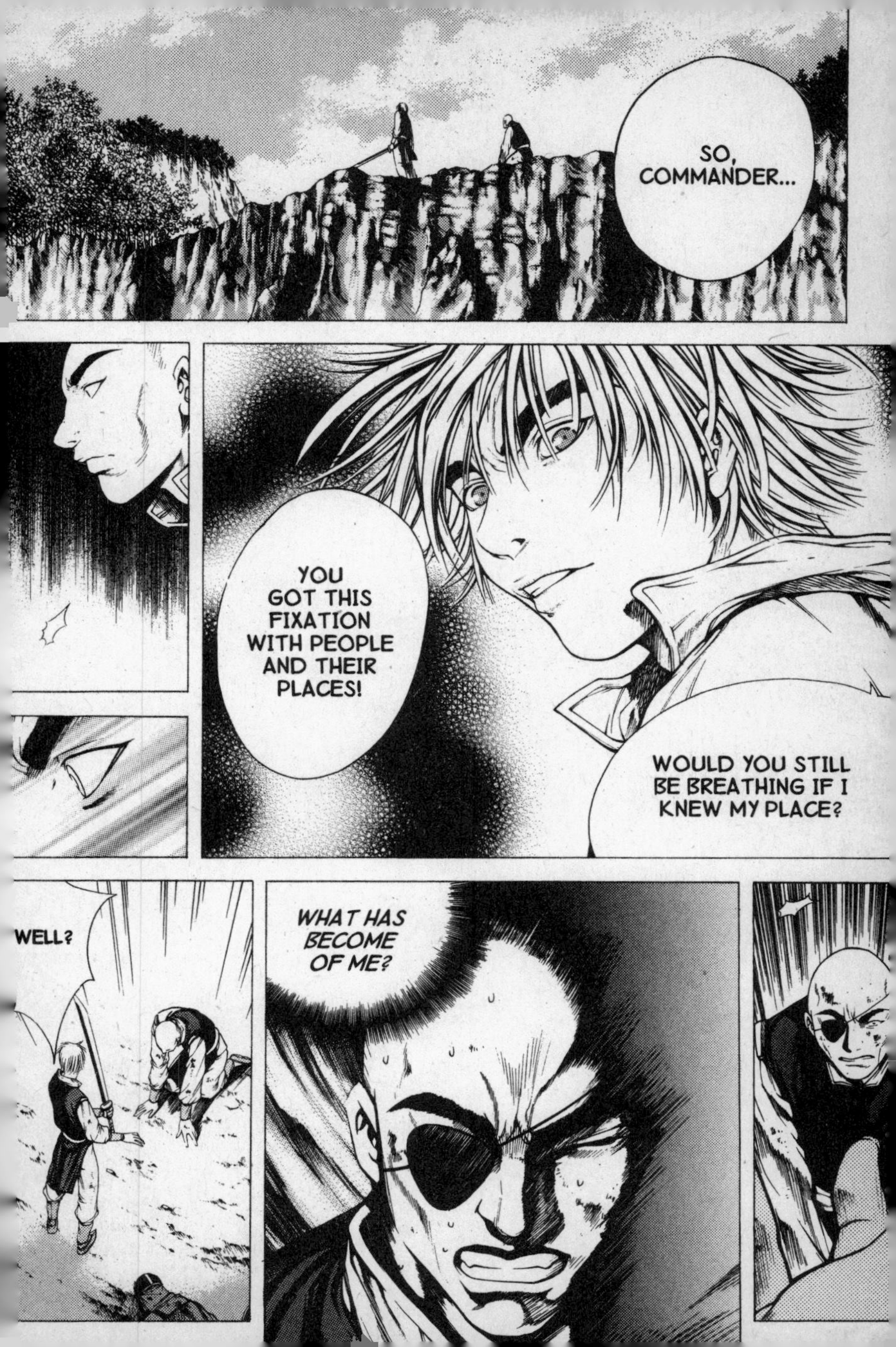
SO, COMMANDER...
YOU GOT THIS FIXATION WITH PEOPLE AND THEIR PLACES!
WOULD YOU STILL BE BREATHING IF I KNEW MY PLACE?
WELL?
WHAT HAS BECOME OF ME?

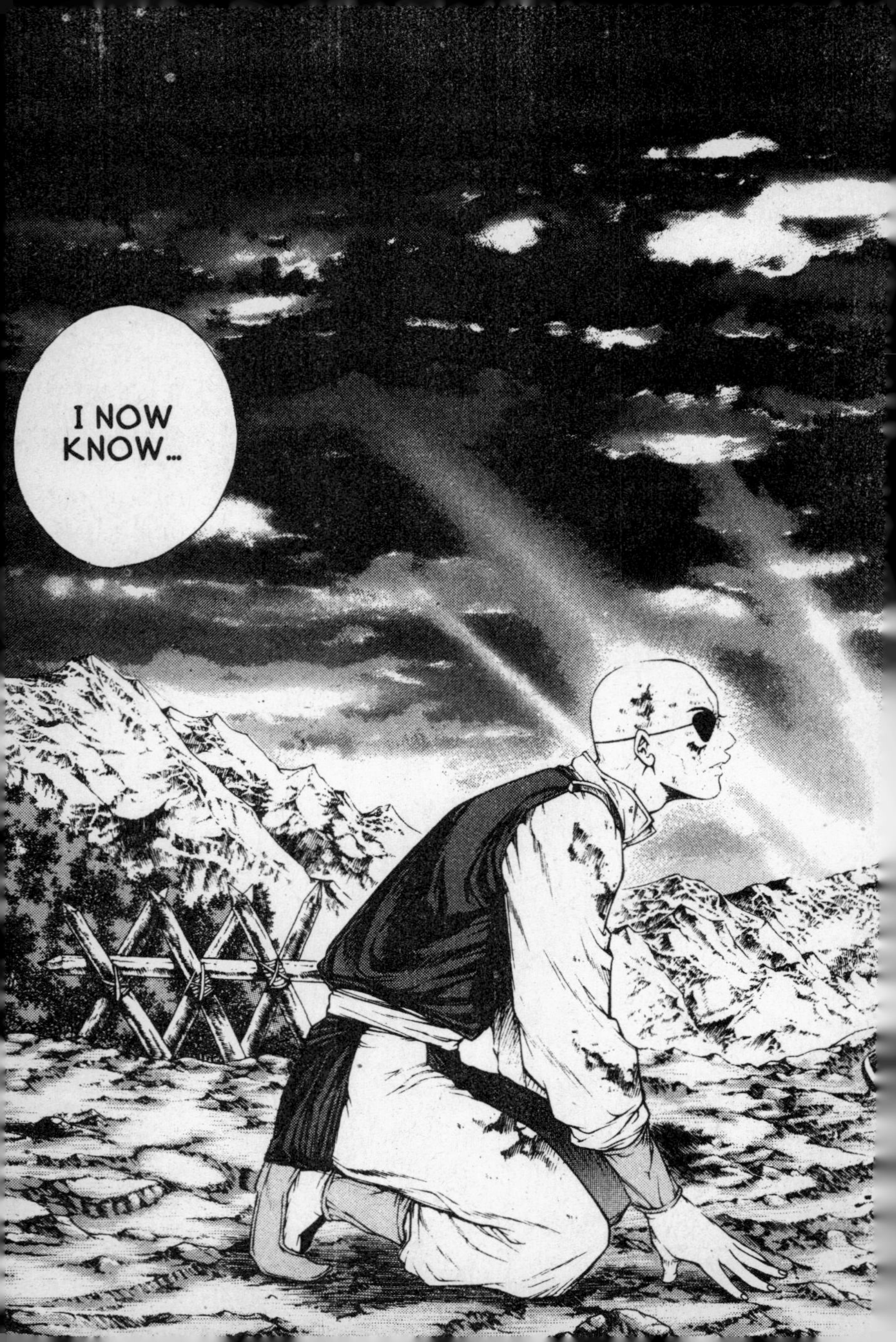
I NOW KNOW...

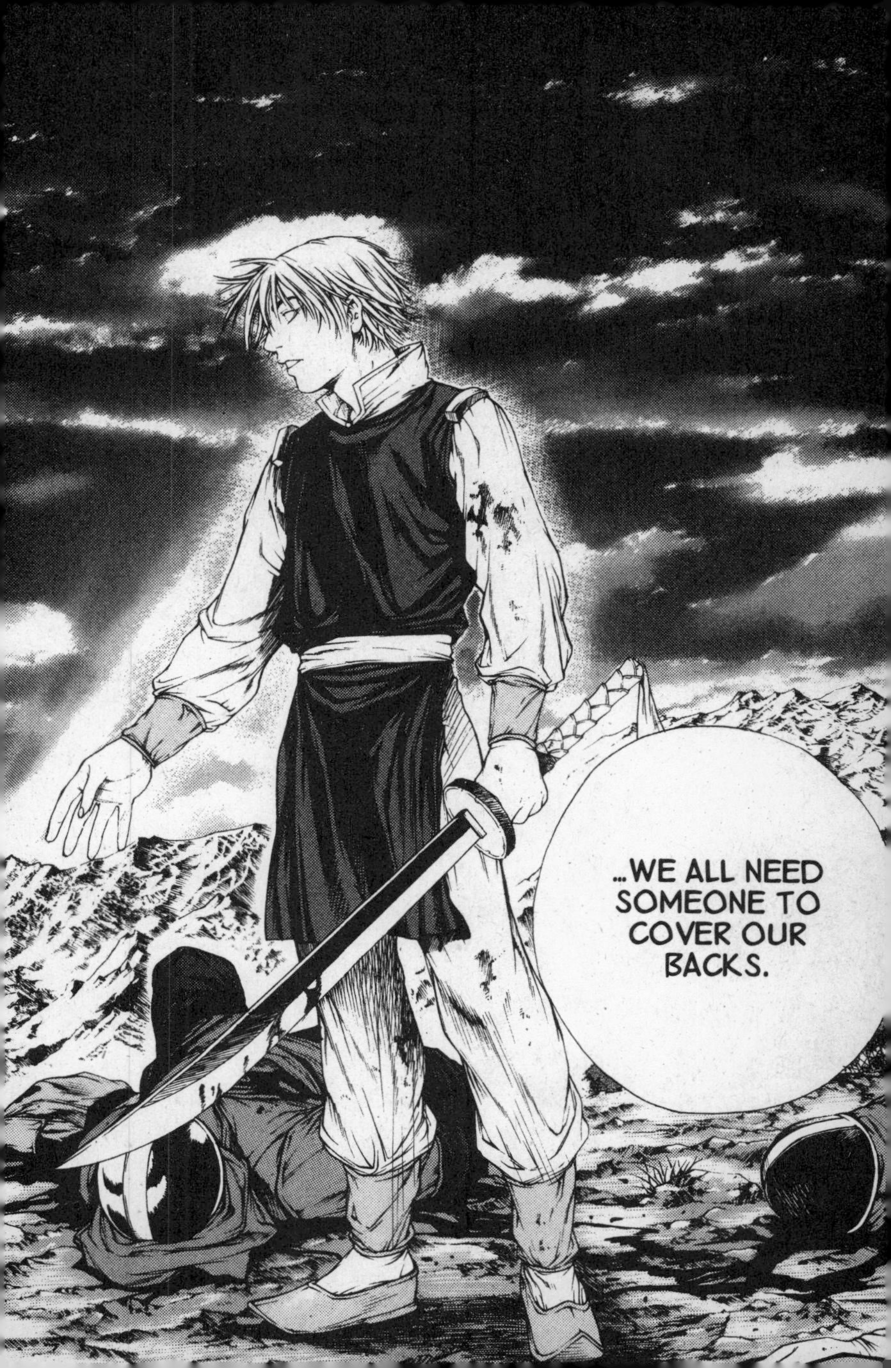
...WE ALL NEED SOMEONE TO COVER OUR BACKS.

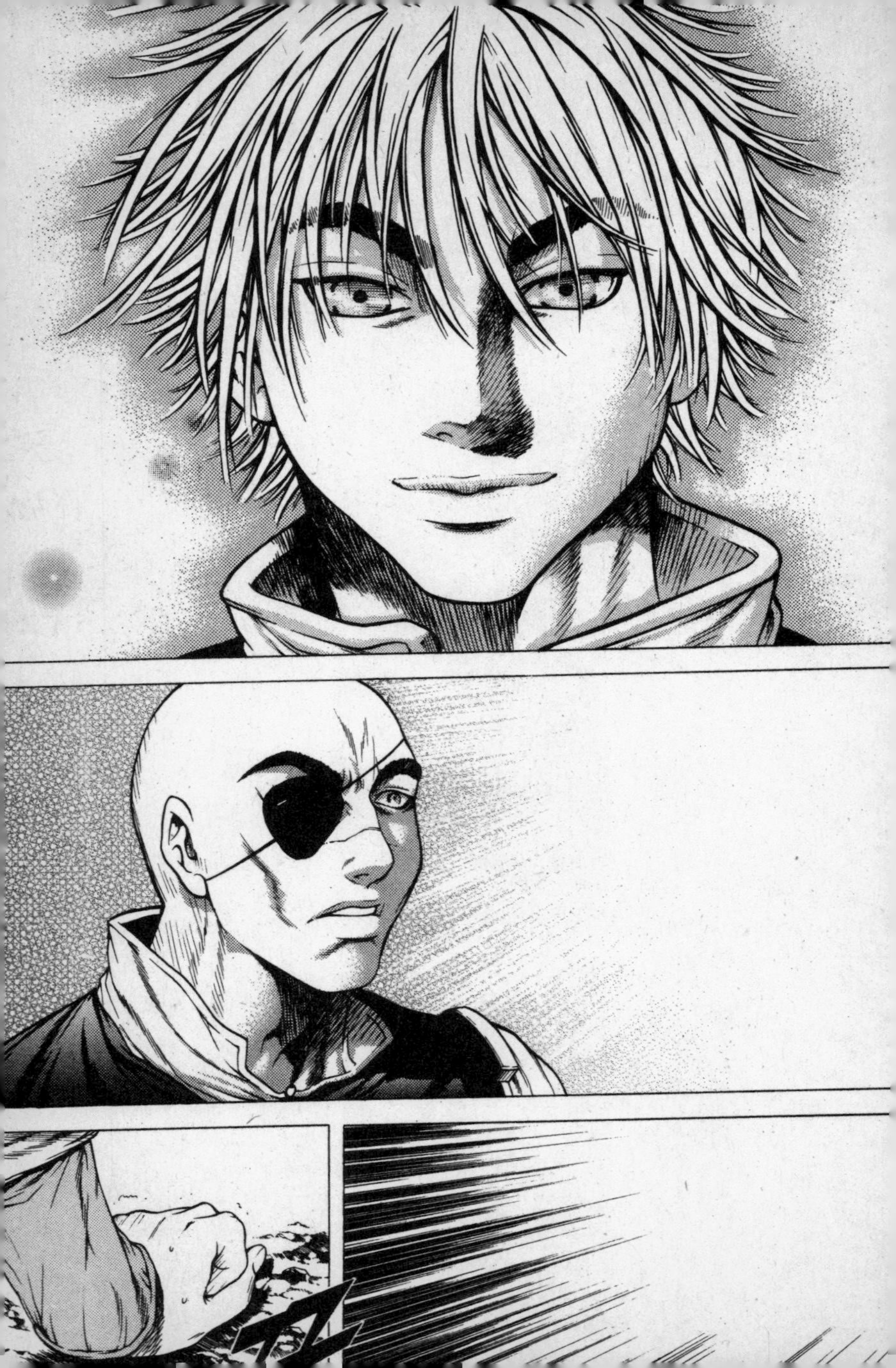

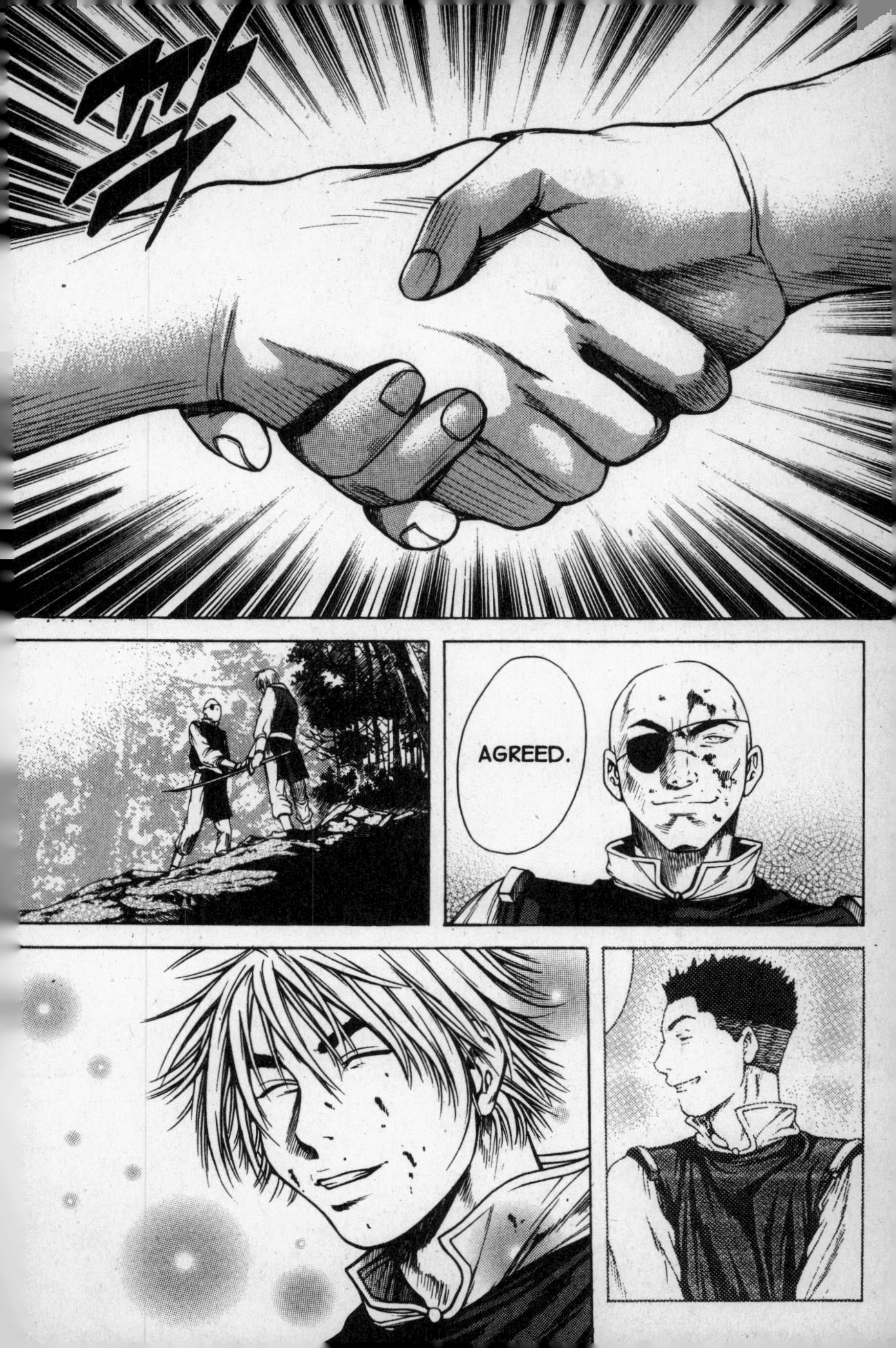
AGREED.

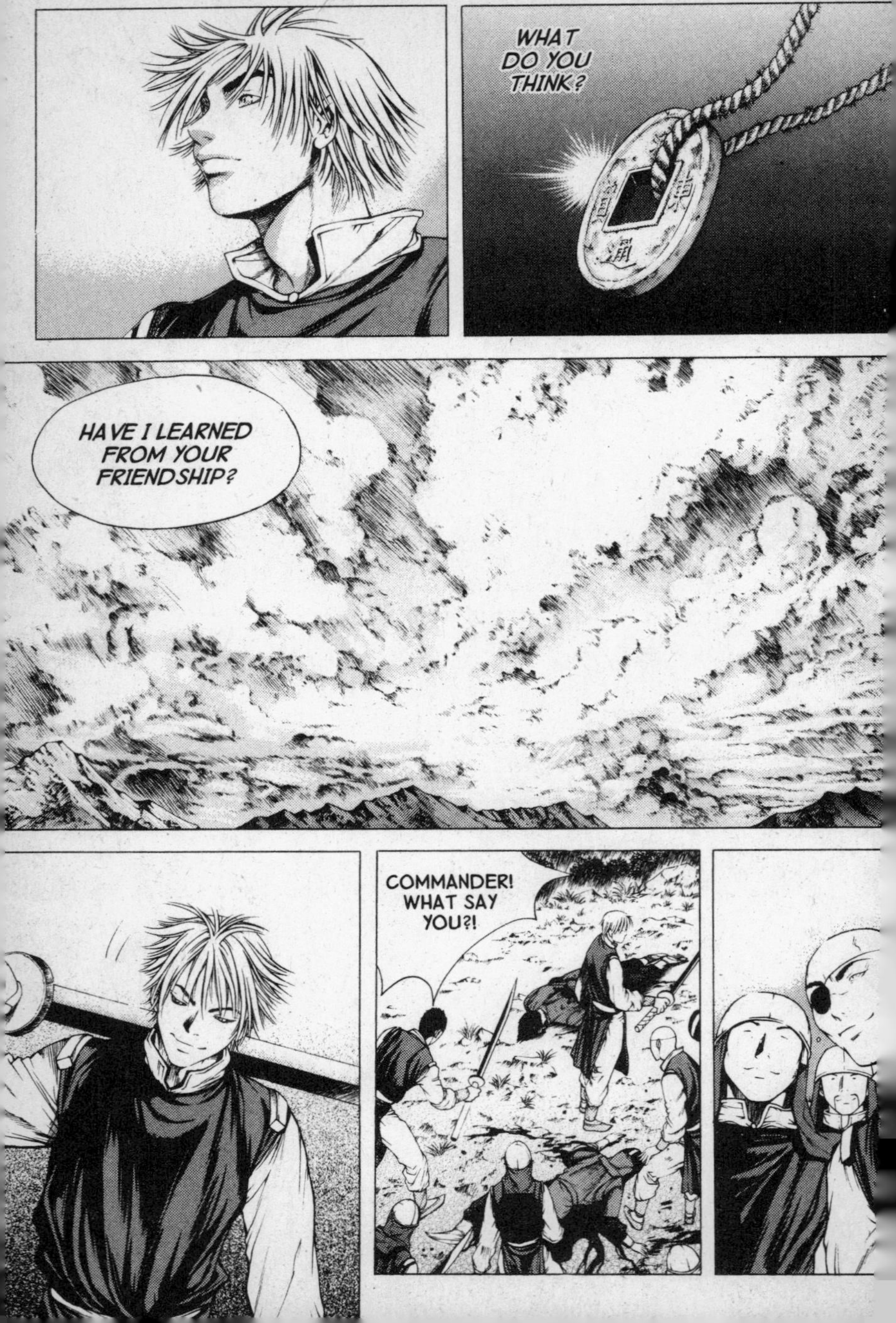
WHAT DO YOU THINK?
HAVE I LEARNED FROM YOUR FRIENDSHIP?
COMMANDER! WHAT SAY YOU?!

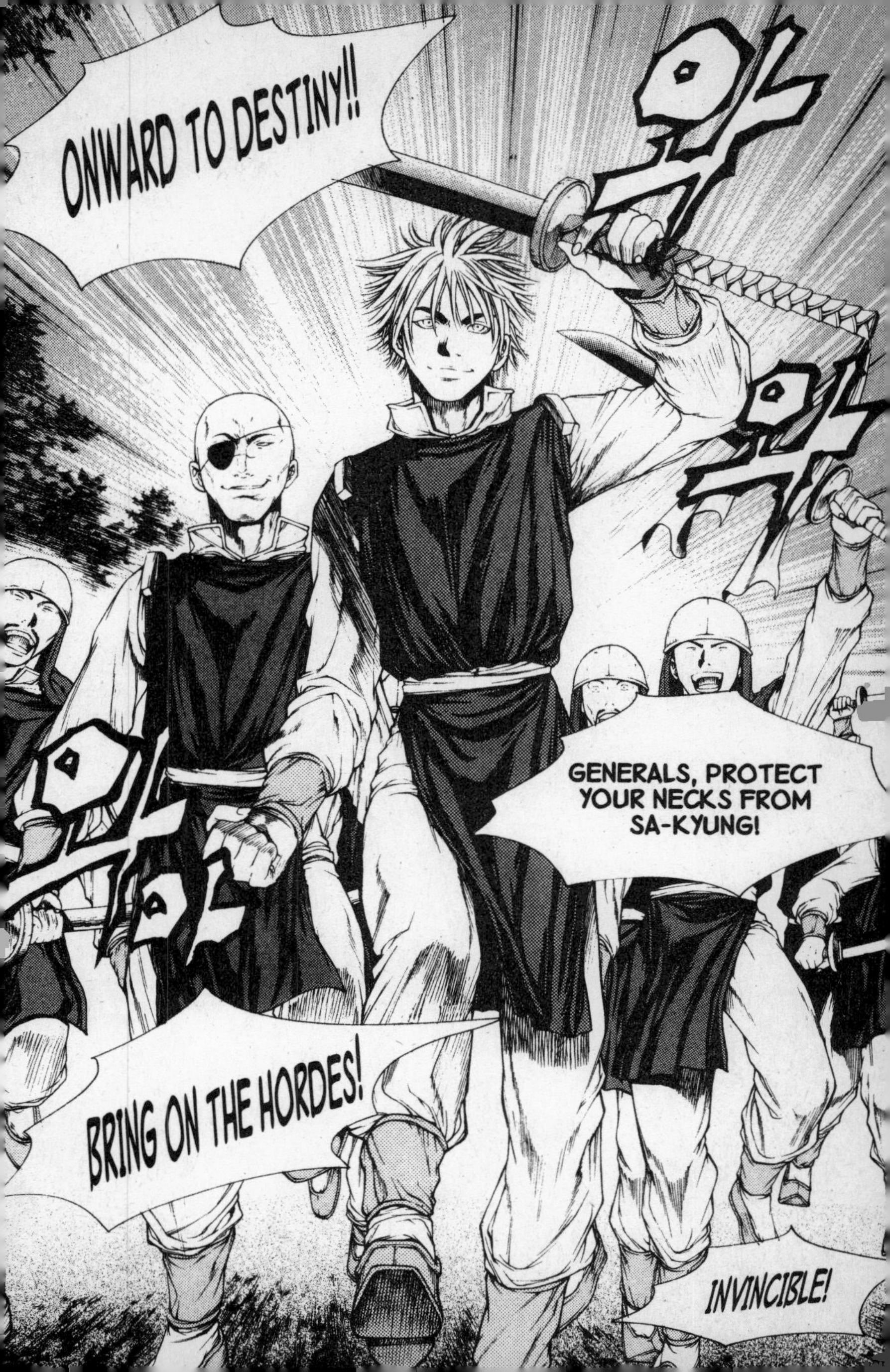
ONWARD TO DESTINY!!
GENERALS, PROTECT YOUR NECKS FROM SA-KYUNG!
BRING ON THE HORDES!
INVINCIBLE!

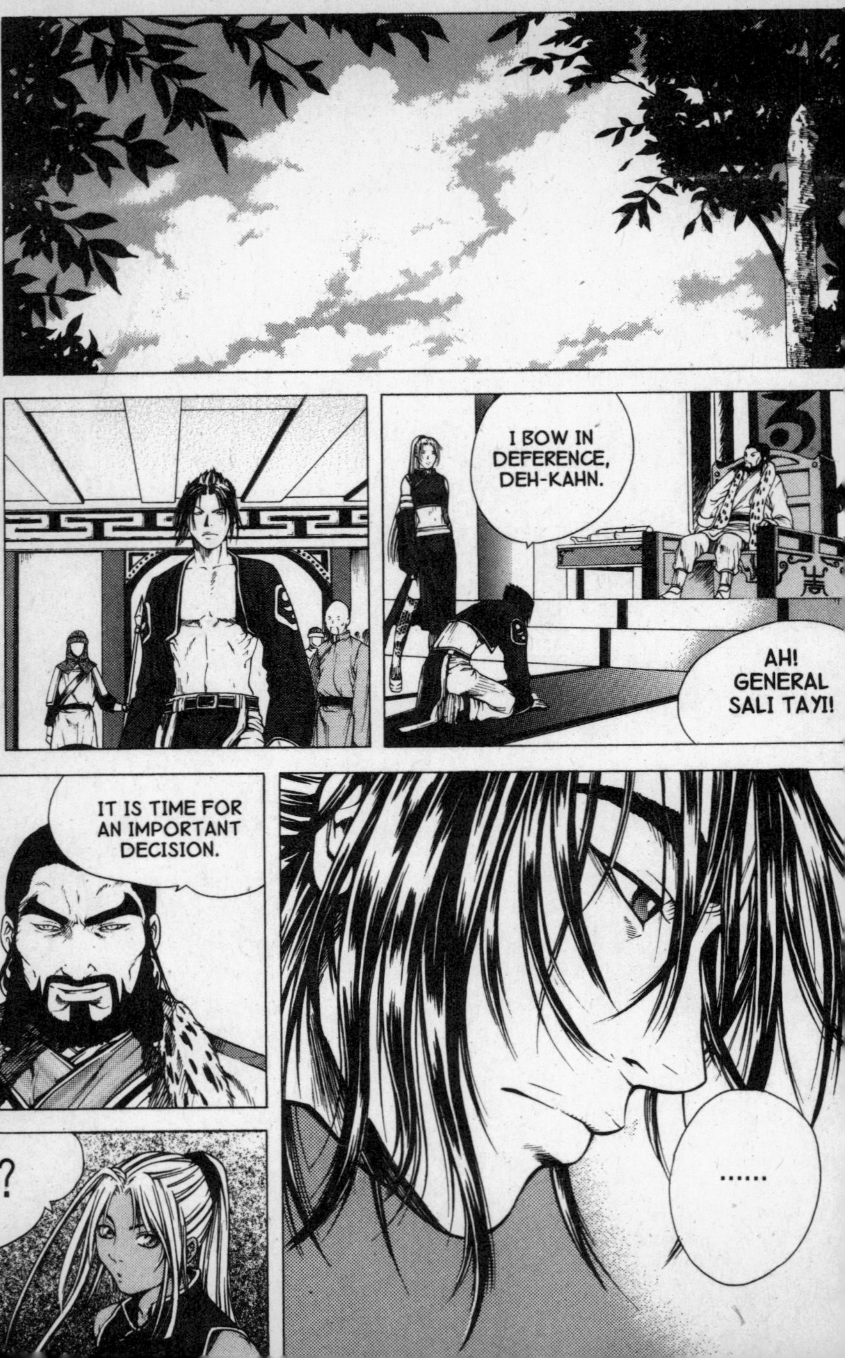
I BOW IN DEFERENCE, DEH-KAHN.
AH! GENERAL SALI TAYI!
IT IS TIME FOR AN IMPORTANT DECISION.
......
?

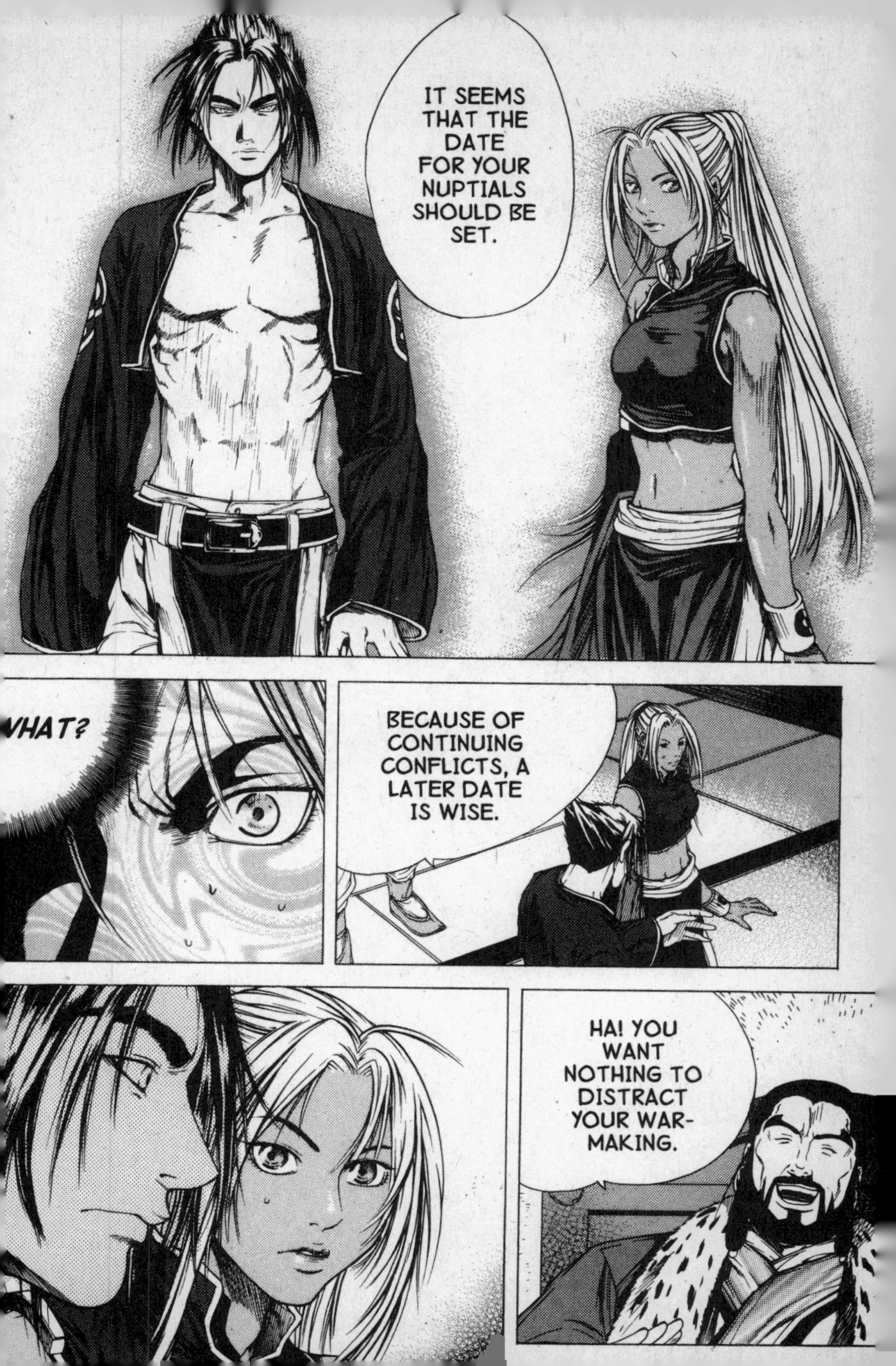
IT SEEMS THAT THE DATE FOR YOUR NUPTIALS SHOULD BE SET.
WHAT?
BECAUSE OF CONTINUING CONFLICTS, A LATER DATE IS WISE.
HA! YOU WANT NOTHING TO DISTRACT YOUR WAR-MAKING.

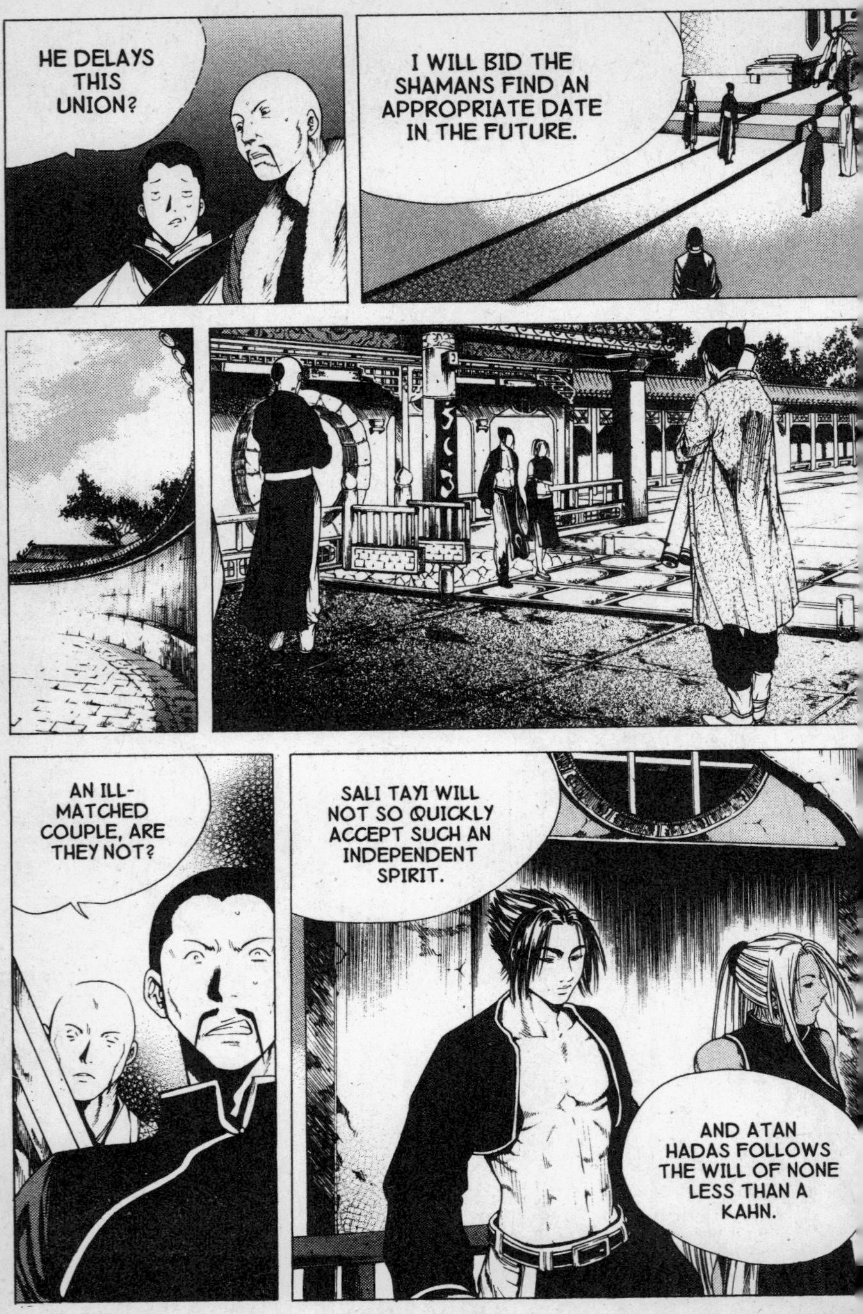
HE DELAYS THIS UNION?
I WILL BID THE SHAMANS FIND AN APPROPRIATE DATE IN THE FUTURE.
AN ILL-MATCHED COUPLE, ARE THEY NOT?
SALI TAYI WILL NOT SO QUICKLY ACCEPT SUCH AN INDEPENDENT SPIRIT.
AND ATAN HADAS FOLLOWS THE WILL OF NONE LESS THAN A KAHN.

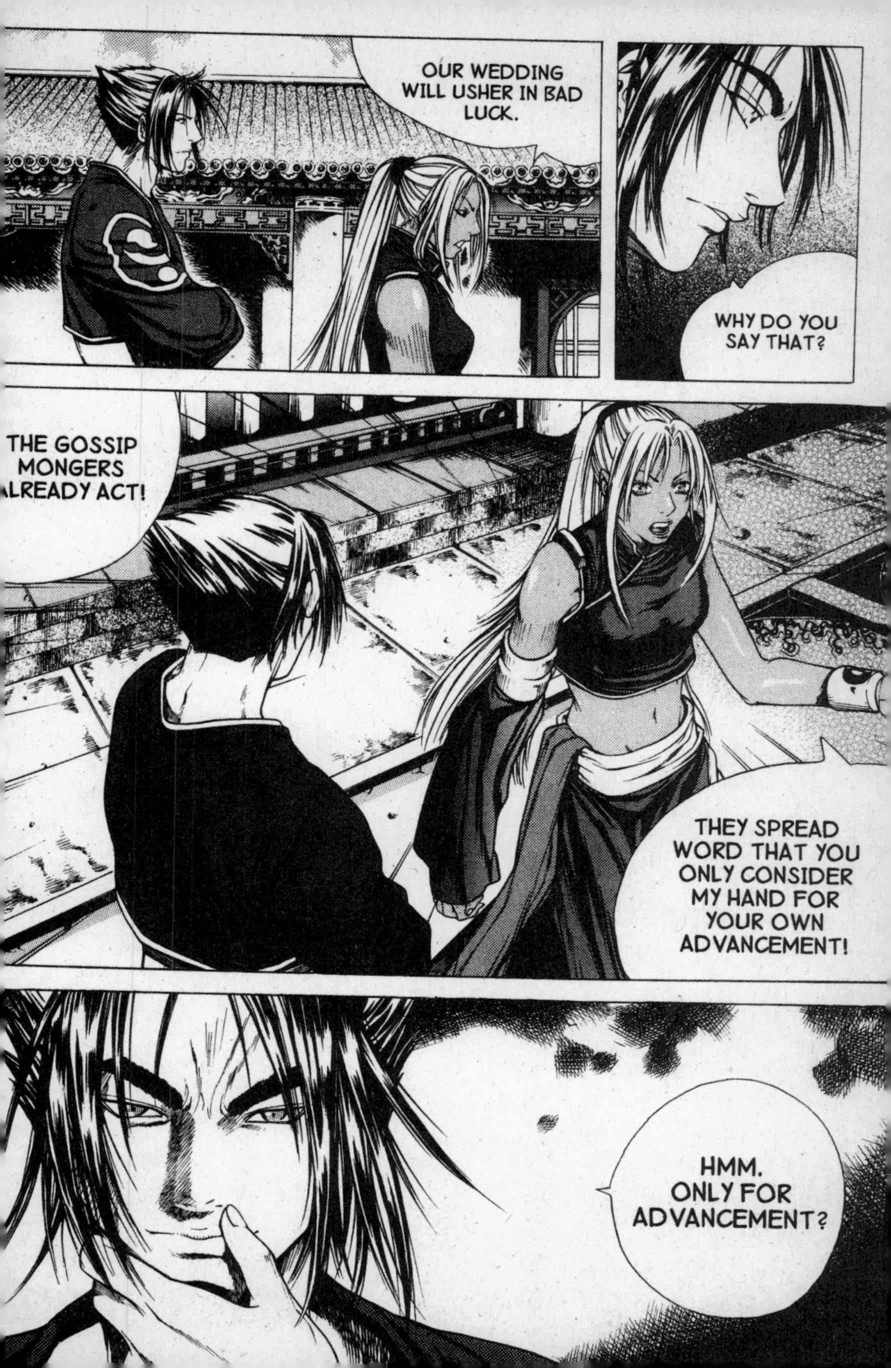
OUR WEDDING WILL USHER IN BAD LUCK.
WHY DO YOU SAY THAT?
THE GOSSIP MONGERS LREADY ACT!
THEY SPREAD WORD THAT YOU ONLY CONSIDER MY HAND FOR YOUR OWN ADVANCEMENT!
HMM. ONLY FOR ADVANCEMENT?

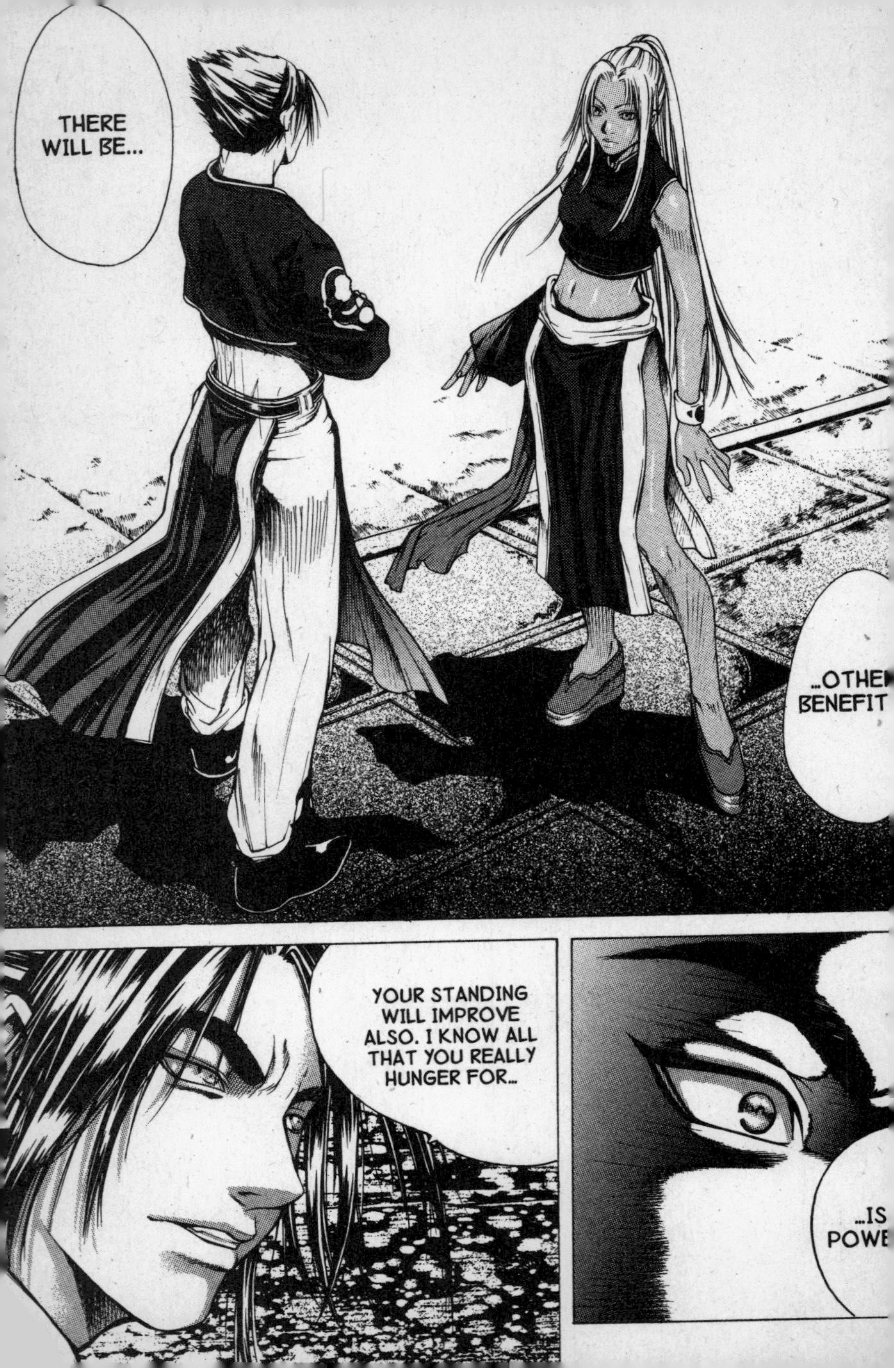
THERE WILL BE...
...OTHE BENEFIT
YOUR STANDING WILL IMPROVE ALSO. I KNOW ALL THAT YOU REALLY HUNGER FOR...
...IS POWE

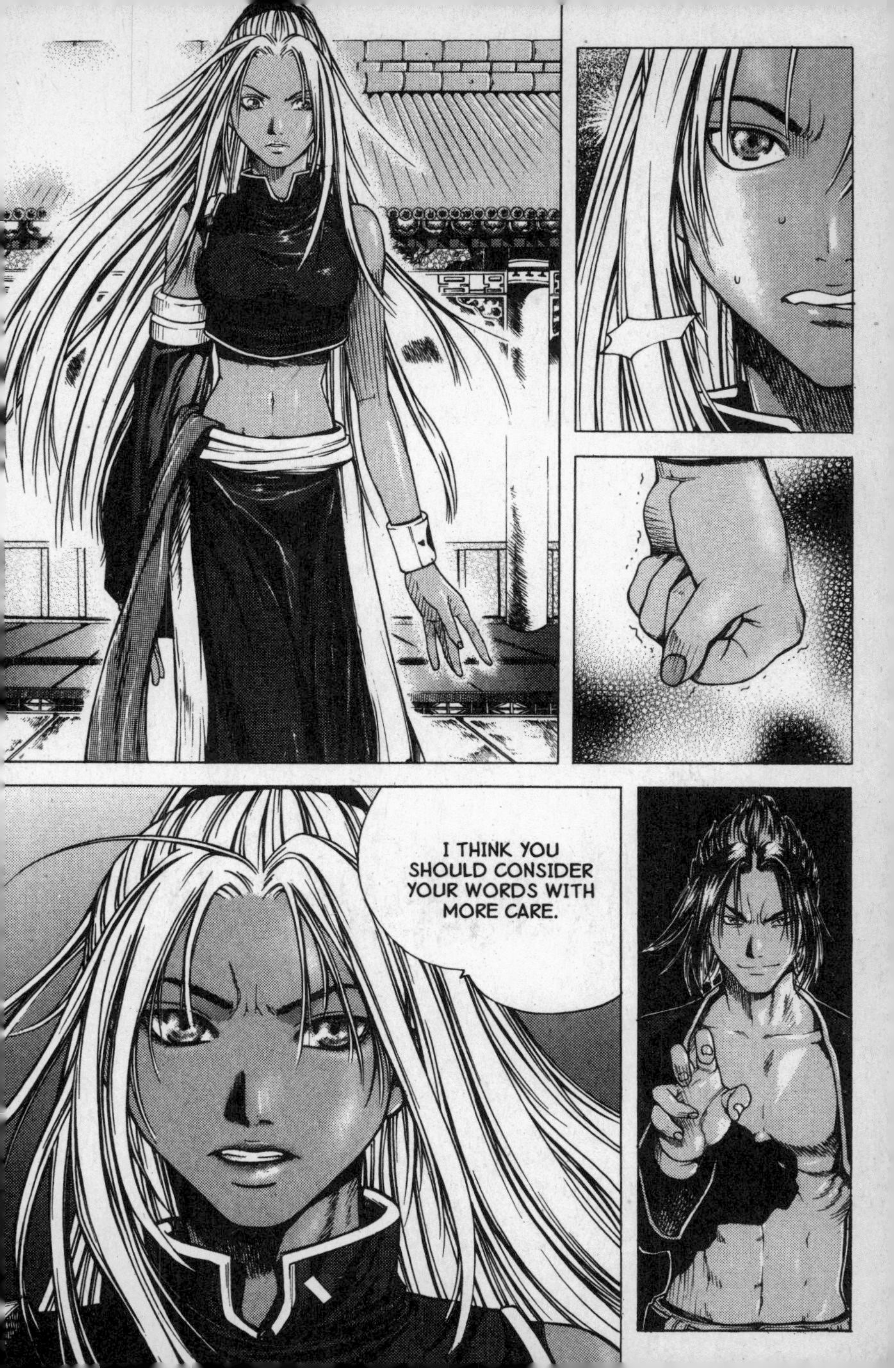
I THINK YOU SHOULD CONSIDER YOUR WORDS WITH MORE CARE.

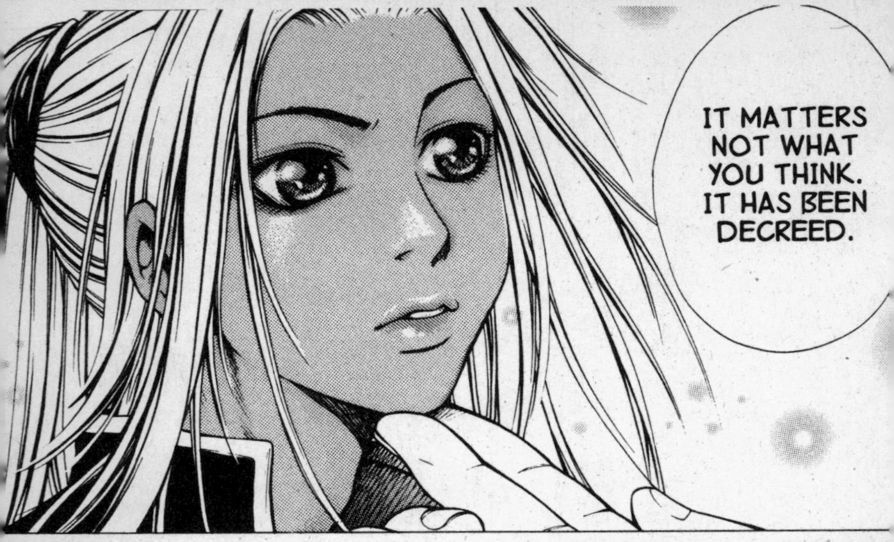
IT MATTERS NOT WHAT YOU THINK. IT HAS BEEN DECREED.
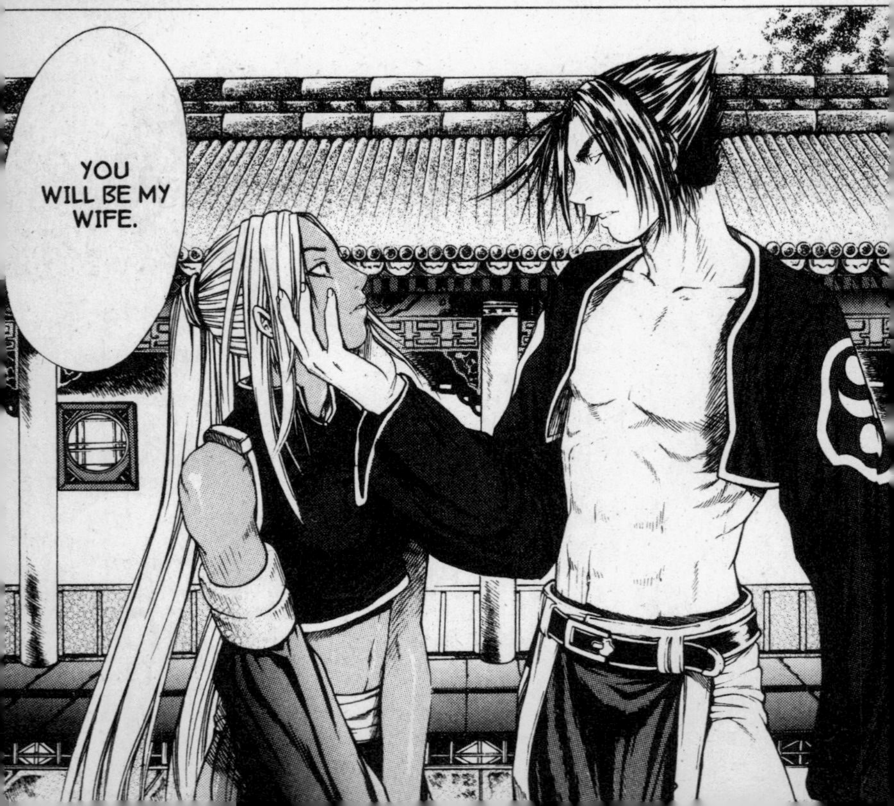
YOU WILL BE MY WIFE.

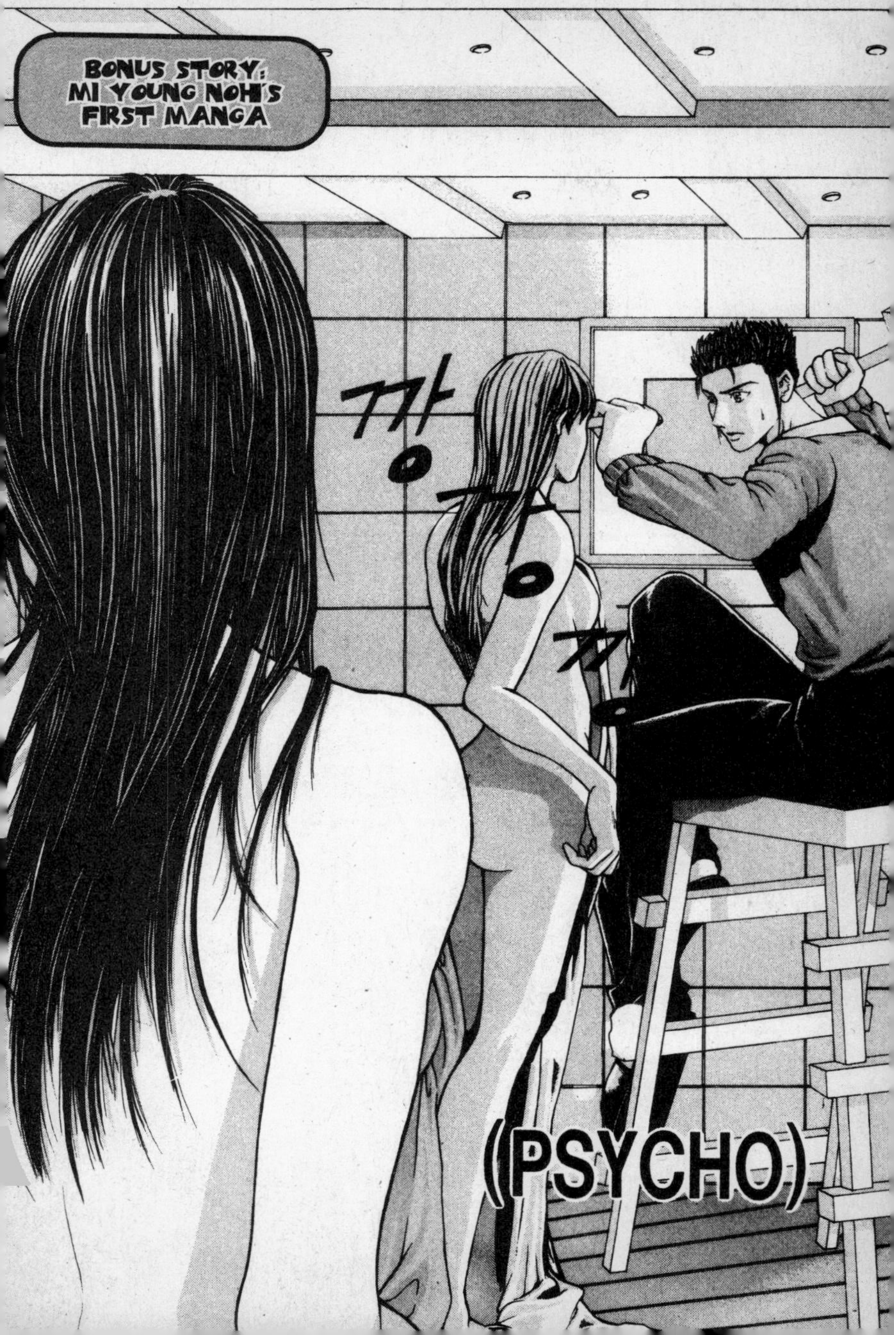
BONUS STORY:
MI YOUNG NOH'S
FIRST MANGA
(PSYCHO)

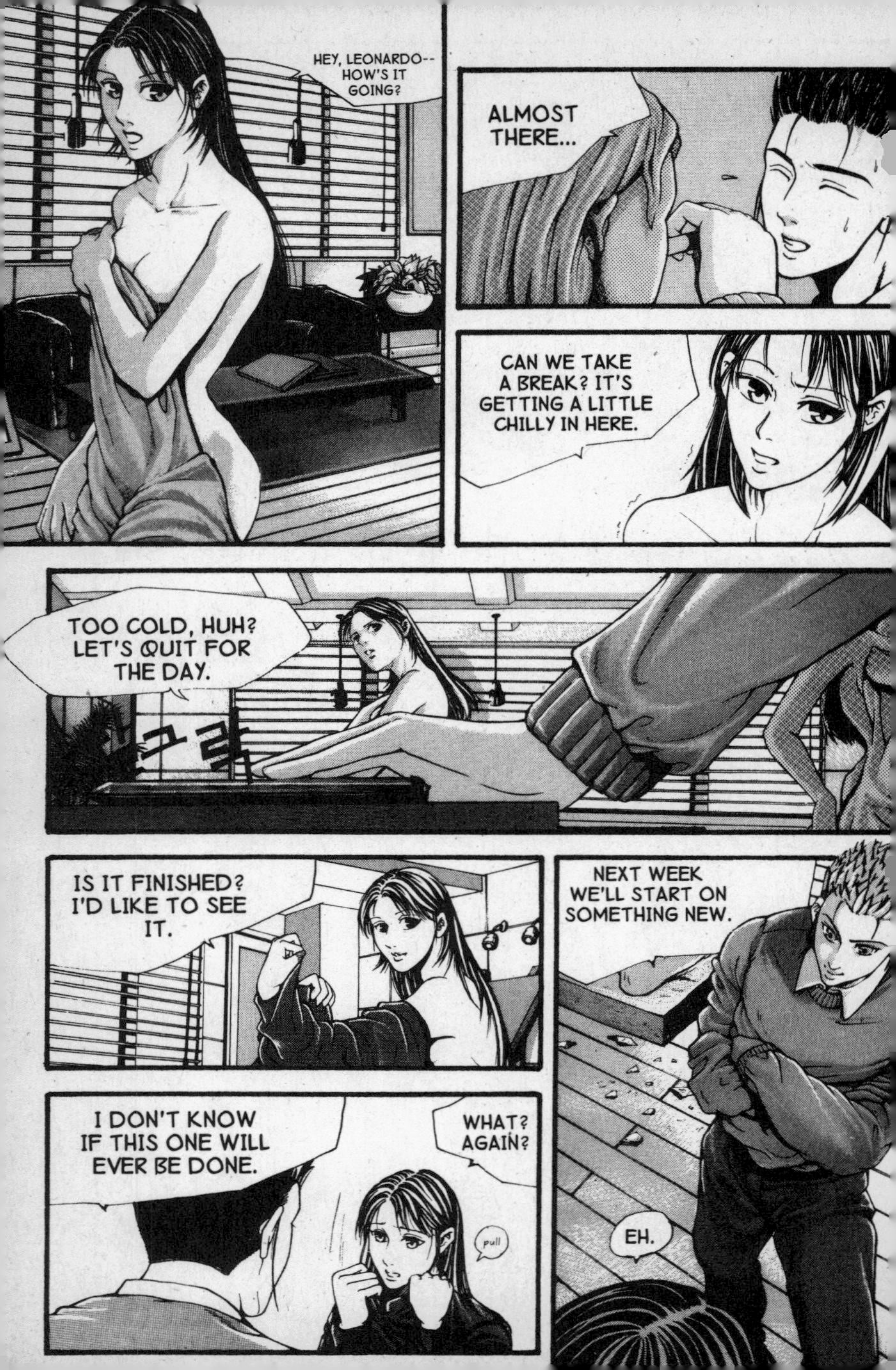
HEY, LEONARDO-- HOW'S IT GOING?
ALMOST THERE...
CAN WE TAKE A BREAK? IT'S GETTING A LITTLE CHILLY IN HERE.
TOO COLD, HUH? LET'S QUIT FOR THE DAY.
IS IT FINISHED? I'D LIKE TO SEE IT.
I DON'T KNOW IF THIS ONE WILL EVER BE DONE.
WHAT? AGAIN?
pull
NEXT WEEK WE'LL START ON SOMETHING NEW.
EH.

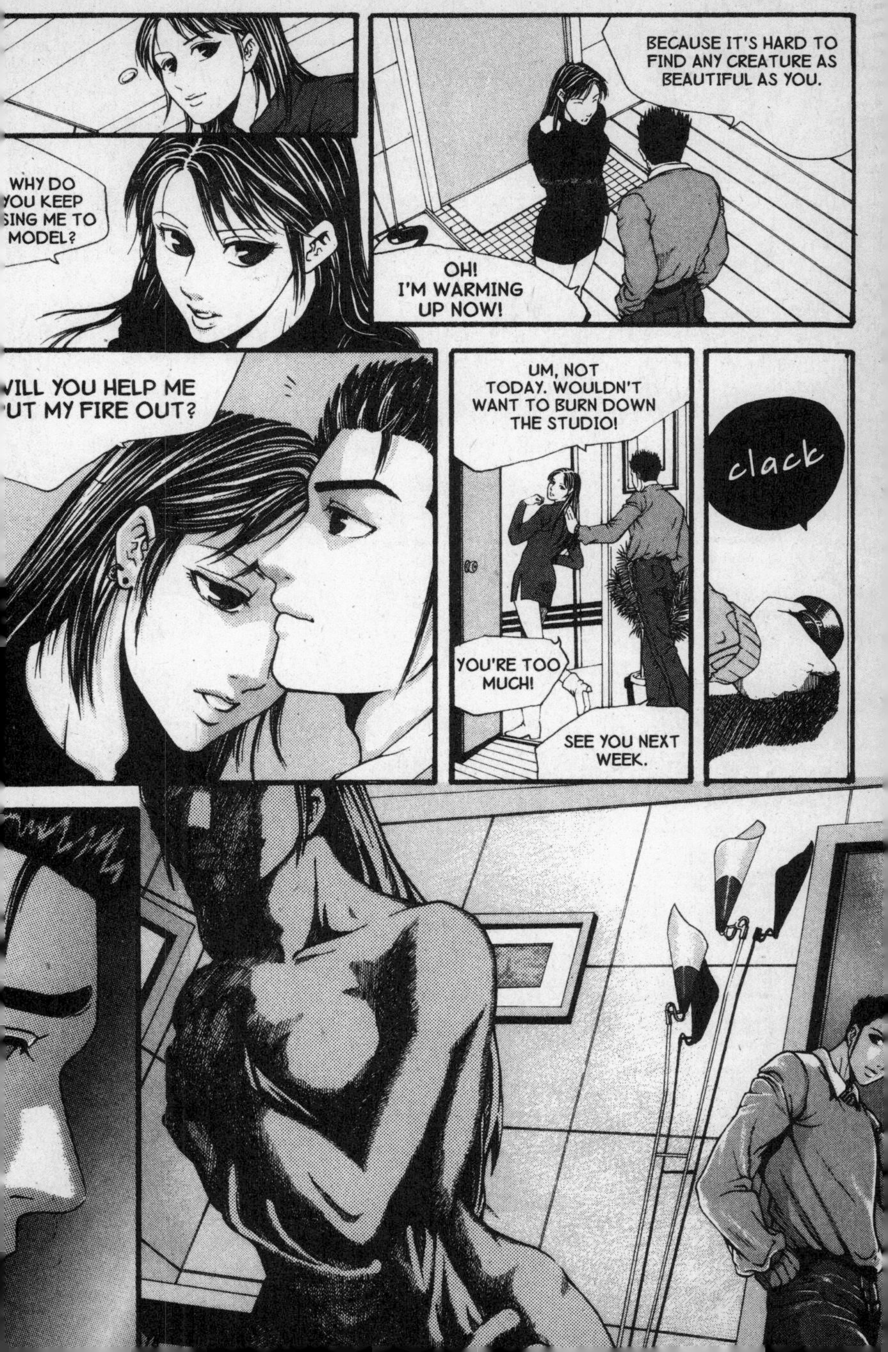
WHY DO YOU KEEP SING ME TO MODEL?
BECAUSE IT'S HARD TO FIND ANY CREATURE AS BEAUTIFUL AS YOU.
OH! I'M WARMING UP NOW!
VILL YOU HELP ME UT MY FIRE OUT?
UM, NOT TODAY. WOULDN'T WANT TO BURN DOWN THE STUDIO!
YOU'RE TOO MUCH!
SEE YOU NEXT WEEK.
clack

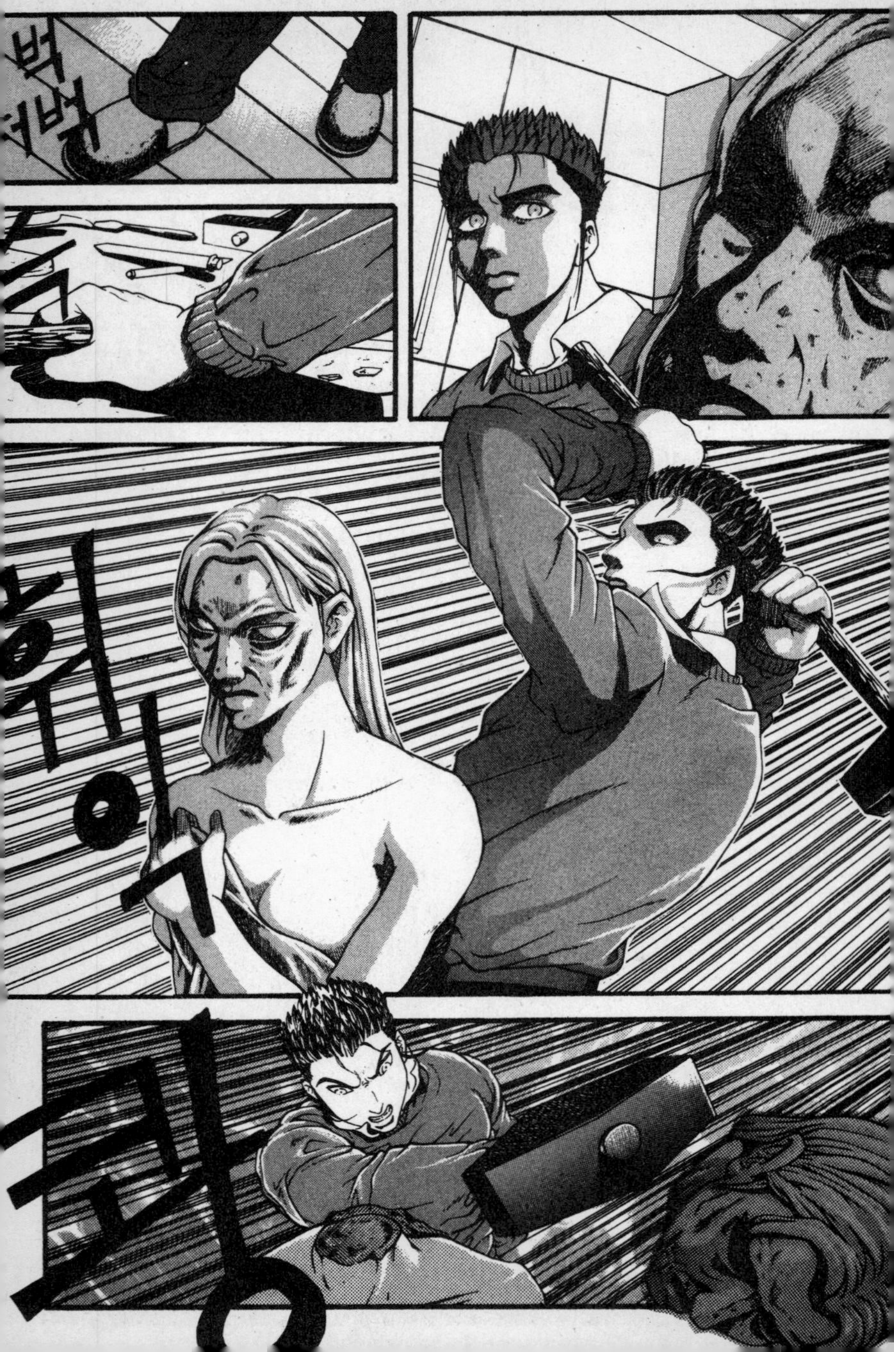
벅벅
휘이익
쾅

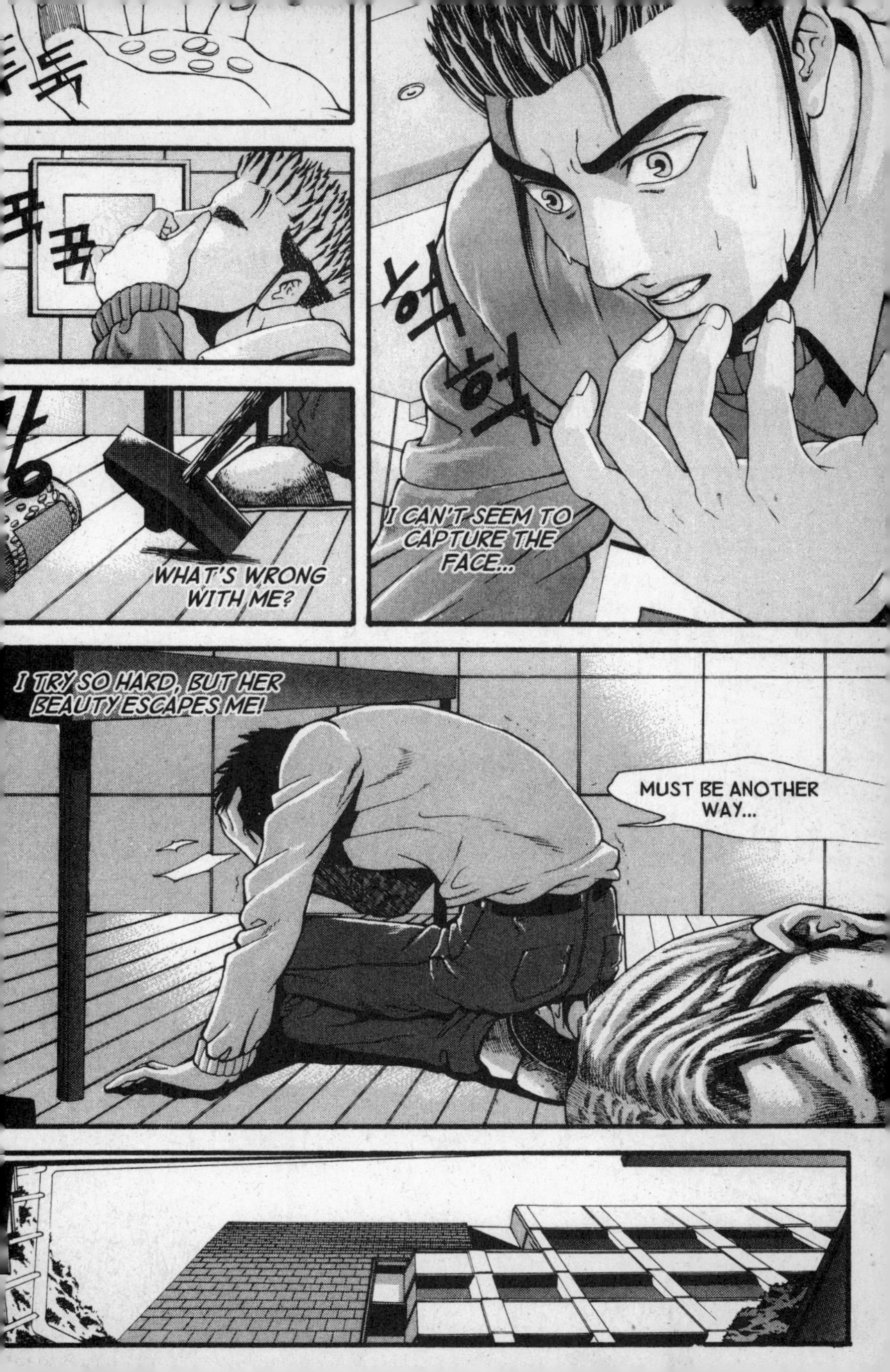
WHAT'S WRONG WITH ME?
I CAN'T SEEM TO CAPTURE THE FACE...
I TRY SO HARD, BUT HER BEAUTY ESCAPES ME!
MUST BE ANOTHER WAY...

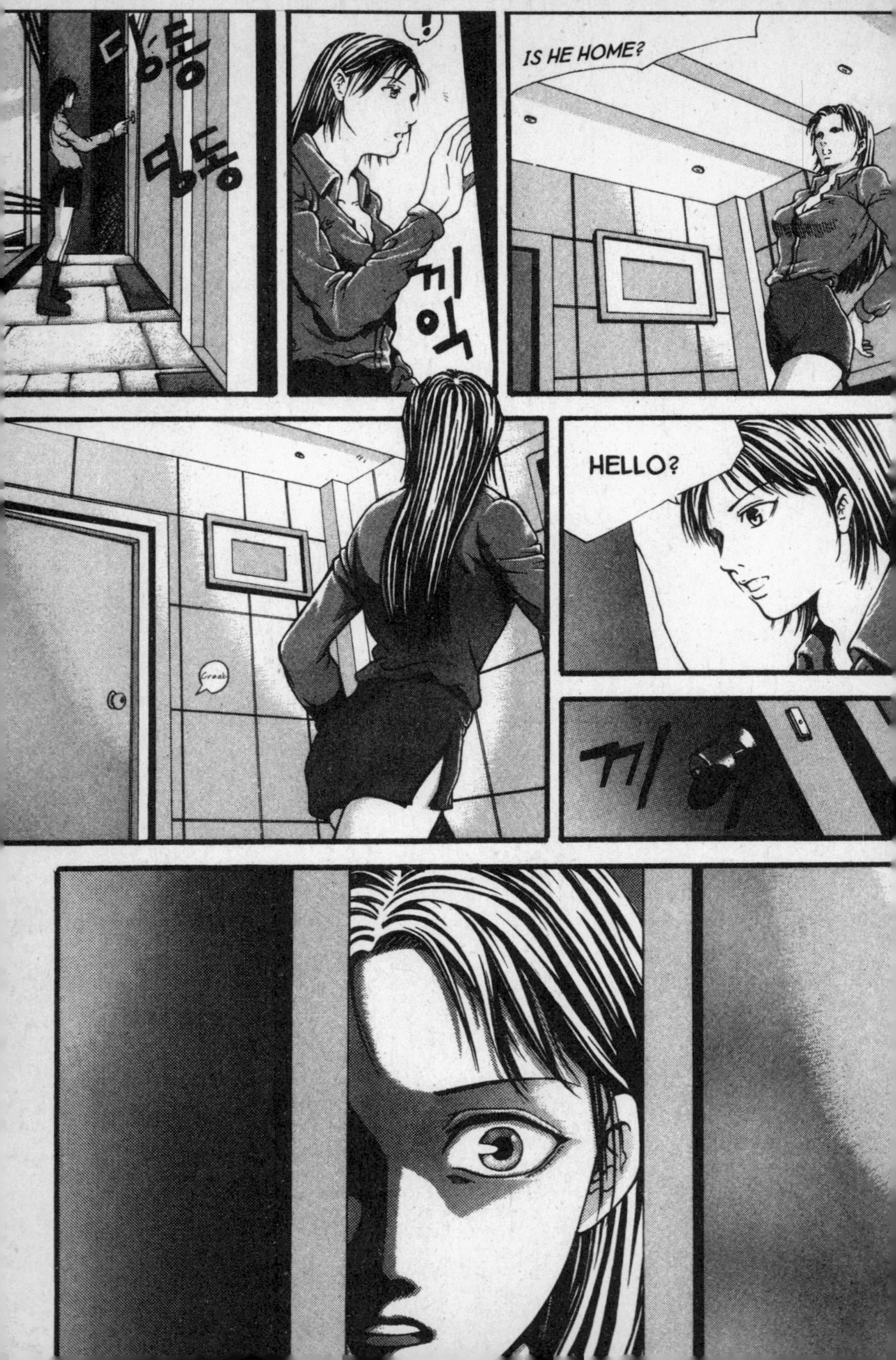
딩동
딩동
!
IS HE HOME?
Creak
HELLO?

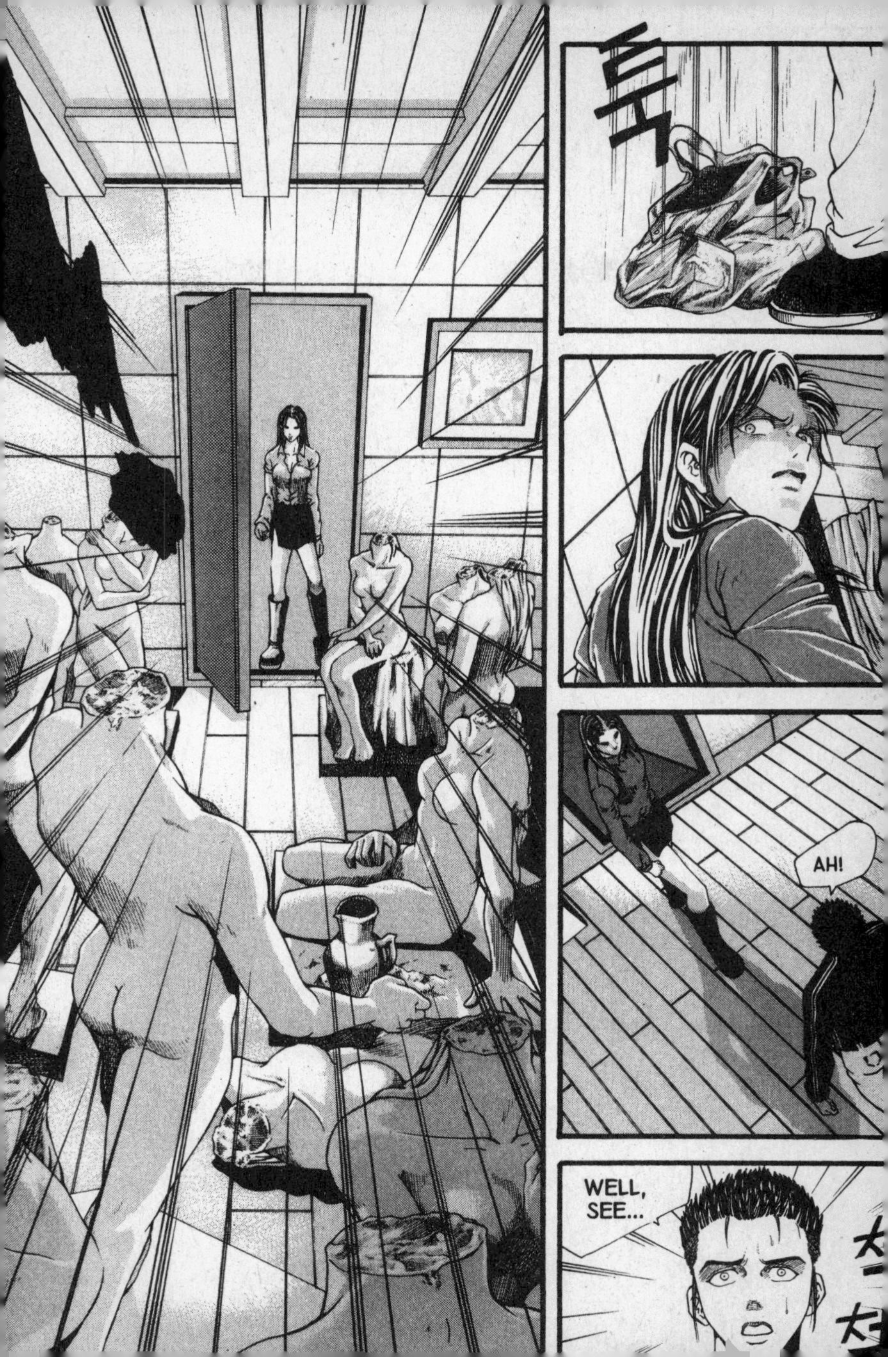
툭
AH!
WELL, SEE...

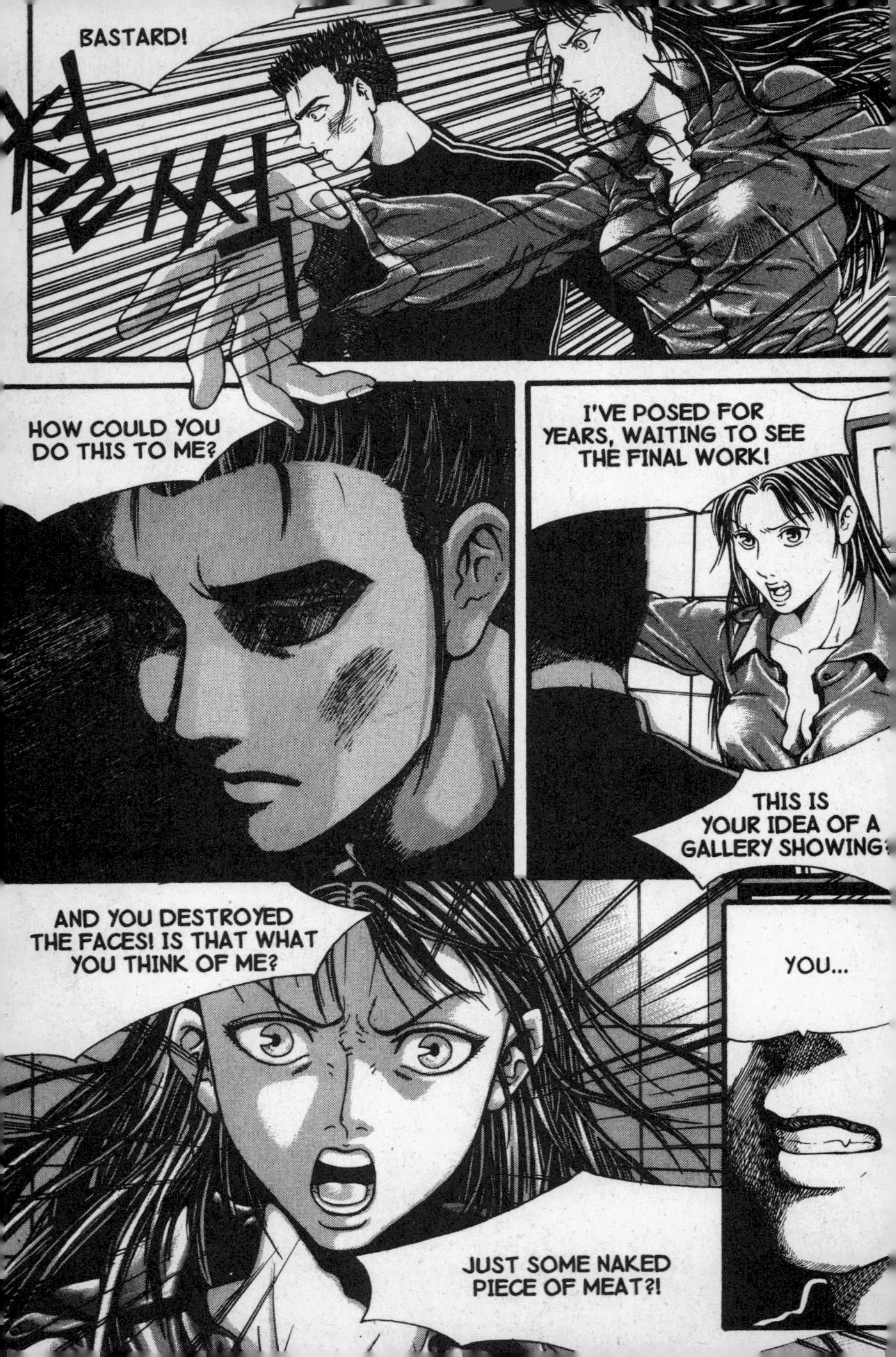
BASTARD!
HOW COULD YOU DO THIS TO ME?
I'VE POSED FOR YEARS, WAITING TO SEE THE FINAL WORK!
THIS IS YOUR IDEA OF A GALLERY SHOWING?
AND YOU DESTROYED THE FACES! IS THAT WHAT YOU THINK OF ME?
JUST SOME NAKED PIECE OF MEAT?!
YOU...

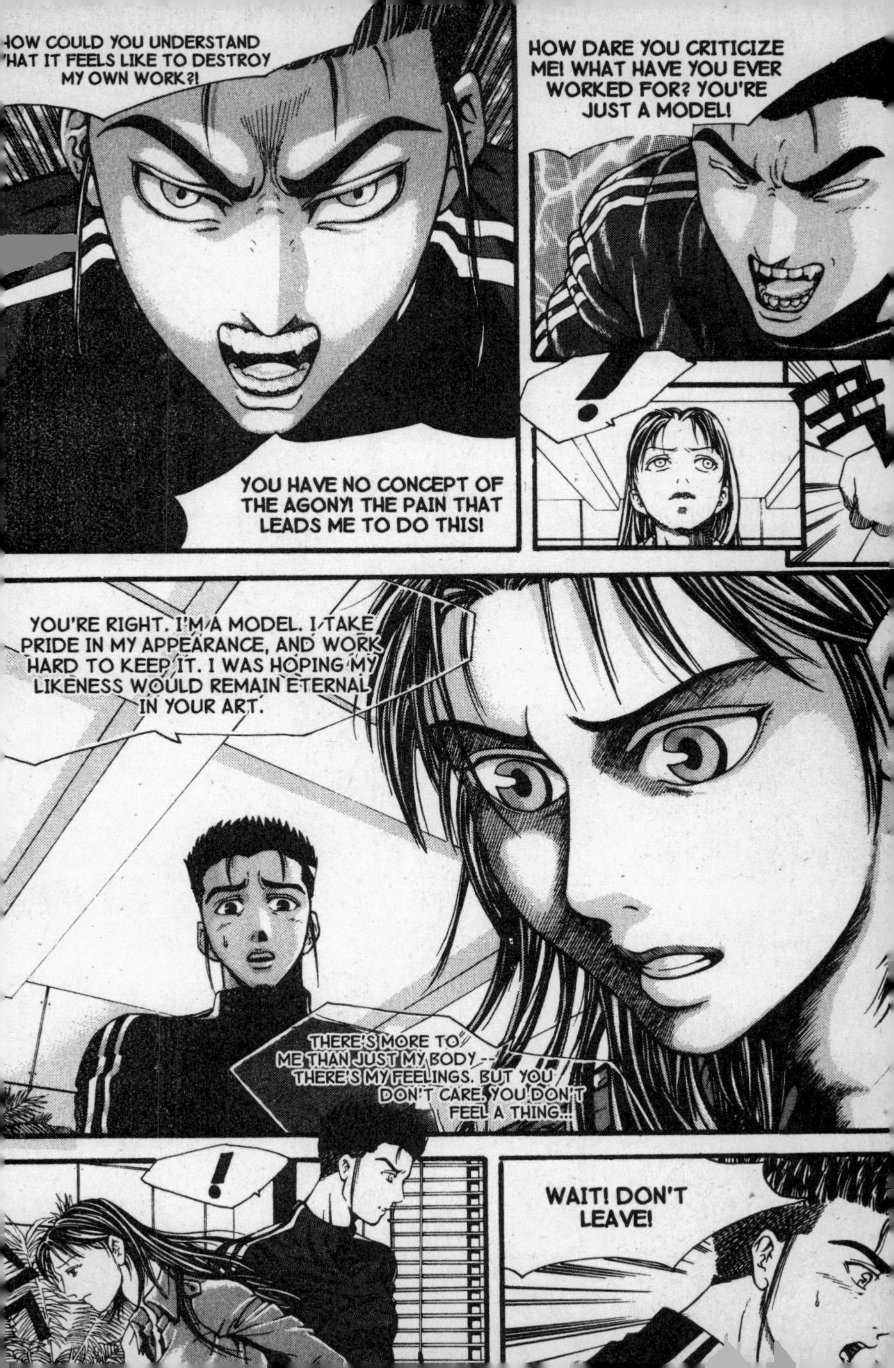
HOW COULD YOU UNDERSTAND WHAT IT FEELS LIKE TO DESTROY MY OWN WORK?!
YOU HAVE NO CONCEPT OF THE AGONY! THE PAIN THAT LEADS ME TO DO THIS!
HOW DARE YOU CRITICIZE ME! WHAT HAVE YOU EVER WORKED FOR? YOU'RE JUST A MODEL!
!
YOU'RE RIGHT. I'M A MODEL. I TAKE PRIDE IN MY APPEARANCE, AND WORK HARD TO KEEP IT. I WAS HOPING MY LIKENESS WOULD REMAIN ETERNAL IN YOUR ART.
THERE'S MORE TO ME THAN JUST MY BODY -- THERE'S MY FEELINGS. BUT YOU DON'T CARE. YOU DON'T FEEL A THING...
!
WAIT! DON'T LEAVE!

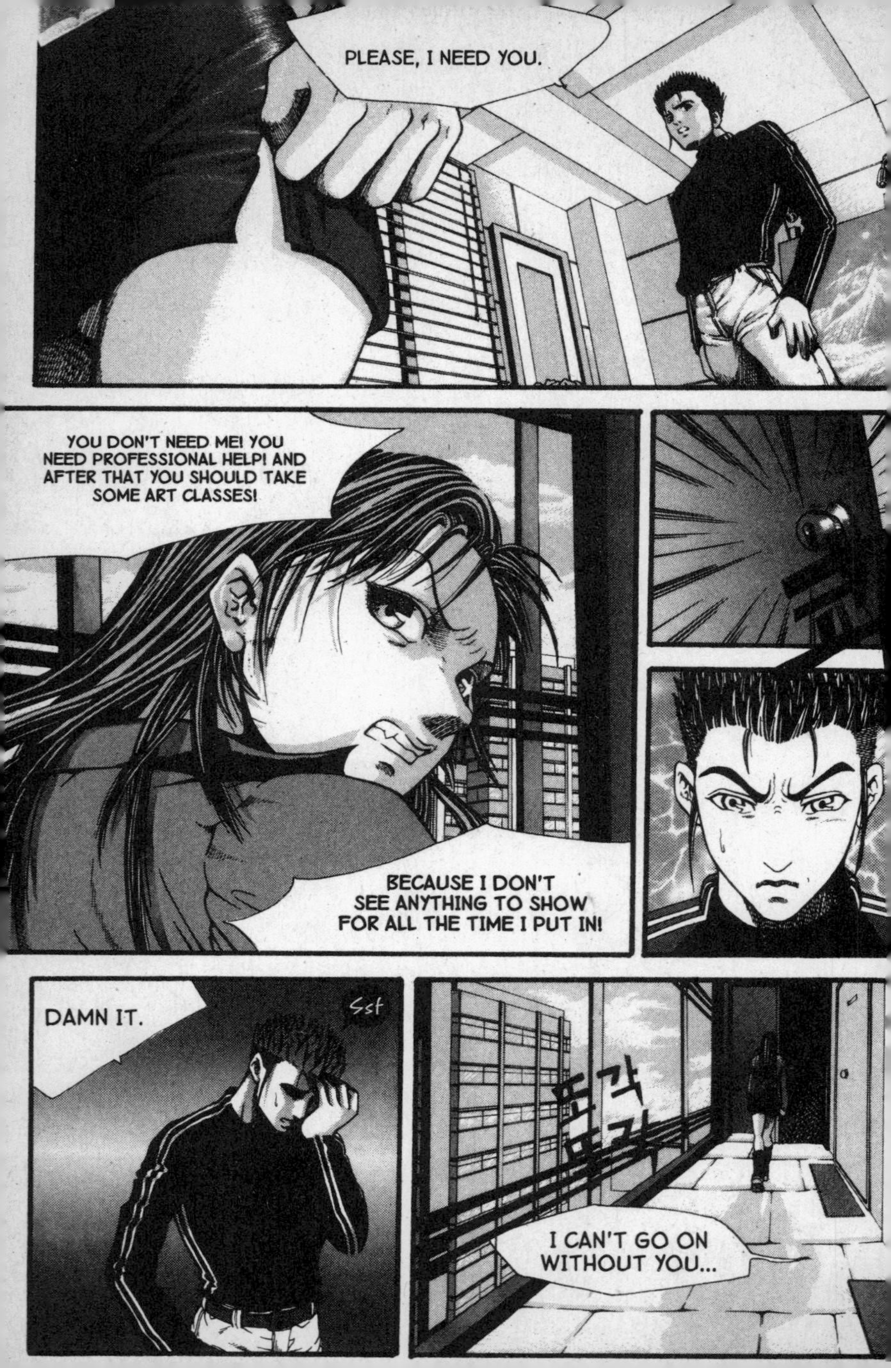
PLEASE, I NEED YOU.
YOU DON'T NEED ME! YOU NEED PROFESSIONAL HELP! AND AFTER THAT YOU SHOULD TAKE SOME ART CLASSES!
BECAUSE I DON'T SEE ANYTHING TO SHOW FOR ALL THE TIME I PUT IN!
DAMN IT.
Sst
I CAN'T GO ON WITHOUT YOU...

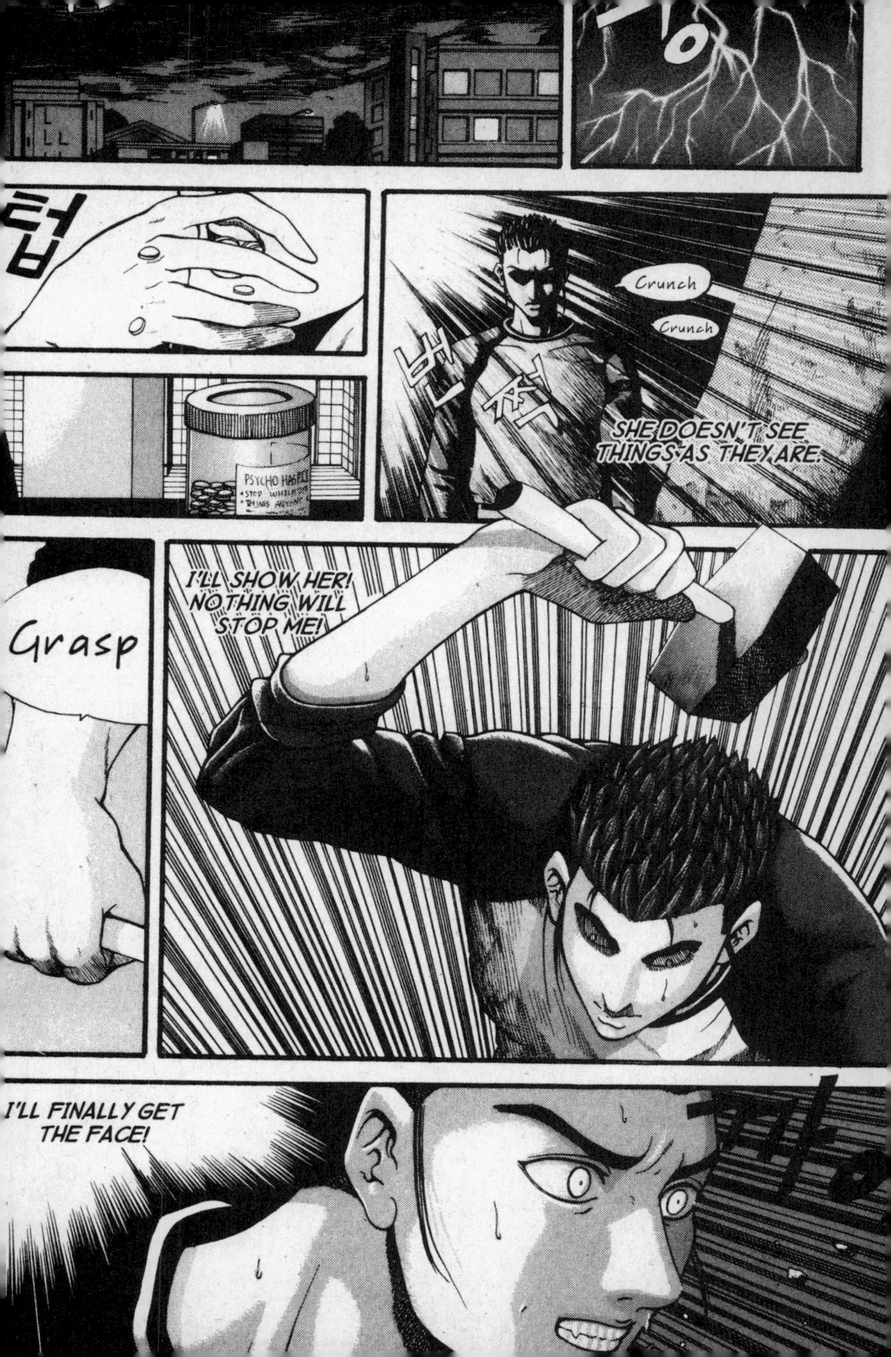
Crunch
Crunch
SHE DOESN'T SEE THINGS AS THEY ARE.
Grasp
I'LL SHOW HER! NOTHING WILL STOP ME!
I'LL FINALLY GET THE FACE!

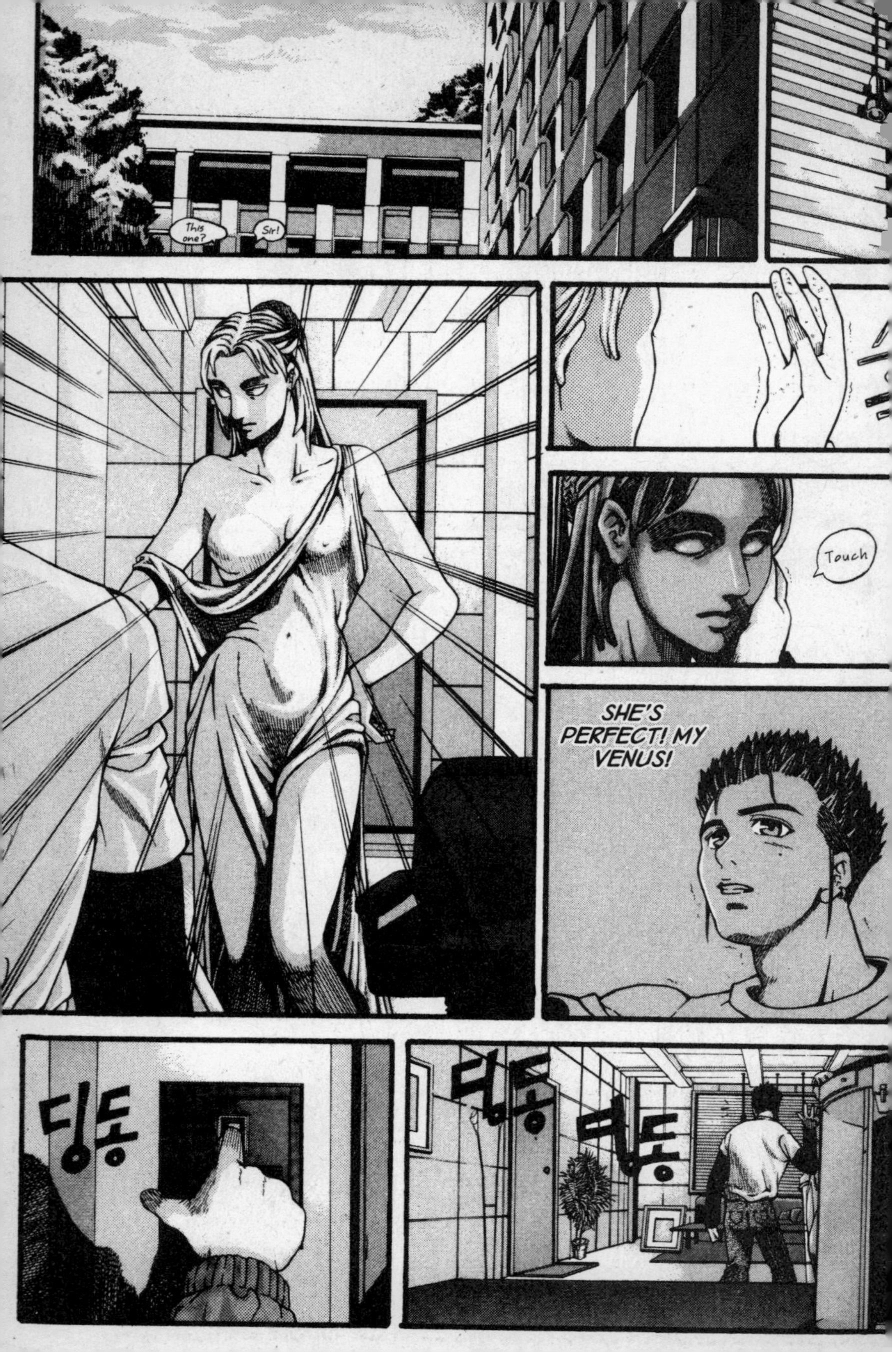
This one?
Sir!
Touch
SHE'S PERFECT! MY VENUS!
딩동
딩동
딩동

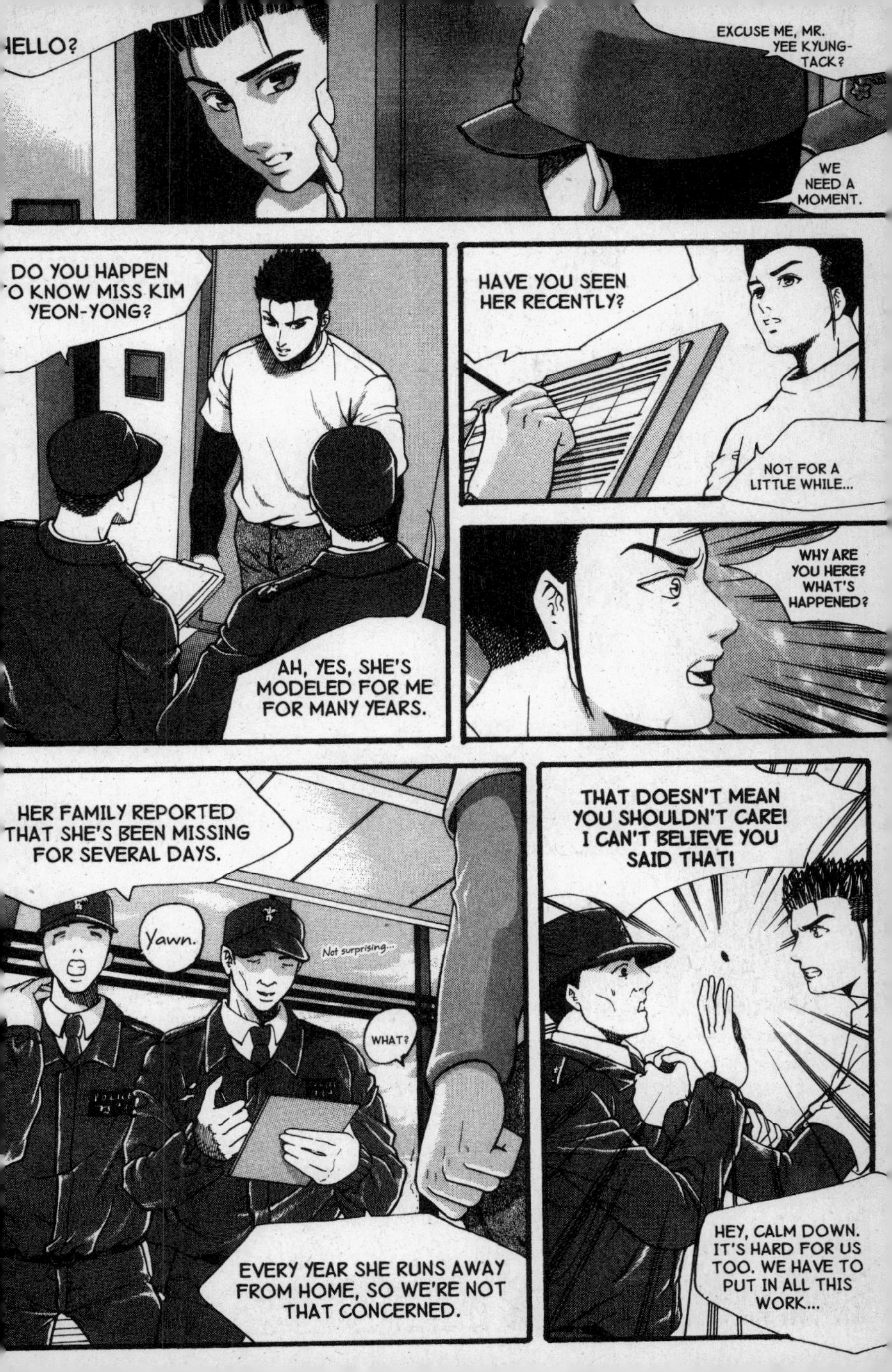
HELLO?
EXCUSE ME, MR. YEE KYUNG-TACK?
WE NEED A MOMENT.
DO YOU HAPPEN TO KNOW MISS KIM YEON-YONG?
AH, YES, SHE'S MODELED FOR ME FOR MANY YEARS.
HAVE YOU SEEN HER RECENTLY?
NOT FOR A LITTLE WHILE...
WHY ARE YOU HERE? WHAT'S HAPPENED?
HER FAMILY REPORTED THAT SHE'S BEEN MISSING FOR SEVERAL DAYS.
Yawn.
Not surprising...
WHAT?
EVERY YEAR SHE RUNS AWAY FROM HOME, SO WE'RE NOT THAT CONCERNED.
THAT DOESN'T MEAN YOU SHOULDN'T CARE! I CAN'T BELIEVE YOU SAID THAT!
HEY, CALM DOWN. IT'S HARD FOR US TOO. WE HAVE TO PUT IN ALL THIS WORK...

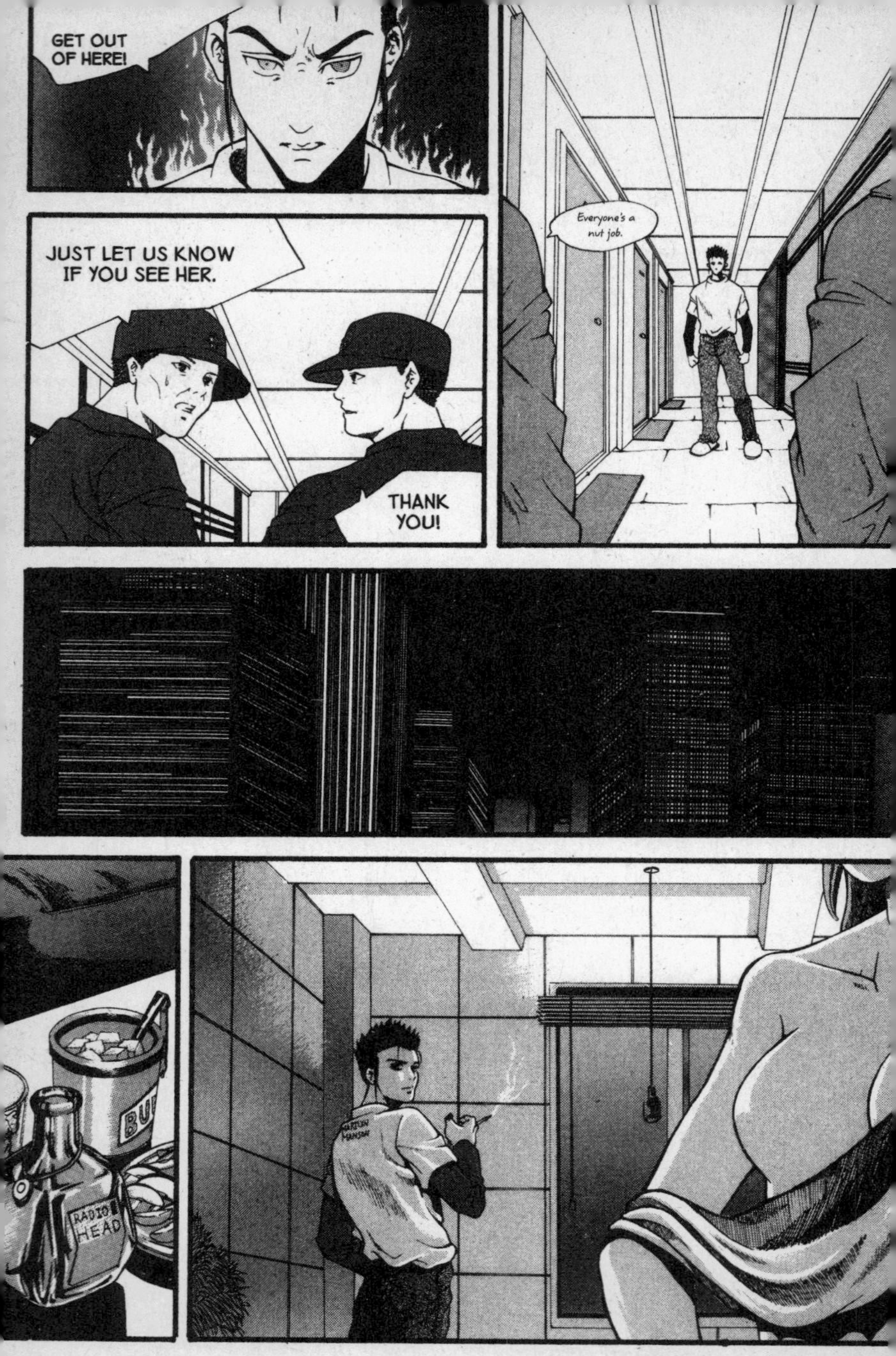
GET OUT OF HERE!
JUST LET US KNOW IF YOU SEE HER.
THANK YOU!
Everyone's a nut job.
RADIO HEAD

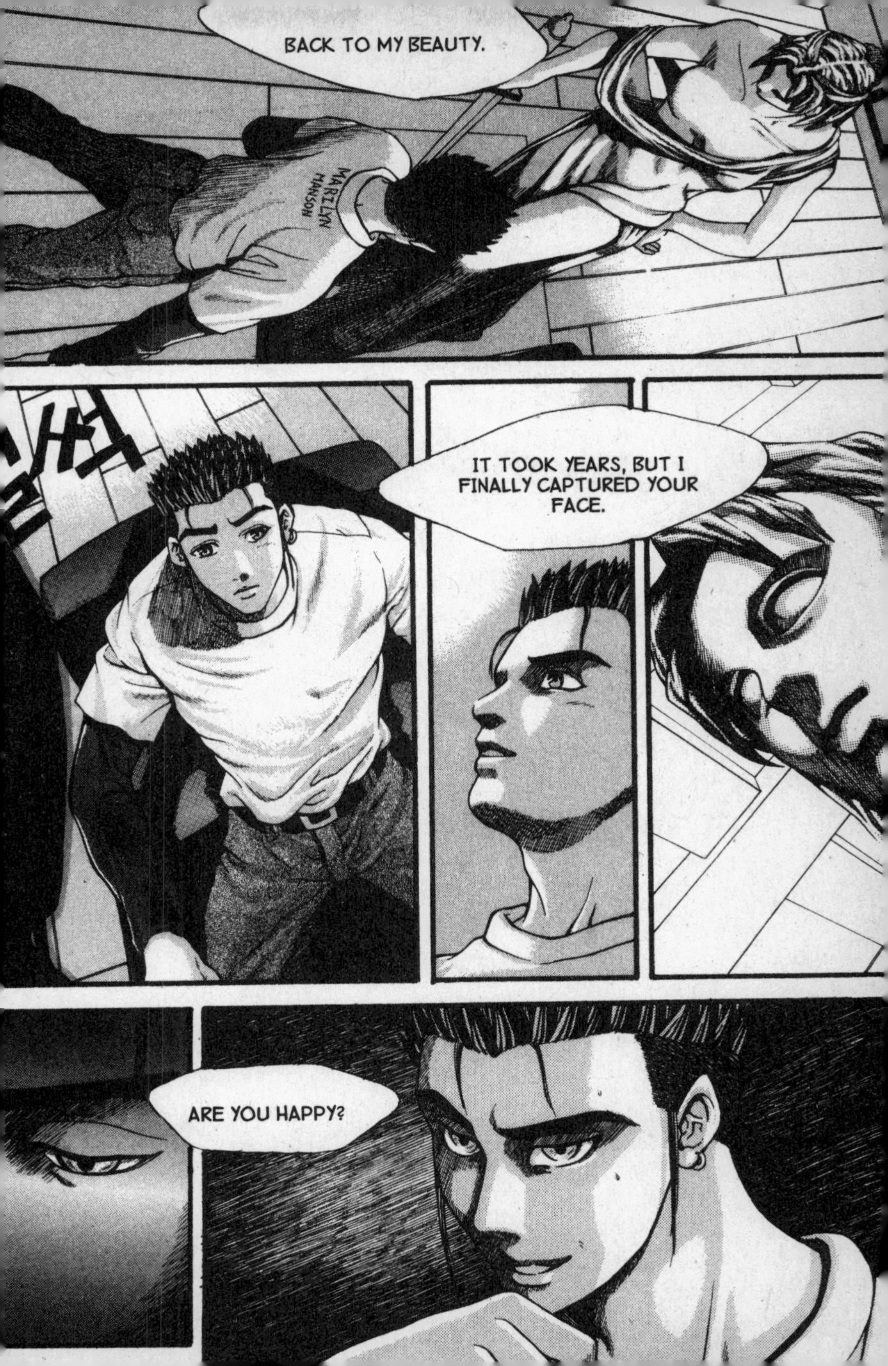
BACK TO MY BEAUTY.
MARILYN MANSON
IT TOOK YEARS, BUT I FINALLY CAPTURED YOUR FACE.
ARE YOU HAPPY?

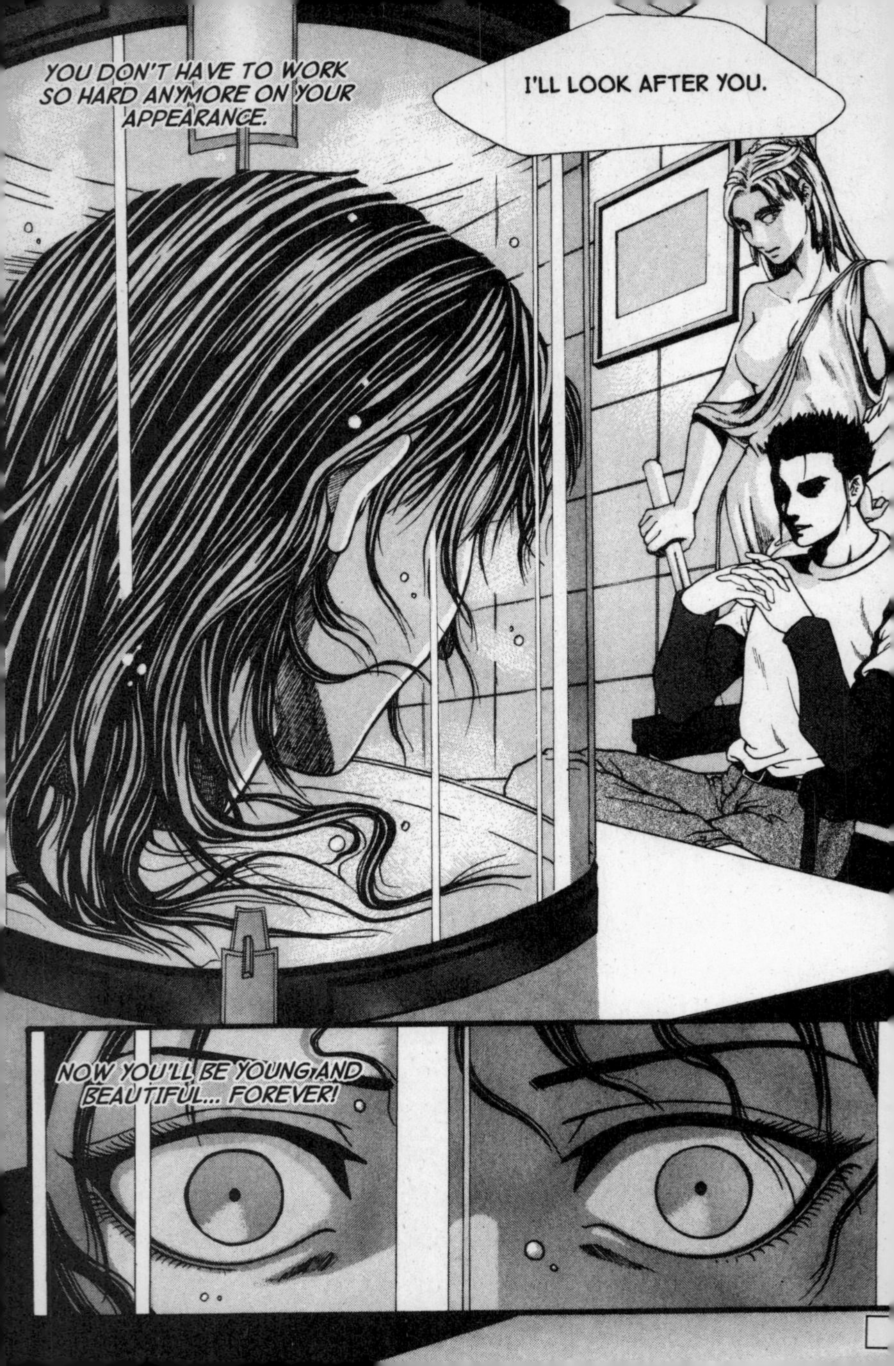
YOU DON'T HAVE TO WORK SO HARD ANYMORE ON YOUR APPEARANCE.
I'LL LOOK AFTER YOU.
NOW YOU'LL BE YOUNG AND BEAUTIFUL... FOREVER!

Threads of Time

In Volume 8

Winning notice in the upper ranks of the Mongol Army,
the slave Moon-Bin--or rather the son of the great
General Kim Kyung-Sohn in the reality that Moon-Bin
now finds himself--may once again be reunited with
the beautiful and compassionate Atan Hadas, who has
becoming increasingly disgusted with the decadence and
carelessness of the Mongol high command. But
Moon-Bin might also soon come to the attention of
General Sali Tayi, a man who has sworn to destroy
the Kyung-Sohn family.

TOKYOPOP presents a special and continuing
supplement to Threads of Time...

The Chronicles Of Koryo

Departure

Art by Karen Remsen
Written by Tim Beedle

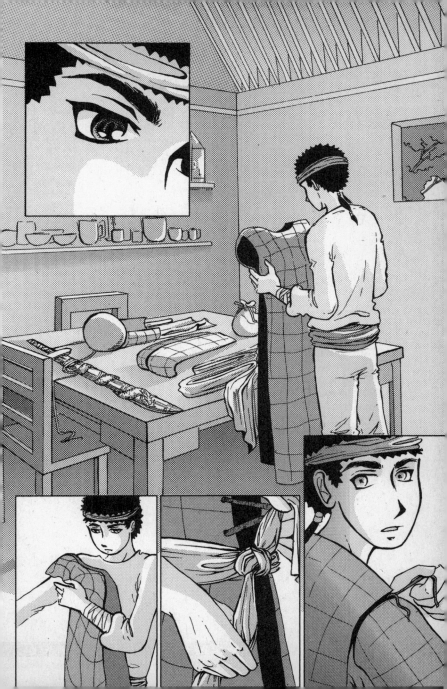

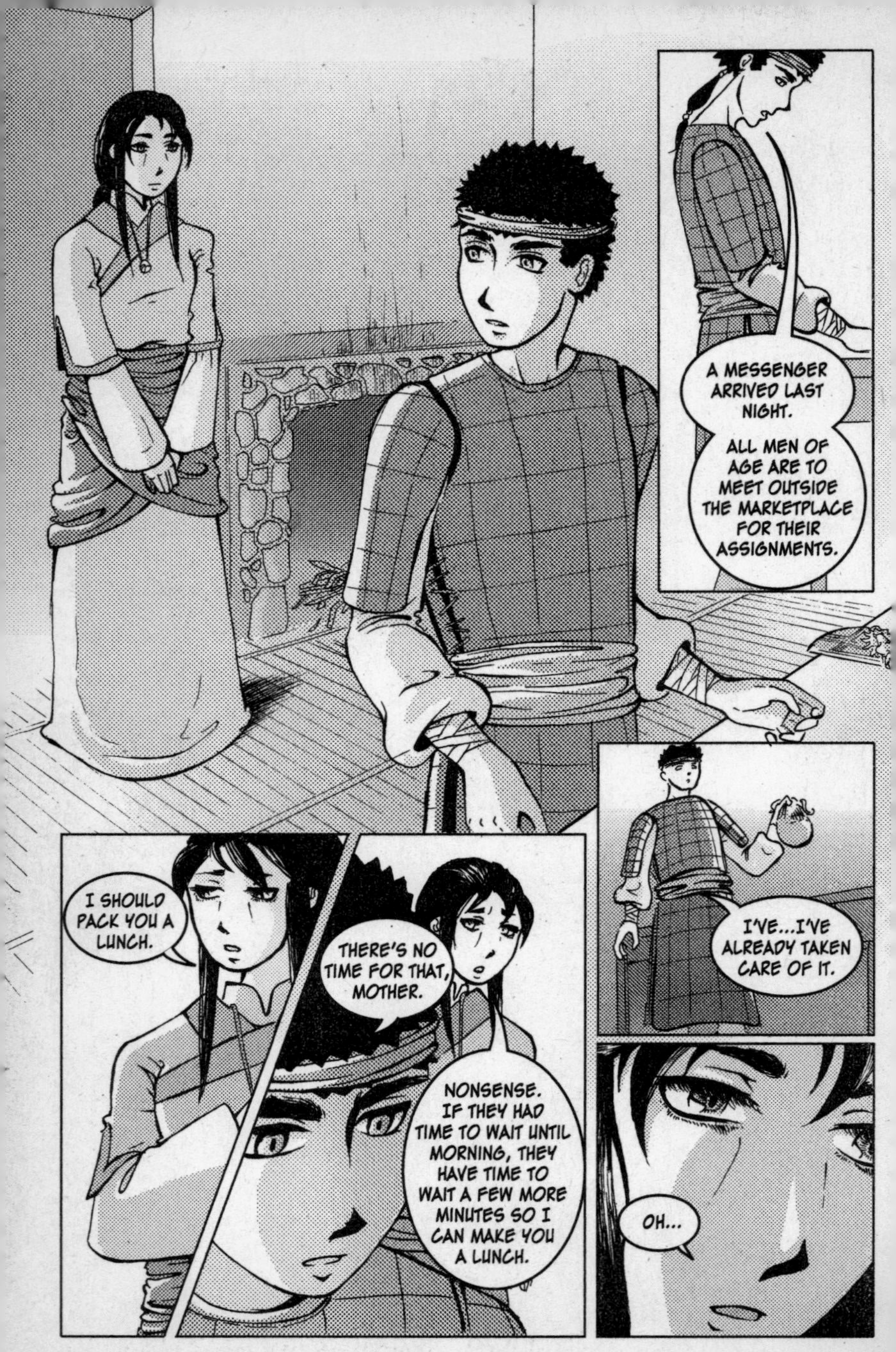
A MESSENGER ARRIVED LAST NIGHT.
ALL MEN OF AGE ARE TO MEET OUTSIDE THE MARKETPLACE FOR THEIR ASSIGNMENTS.
I'VE...I'VE ALREADY TAKEN CARE OF IT.
I SHOULD PACK YOU A LUNCH.
THERE'S NO TIME FOR THAT, MOTHER.
NONSENSE. IF THEY HAD TIME TO WAIT UNTIL MORNING, THEY HAVE TIME TO WAIT A FEW MORE MINUTES SO I CAN MAKE YOU A LUNCH.
OH...

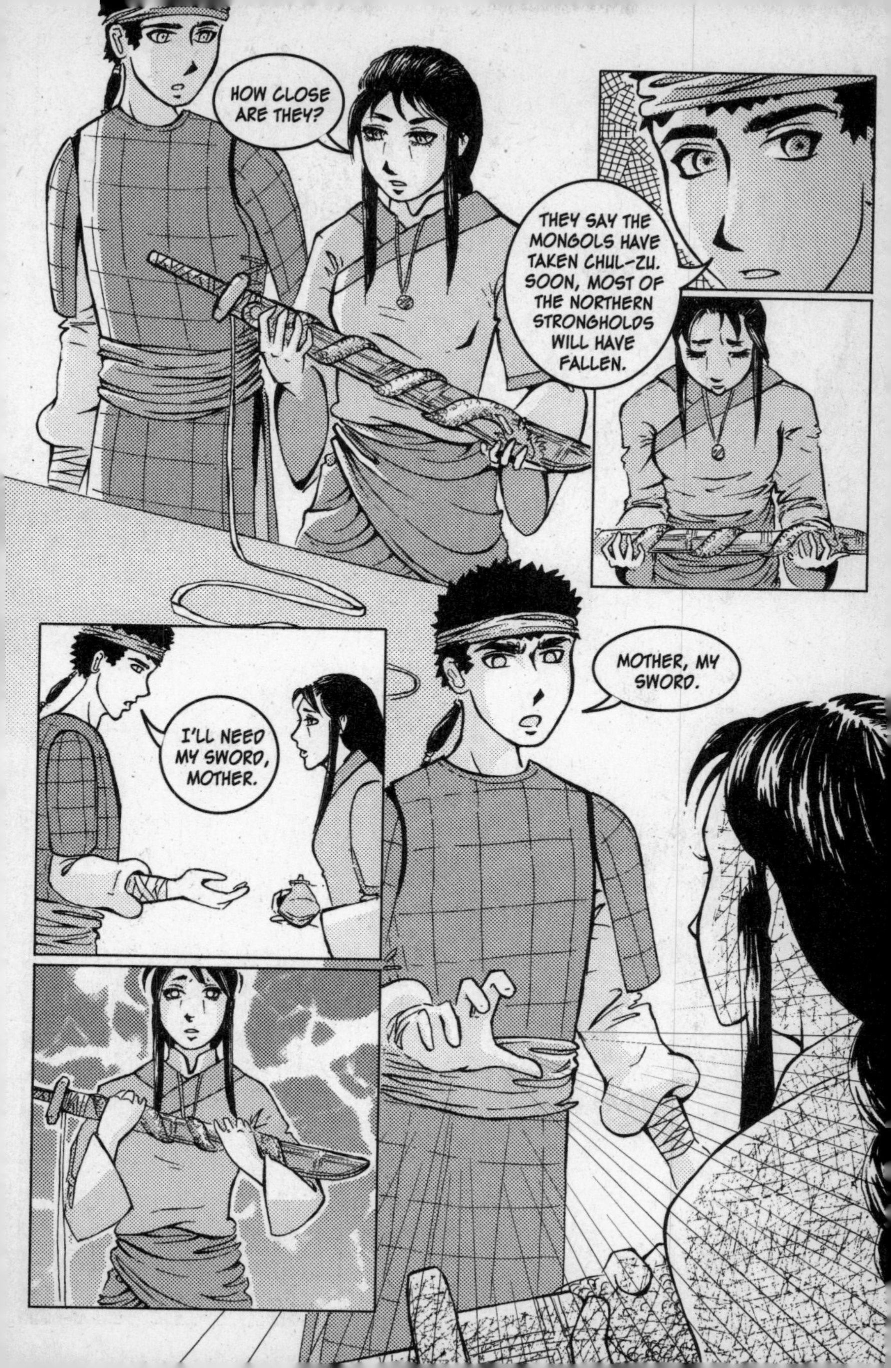
HOW CLOSE ARE THEY?
THEY SAY THE MONGOLS HAVE TAKEN CHUL-ZU. SOON, MOST OF THE NORTHERN STRONGHOLDS WILL HAVE FALLEN.
I'LL NEED MY SWORD, MOTHER.
MOTHER, MY SWORD.

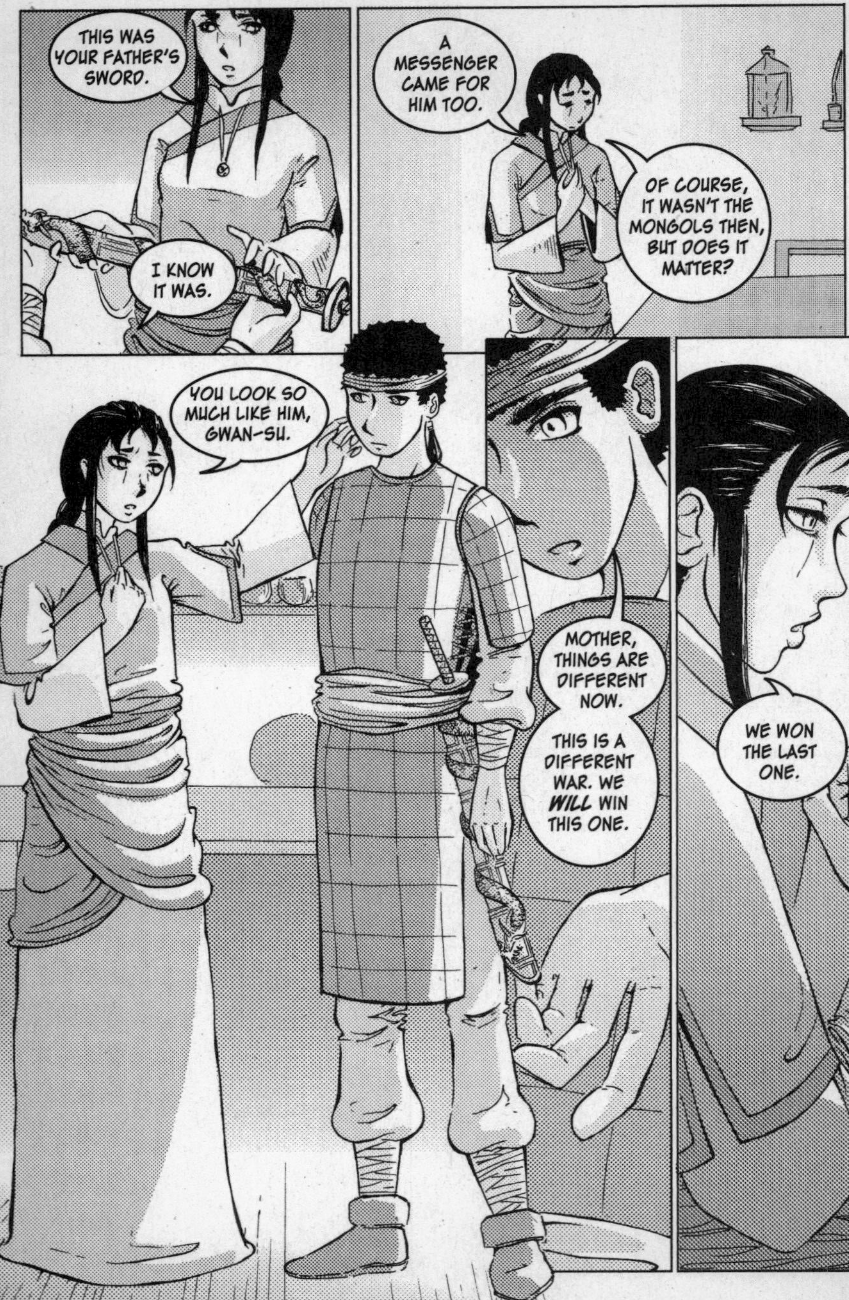
THIS WAS YOUR FATHER'S SWORD.
I KNOW IT WAS.
A MESSENGER CAME FOR HIM TOO.
OF COURSE, IT WASN'T THE MONGOLS THEN, BUT DOES IT MATTER?
YOU LOOK SO MUCH LIKE HIM, GWAN-SU.
MOTHER, THINGS ARE DIFFERENT NOW.
THIS IS A DIFFERENT WAR. WE WILL WIN THIS ONE.
WE WON THE LAST ONE.

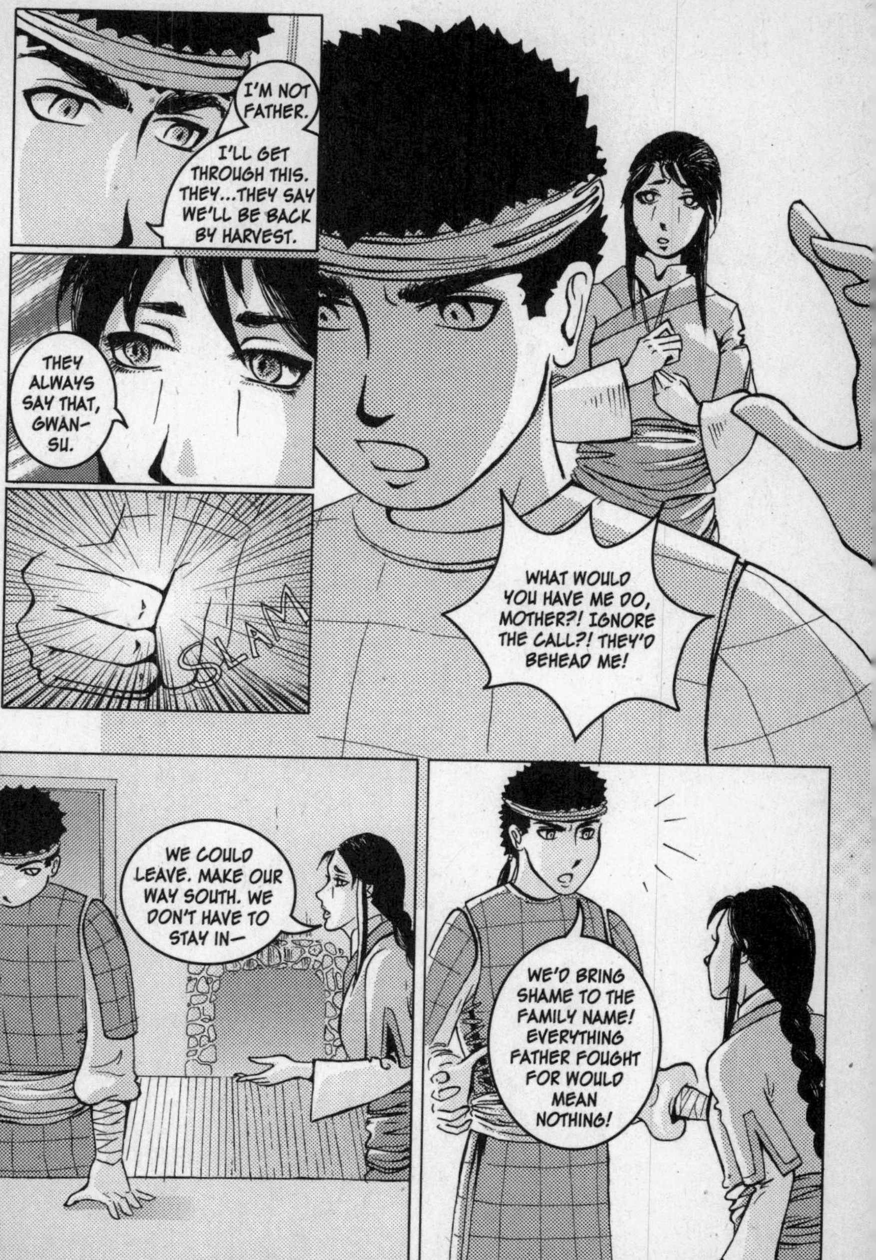

I'M NOT FATHER.
I'LL GET THROUGH THIS. THEY...THEY SAY WE'LL BE BACK BY HARVEST.
THEY ALWAYS SAY THAT, GWAN-SU.
SLAM
WHAT WOULD YOU HAVE ME DO, MOTHER?! IGNORE THE CALL?! THEY'D BEHEAD ME!
WE COULD LEAVE. MAKE OUR WAY SOUTH. WE DON'T HAVE TO STAY IN—
WE'D BRING SHAME TO THE FAMILY NAME! EVERYTHING FATHER FOUGHT FOR WOULD MEAN NOTHING!

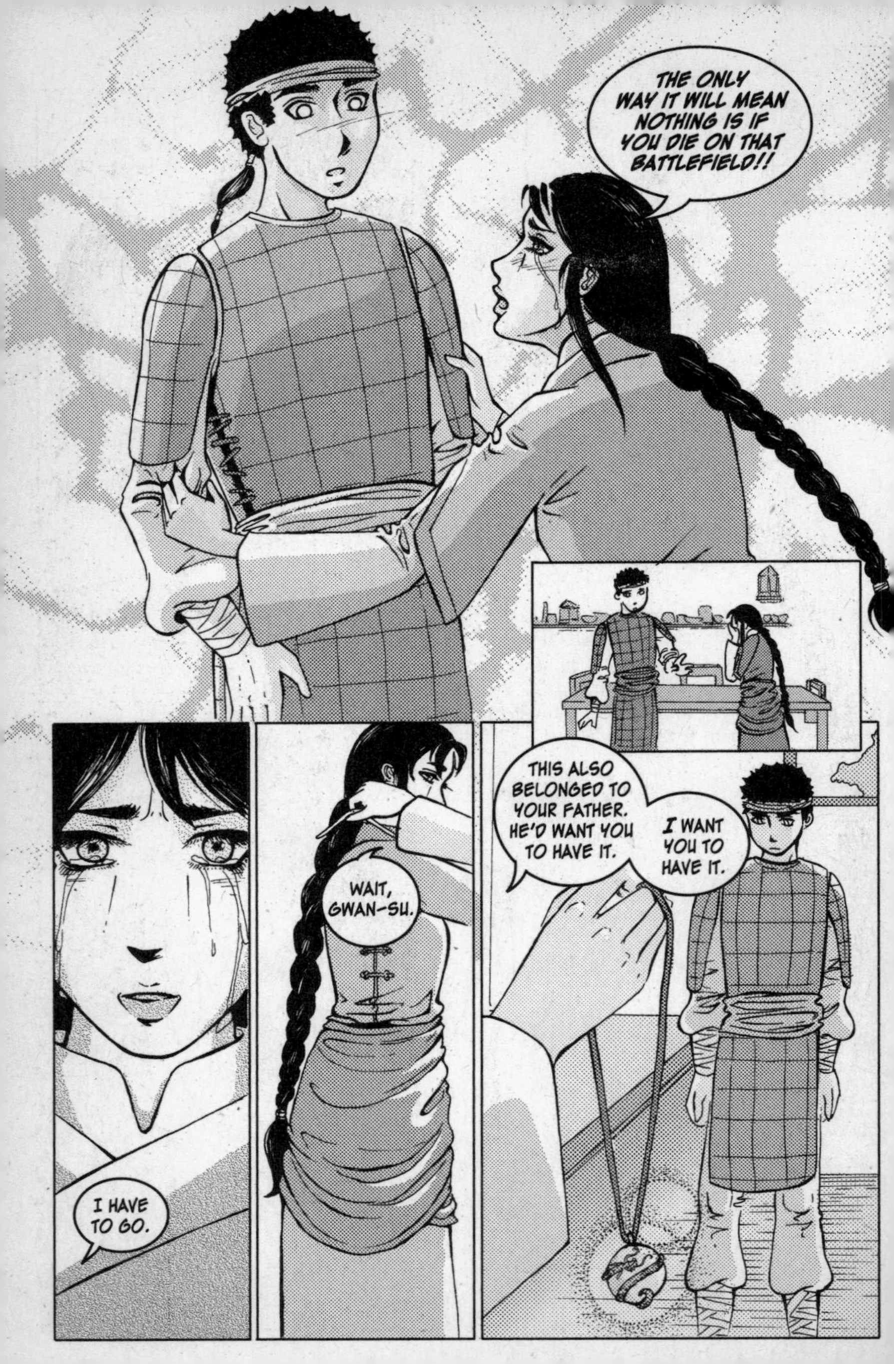
THE ONLY WAY IT WILL MEAN NOTHING IS IF YOU DIE ON THAT BATTLEFIELD!!
I HAVE TO GO.
WAIT, GWAN-SU.
THIS ALSO BELONGED TO YOUR FATHER. HE'D WANT YOU TO HAVE IT.
I WANT YOU TO HAVE IT.

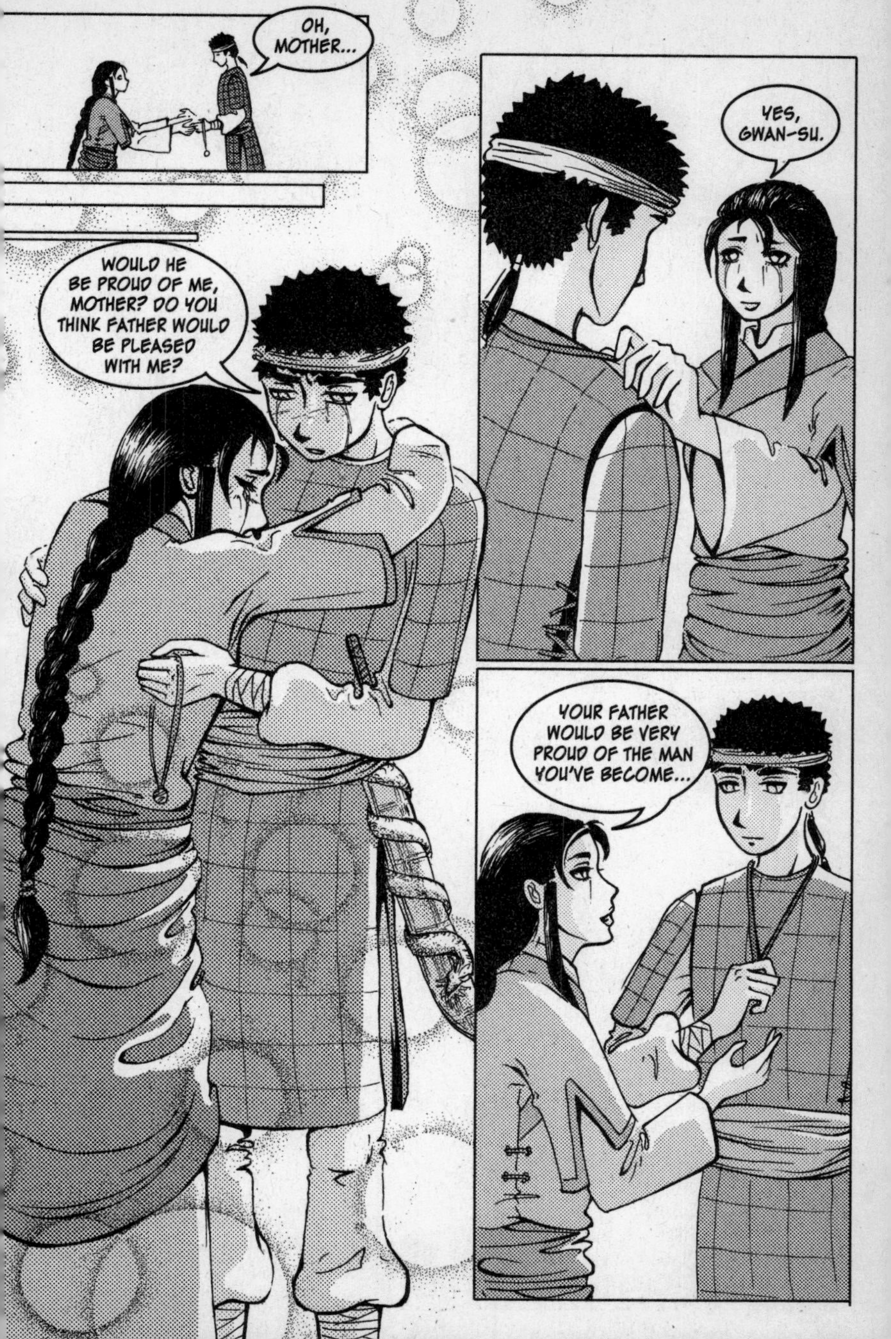
OH, MOTHER...
WOULD HE BE PROUD OF ME, MOTHER? DO YOU THINK FATHER WOULD BE PLEASED WITH ME?
YES, GWAN-SU.
YOUR FATHER WOULD BE VERY PROUD OF THE MAN YOU'VE BECOME...

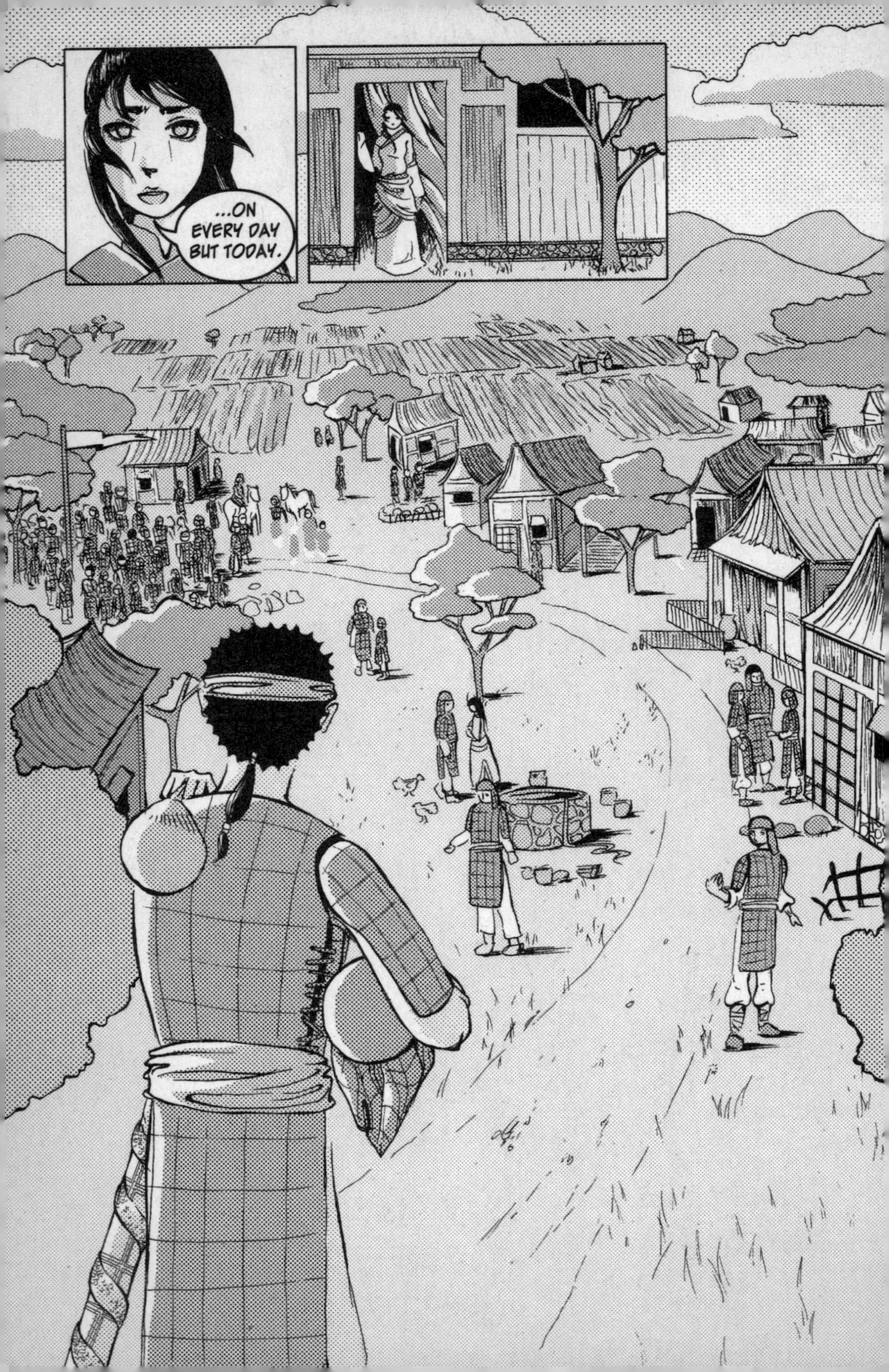
...ON EVERY DAY BUT TODAY.

TOKYOPOP SHOP

DRAMACON™

Sometimes even two's a crowd.

When Christie settles in the Artist Alley of her first-ever anime convention, she only sees it as an opportunity to promote the comic she has started with her boyfriend. But conventions are never what you expect, and soon a whirlwind of events sweeps Christie off her feet and changes her life. Who is the mysterious cosplayer who won't even take off his sunglasses indoors? What do you do when you fall in love with a guy who is going to be miles away from you in just a couple of days?

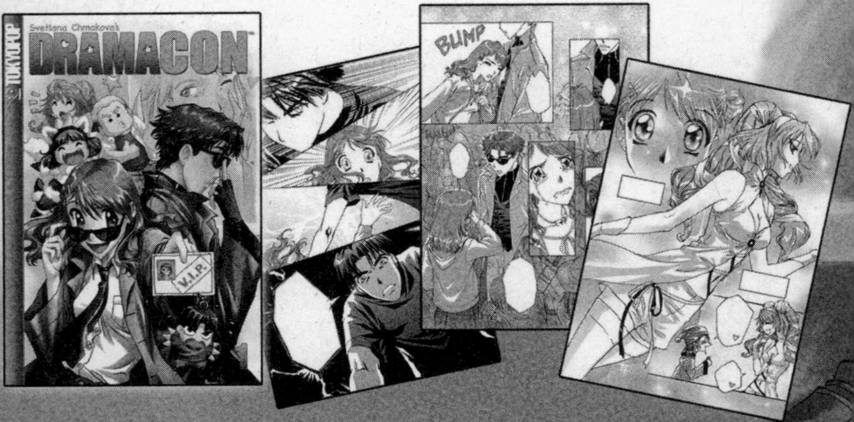
Svetlana Chmakova's
DRAMACON
TOKYOPOP
V.I.P.
BUMP

CREATED BY SVETLANA CHMAKOVA!

"YOU CAN'T AVOID FALLING UNDER ITS CHARM." -IGN.COM

READ AN ENTIRE CHAPTER ONLINE FOR FREE:
WWW.TOKYOPOP.COM/MANGAONLINE

TOKYOPOP MANGA SUPPLEMENT

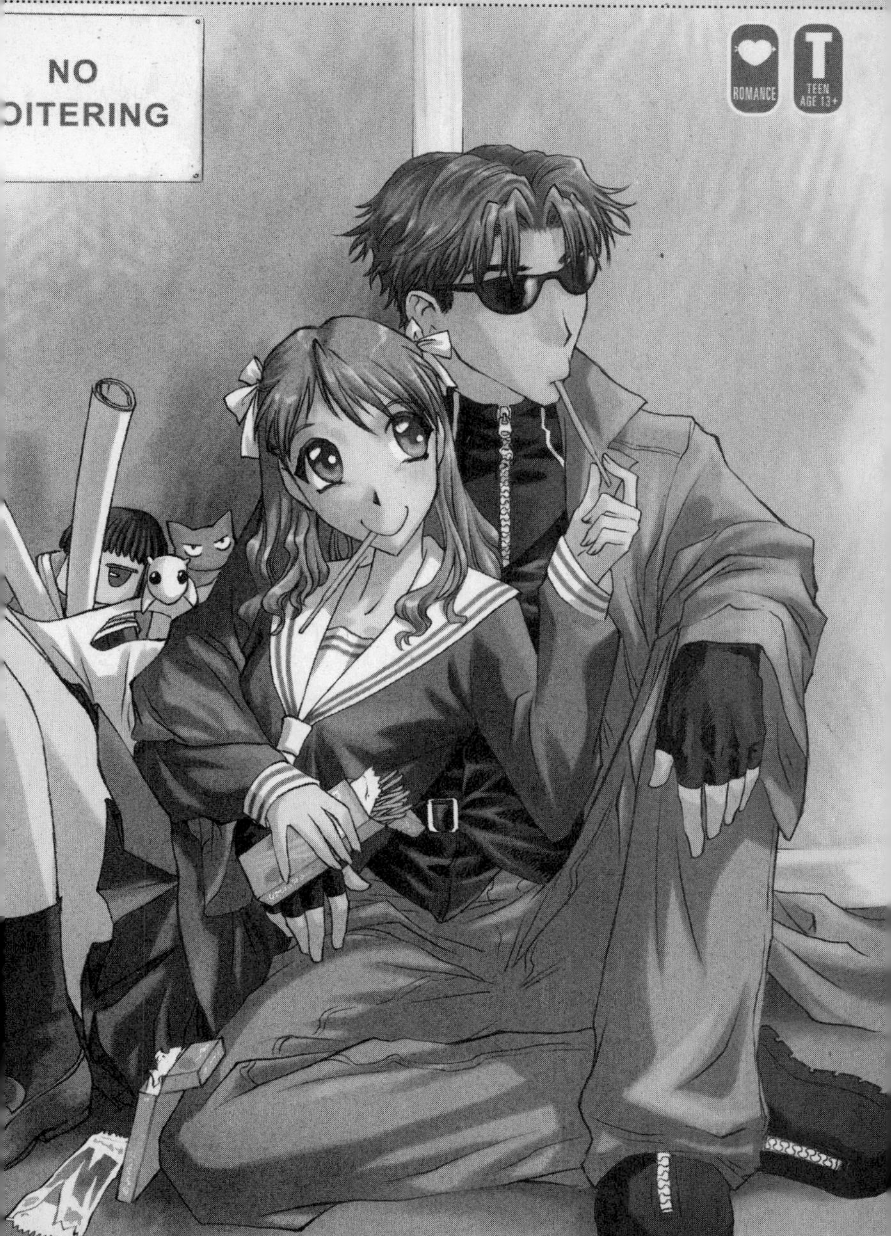

NO
OITERING
ROMANCE
T
TEEN
AGE 13+